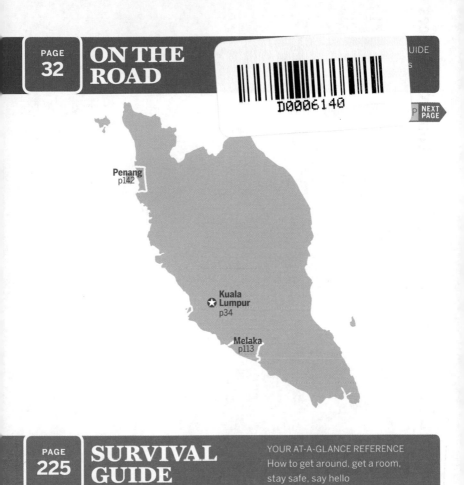

Penang
p142

Kuala
Lumpur
p34

Melaka
p113

PAGE
225

SURVIVAL GUIDE

YOUR AT-A-GLANCE REFERENCE
How to get around, get a room,
stay safe, say hello

Directory
A–Z

THIS EDITION WRITTEN AND RESEARCHED BY

Simon Richmond,
Celeste Brash

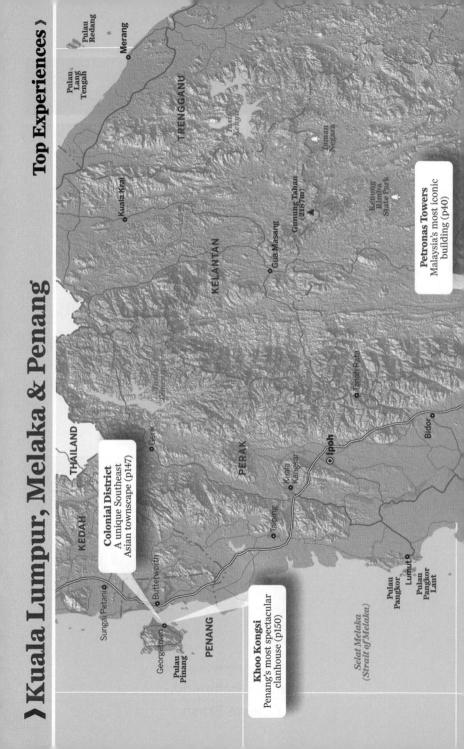

Kuala Lumpur, Melaka & Penang

Top Experiences

Colonial District
A unique Southeast Asian townscape (p147)

Khoo Kongsi
Penang's most spectacular clanhouse (p150)

Petronas Towers
Malaysia's most iconic building (p40)

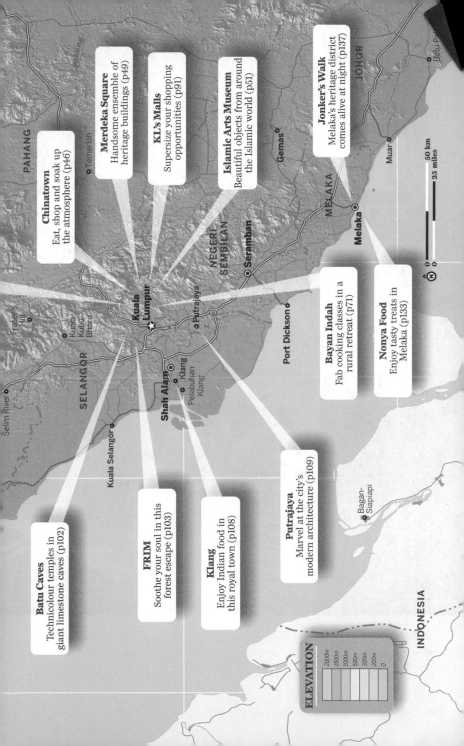

Chinatown
Eat, shop and soak up the atmosphere (p46)

Merdeka Square
Handsome ensemble of heritage buildings (p49)

KL's Malls
Supersize your shopping opportunities (p91)

Islamic Arts Museum
Beautiful objects from around the Islamic world (p51)

Jonker's Walk
Melaka's heritage district comes alive at night (p137)

Bayan Indah
Fab cooking classes in a rural retreat (p71)

Nonya Food
Enjoy tasty treats in Melaka (p133)

Putrajaya
Marvel at the city's modern architecture (p109)

Klang
Enjoy Indian food in this royal town (p108)

FRIM
Soothe your soul in this forest escape (p103)

Batu Caves
Technicolour temples in giant limestone caves (p102)

50 km
25 miles

PAHANG

Temerloh

Fraser's Hill

Kuala Kubu Bharu

Selim River

SELANGOR

Kuala Selangor

Kuala Lumpur

Shah Alam

Klang
Pelabuhan Klang

Putrajaya

Seremban

NEGERI SEMBILAN

Port Dickson

Gemas

MELAKA

Melaka

Muar

Batu Pa

JOHOR

Bagan-Siapiapi

INDONESIA

ELEVATION
2000m
1500m
1000m
500m
300m
200m
0

17 TOP
EXPERIENCES

Petronas Towers

1 It's impossible to resist the magnetic allure of the Petronas Towers (p40): the 452m-high structure is beautiful to look at, as well as being the embodiment of Malaysia's transformation into a fully developed nation. Designed by architect Cesar Pelli, this glistening, steel-wrapped structure is the focal point of the Kuala Lumpur City Centre (KLCC), a 40-hectare development that also includes an imaginatively designed tropical park, a fun aquarium, an excellent kids' museum, a world-class concert hall and one of KL's best shopping malls.

KL's Chinatown

2 Plumes of smoke curl upwards from smouldering coils of incense, flower garlands hang like pearls from the necks of Hindu statues and the call to prayer punctuates the honk of traffic. The temples and mosques of the city's Hindus, Muslims and Chinese Buddhists are crammed shoulder-to-shoulder in this atmospheric neighbourhood along the Klang River that epitomises multicultural Malaysia (see p46). Don't miss eating at the daytime Madras Lane hawker stalls or savouring the bustle and fun of the night market along Jln Petaling.

Batu Caves

3 It's always a very busy and colourful scene at this sacred Hindu shrine (p102) but, if you can, time your visit for a holy day, the biggest of which is Thaipusam. Guarding the 272 steps that lead up to the main Temple Cave is the 43m gilded statue of Lord Murugan, assisted by a platoon of lively macaques who show little fear in launching raids on tourists' belongings. A new train station at the foot of the giant limestone outcrop makes getting here easy. Sri Maha Vishnu statue, Batu Caves

Georgetown's Colonial District

4 It's got the highest concentration of pre-WWII buildings in Southeast Asia, but even more fascinating is the life within. Buddha statuettes, rusty lamps and ancient costume jewellery clutter a Chinese shop tucked behind chipped louvred windows, an old man fabricates bicycle parts with a blow torch and a dim sum shop overflows with chattering locals. Surrounding businesses and homes are golden-arched clanhouses, singing mosques, white churches and pastel Hindu temples, ever reminding us of the cultural mix that built and maintains this eclectic city. See p147.

AUN KOH / LONELY PLANET IMAGES ©

AUN KOH / LONELY PLANET IMAGES ©

Nonya Food

5 Nonya food (see p206), a delicious mix of Chinese and Malay cuisines, headlines in Melaka and is regaining popularity in Penang. Melaka's version takes coconut-laden hints from Indonesia, while Penang gets a fiery chilli injection from its proximity to Thailand. Trying something different at the various restaurants, each with their own family recipes, makes you realise how vast this ancient fusion repertoire is – but a laksa followed by an iced *cendol* (sweet dessert with shaved ice, coconut milk, palm-sugar syrup and condensed milk) is hard to beat.

KL's Malls

6 Come for the air-conditioning, stay for the designer bargains! The role call of brands in malls such as Pavilion KL, Suria KLCC and Starhill Gallery will impress even the most sophisticated of shoppers. Refreshments are never far away with masses of restaurants and excellent food courts always part of the retail mix, along with everything from doctor-fish spas to luxurious multiplex cinemas and karaoke rooms. It's the unexpected finds – the feng shui stores, art galleries and even Hindu temples – that really set these malls apart. See p91.

CHRISTER FREDRIKSSON / LONELY PLANET IMAGES ©

Merdeka Square

7 Stand beside the Victorian fountain next to the empty expanse of lawn and take in the impressive scene (p49). When it was called the Padang, members of the Royal Selangor Club would politely clap as another wicket fell in a colonial cricket match. At midnight on 31 August 1957, the flag of the independent nation of Malaya was hoisted on the 95m flagpole. The eastern flank is dominated by the handsome Sultan Abdul Samad Building, decorated with copper-clad domes and barley-sugar-twist columns. Sultan Abdul Samad Building, Merdeka Square

Thaipusam

8 This Hindu festival of repentance (p104), attended by over a million people when it falls in January or February, is a surreal and memorable experience. A statue of Lord Murugan is carried on a silver chariot for the 15km from the Sri Mahamariamman Temple in KL's Chinatown to the temples at the Batu Caves. Gallons of milk to bathe the statue are carried alongside in structures called *kavadi*, while devotees take part in cleansing rituals and the most dedicated show their penance by piercing their backs, chests, cheeks and tongues.

Khoo Kongsi

9 Whether you follow the screeching sounds of Chinese opera on a balmy August night or pedal through the gates by trishaw, arriving at this over-the-top opulent clanhouse (p150) is unforgettable. Take note of the Sikh statues guarding the elaborately carved entryway, revel in the red lanterns contrasting with ubiquitous gold leaf and get lost in the warriors-riding-on-animals designs on the walls. The interior requires thoughtful lingering to savour each detail of the intricate stonework, woodwork and fine paintings. A photographer's dream.

ANDERS BLOMQVIST / LONELY PLANET IMAGES ©

FRIM

10 The Forestry Research Institute of Malaysia (FRIM; p103) is an emerald jewel, a natural escape from KL's urban grind. Feel your soul start to calm as soon as you enter this 600-hectare reserve where hard concrete and traffic pollution give way to soft foliage and fresh air. Get the blood pumping on the steep hike up to the thrilling 200m-long Canopy Walkway that hangs a vertigo-inducing 30m above the forest floor and provides panoramic views back to the city. Down at ground level take refreshments in the charming Malay Teahouse.

Jonker's Walk Night Market

11 Start with a mysterious looking herbal drink to sip while taking a first lap through the low street stalls. Sniff some incense, try on some fancy flip-flops or cheap sunglasses, get your fortune read. Make your way to the bottom of the street where a crowd is cheering on street performer Dr Ho Eng Hui as he shoves his finger into a coconut. Everyone is smiling and nibbling on something delicious. The night ends at a streetside bar with cold beer and live music. (See p137.)

RICHARD I'ANSON / LONELY PLANET IMAGES ©

Kek Lok Si Temple

12 While it's unnerving getting the hard sell from T-shirt vendors on the ascent to Kek Lok Si Temple (p175), the peace of the place prevails at the pagodas. Get lost in tall circular towers and incense-filled prayer rooms, shop for Buddhist paraphernalia, then cable-car up to the highlight: an overwhelmingly tall (36.5m) statue of Kuan Yin, the goddess of mercy, covered by a tiered roof supported by gargantuan bronze columns. Take a break from the grandness of it all in the adjacent koi-pond gardens with views over the island.

SIMON RICHMOND / LONELY PLANET IMAGES ©

Bayan Indah

13 If constant snacking at hawker stalls leaves you craving to know how all those delicious Malaysian dishes are made, then sign up for the brilliant cooking courses offered by delightful Rohani Jelani. This superb culinary retreat (p71) surrounded by lush gardens offers four ensuite rooms for those who would like to relax into the *kampung* (village) atmosphere. Once here, it's hard to credit that you're still within KL city limits and only 30 minutes' drive from frantic Chinatown!

Klang's Little India

14 Indian immigrant labour built and maintained Malaysia's first railway line connecting the royal port town of Klang with Kuala Lumpur. The community remains in this now sleepy but appealing town where Jln Tengku Kelana forms the spine of Little India (p108), a small but seductive area of silk and sari shops, fortune tellers and spice sellers. Best of all is the delicious array of Indian eateries specialising in the spicy curries and sweets of the subcontinent.

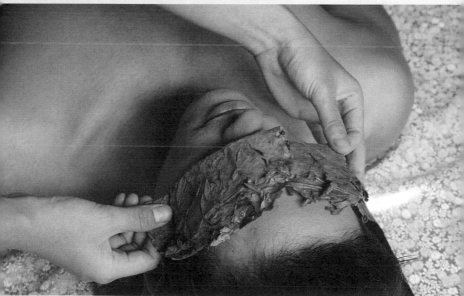

Spa Treatments

15 Steams, body wraps, scrubs, facials and an atlas-hopping range of massage styles are available and affordable in the spas of Kuala Lumpur, the best of which provide ultra luxurious experiences (see p68). Indigenous herbs and flowers, and the essential oils and emollients made from them, are used in some treatments. At some places you can enjoy the initial agony and later ecstasy of a reflexology foot rub, after allowing armies of doctor fish to nibble away the dead skin on your feet.

Putrajaya

16 Touring Malaysia's administrative capital (p109), you may feel a little envious of the bureaucrats and politicians who live and work here, free of the traffic, pollution and stress of KL. Barely two decades old, the striking buildings, futuristic bridges and lush landscaping of this spacious cyber city are a calling card for the country's modern aspirations. Traditional Islamic and Malay designs are incorporated into the structures, many of which are best viewed on a boat trip across the city's central lake. Putra Mosque and Perdana Putra, Putrajaya

ANTONY GIBLIN / LONELY PLANET IMAGES ©

Islamic Arts Museum

17 The dazzling collection of objects housed in this fine museum (p51) on the edge of KL's Lake Gardens prove that religious devotion can be married with exquisite craftsmanship. The building itself – with its Iranian-tiled facade and decorated domes – is a stunner, with natural light–filled galleries stacked with amazing works gathered from around the Islamic world. There's also a good Lebanese restaurant and a gift shop that stocks fabulously designed and expertly made items. Ceiling detail, Islamic Arts Museum

welcome to KL, Melaka & Penang

In these three fascinating areas of Malaysia, beautiful heritage and stunning modern architecture, delicious streetside meals, masses of markets and malls, and an engaging mix of cultures wait to be discovered.

A Modern Country

Malaysia's capital Kuala Lumpur is an ambitious metropolis literally carved from the jungle. Historic monuments, steel-clad skyscrapers, lush parks, mega-sized shopping malls, bustling street markets and trendy nightspots – as well as the incense-wreathed, colourfully adorned mosques and temples of the country's Malay, Chinese and Indian communities – are all parts of its intoxicating mix. The island of Penang and city of Melaka, both mesmerising hodgepodges of heritage buildings and colonial-era monuments, are also paid up members of modern Malaysia with a wealth of fine attractions, hotels, shops and good infrastructure to prove it. In all three places you'll be impressed by how Malaysians balance a reverence for their compilation of centuries-old cultures with a drive to be plugged into the contemporary world, evidenced by a buzzing contemporary art and design scene, as well as citizens embracing the e-economy.

Historical Canvas

In 2008 Melaka and Georgetown (Penang) were inscribed on the Unesco World Heritage list for their unique architectural and cultural townscapes, developed over half a millennium of Southeast Asian cultural and trade exchange. As you wander through the replica of the 15th-century palace of Mansur Shah in Melaka, consider the time when this was the control room of the region's richest port. Imagine Captain Francis Light setting foot on Penang in 1886 where Georgetown's Fort Cornwallis stands today, and claiming it for the British empire. KL, founded barely 150 years ago, may be a youngster in comparison but it, too, has been the scene of history-defining moments. The city's Stadium Merdeka was where, in 1957, the country's first prime minister Tunku Abdul Rahman punched his fist seven times in the air and declared Malaysia independent. And the iconic Petronas Towers were officially the tallest buildings in the world when they opened in 1998.

Delicious Diversions

Reach for the sky by all means, but don't be distracted from what's happening on the ground. To fully connect with the locals, join them in two of their favourite pastimes: shopping and eating. Malaysian consumer culture achieves its zenith in KL, where you could spend all day browsing glitzy air-conditioned malls such as Pavilion KL and Mid Valley Megamall in search of bargains. Alternatively, explore Central Market for locally made souvenirs, then dive into the culinary melting pot of nearby Chinatown. Foodies will also not want to miss sampling the dining delights of Melaka or Penang, the latter acclaimed by many Malaysians as offering the country's best authentic street food. Whatever your opinion, you'll be left in no doubt that this trio are fabulous places to experience the deliciously intertwined traditions of the Malay archipelago.

need to know

Currency
» Malaysian ringgit (RM)

Language
» Bahasa Malaysia and English

When to Go?

Georgetown
GO year-round

Kuala Lumpur
GO year-round

Melaka
GO year-round

Tropical climate, rain year-round
Tropical climate, wet & dry seasons

High Season
(Dec–Feb)

» End-of-year school holidays followed by Chinese New Year push up prices and mean advance booking of transport and hotel rooms is important.

Shoulder
(Jul–Nov)

» July to August, vye with visitors escaping the heat of the Gulf States as Malaysia enjoys what it calls Arab Season. The end of Ramadan, usually in September, also sees increased travel activity in the region.

Low Season
(Mar–Jun)

» The west coast monsoon season is over during this time, when visitor numbers are at their lowest.

Your Daily Budget

Budget less than
RM100

» Dorm bed: RM12–35

» Hawker-stall meal: R10

» Plan sightseeing around walking tours

Midrange
RM100 –400

» Double room in midrange hotel: RM100–400

» Two-course meal in midrange restaurant: RM40–60

» Ticket for theatre show: RM40

Top End more than
RM400

» Double room in five-star hotel: RM450–1000

» Three-course meal plus wine in top-end restaurant plus bottle of wine: RM200

» Half-day Malay cooking course: RM230

Money

» ATMs widely available. Credit cards accepted in most hotels and restaurants.

Visas

» Generally not required for stays of up to 60 days

Mobile Phones

» Local SIM cards can be used in most phones; if not, set your phone to roaming.

Transport

» Plenty of buses connect KL, Melaka and Penang; trains and flights can also be used between KL and Penang.

Websites

» **Tourism Malaysia** (www.tourismmalaysia. gov.my) Official national tourist-information site.

» **Lonely Planet** (www. lonelyplanet.com) Greatest website for preplanning.

» **Malaysiakini** (www. malaysiakini.com) Find out what's really going on in the country.

» **KLue** (www.klue.com. my) Get the lowdown on what's happening in KL.

» **Tourism Penang** (www.tourismpenang. net.my) Details of all the island's attractions.

» **Tourism Melaka** (www.melaka.gov.my) Check out the local government's visitors guide.

Exchange Rates

Australia	A$1	RM3.10
Canada	C$1	RM3.07
Europe	€1	RM4.26
Japan	¥100	RM3.8
UK	UK£1	RM4.94
US	US$1	RM3.09

For current exchange rates see www.xe.com.

Important Numbers

Country code	☑60
International access code	☑00
Police	☑999
Ambulance/Fire	☑994
Directory assistance	☑103

Arriving

» **Kuala Lumpur International Airport**
Trains RM35; every 15 min from 5am to 1am; 30 min to KL Sentral
Buses RM10; every hr from 5am to 1am; 1 hr to KL Sentral
Taxis from RM67.10; 1 hr to KL

» **LCCT**
Buses RM9; every 15 min from 4.30am to 12.45am; 1 hr to KL Sentral
Taxis from RM65; 1 hr to KL

» **Penang Airport**
Buses RM1.50; every hr from 6am to 9pm; 1 hr to Georgetown
Taxis RM40; 45 min to Georgetown.
See p233 for more info.

Responsible Travel

Long, carbon-intensive flights are not the only way to reach Peninsular Malaysia. From Europe and most parts of Asia it's possible to travel overland if you're not in a hurry. The authoritative **Man in Seat 61** (www.seat61.com/Malaysia.htm) reckons it takes a minimum of 3½ weeks to reach KL from London by a combination of trains and buses.

Once in the region consider making your travels more sustainable by taking part in a homestay programme, doing some volunteer work or supporting traditional craft industries when buying souvenirs. **Green Selipar** (http://greenselipar.com) lists some great sustainable travel initiatives around Malaysia while the pressure group and consultancy **Wild Asia** (www.wildasia.net) seeks to raise standards by handing out sustainable-tourism awards. Also see our sustainable picks throughout the guide (indicated by ☑), and p232 for volunteer-work opportunities.

what's new

For this new edition of Kuala Lumpur, Melaka & Penang, *our authors have hunted down the fresh, the revamped, the transformed, the hot and the happening. Here are a few of our favourites. For up-to-the-minute reviews and recommendations, see lonelyplanet.com/kuala-lumpur.*

Georgetown's Heritage Revival

1 Since Georgetown's inscription on the Unesco World Heritage list in 2008 dilapidated buildings in the city's historic centre have been snapped up as savvy investors and conservationists work together to revive this unique urban landscape. Key players include Penang Heritage Trust, the Straits Collection (p160) and the team behind Clove Hall (p163) who have a couple more hotels in restored buildings set to open in 2011–12.

Publika

2 This next-generation mall, in the ritzy KL suburb of Mont Kiara, combines shopping with arts, culture and the fostering of local creative industries and nonprofit organisations (p97).

Bayan Indah

3 Foodie extraordinaire Rohani Jelani is the genial presence behind this stylish culinary retreat teaching the secrets and skills of Malaysian cuisine (p71).

Serendah Tenggiri

4 Landscape architect Ng Seksan has crafted this chic rough-luxe guesthouse that also acts as a gallery for his amazing private collection of contemporary Malaysian art (p73).

Bangsar Shopping Centre

5 The expat-friendly suburb stakes its claim in KL's contemporary dining stakes with the sleek makeover of this mall into a food-focused consumer experience (p96).

Tanarimba

6 Learn jungle survival skills on a three-hour trek through the cool temperate rainforests of this private estate; you can also stay overnight in a handsomely rustic piece of modern architecture (p107).

Melaka Monorail

7 Who knows how long it will take to finish (it's being built in stages) but a functioning monorail could take the edge off Melaka's horrendous traffic problems (p125).

Suffolk House

8 An evolving restoration project spearheaded by Penang Heritage Trust, this grand Georgian mansion sits on the site of Sir Francis Light's (founder of modern Penang) residence (p155).

Malihom

9 There are panoramic views from the nine 100-year-old rice barns, imported from Thailand, that form the Bali-esque accommodation at this idyllic retreat in the hills of Penang (p178).

Performing Arts Centre of Penang

10 By the end of 2011 this new state-of-the-art facility beside the sea in Georgetown will be bringing theatre, films, art shows and other cultural performances to Penang (p170).

if you like...

Great Food

Our Malaysian trio are sensational destinations to enjoy a waistline-expanding menu of delicious meals, from hawker-stall delights to five-star banquets. Each area has local delicacies you must sample as well as colourful fresh-produce markets that are as much a feast for the eyes as they are for the stomach.

Hawker stalls As the contents of woks are tossed, and flames flare, the street-side cooks at hot spots such as Jln Alor in KL provide dramatic theatre as well as scrumptious eats (p76)

Local delicacies Penang and Melaka both have unique food cultures, a product of centuries of ethnic mingling and creative use of ingredients (p200)

Cooking classes Learn how to cook like a native at classes in KL (p59) and Penang (p156)

Tropical fruit Oranges are far from the only fruit – treat your tastebuds to everything from the sweetly perfumed longan to the painfully pungent durian (p204)

Shopping

Although not quite the unparalleled shopping destinations that tourist literature would have you believe, these places are certainly no slouches either when it comes to providing tempting ways to open your wallet and fill your suitcases. Mall culture is highly developed with consumer complexes to satisfy practically all cravings.

Contemporary art Discover the next great Southeast Asian artist in KL's impressive range of commercial galleries (p89)

Suria KLCC Slick and seductive, just as you'd expect for the mall that sits at the base of the Petronas Towers (p97)

Jonker's Walk Browse the curio shops and other emporia any day along this atmospheric Melaka street, then return Friday and Saturday nights for the busy street market with great food and fun performances (p137)

Pewter Royal Selangor (p96) and Penang Pewter (p171) are the two biggest brands for items crafted from this tin alloy

Arts & Crafts

The collections in museums and pieces in antique shops are proof that Malaysians have long had a talent for producing beautiful objects that enhance daily life. Hand-painted batik cloth, giant paper kites, buffalo-hide shadow puppets and expertly woven baskets and boxes are among the crafts still produced locally today.

Kompleks Budaya Kraf Craftspeople and artists work in the cabanas surrounding this government-sponsored craft centre where you can also learn how to make batik (p93)

National Textiles Museum Admire skilful weaving, embroidery, knitting and batik printing in this new museum that gathers together beautiful and rare examples of clothing and fabric (p49)

Islamic Arts Museum Marvel at how craftspeople have been inspired by their Muslim faith to produce gorgeous works of art (p51)

Nonya beaded shoes An intricate fashion beloved by Straits Chinese women and still manufactured in Melaka (p137)

GREG ELMS / LONELY PLANET IMAGES ©

>> A traditional Malay timber house coexists colourfully with more-modern KL architecture

History

Unesco has recognised the World Heritage significance of the townscapes of Melaka and Georgetown. In both these locations and in the capital, KL, significant landmarks and sights provide three-dimensional history lessons on the evolution of Malaysia.

National Museum Join one of the free guided tours of this excellent museum that covers the region's history from prehistoric times to the modern day (p51)

St Paul's Church Dating back to the era of Portuguese rule of Melaka, this Catholic church was the location of miracles performed by St Francis Xavier (p116)

Fort Cornwallis Built on the spot where Captain Light first set foot on Penang and established one of the British Empire's most important strategic outposts (p147)

Stadium Merdeka The heritage conservation body Badan Warisan won an award for its work restoring this open-air stadium built for the declaration of independence in 1957 (p47)

Architecture

Vividly painted and handsomely proportioned wooden Malay houses can still be found in areas of KL, Melaka and Penang. More easily spotted are the distinctive modern skyscrapers and complexes of the capital and its Victorian–Moorish–Mogul mash-up of colonial buildings, such as the old KL railway station, a monument to the grand days of train travel.

Petronas Towers The steel-wrapped twin towers are the poster children of contemporary architecture in Malaysia (p40)

Putrajaya See what a booming economy can buy in this showcase of modern urban planning and vaulting architectural ambition (p109)

Khoo Kongsi Hard to believe that this fabulous example of a Chinese clanhouse was once more ostentatious than it is now (p150)

Masjid Sultan Salahuddin Abdul Aziz Shah Shah Alam's massive Blue Mosque is one of the largest in Southeast Asia and a sight to behold (p108)

Activities

There's plenty more to do in these destinations than eating, shopping and sightseeing. Nature lovers can enjoy treks along jungle trails in the hills that surround KL, and in the hinterland of Penang. It's also possible to learn how to dive, play a round of golf and – for those who'd rather relax indoors – take a course in mediation and yoga, as well as indulge in some bodily pampering at a spa.

Tanarimba Follow a half-day guided trek through the cool temperate rainforest that dominates this private estate less than an hour's drive north of KL (p107)

KL Bird Park Bird spotting is easy in this massive aviary that is the highlight of KL's Lake Gardens (p51)

Eco bike tour Get on your bike to explore the series of *kampung* (villages) and the plantations surrounding Melaka (p124)

Formula 1 racing Don't worry if you can't make to the Malaysian Grand Prix – wannabe Jenson Buttons can take their own spin around the Sepang International Circuit (p111)

month by month

1 **Thaipusam**, January/February

2 **Chinese New Year**, January/February

3 **Petronas Malaysian Grand Prix**, April

4 **Hungry Ghosts Festival**, August

5 **Hari Raya Puasa**, September

Hindus, Muslims and Chinese all follow a lunar calendar, so the dates for many religious festivals vary each year. Muslim holidays typically move forward 11 days each year, while Hindu and Chinese festivals change dates but fall roughly within the same months. Dates have been given where they are known, but may be subject to slight change.

January

Average temperatures vary little through the year across the region. This month can be very busy for travel if Chinese New Year falls within it, so plan ahead. Thaipusam, the other major festival at this time, can also fall in February in some years.

⭐ Chinese New Year

Dragon dances and pedestrian parades mark the start of the new year. Families hold open house and everybody wishes you *kong hee fatt choy* (a happy and prosperous new year). Celebrated on 23 January 2012, 10 February 2013, 31 January 2014.

⭐ Thaipusam

Enormous crowds converge at Batu Caves north of KL and at Nattukotai Chettiar Temple in Penang for this dramatic Hindu festival involving body piercing. Falls between mid-January and mid-February. For more details see p104.

March

⭐ Birthday of the Goddess of Mercy

Offerings are made to the very popular Chinese goddess Kuan Yin at temples across the region; a good one to visit is Thean Hou Temple in KL. The goddess is also honoured three times more during the year, in April/May, July/August and October/November.

👁 Putrajaya International Hot Air Balloon Fiesta

Held over four days in Putrajaya, this festival has hosted hot air balloon pilots from as far afield as New Zealand and Switzerland as well as attracting over 100,000 spectators. Find details at www.myballoonfiesta.com.

April

The end of the light monsoon season on Malaysia's west coast, but not the end of rain, for which you should always be prepared.

☆ Petronas Malaysian Grand Prix

Formula 1's big outing in Southeast Asia is held at the Sepang International Circuit (see p111) over three days, usually at the start of the month. Associated events and parties are held in KL; for more details see www.malaysiangp.com.my.

May

⭐ Wesak Day (Vesak Day)

Buddha's birth, enlightenment and death are celebrated with various events, including the release of caged birds to symbolise the setting free of captive souls, and processions in KL, Melaka and Penang. Celebrated on 17 May 2011, 5 May 2012 and 25 May 2013.

June

Festa San Pedro

This week-long fiesta is celebrated by the Eurasian-Portuguese Christian community of Melaka, and it culminates on 29 June with the main feast day in honour of the patron saint of the fishing community.

Dragon Boat Festival

Commemorates the Malay legend of the fishermen who paddled out to sea to prevent the drowning of a Chinese saint, beating drums to scare away any fish that might attack him. The festival is celebrated from June to August, with boat races in Penang.

August

Festival of the Hungry Ghosts

Chinese Malaysians perform operas, host open-air concerts and lay out food for their ancestors. The ghosts eat the spirit of the food, but thoughtfully leave the substance for mortal celebrants. Celebrated on 14 August 2011, 31 August 2012 and 21 August 2013.

National Day

Join the crowds at midnight on 31 August to celebrate the anniversary of Malaysia's independence in 1957. Events are usually held in Merdeka Sq (Dataran Merdeka) in KL. The next morning there are parades and festivities across the country.

September

Haze from forest and field-clearance fires in Indonesia can create urban smog in KL, Melaka and Penang, so avoid visiting during this month and the next if you are prone to respiratory complaints and asthma.

Hari Raya Puasa

The Muslim fasting month of Ramadan culminates in this major festival traditionally celebrated at home with big banquets. All forms of transport and accommodation fill up at this time as people visit their families or take short vacations.

October

The start of the monsoon season on Malaysia's west coast sees rainfall in Melaka and Penang peak during this month, but it's not so heavy or constant as to affect most travel plans.

Malaysian International Gourmet Festival

Prestigious restaurants and master chefs all pitch in with their best efforts during this month-long celebration of edible creativity in KL that includes food fairs and cooking classes. Full details at www.migf.com.

Deepavali

Tiny oil-lamps are lit outside Hindu homes to attract the auspicious gods Rama and Lakshmi. Indian businesses start the new financial year, and families take a predawn oil bath, put on new clothes and share sweets. Celebrated around 26 October 2011 and 13 November 2012.

December

School holidays can see hotels booked up towards the end of the month when many people arrive in the region to holiday over the Christmas and New Year breaks.

Winter Solstice Festival

Called *Dong Zhi* in Mandarin and *Tang Chek* in Hokkien, this Chinese festival offers thanks for a good harvest and usually occurs between 21 and 23 December. It's celebrated by eating glutinous rice balls served in a clear sugar syrup.

itineraries

Whether you've got six days or 60, these itineraries provide a starting point for the trip of a lifetime. Want more inspiration? Head online to lonelyplanet. com/thorntree to chat with other travellers.

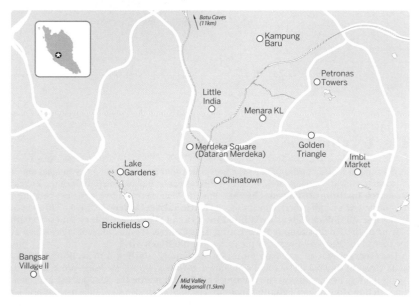

Four Days
Essential KL

❭ For a bird's eye overview of the city take your pick between the skybridge and observation deck of the **Petronas Towers** or the bulbous head of **Menara KL** atop the jungle-clad hill Bukit Nanas. Explore **Chinatown**, dropping by its markets and Hindu and Taoist temples, and admire the colonial buildings around nearby **Merdeka Square** (Dataran Merdeka). Spend the evening in the **Golden Triangle** – dig into delicious food along Jln Alor, then sample the nightlife along buzzing Changkat Bukit Bintang.

Make the **Lake Gardens** the focus of day two, not missing KL Bird Park, the Islamic Arts Museum and the National Museum. Sample authentic Indian cuisine in either **Brickfields** or **Little India**. On day three, having enjoyed breakfast at **Imbi Market**, venture out to **Batu Caves**; exploring the cave temples only takes a couple of hours, leaving time the same day to wander the sleepy streets of **Kampung Baru** back in KL. Set aside day four for some 'me time': enjoy some retail therapy in giant shopping malls such as **Mid Valley Megamall**, or indulge in a luxurious spa treatment at Hamman in **Bangsar Village II**.

Two Weeks
The Terrific Trio

❯ Starting in Kuala Lumpur, follow the previous itinerary, adding on a day to head out of town to view the modern architecture of **Putrajaya** or the lush surrounds of the **Forest Research Institute of Malaysia (FRIM)**. Tap into Malaysia's creative scene by spending a day touring KL's major galleries, including the **National Art Gallery** near Lake Titiwangsa, White Box at **Publika**, **Valentine Willie Fine Art** and **Wei-Ling Gallery**; and see what's playing at the **Kuala Lumpur Performing Arts Centre**, the magnificent concert hall at the base of the Petronas Towers, or the jazz venue **No Black Tie**.

Use **Georgetown** as your base for exploring Penang, starting with **walking tours** of its fascinating colonial district and Chinatown, a Unesco World Heritage–protected area. Along the way be sure to visit the **Cheong Fatt Tze Mansion**, the fabulously ornate clan-house **Khoo Kongsi** and **Penang Museum**. Having prepped your stomach on afternoon tea in the elegant surrounds of the **Eastern & Oriental Hotel** or the restored grandeur of **Suffolk House**, go for broke by night trawling Penang's amazing range of streetside **hawker stalls**.

Lose yourself for half a day at the enormous **Kek Lok Si Temple**, which has an excellent vegetarian restaurant on the premises. Alternatively, stroll the pathways of the lovely **Botanical Gardens** and continue on to the base of **Penang Hill**. Ride the funicular railway to the peak and spend the rest of the afternoon strolling the trails in the cool air. Leave a couple of days to explore the rest of the island, including **Penang National Park** and the beaches and resorts at **Batu Ferringhi**.

Round off your trip with a few days in Melaka, becoming acquainted with the delights of Peranakan cuisine. Tick off the main historic sights, including the **Stadthuys**, **Porta de Santiago**, **St Paul's Church**, the **Sultanate Palace**, **Villa Sentosa** and historic **China-town**, where you'll find the **Baba-Nonya Heritage Museum**. Escape the crowds at **Bukit China** graveyard, with sunset views of the city. Time permitting, enjoy a **riverboat cruise** or an **Eco Bike Tour** and, if it's Friday or Saturday, don't miss the **Jonker's Walk Night Market**.

Shopping

Sale Times

Malaysia Grand Prix Sale March to early April
Malaysia Mega Sale Carnival Mid-July to mid-September
Malaysia Year-End Sale End November to early January

Shopping Hours

Variable, but most places open from around 9.30am to 7pm Monday to Saturday. Big department stores and shopping malls are open 10am to 10pm daily.

Shopping Festivals

The following all take place in Kuala Lumpur.
Hari Kraf Kebangsaan (www.kraftangan. gov.my) February-March
KL Design Week (www.kualalumpurdesign week.com.my) April
Malaysian International Shoe Festival (www.malaysiafootwear.com) April
Malaysian Fashion Week (www.mifa.com. my) November

Refunds

Policies vary from shop to shop; as a rule you'll find more flexible, consumer-friendly service at international brand stores.

The Shopping Scene

When it comes to shopping, Malaysia offers a good range of appealing handicrafts and souvenirs, all the major international brands (in real and fake versions), masses of mega malls and decent sale prices. Kuala Lumpur in particular pitches itself as a star player on the Asian shopping parade, a worthy contender to retail heavyweights Singapore, Bangkok and Hong Kong.

However, when something seems too good to be true it usually is, and the shopping scene is no exception. There are bargain buys, but Malaysia is too middle class a country to offer consistently dirt cheap prices. Counterfeit goods are a problem – not just Prada handbags and Rolex watches, but also software and electronics. Local fashionistas complain that international labels try to palm off the last season's looks on Malaysia. And several retail entrepreneurs lament the conservative nature of the local crafts industry and how skilled artisans are a dying breed.

This said, there is good shopping to be had, from fun, throw-away fashions from across Asia, to quality antique pieces and exquisite local crafts. KL hosts events throughout the year showcasing local retail talent and, while mall culture rules, lively outdoor markets are still very popular. There's also an interesting trend for online niche stores and boutiques, some of which have graduated to bricks-and-mortar retail operations.

BEST BATIK BUYS

iKARRTiNi (KL; p94)

Peter Hoe Evolution (KL; p95)

Pink Jambu (KL; p97)

Where to Shop

See the Shopping sections of the Kuala Lumpur (p91), Penang (p170) and Melaka (p137) chapters to get on the fast track to the best of the best.

Malls

Malaysians adore malls – it's so hot outside who can blame them for wanting to shop in air-conditioned comfort. Nowhere is this love affair more pronounced than in KL and its surrounds, which has become a city of malls; among the latest additions are Fahrenheit88 and Publika. There are malls so big here it would take several days to do them justice – Mid Valley Megamall and Sunway Pyramid, for example, are like communities unto themselves with hotels, entertainment facilities and, in the former, even a hundred-year-old Hindu temple! Melaka's Dataran Pahlawan and Penang's Prangin Mall are two more outsized shopping complexes worth swinging through.

Department Stores & Hypermarkets

Invariably anchoring the malls are department stores specialising in fashion, accessories and homewares. The major operations are **Jusco** (www.jusco.com.my), **Metrojaya** (www.metrojaya.com), **Parkson** (www.parkson.com.my) and **Robinsons** (www.robinsons.com.my). You'll also come across branches of overseas department stores such as Japan's **Isetan** (www.isetankl.com.my) and the UK's Marks & Spencer and Debenhams.

Hypermarkets (giant supermarkets) include the local sell-it-cheap wholesaler **Mydin** (www.mydin.com.my) and the French-owned **Carrefour** (www.carrefour.com.my).

Markets

The street and permanent markets in KL, Melaka and Penang are hugely enjoyable and atmospheric experiences regardless of whether you have a purchase in mind. Day markets are usually focused around fresh produce – the main ones in KL include Chinatown, Chow Kit and Pudu. Vendors at *pasar malam* (night markets) typically sell prepared food, clothing, accessories, DVDs and CDs and the like. Some occur daily, such as the one along Jln Petaling in KL's Chinatown, others once or twice a week, such as Melaka's Jonker's Walk.

There's a trend for flea, fashion and craft markets too (see p93). Georgetown's Little Penang Street Market runs on the last Sunday of the month and is well worth attending.

What to Buy

Traditional craft-making is still practised across Malaysia and you can find great pieces for sale in KL, Melaka and Penang that make ideal souvenirs and gifts. Fashion is another good buy and contemporary art galleries, antique stores and interior design shops are worth a look.

FASHION INSIDER *SUEANN CHONG*

Rising stars of KL's design scene include Nurita Harith, Jonathan Liang, Tengku Syahmi and Justin Yap – all have been singled out for awards given by the **Malaysian International Fashion Alliance** (www.mifa.com.my). There are also more-established names such as Bernard Chandran, Khoon Hooi, Sonny Sam (of the brand Eclipse) and Tom Abang Saufi – her designs include kaftans that adhere to Islamic codes of modesty but are brightly coloured with batik prints and made of silks and chiffon.

In contrast, there are the young girls who cruise the inexpensive boutiques of Bangsar, Mutiara Damansara and the SS15 area of Subang Jaya (all areas in and around KL). You'll find a lot of similar items from Thailand, South Korea and across Asia in these stores that pick up on the fashion trends of the region.

Sueann Chong is the managing editor of fashion blog Tongue in Chic (www.tonguechic.com).

Textiles

Produced by drawing or printing a pattern on fabric with wax and then dyeing the material, batik fabrics can be made into clothes, cushion covers, tablecloths, placemats or simply displayed as works of art. Traditional abstract patterns have largely been replaced by figurative designs inspired by nature.

Another textile to look out for is *kain songket,* a luxurious fabric with gold and silver threads woven throughout the material.

Basketry & Mengkuang

Basketry is a living art in Malaysia. Local people make all sorts of useful household items using rattan, bamboo, swamp nipah grass and pandanus leaves. *Mengkuang* (a local form of weaving) uses pandanus leaves and strips of bamboo to make baskets, bags and mats.

Kites & Puppets

Eye-catching *wayang kulit* (shadow puppets) are made from buffalo hide to portray characters from epic Hindu legends, while kites are made from paper and bamboo strips in a variety of traditional designs. The crescent-shaped *wau bulan* (moon kite) can reach 3m in length and breadth, while the *wau kucing* (cat kite) is the logo of Malaysia Airlines.

Metalwork

Peninsular Malaysia has many skilled silversmiths who specialise in filigree and repoussé work, where designs are hammered through the silver from the underside. Objects crafted out of pewter (an alloy of tin) are synonymous with Selangor – the Royal Selangor Pewter Factory near KL is the largest pewter manufacturer in the world. Penang also has a number of pewter makers.

Woodcarving

The Orang Asli of Peninsular Malaysia are gifted carvers. The Hma' Meri tribe from Pulau Carey off the coast of Selangor are particularly renowned for their sinuous carvings of animist spirits.

Travel with Children

Best of...for Kids

Each place has different draws for families:

Kuala Lumpur

A giant aviary, butterfly garden, waterfall splash pool and canopy walk; going high, high up the Petronas Towers and Menara KL; space-age shopping malls, a modern aquarium and water park; busy markets; easy access to Zoo Negara and the City of Digital Lights at i-City; good public transport.

Melaka

Crazy trishaw rides, museums galore, river cruises, pedestrian-only heritage area; the world's best *cendol* (shave ice), massive shopping malls, nearby beach and water park.

Penang

Best beaches of the three cities; national park with wild monkeys, lizards and a canopy walk; funicular railway up Penang Hill; hawker food; exploring the city by trishaw; mall and trinket shopping; Toy Museum.

Take in the cultural mix of Southeast Asia in these cosmopolitan cities where families can watch temple ceremonies, take trishaw rides, spot monkeys and taste some of the best food on the continent while having access to clean accommodation, modern malls and fun waterparks.

KL, Melaka & Penang for Kids

Once in situ, activity-driven families will have plenty to explore.

Museums, Temples & Heritage Buildings

Many Malaysian museums are a collection of dioramas with few photos and lots of text; see p27 for a list of the more-fun museums. Temples and heritage buildings can be interesting, but a word of advice: see them in small doses, perhaps just two per day, interspersed with stops for drinks or relaxing. Learning a little about the history and culture via books or videos before you visit can also generate enthusiasm and prolong short attention spans.

Parks, Gardens & Beaches

Kuala Lumpur, Melaka and Penang are bustling, often frenetic cities – not generally considered relaxing beach-holiday destinations. That said, there are decent beaches around Penang, and mediocre ones near Melaka. KL

CROWD-PLEASING TREATS

» **Cendol** Shave ice with cane sugar, coconut milk and jellies.

» **Fruit** Finding it at the market is as much fun as eating it.

» **Char kway tiaw** Broad rice noodles fried in soy sauce.

» **Dim sum** Steamed savoury Chinese dumplings and treats.

» **Roti canai** Flaky crepe served with banana and other variations.

» **Sugar cane juice** Watch the cane go through the press and enjoy it cold.

» **Popiah** Spring rolls – to dip or not to dip in sauce.

» **Murtabak** Indian pancake stuffed with meat, veg and/or egg.

» **Chicken rice** Chicken in a light soy-based sauce served with rice and broth.

is dotted with gardens and parks, making it the most family-friendly destination. Penang comes in a close second with its long stretches of coastline and a national park where you can be sure to see wildlife.

Dining Out

Food is a highlight here and there's a lot on offer that kids will love. Contrary to Western impulse, a busy food stall is usually the safest place to eat – you can see the food being prepared, the ingredients are often fresh and if the wok stays hot there's little chance of bacteria. Grownups can also try more adventurous dishes while the kids get some thing more familiar.

Many restaurants attached to hotels and guesthouses will serve familiar Western food, while international fast food is ubiquitous. Mid-range and upscale restaurants often have highchairs but most budget places don't. Breastfeeding in public should be discreet if at all (remember this is a Muslim country so avoid showing any skin); local women breastfeed in public only rarely, using their headscarves for extra coverage.

Malaysian drinks are very sweet and even fresh juices usually have sugar added. To cut down on sugar ask for drinks without sugar or order bottled water. It's not a bad idea to carry a Steripen (www.steripen. com), a battery-run water filter about the size of a small screwdriver that can purify

tap water as well as ice cubes in any kind of drink. (See p240 for more on drinking water in Malaysia.)

Children's Highlights
Energy Burners

» **Parks & Open Spaces** Lake Gardens (KL), KLCC Park (KL), Taman Tasik Titiwangsa (KL), Bukit Nanas Forest Reserve (KL), Botanical Gardens (Penang), Bukit China (Melaka)

» **Water & Theme Parks** Sunway Lagoon (KL), Genting Highlands (KL), Desa Waterpark (KL), Water World (Melaka), Midlands Park Centre (Penang), Mines Resort City (KL)

» **Beaches** Batu Ferhinggi (Penang), Penang National Park (Penang), Tanjung Bidara (Melaka)

Budding Naturalists

» **Canopy Walkways** Forest Research Institute of Malaysia (KL), Penang National Park (Penang)

» **Zoos, Aquariums & Wildlife Centres** Zoo Negara (KL), Kuala Gandah Wildlife Conservation Centre (KL), Bird Park (KL), Butterfly Park (KL), Aquaria KLCC (KL), Melaka Zoo (Melaka), Penang Aquarium (Penang), Penang Butterfly Farm (Penang), Deer Park (KL)

» **Cheeky Monkeys** Penang National Park (Penang), Botanical Gardens (Penang), Batu Caves (KL)

Culture & History

» **Museums** Petrosains (KL), National Museum (KL), Maritime Museum (Melaka), Toy Museum (Penang)

» **Living History** (for ages 9+) Pinang Peranakan Mansion (Penang), Baba-Nonya Heritage Museum (Melaka), Dr Sun Yat Sen's Penang Base (Penang)

» **Temples & Heritage Buildings** Kek Lok Si Temple (Penang), Batu Caves (KL), Snake Temple (Penang), St Paul's Church (Melaka)

GROWN-UP TIME

There are dedicated play spaces and crèches for younger kids in KL, including Megakidz and Kizsports & Gym (p62).

WHAT TO PACK

All ages need the usual suspects: sunscreen, insect repellent and rain gear (an umbrella is fine).

Babies & Toddlers

☐ A folding pushchair is practical for most areas – think naps through longer trips to museums and temples.

☐ A portable changing mat, hand-wash gel et al (baby changing facilities are a rarity).

Ages 6–12

☐ Binoculars for young explorers to zoom in on wildlife, intricate temple latticework, etc.

☐ A camera to inject newfound fun into 'boring' grown-up sights and walks.

☐ Field guides to Malaysian flora and fauna.

Teens

☐ Malaysia-related iPhone apps.

☐ Bahasa Malaysia phrasebook.

☐ Mask, snorkel and flippers.

High-Tech Forays

» **Viewing Towers** Petronas Towers (KL), Menara KL (KL), Menara Tamin Sari (Melaka)

» **Indoor Action** Cosmo's World (KL), City of Digital Lights at i-City (KL), Cosmic Bowl (KL)

Planning
When to Go

The region is hot pretty much all the time. All three cities are crowded and traffic clogged, which escalates during festival times and weekends (particularly in Melaka). If your family doesn't enjoy packed streets, it's best to avoid the busier periods; otherwise, festivals are a time to experience the culture at its fullest.

Accommodation

Cleanliness standards in Malaysia are high and getting better all the time. Family rooms are available everywhere from certain budget guesthouses to the some of the most deluxe hotels. These rooms generally sleep three or four people; in budget places this might mean a dorm room with two bunk beds or a double bed plus one or two single beds, while at midrange and top-end hotels there's usually a double bed and a lounge area with a pull-out couch. The most comfortable choices are two-bedroom suites or two rooms with an adjoining door, found at larger hotels. Occasionally, guesthouses and hotels that don't have family rooms can provide cots but will usually charge a fee. Budget options will sometimes have shared bathrooms.

TOILETS

It's easy to find an emergency toilet – public parks and museums have them (usually quite clean) and in a bind you can duck into a restaurant where most proprietors will be understanding. Most facilities in Malaysia have Western-style toilets but not all have toilet paper – carry some with you.

regions at a glance

Malaysia's capital of Kuala Lumpur (or KL as it's commonly called) is where you'll most likely arrive and spend the bulk of your time. Surrounding it is the state of Selangor, a prosperous industrial powerhouse with an excellent range of easily accessible tourist attractions including the urban planning showcase of Putrajaya, the federal government's administrative hub.

Two hours' drive south is the historic city and state of Melaka; its glory days as a leading Southeast Asian entrepôt may be long over, but this charming low-rise community continues to draw the tourist crowds. The island of Penang, 350km north of KL, may be Malaysia's smallest state but it packs a considerable multicultural punch with its fantastic food scene, heritage buildings of Georgetown and cool hill station.

Kuala Lumpur

Shopping✓✓
Food✓✓✓
Art Galleries✓✓✓

Super Shopping
Shopaholics will be thrilled by KL's multiplicity of malls. There's also classic Southeast Asian fresh-produce day markets and several atmospheric night markets, the most famous of which is the one along Chinatown's Jln Petaling. Also don't miss the Central Market, an Art Deco souvenir treasure house.

Fantastic Food
Allow your stomach to lead the way around KL. Tuck in with locals at the fantastic hawker stalls along Jln Alor, Imbi Market or Madras Lane. Sample Indian food in Brickfields and Little India and a brilliant array of international options in Bangsar and along the city's party strip, Changat Bukit Bintang.

Contemporary Art
Access Malaysia's vibrant contemporary art scene at the National Art Gallery or at exhibitions held in commercial galleries such as the Annexe Gallery and Valentine Willie Fine Art.

p34

Melaka

Shopping ✓
Food ✓✓✓
Heritage ✓✓✓

Funky or Modern
Shop Chinatown's Southeast Asian hippie-ish clothing, masterfully beaded Nonya shoes, and trinkets from sunglasses to incense holders. Or go modern in massive air-con malls to shop for camera equipment and name brands. Don't miss Jonker's Walk Night Market with sale stalls alongside food vendors.

Sit-down Meals
Take a dim-sum breakfast, banana-leaf curry for lunch and Nonya specialities for dinner. Melaka isn't swarming with hawker stalls like KL and Penang but offers an exceptional choice of eateries boasting international and regional cuisines.

Walkable Heritage
Wander past Chinese shophouses, Dutch colonial architecture, Chinese and Hindu temples, mosques and churches. Learn about history, culture and architecture at abundant museums and experience it alive today within the ancient buildings.

p113

Penang

Shopping ✓✓
Food ✓✓✓
Heritage ✓✓✓

Malls to Local Artists
Mall-crawl from souk-like markets to antiseptic labyrinths of computer and watch stores. Head to Jln Penang to get lost in Sam's Batik House for funky clothes or antique and pewter shops for precious trinkets. Don't forget Penang artists' romantic paintings, glass objects and more.

Hit the Street Stalls
As Parisians have mastered patisseries, Penangites are street-food virtuosos. Try the specialities, seek out twists on old favourites then move on to Indian curries, Nonya dishes, good sushi and fusion cuisine at chic restaurants.

Historic Elegance
Once-dilapidated Chinese shophouses are being revamped to become silk-cushioned boutique hotels. Walk down hidden, paint-chipped alleys, duck into ornate temples then sleep it all off in a heritage suite with louvred shutters and antique furniture.

p142

Look out for these icons:

 TOP CHOICE Our author's recommendation

 A green or sustainable option

 FREE No payment required

See the Index for a full list of destinations covered in this book.

On the Road

Kuala Lumpur

TELEPHONE CODE: 03 / POPULATION: 1.8 MILLION / AREA: 243 SQ KM

Best Places to Stay

» Bayan Indah (p71)

» Fraser Place (p68)

» G City Club Hotel (p71)

» Sahabat Guest House (p67)

» Serendah Tenggiri (p73)

Best Places to Eat

» Imbi Market (p75)

» Frangipani (p75)

» Madras Lane (p74)

» Nathalie's Gourmet Studio (p83)

» Jalan Alor (p76)

» Sek Yuen (p81)

Why Go?

Kuala Lumpur (KL) is the consummate Asian cyber-city: historic temples and mosques rub shoulders with space-age towers and shopping malls; traders' stalls are piled high with pungent durians and counterfeit handbags; monorail cars zip by lush jungle foliage; and locals sip cappuccinos in wi-fi–enabled cafes or feast on delicious streetside hawker food.

One hundred and fifty years since tin miners hacked a base out of the jungle, KL has evolved into an affluent 21st-century metropolis remarkable for its cultural diversity. Ethnic Malays, Chinese prospectors, Indian immigrants and British colonials all helped shaped the city, and each group has left its indelible physical mark as well as a fascinating assortment of cultural traditions.

Eating and shopping are highlights of any visit, but don't restrict yourself just to the heart of the city – there are many easy day trips when you need relief from the hustle and bustle.

When to Go?

If shopping is your aim, coincide your trip with the general sales that happen in March and from the end of November through early January. The end of March and early April is also a good time to visit to take in both KL Design Week and the events around the Malaysian Grand Prix. Foodies can dig into special treats at Ramadan markets and buffets across the city, usually in August and early September.

Good Food Blogs

If KLites have strong opinions about anything, it's on their favourite places to eat – and they're very happy to share recommendations online. **Friedchillies** (www.friedchillies.com) is the go-to website for spot-on reviews and fun video clips by some of the most enthusiastic foodies we've met. Other blogs guaranteed to get you salivating:

» **Eating Asia** (www.eatingasia.typepad.com)
» **Masa Masa** (www.masak-masak.blogspot.com)
» **A Whiff of Lemongrass** (www.awhiffoflemongrass.com)
» **Cumi & Ciki** (www.cumidanciki.com)

KL'S DAY & NIGHT MARKETS

Daily daytime wet markets in Chinatown, Chow Kit and Pudu, with stalls selling live chickens, fresh fish and an eye-boggling selection of exotic fruit and vegetables, are a truly Asian experience. KL also hosts several atmospheric *pasar malam* (night markets) once a week. From mid-afternoon until around midnight whole streets vanish under a sea of hawker stalls, traders' tables and motorcycles modified into mobile kitchens. Apart from stocking up on all kinds of cheap garments, shoes, accessories and gadgets, night markets are brilliant for eating.

Top Four Night Markets

» **Kampung Baru** (Map p60) Around Jln Raja Muda Musa and Jln Raja Alang on Saturday continuing through to Sunday morning (hence it's known as the Sunday Market). Sample satay and spicy Indonesian food and southern Thai seafood dishes.

» **Little India** (Map p60) From 1.30pm on Saturday along Lg TAR. Search out the stall selling freshly made chocolate cakes slavered in chocolate sauce.

» **Bangsar Baru** (Map p59) Sunday, next to a car park off Jln Telawi 1. Sample wonderful sour-spicy *asam laksa*, freshly made *popiah* (spring rolls), *otak otak* (spicy fish paste grilled in banana leaves) and the crepelike *apam balik*.

» **Taman Connaught, Cheras** In the southeast of the city, stretching along Jln Cerdas, this is the longest *pasar malam* in Malaysia. At the western end near Jln Pantas, fuel up on *kway teow mee goreng* (noodles), fresh juices and baked birds' eggs on a stick. Take the LRT or Komuter Train to Bandar Tasik Selatan, then hop in a taxi (around RM7).

TOP FIVE SHOPPING MALLS

» Pavilion KL (p91)
» Suria KLCC (p97)
» Sungei Wang Plaza (p97)
» Mid Valley Megamall (p95)
» Bangsar Village I & II (p96)

Best KL Day Trips

» Batu Caves (p102)
» FRIM (p103)
» Sunway Lagoon (p106)
» Klang (p108)
» Putrajaya (p109)

Internet Resources

» KLue (www.klue.com.my) Features and listings

» KL Tourist Association (www.klta.org.my) Tourist information

» Time Out Kuala Lumpur (www.timeoutkl.com) What's on in KL

» Visit KL (www.visitkl.gov.my) Official city site

Kuala Lumpur Highlights

1 Admire the glittering exterior of the **Petronas Towers** (p40), then head up to the top-floor observation deck

2 Day or night, bustling **Chinatown** (p46) is a dynamic place to eat, shop and people watch

3 Climb the 272 steps up the side of a limestone outcrop to enter the **Batu Caves** (p102), home to vividly decorated Hindu temples

4 Stand at KL's colonial heart on **Merdeka Square** (p49) and admire the handsome ensemble of heritage buildings

5 All kinds of feathered beauties can be spotted in **KL Bird Park** (p51), showpiece of the lush Lake Gardens

6 Get a treetop perspective on KL from the canopy walkway at **FRIM** (p103)

7 Admire the beautiful objects gathered from around the Islamic world in the **Islamic Arts Museum** (p51)

8 Pay respects to the heavenly mother at the riotously colourful **Thean Hou Temple** (p56)

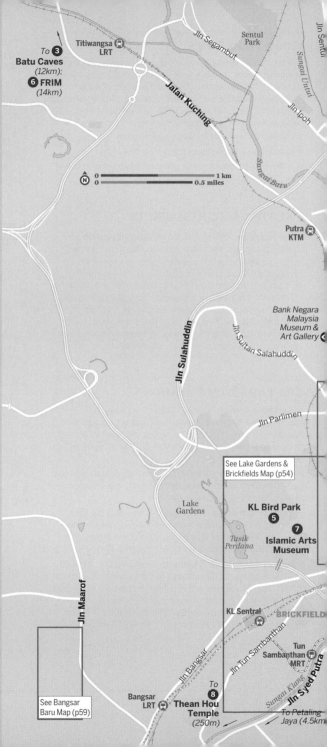

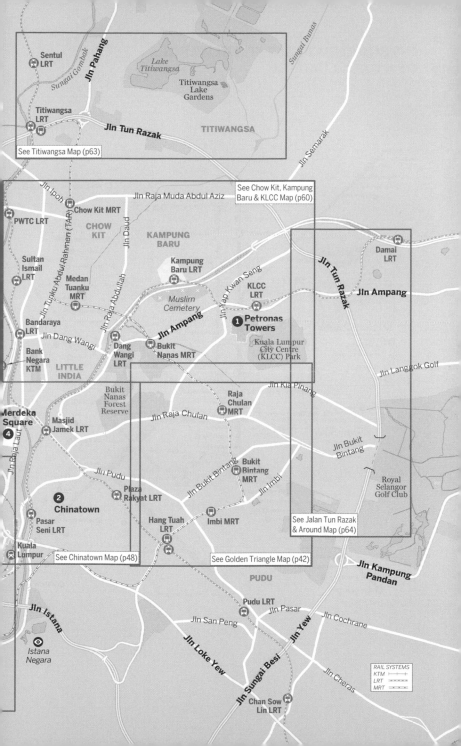

INTEGRATED TRANSIT NETWORK OF KUALA LUMPUR

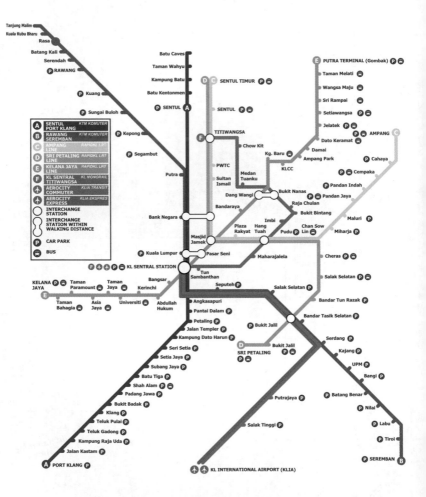

History

In 1857, 87 Chinese prospectors in search of tin landed at the meeting point of the Klang and Gombak rivers and set up camp, naming the spot Kuala Lumpur, meaning 'muddy confluence'. Within a month all but 17 of the prospectors had died of malaria and other tropical diseases, but the tin they discovered in Ampang attracted more miners and KL quickly became a brawling, noisy, violent boomtown, ruled over by so-called 'secret societies', a network of Chinese criminal gangs.

As in other parts of the Malay Peninsula, the local sultan appointed a proxy (known as Kapitan China) to bring the unruly Chinese fortune-seekers and their secret societies into line, the most famous of these being Yap Ah Loy. According to legend, Yap was able to keep the peace with just six policemen, such was the respect for his authority within the Chinese community.

Yap had only just established control when local sultans went to war over the throne of Perak and its tin mines, marking the start of the Malay Civil War. KL was swept up in the conflict and burnt to the ground in 1881. This allowed the British government representative, Frank Swettenham, to push through a radical new town plan that transferred the central government from Klang to KL. By 1886 a railway line linked KL to Klang. A year later a new city was constructed in fire-resistant brick, and in 1896 KL became the capital of the newly formed Federated Malay States.

During WWII, Japanese forces occupied KL. Many Chinese were tortured and killed, and many Indians and British prisoners of war were sent to work on Burma's notorious 'Death Railway' or interned in Pudu Jail. The British temporarily returned after WWII, only to be ousted when Malaysia finally declared its independence in 1957.

KL continued to thrive but was shaken to the core on 13 May 1969, when race riots between Chinese and Malays claimed hundreds, perhaps thousands, of lives. (Authorities have acted quickly to quell any race-related street protests ever since, with police using tear gas and water cannons to disperse antidiscrimination marches by thousands of ethnic Indians in 2007 and 2008.)

In 1974, the sultan of Selangor ceded the city's land to the state so that it could officially become the Federal Territory of Kuala Lumpur. There are no elections for KL's mayor and councillors, who are appointed by the Federal Territories Minister; the current mayor, in office since December 2008, is Ahmad Fuad bin Ismail.

In 1996, Prime Minister Mahathir Mohammed approved the construction of a new political capital 20km south of KL at Putrajaya (p109). Putrajaya was made the official seat of the Malaysian government in 1999 and many government ministries are now located there. This has left KL to concentrate on doing business deals and property development, its latest project being the construction of Malaysia's tallest building (see p186).

◎ Sights

Six-lane highways and flyovers slice up the city, but even so, the best way to get a feel for KL's vibrant atmosphere is to walk. The city centre is surprisingly compact – from Chinatown to Little India takes little more than 10 minutes on foot – and some sights are so close together that it's often quicker to walk than take public transport or grab a cab (which can easily become snarled in traffic and KL's tortuous one-way system). For a couple of walking routes, see p52 and p58. Apart from the sights listed here, be sure to explore some of the eye-boggling

---

THE FOUNDER OF KUALA LUMPUR

He was only 17 when he left his village in southern China in search of work in Malaya. Fifteen years later, Yap Ah Loy had shown sufficient political nous, organisation ability and street smarts to secure the role of KL's third Kapitan China. He took on the task with such ruthless relish that he's now credited as the founder of KL.

Yap's big break was being the friend of KL's second Kapitan China, Liu Ngim Kong. When Liu died in 1869, Yap took over and managed within a few years to gather enough power and respect to be considered the leader of the city's previously fractured Chinese community. He amassed great wealth through his control of the tin trade as well as more nefarious activities, such as opium trading and prostitution, which thrived in the mining boomtown. Yap founded the city's first school in 1884 and, by the time he died a year later, it's said he owned a quarter of the buildings in KL.

shopping malls (p91) – all part of the essential KL experience.

GOLDEN TRIANGLE, KLCC & AROUND

KL's most iconic modern building – the Petronas Towers – is the focal point of the Kuala Lumpur City Centre (KLCC), built across the former site of the Selangor Turf Club. This 40-hectare development includes a sprawling tropical park, huge convention centre, aquarium, excellent kids' museum, world-class concert hall and Suria KLCC (p97), one of KL's best shopping malls.

Around 15 minutes' walk west of the KLCC back towards Chinatown, Bukit Nanas Forest Recreational Park is crowned by another of the city's iconic structures: Menara KL. South of here, the intersection of Jln Sultan Ismail and Jln Bukit Bintang marks the heart of the Golden Triangle, KL's premier business, shopping and entertainment district.

Petronas Towers   MODERN ARCHITECTURE

(Map p60; www.petronastwintowers.com.my; KLCC, Jln Ampang) Epitomising modern KL are these shimmering stainless steel–clad towers, the headquarters of the national oil and gas company Petronas. Resembling twin silver rockets plucked from an early episode of *Flash Gordon,* they are the perfect allegory for the meteoric rise of the city from tin miners' hovel to space-age metropolis.

Opened in 1998, the 88-storey twin towers are nearly 452m tall, making them the seventh-highest built structures in the world (as of 2010). Designed by Argentinian architect Cesar Pelli, the twin towers' floor plan is based on an eight-sided star that echoes arabesque patterns. Islamic influences are also evident in each tower's five tiers – representing the five pillars of Islam – and in the 63m masts that crown them, calling to mind the minarets of a mosque and the Star of Islam. Apart from Petronas the towers also house the offices of several other companies, including Al Jazeera's Asian broadcasting centre.

There are three packages for going up the towers, all of which can be purchased from the ticket counter in the basement. The cheapest deal only allows access to the 41st-floor **Skybridge** (ticket RM10; ☺9am-7pm Tue-Sun, closed 1-2.30pm Fri) connecting the two towers, a modest 170m above ground. For RM40 you can continue up to the 88th floor observation deck in Tower 2, while a premium package (including lunch/dinner RM200/350) also gains you access to the tower's exclusive members-only Malaysian Petroleum Club for a meal. Avoid visiting at weekends and public holidays when the complex is at its busiest.

Menara KL   OBSERVATION TOWER

(KL Tower; Map p42; ☏2020 5448; www.menarakl.com.my; 2 Jln Punchak) Although the Petronas Towers are taller, the 421m Menara KL, rising from the crest of Bukit Nanas, offers the best city views. Surrounded by a dense area of pristine jungle, this lofty spire is the world's fourth-highest telecommunications tower – the bulb at the top (its shape inspired by a Malaysian spinning toy) contains the revolving restaurant Seri Angkasa (p80) and an **observation deck** (adult/child RM38/28; ☺9am-10pm, last tickets 9.30pm). This is the best place to appreciate the phenomenal growth of the city.

A **shuttle bus** (every 15 min; free; ☺9am-9.30pm) runs up to the tower from the gate on Jln Punchak opposite the PanGlobal building.

Bukit Nanas Forest Reserve   NATURE RESERVE

(Map p42; ☺7am-6pm) If you fancy a bit of a workout, an alternative to the shuttle bus to the tower is by climbing the short and well-labelled nature trails through the Bukit Nanas Forest Reserve. This lowland dipterocarp forest reserve was gazetted in 1906 making it the oldest protected piece of jungle in Malaysia. Explore it alone, or on a free guided tour starting from the entrance to Menara KL at 11am, 12.30pm, 2.30pm and 4.30pm daily and lasting about 45 minutes. There are good displays and leaflets in the **Forest Information Centre** (☏2026 4741; www.forestry.gov.my; Jln Raja Chulan; ☺9am-5pm) at the base of the hill.

Aquaria KLCC   AQUARIUM

(Map p42; ☏2333 1888; www.klaquaria.com; concourse level, KL Convention Centre; adult/child aquarium RM45/35; aquarium & aquazone RM80/52; ☺11am-8pm) This impressive aquarium is a short stroll from Suria KLCC, in the basement of the KL Convention Centre. As well as tanks of colourful fish and touch-a-starfish–type activities, you can walk through a 90m underwater tunnel to view sinister-looking (but mostly harmless) sand tiger sharks and giant gropers. Time your trip to coincide with the shark feeding (3pm on Monday, Wednesday and Saturday). If you're a certified diver you can also get into the tanks with the sharks (RM400).

TRADITIONAL CHINESE MEDICINE

In 1997 Ng Chee Yat, a University of Birmingham–trained pharmacist, started the **KL Academy of Traditional Chinese Medicine** (Map p48; ☑2026 5273; www.klatcm. com; 138-140 Jln Petaling; ☺Mon-Fri 7-10pm, Sat 2-10pm, Sun 9am-6pm) along with some friends. The academy provides training for those wanting to learn the ancient practices of traditional Chinese medicine (TCM). It runs year-long courses in English and French and operates as a drop-in clinic for patients.

What kind of ailments do patients come here to get treated for?

A variety of things, but mainly aches and pains, soft-tissue injuries and spinal diseases.

What's the fundamental difference between Western medicine and TCM?

I could write a dissertation for you about that! Essentially, though, Chinese medicine is more holistic – a TCM doctor may talk about your body's fire, for example, and prescribe a course of treatment to reduce the heat, cool your system. That may involve acupuncture, cupping, reflexology or a course of herbal remedies.

How much does a consultation cost?

It's RM6 to see the doctor and RM10 if that's followed by a session of acupuncture.

How safe is acupuncture?

Very safe. The needles are only used once and they are swabbed with alcohol before being used, too.

What kind of training do TCM doctors go through?

The majority of students here are working adults, so they come three or four times a week in the evenings to study for three hours each session over five years. To graduate they then have to spend six months on practical training at the Heilongjiang University of Chinese medicine in Harbin, China.

What regulatory control is there of TCM in Malaysia?

At present there are no specific laws to control complementary medicine, but a government bill is in the works.

Ng Chee Yat is the second-generation owner of Kien Fatt Medical Store (p97), a family concern that has been operating in Chinatown since 1943.

To feed some of the fish directly, dip your feet into pools of *Garra rufa* (doctor fish) at the Aquazone Fish Therapy Centre (adult/child RM38/22); for more about these fishy podiatrists see p69.

Petrosains   SCIENCE MUSEUM
(Map p60; ☑2331 8181; www.petrosains.com. my; Level 4, Suria KLCC; adult/child RM12/4; ☺9.30am-4pm Tue-Thu, 1.30-4pm Fri, 9.30am-5pm Sat & Sun) Kids and kidults can fill an educational few hours at this interactive science discovery centre in Suria KLCC with all sorts of buttons to press and levers to pull. Many of the activities and displays focus on the wonderful things that petrol has bought to Malaysia –

no prizes for guessing who sponsors the museum.

FREE **Galeri Petronas**   ART GALLERY
(Map p60; ☑2051 7770; www.galeri petronas.com.my; 3rd fl, Suria KLCC; ☺10am-8pm Tue-Sun) Swap consumerism for culture at this excellent art gallery showcasing contemporary photography and paintings. It's a bright, modern space with interesting, professionally curated shows that change every few months.

KLCC Park   PARK
(Map p60; ☺24hr) Having admired the towers and done a little shopping in Suria KLCC, leave time to wander through the attached park. Here you'll

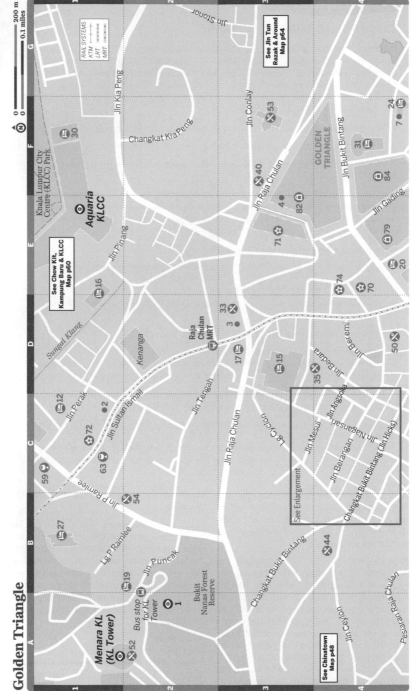

Golden Triangle

0 200 m
0 0.1 miles

N

RAIL SYSTEMS
KTM
LRT
MRT

See Jln Tun
Razak & Around
Map p54

GOLDEN
TRIANGLE

See Chow Kit,
Kampung Baru & KLCC
Map p60

Kuala Lumpur City
Centre (KLCC) Park

Aquaria
KLCC

Jln Kia Peng

Changkat Kia Peng

Jln Stonor

Jln Conlay

Jln Bukit Bintang

Jln Pinang

Jln Gading

Sungai Klang

Kenanga

Raja
Chulan
MRT

Jln Raja Chulan

Jln Tengah

Jln Sultan Ismail

Jln Perak

Jln P Ramlee

Lg P Ramlee

Jln Raja Chulan

Le Cyclon

Jln Beremi

Jln Beddara

See Enlargement

Jln Mesui

Jln Angsoka

Jln Nagasari

Jln Berangan

Changkat Bukit Bintang (Jln Hicks)

Changkat Bukit Bintang

Jln Puncak

Bukit
Nanas Forest
Reserve

Bus stop
for KL
Tower

Menara KL
(KL Tower)

See Chinatown
Map p48

Jln Ceylon

Jln Raja Chulan

Pesiaran Raja Chulan

30
53
40
4
82
71
24
7
31
84
79
20
74
70
16
33
3
17
15
35
50
12
72
2
63
59
27
54
44
19
1
52

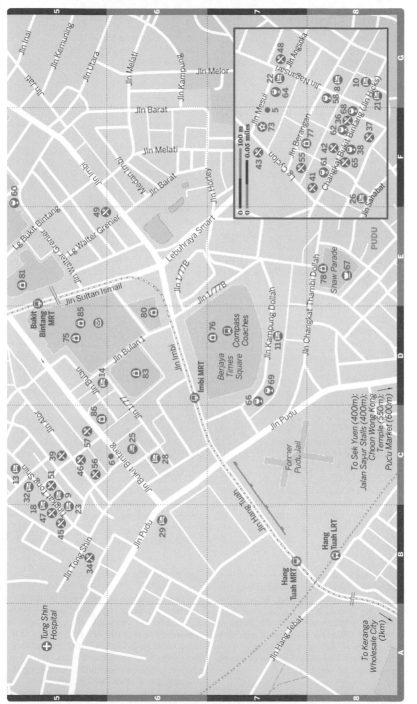

Golden Triangle

Top Sights

Aquaria KLCC ... E1
Menara KL (KL Tower) ... A1

Sights

1 Bukit Nanas Forest Reserve ... A2
Flying Fox Park ... (see 1)

Activities, Courses & Tours

Ampang Superbowl ... (see 76)
Asianel Reflexology Spa ... (see 84)
Berjaya Times Square Theme Park ... (see 76)
Celebrity Fitness ... (see 81)
Cosmo's World Theme Park Theatre ... (see 76)
Donna Spa ... (see 84)
2 Fitness First ... C1
Foot Master Dr Fish Spa ... (see 76)
3 Genting Highlands Sales Office ... D3
JoJoBa Spa ... (see 76)
4 Kenko ... E3
Kings Kitchen Klub ... (see 31)
5 Lightworks ... F7
Morino Kaze ... (see 20)
6 Old Asia ... C6
7 Spa Village ... F4

Sleeping

8 41 Berangan ... G8
9 Anggun Boutique Hotel ... C5
10 Bedz KL ... G8
11 Classic Inn ... D7
12 Fraser Place Kuala Lumpur ... C1
13 Green Hut Lodge ... C5
14 Hotel Capitol ... D5
15 Hotel Istana ... D3
16 Impiana ... E1
17 Lodge Paradise Hotel ... D3
18 Number Eight Guesthouse ... B5
19 Pacific Regency Hotel Suites ... B2
20 Piccolo Hotel ... E4
21 Radius International Hotel ... G8
22 Rainforest Bed & Breakfast ... G7
23 Red Palm ... B5
24 Ritz Carlton ... F4
25 Royale Bintang Kuala Lumpur ... C6
26 Sahabat Guest House ... F8
27 Shangri-La Hotel ... B1
28 Sky Hotel ... C6
29 Swiss-Garden Hotel ... B6
30 Traders Hotel Kuala Lumpur ... F1
31 Westin Kuala Lumpur ... F4
32 YY38 Hotel ... C5

Eating

33 Betty's Café ... D3
Bibitus ... (see 38)
Bijan ... (see 44)
34 Blue Boy Vegetarian Food Centre ... B5
35 Chiaroscuro ... D4
36 Daikanyama ... F8
Din Tai Fung ... (see 82)
Dragon-i ... (see 82)
37 Elcerdo ... F8
Enak ... (see 84)
Food Republic ... (see 82)
38 Frangipani ... F8
39 Frog Porridge Stall ... C5
Gonbei ... (see 84)
40 Hakka ... F3
41 Le Bouchon ... F8
Loaf ... (see 82)
Lot 10 Hutong ... (see 81)
42 Magnificent Fish & Chip Bar ... F8
Mythai Jim Thompson ... (see 84)
43 Neroteca ... F7
44 Nerovivo ... B4
45 Ngau Kee Beef Ball Noodles ... B5
46 One Plus One ... C5
Prego ... (see 31)
47 Restaurant Muar ... B5

find a soft-surface jogging track, synchronised fountains, a fantastic (under 12s only) **playground & paddling pool** (10am-7.30pm Tue-Sat) and – of course – great views of the Petronas Towers. In the early evening, it can seem like everyone in town has come down here to watch the glowing towers punching up into the night sky.

Badan Warisan Malaysia TRADITIONAL ARCHITECTURE

(Heritage of Malaysia Trust; Map p64; 2144 9273; www.badanwarisan.org.my; 2 Jln Stonor; 10am-5.30pm Mon-Sat) Find out about the work of this built heritage preservation society at its head office in a 1925 colonial bungalow in the shadow the Petronas Towers. The property's grounds contain the **Rumah Penghulu** (suggested donation RM10; tours 11am & 3pm Mon-Sat), a handsome example of a restored

Malay-style wooden house from Kedah. The trust also holds exhibitions in the bungalow, where there's a good bookshop and an excellent gift store stocking wooden antique furniture and local handcrafted items.

Dharma Realm Guan Yin Sagely Monastery   BUDDHIST TEMPLE
(Map p60; 161 Jln Ampang; ⊘7am-4pm) The calm spaces, potted plants, mandala ceilings and giant gilded statues create an appropriately contemplative mood for quiet meditation at this colourful modern temple. The complex is dedicated to Guan Yin, the Buddhist goddess of compassion, represented by the central statue in the main building.

Tabung Haji   MODERN ARCHITECTURE
(Map p64; 201 Jln Tun Razak) Designed by Hijjas Kasturi, this distinctive tower houses the *hajj* pilgrimage funding body. The five main exterior columns represent the five pillars

HERITAGE UNDER THREAT

Malaysia's National Heritage Act is supposed to protect outstanding examples of the nation's architecture, but with development rampant it doesn't always work, as proved by the destruction of KL's historic Bok House in 2006. Campaigning to save other heritage buildings is **Badan Warisan Malaysia** (BWM; www.badanwarisan.org.my), a nongovernmental organisation that is Malaysia's equivalent of the UK's National Trust.

As Elizabeth Cardosa, executive director of BWM, explains, the organisation goes about its work in several ways: 'By advocacy, trying to have an impact on official policy from top level government down to the local level; by influencing public opinion through our publications; and by education – going into schools and getting people involved at the community level. We also provide practical conservation and heritage consultancy services.'

BWM were the lead conservation consultants for the restoration of **Stadium Merdeka** (p47), for which they won a Unesco award for excellence. They also manage **8 Heeren St** (p120) in Melaka and **Suffolk House** (p155) in Penang.

Such success aside, it's the relentless demolition of modest and unprotected – but notable – buildings, such as **Pudu Jail** (see p56), that concerns Cardosa and her colleagues the most. 'Alone they may not be outstanding,' she says, 'but together they define the character of the area.'

A case in point is the inner-city Malay area of Kampung Baru (p59). 'Local government has an area plan but there's a lot of conflict resolution needed to get an outcome that pleases everyone,' notes Cardosa. 'When it comes to saving old buildings, unless someone has a personal connection to the structure it's difficult to convince them of the worth of preservation.'

---

of Islam while the overall structure recalls the drum used to summon pilgrims to the *hajj* and the shape of a traditional Arabic perfume vessel.

Hijjas, an acclaimed local architect, is also responsible for the Menara Maybank in Chinatown, the shape of which was inspired by a kris, the traditional Malay dagger, and the 55-storey finlike Menara Telekom tower, KL's third-tallest building on the border between the city and Petaling Jaya. It's occasionally possible to visit the architect's private estate Rimbun Dahan (p105).

CHINATOWN

Despite its name, atmospheric, perpetually bustling Chinatown is a true microcosm of the city, home not just to the scions of KL's original Chinese immigrants but also to Indians and Malays. Its central spine, bracketed by traditional arch gates, is Jln Petaling between Jln Tun Tan Cheng Lok and Jln Sultan. From 4pm to midnight this stretch is pedestrianised when one of KL's best night markets (p94) opens for business.

Running west of the main market towards Jln Tun HS Lee is Chinatown's pungent **wet market** (⊘7am-3pm), where locals shop for fresh fish, vegetables and gruesome anatomical cuts of meat. If you're up early

enough, there's also a **flea market** (⊘6am-10am) on the alley running between Jln Petaling and Jln Sultan. Poke around the streets and you'll find all manner of businesses, from traditional medicine shops (see p41) to barbers and songbird sellers.

Sri Mahamariamman Temple   HINDU TEMPLE
(Map p48; 163 Jln Tun HS Lee; ⊘6am-8.30pm) Looking grand after the completion of its once-every-12-years repaint and repair in 2010, this venerable Hindu shrine – the oldest in Malaysia – was founded by migrant workers from the Indian state of Tamil Nadu in 1873. Flower-garland vendors crowd the entrance and the temple is crowned by a huge *gopuram* (temple tower) covered in riotously colourful statues of Hindu deities. Locals leave incense, flowers, coconuts and strings of limes as offerings to Mariamman, the south Indian mother goddess, an incarnation of Durga. An idol from the temple is paraded to Batu Caves (p102) in a silver chariot during the Thaipusam festival in January or February each year. Non-Hindus are welcome to visit, but leave your shoes at the entrance.

Masjid Jamek   MOSQUE
(Friday Mosque; Map p48; off Jln Tun Perak; ⊘8.30am-12.30pm & 2.30-4pm Sat-Thu, 8.30-

11am & 2.30-4pm Fri) Chinatown's Muslim population prays at this beautiful onion-domed mosque. Constructed in 1907 at the confluence of the Klang and Gombak rivers, the mosque is an island of serenity, with airy open pavilions shaded by palm trees. The designer was British architect AB Hubbock, who sought inspiration from the Mughal mosques of northern India. Visitors are welcome outside prayer times, but shoes should be removed and female visitors should cover their heads, legs and shoulders (scarves and sarongs are available at the entrance).

Sze Ya Temple CHINESE TEMPLE
(Map p48; Jln Tun HS Lee; ⊗7am-5pm) On a narrow alleyway near the Central Market, this is probably the most atmospheric Chinese temple in KL. The Taoist temple was constructed in 1864 on the instructions of 'Kapitan China' Yap Ah Loy. You can see a statue of the man just left of the main altar. Its odd position, squished between rows of shophouses, was determined by feng shui. Fortune-telling sticks are provided for devotees; just rattle the pot until a stick falls out, then find the paper slip corresponding to the number on the stick. Staff will translate the fortune on the slip for RM1. On your way out, note the two gilded sedan chairs used to carry the deity statues during religious processions. You can enter the temple through the stucco gatehouse on Jln Tun HS Lee or the back gate on the next alley west.

Guandi Temple CHINESE TEMPLE
(Map p48; Jln Tun HS Lee; ⊗7am-5pm) Similar in atmosphere to the Sze Ya Temple is the 1886 Guandi Temple. The main hall is hung with fragrant coils of spiral incense, paper clothes and money that are burned to bring good fortune to the ancestors. The temple is dedicated to Kwan Ti, a historical Chinese general revered by Taoists as the god of war. It is also known as Kwong Siew Free School after the clan association who originally built it.

Central Market MARKET
(Pasar Seni; Map p48; ☑2031 0399; www.central market.com.my; Jln Hang Kasturi; ⊗10am-9pm) Housed in a handsome Art Deco building that looks more Miami than Southeast Asia, Central Market was built in 1888 as the wet market for the miners of old Kuala Lumpur. The building was nearly demolished in the 1970s before the Malaysian Heritage Society intervened to save it for future generations. The main building now houses a touristy market with some fine handicrafts and souvenirs (see p47), while the adjoining modern Annexe building has more stalls and the interesting Annexe Gallery (p89).

Stadium Merdeka HERITAGE BUILDING
(Map p48; Jln Stadium) Purpose-built for the declaration of independence in 1957, this recently restored open-air stadium is the only building of its type in Southeast Asia. This is where Malaysia's first prime minister, Tunku Abdul Rahman, punched his fist seven times in the air shouting 'Merdeka!' (Independence!) The Asian financial crisis of 1997 saved the structure from being demolished for redevelopment and the Merdeka Heritage Trust is now working with Badan Warisan Malaysia to restore the adjacent **Stadium Negara**, built in 1962 and Malaysia's first indoor stadium. Plans are afoot for tours of Stadium Merdeka: there are panoramic views of the city from the grandstands and a couple of evocative photographic murals in the entrance hall.

Land around the stadia will be developed as part of the construction of the 100-storey Warisan Merdeka tower, optimistically slated for completion in 2015.

Kompleks Dayabumi MODERN ARCHITECTURE
(Map p48; Jln Sultan Hishamuddin) The former headquarters of Petronas, Kompleks Dayabumi was designed by Nik Mohammed and built in 1981 on land formerly occupied by the workshops for the Malayan Railway. In profile, the 35-storey marble-clad tower, cloaked in delicate fretwork screens, forms a four-pointed star intersected by a square, a recurring symbol in Islamic art. To get here, walk over the footbridge behind Central Market. Next door is KL's main **post office** where philatelists will want to

---

GAMES ON THE SQUARE

Apart from on New Year's Eve and National Day, crowds rarely gather at Merdeka Sq, which became the city's property in 1987. In an attempt to reclaim the public space the group **Main Dengan Rakyat** (www.facebook.com/group.php?gid=158695034017) has been organising games sessions from 5pm on the last Sunday of the month on the grassy square. Turn up to learn some traditional Malay schoolyard games, take part in a game of rounders or perhaps play scrabble and have a picnic.

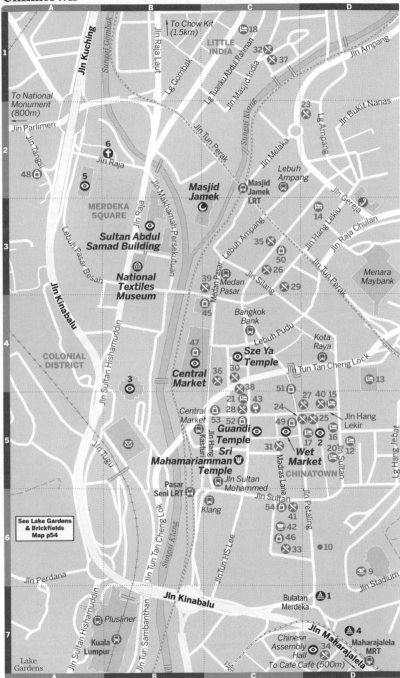

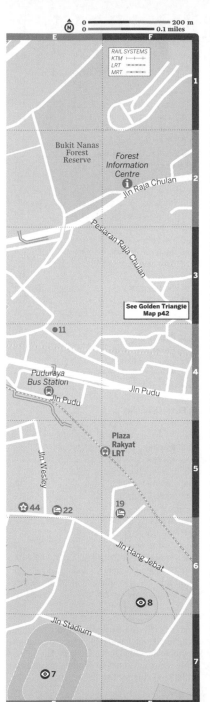

inspect and buy the beautiful selection of stamps and first day covers.

Chan She Shu Yuen Temple BUDDHIST TEMPLE
(Map p48; Jln Petaling; ⊘9am-6pm) Features KL's finest example of a Kwangtung pottery shard–decorated roof, with dioramas of celestial scenes and dramatic woodcarvings inside the main shrine.

Koon Yam (Guanyin) Temple BUDDHIST TEMPLE
(Map p48; cnr Jln Stadium & Jln Maharajalela; ⊘7am-5pm) Up some steps from the street is this pretty Hokkien temple, which displays golden Chinese Buddhist statues.

MERDEKA SQUARE
Ringed by handsome heritage buildings, Dataran Merdeka (Independence Sq, but commonly called Merdeka Sq) is KL's most impressive architectural ensemble. Once known as the Padang, until 1987 this vast lawn was the cricket pitch belonging to the neighbourbouring Royal Selangor Club. At midnight on 31 August 1987, the Union flag was lowered and that of the Malayan States hoisted on the Padang's 95m flagpole – a hugely symbolic event commemorated in 1990 when the square was renamed Dataran Merdeka.

FREE **National Textiles Museum** MUSEUM
(Muzium Tekstil Negara; Map p48; ☏2694 3457; www.jmm.gov.my; Jln Sultan Hishamuddin; ⊘daily 9am–6pm) On the square's southeast corner and entered off Lebuh Pasar Besar is this interesting new museum. Four darkened exhibition spaces help preserve the delicate textiles on display – there are some beautiful pieces and plenty of explanation of how they are made. The sad thing is that many of the time-consuming skills necessary for the production of such textiles are dying out, making these pieces increasingly rare.

Sultan Abdul Samad Building
HERITAGE BUILDING
(Map p48; Jln Raja). Gracing the east side of the square are the Moorish domes and 41m clocktower of this glorious brick building, built as the secretariat for the colonial administration in 1897. It was designed by the India-obsessed architect AC Norman (an associate of AB Hubbock) and now houses the national Ministry of Information, Communications and Culture.

St Mary's Cathedral CHURCH
(Map p48; ☎2692 8672; www.stmaryscathedral.org.my; Jln Raja) AC Norman is also responsible for the rather less florid St Mary's Cathedral at the north end of the square. Looking every inch the whitewashed English country church, it was built in 1894 and it still maintains a small Anglican congregation. Inside is a fine pipe-organ dedicated to Sir Henry Gurney, the British high commissioner to Malaya, assassinated in 1951 during the Emergency.

Royal Selangor Club HERITAGE BUILDING

(Map p48; www.rscweb.my; Jln Raja) Built in mock Tudor style and founded in 1884, this exclusive social club for the KL elite is where the running-and-drinking club, the Hash House Harriers, kicked off in 1938. Women are still said to be barred from its long bar, which has a view of the former playing fields.

LAKE GARDENS & AROUND

Just a few hundred metres from Chinatown, the urban landscape gives way to sculpted parks and dense tropical jungle. Covering 92 hectares, the Lake Gardens were created during the colonial era as an urban retreat where the British administrators could escape the hurly burly of downtown (as well as people of other races). Atop the tallest hill, the official residence of British government representative Frank Swettenham is now the luxury hotel Carcosa Seri Negara (p72), while on the garden's northern fringes is the giant honeycomb tower containing the Malaysian Parliament.

Although the area seems cut off by railway lines and highways, it is possible to walk here from Chinatown: take the pedestrian bridge across from the Central Market to Kompleks Dayabumi and then head south around the back of the post office to the underpass leading to the Masjid Negara. There's also a bridge into the Lake Gardens from the National Museum. Alternatively the KL Hop-On-Hop-Off bus (p65) stops at Masjid Negara, KL Bird Park, the National Monument and the National Museum. Once in the Lake Gardens you're at the mercy of taxi drivers who insist on charging at least RM15 to cover the short distance back to the city and refuse to use the meter.

KL Bird Park AVIARY

(Map p54; ☑2272 1010; www.klbirdpark.com; Jln Cenderawasih; adult/child RM45/35; ☺9am-6pm) This fabulous aviary brings together some 200 species of (mostly) Asian birds flying free beneath an enormous canopy. Star attractions include ostriches, hornbills, eagles, flamingos and parrots. It's worth getting to the park for feeding times (hornbills 11.30am, eagles 2.30pm) or the bird shows (12.30pm and 3.30pm), which feature plenty of parrot tricks to keep youngsters amused. The park's Hornbill Restaurant (p81) is also good.

TOP CHOICE Islamic Arts Museum MUSEUM

(Muzium Kesenian Islam Malaysia; Map p54; ☑2274 2020; www.iamm.org.my; Jln Lembah Perdana; adult/child RM12/6; ☺10am-6pm) This outstanding museum is home to one of best collections of Islamic decorative arts in the world. Aside from the quality of the exhibits, which include fabulous textiles, carpets, jewellery and calligraphy-inscribed pottery, the building itself is a stunner, with beautifully decorated domes and glazed tilework. There's a good Middle Eastern restaurant (set lunch RM43, Friday buffet RM28; ☺closed Mon) and one of KL's best museum gift shops stocking beautiful products from around the Islamic world.

National Museum MUSEUM

(Muzium Negara; Map p54; ☑2282 6255; www.muziumnegara.gov.my; Jln Damansara; adult/child RM2/free; ☺9am-6pm) Housed in a building with a distinctive Minangkabau-style roof and decorated with two beautiful front murals made of Italian mosaic glass depicting Malaysian life, this museum is one of the city's best. A major renovation has resulted in four main galleries with interesting, well

---

LOCAL KNOWLEDGE

ADLINE BINTI ABDUL GHANI: CURATOR

My personal highlights of the Islamic Arts Museum:

» **Ottoman Room** A reconstruction of an 1820s decorative room from Syria.

» **Kiswah** An embroidered door panel from the holy Ka'aba in Mecca, rare because it is usually cut into small pieces to be distributed to pilgrims.

» **Chinese calligraphy scolls** Only from the 1980s and '90s but the use of reed brushes for the strokes is very expressive.

» **19th-century Qurans** From Malaysia's east coat, decorated in red, gold and black.

» **Limar** There's Islamic calligraphy in the pattern of this weft silk ikat fabric. The tradition of making these pieces has now died out.

» **Uzbek pectoral plates** Shatters the idea of jewellery being only delicate objects.

Adline binti Abdul Ghani is the curator of the Islamic Arts Museum.

START MASJID JAMEK
LRT STATION
FINISH PETALING
STREET MARKET
DISTANCE 1.6KM
DURATION 1½ HOURS

Walking Tour
Chinatown

> From the station head south down Jln Ben-
teng across which you'll get a great view of
1 **Masjid Jamek**. At the junction with Lebuh Ampang is **2** **Medan Pasar**, site of KL's
original market square. In the centre stands
a clock tower built in 1937 to commemorate
the coronation of King George IV.

Where Medan Pasar meets Lebuh Pasar
Besar you'll see the **3** **OCBC Building**, a
graceful Art Deco structure built in 1938 for
the Overseas Chinese Banking Company.
Around the corner with Jln Tun HS Lee is
4 **MS Ally Company**, a pharmacy in business since 1909.

Cross Lebuh Pudu, turn right and, after
25m, duck left into an alleyway leading to the
atmospheric **5** **Sze Ya Temple**. Exit the way
you came in, cross the street and walk through
the alley opposite to hit **6** **Central Market**.

Exit the market, turn left onto Jl Cheng Lock,
then right onto Jln Tun HS Lee. The shophouses along here are among Chinatown's oldest;
note the unique feature of a five-foot way
(pavement) lower than the road level.

On the south corner is the pale yellow-
painted Art Deco **7** **Lee Rubber Building**;
on the second floor is Peter Hoe Evolution
(p95) where you can pause for refreshments.

Opposite, next to the bright-red, incense-
wreathed **8** **Guandi Temple** is Jln Sang
Guna, a covered arcade housing Chinatown's
atmospheric **9** **wet market**. Back on Jln
Tun HS Lee pause to admire the **10** **Sri Mahamariamman Temple** and to breathe in the
sweet jasmine of the flower sellers outside.

At the junction with Jln Sultan turn left,
then right onto Jln Petaling. Further south,
around the busy traffic roundabout of Bu-
latan Merdeka, you find the ornate ancestral
11 **Chan See Shu Yuen Temple** and, across
Jln Stadium, the **12** **Guan Yin Temple**, dedicated to the goddess of mercy.

Finish at **13** **Maharajalela MRT station**
or, if it's evening, return to Jln Petaling to
browse the **14** **Petaling Street Market**.

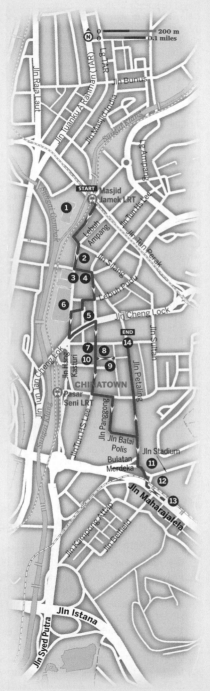

-organised displays: Early History, where you'll find the bones of Perak Man (see p189); Malay Kingdoms, including the history of the Melaka; Colonial Era, from the Portuguese through to the Japanese occupation; and Malaysia Today, which charts the country's post-WWII development. There are more things to see outside, including a regularly changing exhibition (extra charge) and a couple of small free galleries: the **Orang Asli Craft Museum** and **Malay World Ethnology Museum**, which has good displays of batik and other fabrics.

Time your visit to coincide with one of the free **tours** (⊙10am Mon-Thu & Sat in English; Tue & Thu in French, Thu in Japanese) given by enthusiastic volunteer guides. Although the museum is very close to KL Sentral station, it's surrounded by a snarl of highways – the easiest way to get here is by taxi, the hop-on-hop off bus, or via the walkway over the highway south of the Lake Gardens.

KL Train Station   HERITAGE BUILDING
(Map p54; Jln Sultan Hishamuddin) Midway between Chinatown and KL Sentral is another of AB Hubbock's Moorish-inspired fantasies. Opened with much pomp and circumstance in 1911 to receive trains from Butterworth and Singapore, KL's old train station is a wonderful confection of turrets and towers. The soaring domes and arches were restored in the 1980s, but the station was replaced as the city's main transport hub by KL Sentral station in 2001. Today the platforms are mainly used for KTM Komuter trains to the suburbs and further afield to Seremban and Ipoh. It's looking dishevelled and forlorn, but it's still worth coming here to imagine the glory days.

The station is mirrored by the **Malayan Railway Administration Building** across the road. Walking here from Chinatown, the best route to follow is to take the pedestrian bridge across from the Central Market to Kompleks Dayabumi and then head south around the back of the post office to the underpass leading to the Masjid Negara.

Masjid Negara   MOSQUE
(National Mosque; Map p54; Jln Lembah Perdana; ⊙9am-noon, 3-4pm & 5.30-6.30pm, closed Fri morning) The main place of worship for KL's Malay Muslim population is this gigantic mosque, inspired by Mecca's Grand Mosque. Its umbrella-like blue-tile roof has 18 points symbolising the 13 states of Malaysia and the five pillars of Islam. Rising above the mosque, a 74m-high minaret issues the call to prayer, which can be heard across Chinatown. Non-Muslims are welcome to visit outside prayer times but dress appropriately and remove your shoes before entering.

Butterfly Park   BUTTERFLY RESERVE
(Taman Rama Rama; Map p54; ☑2693 4799; Jln Cenderawasih; adult/child RM18/9; ⊙9am-6pm) Flying creatures of a different sort are showcased at this enclosure near the Bird Park. Some of the 120 different species of colourful butterflies fluttering around the covered grounds are real monsters, and there's a bug gallery where you can shudder at the size of Malaysia's giant centipedes and spiders.

National Planetarium   PLANETARIUM
(Map p54; ☑2273 4303; www.angkasa.gov.my/planetarium; 53 Jln Perdana; gallery admission RM1; ⊙9.30am-4.30pm Tue-Sun) Looking more like a mosque than a centre for scientific research, this planetarium is part of the National Space Agency. Parts of the rocket that launched Malaysia's first satellite are displayed in the main gallery. **Planetarium shows** (adult/child RM3/2 or RM6/4 depending on the programme) take place throughout the day in English and Bahasa Malaysia. In the

SECRET SOCIETIES

Although nominally loyal to the local sultans, the Chinese prospectors who founded Kuala Lumpur maintained their own network of 'secret societies', responsible for most of the organised crime in Malaya. These forerunners of modern-day Triads accumulated vast fortunes from smuggling and racketeering, carrying out robberies and assassinations, stage-managing strikes and riots, and pushing forward the political agenda of the Hokkien and Hakka communities. Their reach extended across Malaya and Singapore. During the 1860s, Penang faced all-out war between the Hai San and Gheen Hin gangs over the Perak Mines, triggering a massive crackdown on gang membership by the colonial police. The power of the secret societies waned as the Malay community took control of Malaysian politics. You can see some of the brutal weapons confiscated from gang members in the Royal Malaysia Police Museum.

grounds are small-scale models of famous historic observatories, including Jai Singh's Delhi observatory and Stonehenge.

National Monument   MONUMENT

(Plaza Tugu Negara; off Map p48; Jln Parlimen; ☺7am-6pm) At the northern end of the Lake Gardens, this impressive monument commemorates the defeat of the Communists in 1950. The militaristic bronze sculpture was created in 1966 by Felix de Weldon, the artist behind the Iwo Jima monument in Washington, DC. Nearby is a monument to the Malay fighters who died in WWI and WWII. Creating an interesting juxtaposition to the triumphalism of the monument, members of the **Tugu Drum Circle** (http://tugudrumcircle.blogspot.com) meet here every Sunday from 5.30pm for some therapeutic drumming.

FREE Royal Malaysia Police Museum

MUSEUM

(Map p54; www.muziumpolis.com; 5 Jln Perdana; ☺10am-6pm Tue-Sun, closed 12.30-2.30pm Fri) Between the Islamic Arts Museum and the Planetarium is this surprisingly interesting museum. Inside you can watch videos, see police uniforms and vehicles, a collection of old swords, cannons and kris, plus some sinister-looking handmade guns and knives seized from members of criminal 'secret societies' and communists during the Emergency.

Lake Gardens Park   PARK

(Taman Tasik Perdana; Map p54; Jln Tembusu; ☺daylight hours) The focal point of the Lake Gardens is this vast park planted with a variety of native plants, trees and shrubs. In the middle is a good children's adventure playground and nearby is the sprawling lake for which the gardens are named. You can rent boats for RM6 per hour and watch t'ai chi practitioners in the early morning.

Deer Park   PARK

(Taman Rusa & Kancil; Map p54; Jln Perdana; ☺10am-6pm, closed noon-2pm weekdays) Close to the children's playground, and home to a collection of tame deer including the tiny *Tragulus kanchil* (lesser mouse deer), the world's smallest hoofed mammal.

Orchid Garden   GARDEN

(Taman Orkid; Map p54; Jln Cenderawasih; Sat & Sun RM1, weekdays free; ☺9am-6pm) Some 800-odd species of these beautiful blooms are planted uphill from the lake.

Hibiscus Garden   GARDEN

(Taman Bunga Raya; p54; Jln Cenderawasih; Sat & Sun RM1, weekdays free; ☺9am-6pm) Adjacent to the Orchid Garden, this garden is dedicated to Malaysia's national flower and surrounds a small art gallery.

BRICKFIELDS & AROUND

Following devastating fires in the late 19th century, KL's colonial administration decreed that bricks would henceforth be used to construct the city's buildings. The area where they were manufactured naturally became known as Brickfields. Many Indian labourers, mainly Tamils from southern India and Sri Lanka, settled here, giving the area its still-predominant Indian atmosphere, although as in other areas of KL, the ethnic mix is readily apparent.

Old Brickfields is stealthily becoming overshadowed by the continued rise of **KL Sentral**, the city's transportation hub around which several new shopping com-

Lake Gardens & Brickfields

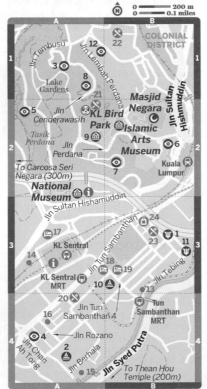

During 2010 the city's redevelopment of Brickfields got underway with Indian prime minister Manmohan Singh being a guest at the area's official reopening in October of that year. Pavements around Jln Tun Sanbantham were widened, a one-way road system introduced, Indian-style street lighting installed and a new three-storey Indian shopping mall and food court commenced construction. Also on the drawing board is a ceremonial arch on Jln Brickfields and a fountain at the junction with Jln Travers.

A probable casualty of this civic plan is the parallel rows of concrete houses known as the **Hundred Quarters**. Built in 1915 to house railway employees and other civil servants, this multi-ethnic neighbourhood has two roads, Jln Rozario and Jln Chan Ah Tong, that were named after former chief clerks of the colonial civil service. Although the houses were recently renovated, in May 2010, residents were given notice to vacate, with an assurance that no one would be moved until suitable alternative accommodation could be found.

plexes and offices towers are sprouting. Apart from the sights listed below, Brickfields also has the Temple of Fine Arts (p64) and the Wei-Ling Gallery (p89).

To the south across Jln Syed Putra rise up the green hills that are home to KL's main Chinese Cemetery as well as the spectacular Thean Hou Temple and Istana Negara.

One stop further south on the Ipoh–Seremban train line will bring you to **Mid Valley City** (www.midvalleycity.com) dominated by its twin malls Mid Valley Megamall and the Gardens (p95). Immediately north of here is **Bangsar**, a century ago a rubber plantation, now an upscale residential area of luxury bungalows and condominiums.

Lake Gardens & Brickfields

THE END OF PUDU JAIL

For over a century Pudu Jail (Map p42) stood on the corner of Jln Imbi and Jln Pudu. Completed in 1895, the star-shaped penitentiary is where notorious gangster Botak Chin and sometime pop singer, witch doctor and murderess Mona Fandey were both incarcerated. The jail was also commandeered by the Japanese to intern Commonwealth soldiers during WWII. Most famously, tropical scenes covered 394 metres of its outer wall, hand-painted by inmates in the 1980s, and at the time noted by the Guinness *Book of World Records* as the world's longest such mural.

Little was done to preserve the mural since the jail closed in 1996. When plans finally got underway to redevelop the land into a mix of commercial and residential properties in June 2010, the city took the opportunity to demolish the wall along Jln Pudu for a road-widening and traffic underpass project. The night of the demolition, hundreds of spectators gathered to protest and mourn the loss of a building that they thought should always be part of KL's fabric.

A small piece of it might continue to be. At the time of reseach, the section of painted wall and main entrace gate to the jail along Jln Imbi remained standing, with a vague commitment from the developer that it will be incorporated into their final plans.

Bangsar Baru is one of the most pleasant places to eat and shop in the city.

TOP CHOICE **Thean Hou Temple**   BUDDHIST TEMPLE
(off Map p54; ☑2274 7088; www.hainannet. com; 65 Persiaran Endah, ☺9am-6pm) Off Jln Syed Putra, this multilayered and highly ornate temple is one of the most visually impressive in Malaysia. It's dedicated to the heavenly mother, Thean Hou. Her statue takes centre stage in the main hall, with Kuan Yin (the Buddhist goddess of mercy) on her right and Shuiwei Shengniang (the goddess of the waterfront) to her left. Statues of Milefo (the laughing Buddha), Weituo and Guandi further contribute to this Taoist–Buddhist hodgepodge.

There are great views from the temple's upper decks, while at its base are tourist restaurants and shops. To reach the temple, 3km south of the centre of town, take either a taxi or bus 27 or 52 from Klang bus station and then walk up the hill (ask to be dropped off near the temple). Alternatively take the monorail to Tun Sambanthan station, cross Jln Syed Putra using the overpass and walk up the hill.

Sri Kandaswamy Kovil   HINDU TEMPLE
(Map p54; ☑2274 2987; www.srikandaswamyko vil.org; 3 Lg Scott; ☺5.30am-9pm) Founded by the Jaffna Sri Lankan community in 1909, Brickfield's major Hindu temple is dedicated to Lord Murgan and the mother goddess Sri Raja Rajeswary. It's marked by an elaborate *gopuram* (gateway), which was being renovated at the time of research.

Nearby is the smaller **Arulmigu Sree Veera Hanuman Temple** (Jln Scott; ☺7am-9pm) honouring Hanuman, the Hindu monkey god, and notable for its *gopuram*, which is a coiled tower of his tail.

Istana Negara   HERITAGE BUILDING
(off Map p54; Jln Istana) Built in 1928 by Chinese millionaire Chang Wing, this grand building was requisitioned by the government in 1957 and turned into the National Palace of the Sultan of Malaysia. The palace itself is only distantly visible through the ornate gates and trees, but Malaysians come here to see the hourly **changing of the palace guard** (from 8am to 4pm weekdays). After the enormous new Sultan's Palace on Jln Duta near Mont Kiara opens in 2011, this building may be turned into a museum.

Sam Kow Tong Temple   BUDDHIST TEMPLE
(Map p54; 16 Jln Thambapillai; ☺7am-5pm) Has an impressive dragon-decorated roof that contrasts with the soaring towers above KL Sentral.

Buddhist Maha Vihara   BUDDHIST TEMPLE
(Map p54; ☑2274 1141; www.buddhistmahavi hara.com; 123 Jln Berhala) Centred on a stucco Buddhist shrine dating from 1895, founded by Sinhalese Buddhists.

PUDU

Once a Chinese village on the edge of the city, Pudu is now firmly part of KL, hosting a lively fresh produce market, a street of wonderful hawker stalls (p81) and one of the city's best Chinese restaurants (p81).

Its most famous landmark was Pudu Jail, little of which now remains (see p56). The potentially interesting **Pudu Community Art Project** (http://puducommunityartproject. blogspot.com) kicked off in late 2010; see their website for details of events.

Pudu Market   MARKET
(Map p42; Jln Pasar Baru; ☺6am-2pm) KL's biggest wet and dry market is a frenetic place, full of squawking chickens, frantic shoppers and porters forcing their way through the crowds with outrageous loads. Stalls here sell everything from goldfish to pigs' heads, cows' tongues and durians in baskets. Arrive early in the morning to experience the market at full throttle.

The market is five minutes' walk from Pudu LRT station; go south along Jln Pudu, right onto Jln Pasar, then right down Jln Pasar Baharu, passing the colourful **Choon Wan Kong**, a Chinese temple dating from 1879.

LITTLE INDIA & AROUND
Centred on the southern end of Jln TAR and parallel Jln Masjid India, Little India is another area that is best explored on foot (see p58). Late on Saturday afternoon Lg TAR fills up with the area's night market (see p35).

Loke Mansion   HERITAGE BUILDING
(Map p60; ☑2691 0803; 273A Jln Medan Tuanku) Rescued from the brink of dereliction by the law firm Cheang & Ariff, Loke Mansion was once the home of self-made tin tycoon Loke Yew, although the original part of the structure was built in the 1860s by another rich merchant, Cheow Ah Yeok. The Japanese high command also set up base here in 1942. After years of neglect, the mansion has been beautifully restored; access to the interior is by appointment only, but there's nothing to stop you walking by and admiring the whitewashed exterior.

CapSquare   ENTERTAINMENT COMPLEX
(Map p60; www.capsquare.com.my; cnr Jln Munshi Abdullah & Jln Dang Wangi) On the area's eastern flank is this attractive business, residential and entertainment complex that rests on the bank of the muddy Klang River – it's not taken off as hoped since it opened in 2009 but there's still some decent places to eat and drink here.

**Bank Negara Malaysia Museum &
Art Gallery**   MUSEUM
(Map p36; http://museum.bnm.gov.my) After much delay this place is slated to open

in October 2011. Housed in a futuristically designed metal-clad complex west of Jln Kuching and within walking distance of Bank Negara train station, it looks promising.

CHOW KIT & TITIWANGSA
Spread around the northern end of Jln TAR, Chow Kit is named after tin miner and city councillor Loke Chow Kit. One of KL's red light districts, it is best known for its wet market. Further north Chow Kit's grimy streets give way to the greenery, mansions and public buildings ranged around the spacious Titiwangsa Lake Gardens. Both areas can be accessed by the monorail.

FREE **National Art Gallery**   ART GALLERY
(Balai Seni Lukis Negara; Map p63; ☑4026 7000; www.artgallery.org.my; 2 Jln Temerloh; ☺10am-6pm) Occupying a pyramid-shaped block between Jln Tun Razak and Lake Titiwangsa, this fine gallery showcases contemporary Malaysian art. There are often interesting temporary shows of local and regional artists, as well as pieces from the gallery's permanent collection of 4000 pieces including paintings by Zulkifi Moh'd Dohalan, Wong Hoi Cheong, Ahad Osman and the renowned batik artist Chuah Than Teng. Art-loving ex-ambassador Mohd Yusof Ahmad was appointed the gallery's director-general in 2010, and there are plans to expand the exhibition space, the interior of which is dominated by a swirly Guggenheim Museum–style staircase.

Next to the gallery is the theatre **Istana Budaya** (p90). Designed by Mohammed Kamar Ya'akub, the building's soaring roof is based on a traditional Malay floral decoration of betel leaves, while its footprint resembles a *wau bulan* (Malay moon kite).

Bazaar Baru Chow Kit   MARKET
(Chow Kit Market; Map p60; 469-473 Jln TAR; ☺8am-9pm) Middle- and upper-class KLites give this chaotic and less than sanitary wet market a wide berth but tourists and the less moneyed locals love it. Apart from freshly butchered meat and filleted fish, there's a staggering array of weird and wonderful tropical fruit and vegetables on sale here, as well as clothes, toys, buckets, stationery, noodles, spices and other commodities. Pushing through the narrow aisles is a heady, sensory experience, particularly for the sense of smell.

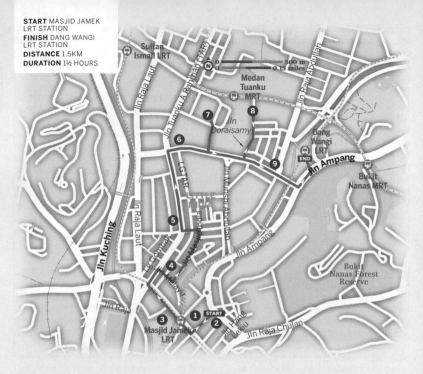

START MASJID JAMEK
LRT STATION
FINISH DANG WANGI
LRT STATION
DISTANCE 1.5KM
DURATION 1½ HOURS

Walking Tour
Little India

❯ From the LRT station walk one block southeast to Lebuh Ampang. Lined with moneychangers, Indian cafes, and street vendors selling sweets and flower garlands, this street has long been the preserve of the Chettiars from south India. Note the striking ❶ **old shophouses** at Nos 16 to 18 and Nos 24 to 30, and the ceramic peacock tiles on the ❷ **Chettiar House** at No 85.

Return to the station next to which is the venerable ❸ **Masjid Jamek** (p46). Opposite, Jln Melayu curves around to the covered arcade of market stalls at the pedestrianised end of Jln Masjid India. Pick your way through the tightly packed stalls to find the Indian Muslim mosque ❹ **Masjid India**. You're now in the thick of Little India, surrounded by a preponderance of sari and scarf stalls, gold jewellers and DVD and CD shops playing Bollywood soundtracks at full blast. The bazaar-like atmosphere is enhanced every Saturday from late afternoon when a *pasar malam* (night market) sets up along Lg TAR, the lane sandwiched between Jln TAR and Jln Masjid India.

A colonial relic surviving at the south end of Jln TAR is the ❺ **Coliseum Hotel**, where Somerset Maugham once drank; stop here for a reviving beer or meal at the Coliseum Café (p80). The Coliseum Cinema next door is of the same era, while heading north along Jln TAR you'll pass scores of colourful fabric shops.

Another Art Deco movie house, the ❻ **Odeon**, is on the corner at the crossroads of Jln Dang Wangi and Jln TAR, opposite Sogo department store. Head east along Jln Dang Wangi, taking the first road on the left: on the next corner, opposite the car park, is the grand colonial era ❼ **Loke Mansion**.

The parallel street to the east is Jln Doraisamy, a strip of restored shophouses turned into bars, clubs and restaurants and rebranded ❽ **Asian Heritage Row**. Continue down Jln Dang Wangi to the venerable *kopitiam* (coffee shop) ❾ **Yut Kee** (p80). Dang Wangi LRT is nearby.

Bangsar Baru

Titiwangsa Lake Gardens PARK
(Taman Tasik Titiwangsa; Map p63; Jln Tembeling; ☉daylight hours) Head to this relaxing recreational park surrounding Lake Titiwangsa for a picture-postcard view of the city skyline. As well as walking paths and jolly boating on the lake (from RM3 per hour), there are tennis courts, squash courts and a remote-controlled-car racing track where enthusiasts stage miniature Formula 1 races. The park is a favourite spot for courting Malaysian couples (and the religious police on the lookout for improper behaviour).

The park is a 10-minute walk east of the Titiwangsa monorail station. Or take Rapid KL bus B101 here from KL Sentral, via Jln Cheng Lock in Chinatown; bus B102 from Jln Bukit Bintang; or bus B103 from the KLCC.

Tatt Khalsa Diwan Gurdwara SIKH TEMPLE
(Map p60; www.tattkhalsa.org; 24 Jln Raja Alang) A short stroll east along Jln Raja Alang behind Bazaar Baru Chow Kit brings you to the largest Sikh temple in Southeast Asia, spiritual home of KL's 75,000 Sikhs. There's been a temple and school here since 1924 – the present building dates from the 1990s and is open to visitors.

KAMPUNG BARU

The Malay neighbourhood of Kampung Baru, meaning 'new village', looks like a piece of rural Malaysia smuggled into the heart of modern KL. The land here was reserved for Malays by the colonial administration in the

Bangsar Baru

KUALA LUMPUR ACTIVITIES

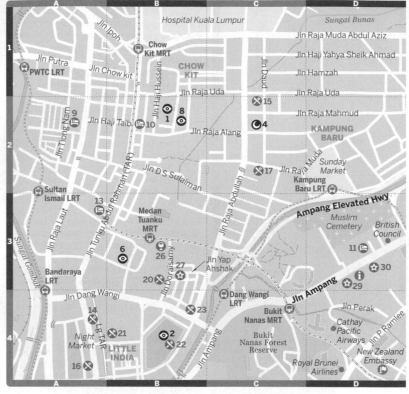

1890s, and the leafy residential streets are still lined with quaint wooden houses that in recent years have also become homes to Indonesians and Thai Muslims.

Relentless development pressures on this central area mean it's unlikely to remain so peaceful or low rise forever, although, with an estimated 4300 lot owners across the 153-hectare site, overnight changes are unlikely. The area is at its most lively on Saturday night when a bustling *pasar malam* (night market) springs up around Jln Raja Muda Musa (see p35). It's also a great area to visit during Ramadan when **street markets** (☺3pm-midnight) offer delicacies prepared specially to break the daily fast.

On Jln Raja Alang is the **Kampung Baru Mosque** (Map p60), built in 1924, with a handsome gateway decorated with eye-catching tiles in traditional Islamic patterns. Stalls around the mosque sell religious paraphernalia, including white *kopia* and black

songkok, the traditional head coverings for Malay Muslim men. It's a short stroll west from here to Chow Kit Market.

Kampung Baru LRT station provides easy access to the area and it's worth coming here for lunch any day of the week; Jln Raja Muda Musa is lined with hawker-style restaurants serving excellent Malay food to hordes of hungry city workers.

🏃 Activities

KL has plenty of activities that can be enjoyed both indoors and outdoors, from a sybaritic pampering in a luxurious spa to a game of ten-pin bowling. If you feel the humidity lulling you into a stupor, freshen up at one of the public swimming pools or hit the treadmills of numerous air-con gyms, many of which also offer yoga classes.

Ampang Superbowl　　　BOWLING
(Map p42; ☎2134 0900; www.ampangsuperbowl. com; 5th fl, Berjaya Times Sq, 1 Jln Imbi; admission

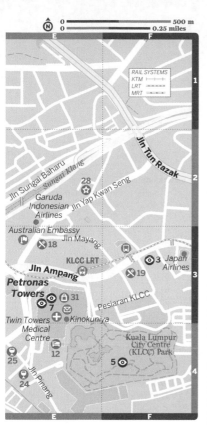

RAIL SYSTEMS
KTM
LRT
MRT

per hr off peak/peak RM40/60; ⊘noon-midnight) Playing an actual round of golf in Kuala Lumpur is a sweaty business, so why not give these golf simulators a go, the brilliant thing being you can choose your course from famous ones around the world. In addition there's a pretty swish bar and restaurant run by the La Bodega group, and a couple of pool tables.

Cosmic Bowl BOWLING
(☑2287 8280; www.cosmicbowl.com.my; 3rd fl, Mid Valley Megamall, Mid Valley City; admission RM5-7 depending on time of day; ⊘11am-1am Sun-Thu, to 2am Fri & Sat) Glow in the dark lanes jazz up this 38-lane bowling alley.

Berjaya Times Square Theme Park
AMUSEMENT PARK
(Map p42; ☑2117 3118; www.timessquarekl.com; Berjaya Times Sq, 1 Jln Imbi; adult/child RM25/15; ⊘noon-10pm Mon-Fri, 11am-10pm Sat & Sun) Despite the mall location, there's a full-sized looping coaster plus a good selection of thrill rides for teenagers and gentler rides for families. (Avoid the DNA Mixer unless you want to see your *nasi lemak* a second time.)

Desa Waterpark SWIMMING
(☑7118 8338; www.desawaterpark.com.my; Taman Danau Desa; adult/child RM20/14; ⊘noon-6pm Mon-Fri, 10am-6pm Sat & Sun). This park is smaller than Sunway Lagoon, but also generally less crowded. You can travel here by taxi from Salak Selatan KTM Komuter station (on the Rawang–Seremban line).

Fitness First GYM
(Map p42; ☑2711 3299; www.fitnessfirst.com.my; Wisma SPK, 22 Jln Sultan Ismail; ⊘6.30am-11pm Mon-Fri, 7am-7pm Sat & Sun) Also has a branch at Menara Maxis at the KLCC.

Kelab Darul Ehsan GOLF
(☑4257 2333; www.berjayaclubs.com/kde/; Taman Tun Abdul Razak, Jln Kerja Air Lama; 9/18 holes Mon-Fri RM50/80, Sat & Sun RM80/120; ⊘7am-10pm Mon-Fri, to 8.30pm Sat & Sun) Respected nine-hole course on the northeast city limits; last tee-off is 90 minutes before closing.

Kompleks Sukan Bangsar SWIMMING, BADMINTON & TENNIS
(off Map p59; ☑2284 6065; 3 Jln Terasek 3, Bangsar Baru; adult/child RM2/1 ⊘9.30am-noon, 2-4.30pm & 6-8.30pm, closed Sun morning) Entry fee covers one 2½-hour swimming session. You can also rent courts for badminton from 8am to

RM5-7 depending on time of day; ⊘10am-1am Sun-Thu, to 3am Fri & Sat) State-of-the-art ten-pin bowling with 48 lanes equipped with giant plasma screens.

Celebrity Fitness GYM
(Map p42; ☑2145 1000; www.celebrityfitness.com. my; Rooftop, Lot 10, 50 Jln Sultan Ismail; day entry RM60; ⊘6.30am-midnight Mon-Fri, 8am-8pm Sat & Sun) Fully equipped gym with classes, including yoga. There are also branches at Bangsar Village II and Mid Valley Megamall.

Chin Woo Stadium SWIMMING
(Map p48; ☑2072 4602; www.chinwoo.org.my; Jln Hang Jebat, Chinatown; admission RM4; ⊘2-8pm Mon-Fri, 9am-8pm Sat & Sun) Great city views at this 50m outdoor pool. All swimsuits must be tight fitting. Access uphill off Jln Hang Jebat.

TOP CHOICE **CityGolf** SIMULATED GOLF
(☑2282 0011; www.citygolf.com.my; Bangsar Shopping Centre, 285 Jln Maarof, Bangsar;

2am (per hour RM4) and tennis from 7am to 11pm (per hour RM4).

Lightworks   YOGA
(Map p42; ☎2143 2966; www.lightworks.com.my; 19 Jln Mesui) New Age centre that offers relaxing hatha yoga classes with an expat instructor. Drop-in classes are RM40 per session and are held at noon on Tuesday, and 7pm on Monday and Wednesday.

Titiwangsa Golf Club PDRM   GOLF
(Map p63; ☎2693 4964; Jln Temerloh, TamanTasik Titiwangsa; 9 holes RM60; ⏰7am-6pm Tue-Sun, 2-6pm Mon) Nine-hole course behind Taman Tasik Titiwangsa.

Yogshakti   YOGA
(☎4252 4714; www.yogshakti.com; 1 Lg Damai 13; classes RM45; ⏰beginners 7pm Mon-Wed, intermediate 7pm Thu, Sat & Sun) This Hatha yoga centre is in the embassy district east of Jln Tun Razak, off Jln Ampang.

Megakidz   CHILDREN
(☎2282 9300; www.megakidz.com.my; 3rd fl, Mid Valley Megamall; under 2/2-16 years RM11/22, Sat & Sun RM14/28) Offers storytelling sessions, art activities, Mandarin lessons, indoor adventure playground and a **crèche service** (under/over 4 years RM30/35 for two hours).

Kizsports & Gym   CHILDREN
(Map p59; ☎2284 6313; www.kizsports.com; 3rd fl, Bangsar Village II; Mon-Fri RM24, Sat & Sun RM30) Your little ones will be sure to have fun in their large soft play area and there's an extensive list of programmes from belly dancing to taekwondo. Child-minding for children 3 years and over is RM35 per hour.

🏃 Courses

There are some unusual cultural courses and classes on offer but to take some you'll have to be in KL for a while. Check directly with each of the listings for prices and exact course times and details.

TOP CHOICE **Rohani Jelani** COOKING
(www.rohanijelani.com/intro.htm)
Learn to cook traditional Malaysian dishes at these hands-on classes run by friendly cookbook author Rohani Jelani in a beautiful countryside retreat where you can also stay the night (p71). Each class ends with a sit-down meal of the dishes prepared that day.

Nathalie's Gourmet Studio COOKING
(✉6207 9572; www.nathaliegourmetstudio. com; Unit 4-1-5 Publika, Jln Dutamas, Mont Kiara) Cooking classes for adults (RM220) and occasionally children (RM150) from a self-taught French chef. Her speciality is macaroons. There's also an excellent restaurant here (p83).

C Woks Design BATIK
(Map p48; ✉012 257 2344; http://batikcwok. blogspot.com; Central Market Annexe; ⊙10am-9pm) Paint your own batik panel from RM15. Either choose a readily prepared design or create your own. The C Woks team also have an outlet at Kompleks Budaya Kraf.

Dance KL DANCE
(Map p59; ✉2282 3456; www.dancekl.com; 54-2 Jln Telawi, Bangsar) Salsa, hip hop, belly dancing and jazz dance classes are all on the schedule. Dance KL also runs a salsa social night every Wednesday at a nearby restaurant.

Kings Kitchen Klub COOKING
(Map p42; ✉2731 8333; www.westindining.com. my; Westin Kuala Lumpur, 199 Jln Bukit Bintang;

classes RM188) On fixed Saturday and Sunday mornings throughout the year, the chefs at the Westin's prestigious restaurants offer 12-person cooking classes covering everything from Indian and Malay cooking to Italian pasta and Chinese dim sum. Classes include lunch or high tea.

Kompleks Budaya Kraf ARTS & CRAFTS
(Map p64; ✉2162 7533; www.malaysiancraft. com; Jln Conlay; ⊙9am-8pm Mon-Fri, until 7pm Sat & Sun) Try your hand at traditional Malay crafts such as batik or pottery at the craft village in the grounds of this one-stop crafts complex. See also p93.

Kuala Lumpur Performing Arts Centre MUSIC & DANCE
(KLPac; ✉4047 9060; www.klpac.com; Sentul West, Jln Strachan) A variety of performing arts courses are offered here, including

---

Titiwangsa

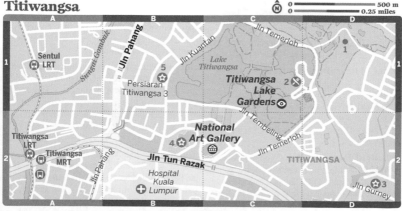

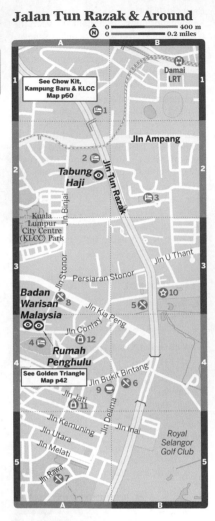

courses in traditional instruments such as the *gamelan* (traditional Malay orchestra).

LaZat Malaysian Home Cooking Class
                       COOKING
(☑019 238 1198; www.malaysia-klcookingclass. com) Held on Tuesday and Saturday mornings, a 25-minute drive from central KL; check the website for the different menus on offer.

School of Hard Knocks   ARTS & CRAFTS
(☑4145 6122; http://visitorcentre.royalselangor. com/vc; 4 Jln Usahawan 6, Setapak Jaya; classes RM50; ⏰9am-5pm) This famous pewter cen-

tre offers entertaining classes (30 minutes) where you make your own pewter bowl; advance booking required.

Dive Station Explorer   DIVING
(www.divestation.com.my; 3rd fl, Mid Valley Megamall, Mid Valley City, Lingkaran Syed Putra) Experienced operator and dive shop through which you can arrange 3-day/2-night PADI open water courses (RM1750) and other dive courses.

Sutra Dance Theatre   MUSIC & DANCE
(Map p63; ☑4021 1092; www.sutradancethe atre.com; 12 Persiaran Titiwangsa 3, Titiwangsa) Courses in Odissi and other forms of classical Indian dance are offered at this cultural centre near Taman Tasik Titiwangsa.

Temple of Fine Arts   MUSIC & DANCE
(Map p54; ☑2274 3709; www.tfa.org.my; 114-116 Jln Berhala, Brickfields) This Indian cultural centre offers courses in classical Indian

dance, song and music. Stage shows take place here throughout the year.

Buddhist Maha Vihara   MEDITATION
(Map p54; ☎2274 1141; www.buddhistmahavihara. com; 123 Jln Berhala) This Brickfields landmark offers a variety of courses. Meditation and chanting classes plus dharma talks take place most days. Classes are run on a donation basis.

YMCA   LANGUAGE
(Map p54; ☎2274 1439; www.ymcakl.com; 95 Jln Padang Belia, Brickfields) Offers Bahasa Malaysia classes as well as courses studying Thai, Mandarin, Cantonese, and Japanese. You can also study martial arts and different types of dancing here.

Vivekananda Ashram   YOGA
(Map p54; ☎4021 4657; www.sivananda.org. my; 220 Jln Tun Sambanthan, Brickfields) This historic ashram, part of the global Ramakrishna movement, offers three-month courses in kundalini yoga.

☞ Tours
If you need a guide or assistance getting around many local agencies offer various tours of the city and attractions around KL.

KL Hop-On Hop-Off   CITY TOURS
(☎2166 6162; www.myhoponhopoff.com; adult/ child 24hr RM38/17, 48hr RM65/29; ☉8.30am-8.30pm; ☜) This double-decker wifi-enabled air-con tourist bus makes a circuit of the main tourist sites half-hourly throughout the day. Stops include KLCC, Jln Bukit Bintang, Menara KL, Chinatown, Merdeka Square and the attractions of Lake Gardens. Tickets, which can be bought on the bus, last all day and you can get on and off as often as you like.

Going Places Tours   ADVENTURE TOURS
(Map p48; ☎2078 4008; www.goingplaces-kl. com; Original Backpackers Inn, 60a Jln Sultan, Chinatown) Offers tours tailored to the backpacker market, including more adventurous options such as rafting, caving and rock-climbing adventures.

Tour 51 Malaysia   CITY TOURS, DAY TRIPS
(☎2161 8830) Runs a decent selection of half-day city tours (RM60) and day trips to places such as Putrajaya, Kuala Selangor and Pulau Ketam (RM150–190). Can be booked via **Malaysian Travel Business** (☎2163 0162), an agency with desks at the Malaysian Tourist Centre.

Travel Han   NATURE TOURS
(Map p48; ☎2031 0899; han-travel.com; Kompleks Selangor, Jln Sultan) One of the many agents offering tours to Taman Negara National Park in the north of Peninsular Malaysia, which is a 4343-sq-km reserve protecting one of the world's oldest tropical rainforests. Three-day, two-night packages from KL start from RM160 per person.

★ Festivals & Events
The capital is a good venue for Malaysia's major holidays and festivals, including Chinese New Year, Deepavali and Thaipusam; see p19 for more information. Note that dates for some events can shift from year to year so check the exact timings locally before making plans.

City Day   ARTS & CULTURE
KL commemorates becoming a federal territory on 1 February each year with celebrations at Tasik Perdana and Titiwangsa Lake Gardens.

KL Design Week   DESIGN
(www.kualalumpurdesignweek.com.my) Events across the city provide a great opportunity to catch up on the latest in design from Malaysia and beyond. End of March/early April.

Malaysian Grand Prix   CAR RACE
(www.malaysiangp.com.my) Special shopping promotions and events along Jln Bukit Bintang accompany the Formula 1 race at Sepang International Circuit (p111). March/April.

DON'T MISS

PECHA KUCHA

Guaranteed to be surprising and entertaining are the **Pecha Kucha** (www.pecha-kucha. org/night/kuala-lumpur) nights organised by the British Council roughly every three months. Sometimes organised around a theme or event such as KL Design week, these entertaining evenings see presenters each allotted 20 slides for 20 seconds for show-and-tell presentations. Check the website for the venue, which changes for each event.

Malaysia Fest (Colours of Malaysia)
ARTS & CULTURE

This celebration lasts for two weeks in May, with exhibits of traditional arts and special cultural performances around town.

Shopping Carnival
SHOPPING

Shopping in KL becomes even more of a bargain as prices plummet during this annual June sale.

Standard Chartered KL Marathon
SPORTS

(www.kl-marathon.com) June sees over 17,500 runners take to the streets for this international marathon event.

KL Festival
ARTS & CULTURE

July is a month of events showcasing Malaysian art, dance, theatre and music.

National Day
ARTS & CULTURE

Join the crowds in Merdeka Sq at midnight on 31 August to celebrate the anniversary of Malaysia's independence. There are parades and festivities the next morning.

KL International Tower Jump
ADVENTURE SPORTS

(www.kltowerjump.com) The only time you'll be able to see people legally flinging themselves off Menara KL is when the international BASE-jumping fraternity are in town in September/October.

Freedom Film Fest
FILM

(www.freedomfilmfest.komas.org) Local independent film-makers get to show their cutting-edge and controversial docos and shorts in this November festival with a political/social theme.

KL International Film Festival
FILM

(www.sinemamalaysia.com.my) Catch screenings and symposiums on local and international films in November.

🛏 Sleeping

KL is awash with both budget and luxury hotels, but characterful midrange options are thin on the ground. Many of the cheapies are grubby fleapits offering windowless boxy rooms, appealing only for their rock-bottom rates. The best places do fill up, so book well ahead.

Always ask about special deals as practically all midrange and top-end places offer promotions that can slash rack rates by 50% or more. On public holidays, room discounts will not apply. Chinatown is crammed with budget places (mostly pretty awful) but there's also a very healthy backpacker scene in the Golden Triangle – this is where you'll find the pick of budget guesthouses and hostels as well as many international-brand luxury hotels. If everywhere is full, Little India and the seedy Chow Kit area further north also have plenty of low-priced accommodation, although many places are brothels, or close enough. If you don't mind being away from the centre, Bangsar or Mid Valley are also worth considering.

Budget ($) hotels and hostels are those offering a double room with attached bathroom or dorm bed for under RM100; midrange ($$) properties have double rooms with attached baths for RM100 to RM400; top-end ($$$) places charge over RM400 including 10% service and 5% tax (expressed as '++').

CHINATOWN

This atmospheric area is the common first stop for backpackers looking for a hostel or budget hotels. However, some of the cheaper places are basically brothels. The following options are legit.

🔝 BackHome
CHOICE | HOSTEL $

(Map p48; ☑2078 7188; www.backhome.com.my; 30 Jln Tun HS Lee; dm/d with breakfast from RM42/100; ❄@🗢) At the Little India end of Chinatown, this new hostel is a chic pit stop for flashpackers with its polished concrete finishes, Zen simple decoration, fab rain showers and a blissful central courtyard sprouting spindly trees. It's noisy on the street outside, but they've got that covered by offering earplugs for light sleepers.

5 Elements Hotel
HOTEL $$

(Map p48; ☑2031 6888; www.the5elementshotel.com.my; Lot 243 Jln Sultan; s/d with breakfast from RM170/200; ❄@) Offering a good range of rooms, some with views towards KL Tower, this hotel makes a credible stab at boutique stylings. We particularly liked the sensuous design motif snaking its way across the corridor and bedroom walls.

Hotel Chinatown (2)
HOTEL $

(Map p48; ☑2072 9933; www.hotelchinatown2.com; 70-72 Jln Petaling; s/d from RM69/90; ❄@🗢) The slightly cheaper and more appealing of the two Hotel Chinatowns instantly pleases with a sparkling lobby equipped with comfy lounge area, water feature, book exchange and piano. The cheapest rooms have no windows but are also away from the noisy main street.

AnCasa Hotels & Resorts (www.ancasa-hotel.com) offers seven different **homestays** in rural parts of Penisular Malaysia, including a couple of destinations easily accessible from Kuala Lumpur. During a three-day, two-night stay with a rice-farming family in Kampung Tebuk Pulai, near Sabak Bernam in Selangor, activities may include kayaking, fishing and visiting fruit plantations and a monkey park. Alternatively, relax in the cool climes of the Cameron Highlands in the village of Kampung Taman Sedia. Here you can take jungle walks and visit various fruit and flower farms as well as watch traditional dance performances. Both programmes cost RM200 per person, not including public transport and transfers from KL, which AnCasa can help you arrange.

AnCasa Hotel & Spa Kuala Lumpur
HOTEL **$$**

(Map p48; ☎2026 6060; www.ancasa-hotel.com; Jln Tun Tan Cheng Lock; d from RM360; ❋@) Promotions halve the rack rates at one of Chinatown's best midrange options, although there's a small surcharge for weekend stays and internet access is chargeable. The comfortable rooms are well equipped. The hotel also has a Balinese-style spa and can arrange homestays around the peninsula.

Olympic Sport Hotel
HOTEL **$$**

(Map p48; ☎2078 7888; www.olympichotelkl.com.my; Jln Hang Jebat; d with breakfast from RM148; ❋🛜) In a building belonging to Malaysia's National Olympic Committee (hence the name), this is a respectable performer for its price bracket. The location, close to Chinatown and both monorail and LRT terminals, is convenient yet quiet. The pleasantly decorated rooms are spacious.

Chinatown Boutique Hotel
HOTEL **$$**

(Map p48; ☎2072 3388; www.chinatownboutiquehotel.com; 34-36 Jln Hang Lekir; d or tw from RM100; ❋🛜) In the thick of Chinatown, this place is egging the pudding to bill itself as 'boutique', even though some creative design effort has gone into jazzing up functional rooms with colourful and interesting wall decorations. Add RM20 to rates for stays Friday to Sunday and on public holidays.

Wheelers Guest House
HOSTEL **$**

(Map p48; ☎2070 1386; www.backpackerskl.com/wheelers.htm; level 2, 131-133 Jln Tun HS Lee; dm/r with shared bathroom RM13/30, r with private bathroom RM60; ❋@) One of KL's quirkier hostels, Wheelers has a mini-aquarium, gay-friendly staff and great rooftop terrace where free Friday-night dinners are hosted. We also love the fact that they offer homemade yoghurt and muesli for breakfast.

Grocer's Inn
HOSTEL **$**

(Map p48; ☎2078 7906; www.grocersinn.com.my; 78 Jln Sultan; dm/s/d from RM15/35/45; ❋@) Occupying a handsome century-old building that was once home to the grocers' association, this backpackers has a decent range of fan and air-con rooms as well as a rooftop dorm and balconies overlooking Chinatown's bustle. The entrance is in an alley just off Jln Sultan.

YWCA
HOSTEL **$**

(Map p48; ☎2070 1623; www.ywcamalaysia.org/ywca_kl.html; 12 Jln Hang Jebat; s/d/tr with shared bathroom RM30/50/70) This quiet, simply decorated establishment tucked away east of Chinatown offers plain but very acceptable rooms with fan, desk and wardrobe. Only for women, couples and families.

Original Backpackers Travellers Inn
HOSTEL **$**

(Map p48; ☎2078 2473; www.backpackerskl.com; 60 Jln Sultan; dm/s/d with shared bathroom RM11/28/30, r with private bathroom from RM54; ❋@) The highlight of this long-established, well-run hostel with cell-like rooms is its rooftop bar where you can get breakfast as well as hook up with fellow travellers. It also runs a travel agency and can arrange a variety of trips (p65).

GOLDEN TRIANGLE

The best place to hunt for characterful budget and midrange options, although note that anything on Changat Bukit Bintang will be plagued by noise from the many bars and restaurants along this party strip.

TOP CHOICE Sahabat Guest House
GUESTHOUSE **$$**

(Map p42; ☎2142 0689; www.sahabatguesthouse.com; 41 Jln Sahabat; d with breakfast from RM96; ❋@🛜) Rush to book this adorable blue-painted eight-room guesthouse tucked away off Tingkat Tong Shin. Small but

A KL PAMPERING

The perfect way to unwind after a long journey to KL is to visit one of the city's many spas or massage parlours. The city is awash with options from exotic and luxurious retreats to simple salons for foot reflexology or a nibble from the doctor fish.

Luxury Spas

Indulgence central is the 'Pamper' floor of swish shopping mall Starhill Gallery (p92), dedicated to exclusive spa and beauty treatments. Among the less pricey options here are **Asianel Reflexology Spa** (Map p42; ☑2142 1397; www.asianel.com; ⊙10am-9pm) and the Balinese-style **Donna Spa** (Map p42; ☑2141 8999; www.donnaspa.net; ⊙10am-9pm).

If money is no object, practically all KL's five-star hotels offer a luxurious spa experience. One of the best is the Ritz Carlton's **Spa Village** (Map p42; ☑2782 9090; www.spavillageresort. org; Ritz Carlton, 168 Jln Imbi; ⊙9am-9pm) with its resort-like atmosphere and wide-ranging menu of Chinese, Indian and Southeast Asian healing and toning therapies.

Other sybaritic possibilities:

» **Hammam** (Map p59; ☑2282 2180; www.hammambaths.com; Lot 3F-7 & 8 Bangsar Village II, Bangsar Baru; ⊙10am-10pm) The Moroccan steam bath comes to KL at this small but beautifully mosaic-tiled operation. A simple steam and scrub (called 'gommage') is RM150; throw in a massage or other treatment and you're looking at RM235 and up.

» **JoJoBa Spa** (Map p42; ☑2141 7766; www.jojoba.com.my; 15th fl, East Wing, Berjaya Times Square Hotel, 1 Jln Imbi; ⊙11am-midnight) Claims to be Malaysia's largest tourist spa – come for seaweed wraps, coffee scrubs and ginger tea.

» **Touches de Siam** (Map p59; ☑2287 2866; www.thaiodyssey.com.my; 2a Jln Telawi; ⊙10am-10pm) Specialises in Thai massage, which focuses on the entire skeletomuscular system.

» **Senjakala** (Map p48; ☑2031 8082; www.senjakala.com; 20 Jln Pudu Lama; ⊙noon-10pm) Tastefully designed men-only spa. Discount available for massage and scrub packages on Tuesday and Thursday.

» **Tanamera Wellness Spa** (Map p54; ☑2785 1815; www.tanameraspa.com.my; 3-5 Sooka Sentral, Jln Stesen Sentral; ⊙noon-10pm) Discover a wide variety of Malay beauty treatments using indigenous herbs and flowers; it's also handy for KL Sentral.

comfy bedrooms, with small en suite bathrooms, are brightened up with a feature wall plastered in vivid patterned wallpaper. There's a small kitchen and a grassy front garden in which to relax. Rates are slightly higher from Friday to Sunday.

TOP CHOICE **Fraser Place Kuala Lumpur**

SERVICED APARTMENTS **$$**
(Map p42; ☑2118 6288; http://kualalumpur.fra sershospitality.com; Lot 163, 10 Jln Perak; apt with breakfast from RM350; ❄@☎❄) Even if you're not planning a long-term stay, these serviced self-catering studios and apartments are super stylish and can be booked for as little as one night. The facilities, including an outdoor infinity pool, gym, sauna and games room, are top notch.

41 Berangan GUESTHOUSE **$$**
(Map p42; ☑2144 8691; www.41berangan.com; 41 Jln Berangan; d with breakfast from RM100; ❄@☎) This sleek property offers zen-style simplicity and innovation: two courtyard

rooms have been built inside shipping crates and they're planning to stack a couple more on top. There are a couple of cheaper rooms (RM80) with shared bathrooms.

Number Eight Guesthouse GUESTHOUSE **$$**
(Map p42; ☑2144 2050; www.numbereight.com. my; 8-10 Jln Tingkat Tong Shin; dm RM30, r without/with private bathroom RM85/135; ❄@☎) Although it's looking a little worn, Number Eight's minimalist design remains appealing and its value-for-money rooms, some with TVs and DVD players, leave most competitors standing. We love the tea-lit tables on the patio, the comfy sofas in the TV lounge and the fact that the rooms have sturdy wooden furniture and eccentric light fittings. It also does its bit for the environment with solar-heated water. Rates include breakfast.

Anggun Boutique Hotel HOTEL **$$**
(Map p42; ☑2145 8003; www.anggunkl.com; 7-9 Jln Tingkat Tong Shin; d with breakfast from RM250;

Massages & Foot Reflexology

If the top-end spas are beyond your budget, there are numerous Chinese massage and re-flexology centres strung along Jln Bukit Bintang. Pricing is fairly consistent – around RM75 per hour for a full body massage and RM25 for 30 minutes of foot reflexology, though you can bargain down – but standards vary and some places are slightly seedy. A reliable option on the strip is **Old Asia** (Map p42; ☑2143 3778; 14 Jln Bukit Bintang; ⊙10am-2am); as well as mas-sages and reflexology, you can try ear candling and hot stone treatments.

Alternatively visit one of the blind masseurs in Brickfields. There are numerous massage centres here, employing blind people who might otherwise be forced to beg for a living. Con-tact the **Malaysian Association for the Blind** (Map p54; ☑2272 2677; www.mab.org.my; Kompleks MAB, Jln Tebing, Brickfields) for recommendations.

Fish Spas

Often combined with foot reflexology, KL's popular fish spas bring a new meaning to feeding the fish. Immerse your feet in a tank filled with the small *Garra rufa* and *Cyprinion macros-tomus*, also known as doctor fish, and allow the flapping podiatrists to gently nibble away at the dead skin. It's an initially ticklish but not wholly unpleasant experience lasting 30 minutes (or as long as you can stand it!).

Among the places you can sample this service, which costs around RM30, are the KLCC aquarium (Aquaria KLCC; see p40) and the following:

» **Foot Master Dr Fish Spa** (Map p42; ☑2141 6651; www.kenko.com.sg; Level 5, Pavilion Kuala Lumpur; ⊙10am-10pm) You can also have a full-body fish spa here for RM108. There's another branch at Mid Valley Megamall.

» **Kenko** (Map p42; ☑2141 6651; www.kenko.com.sg; Level 5, Pavilion KL, 169 Jln Bukit Bintang; ⊙10am-10pm)

» **Morino Kaze** (Map p42; ☑2141 1916; www.morinokaze.com.my; 2nd fl, Piccolo Galleria, 101 Jln Bukit Bintang; ⊙noon-midnight)

❀❀) A far superior grade of property com-pared with its lacklustre guesthouse across the street, the Anggun is a welcome addi-tion to a busy strip. The rooftop restaurant and bar is a leafy oasis hung with twinkling lights. Unfortunately, the largest, top-grade rooms face the noisy street.

Rainforest Bed & Breakfast   HOSTEL **$$**
(Map p42; ☑2145 3525; www.rainforestbnbho tel.com; 27 Jln Mesui; dm/d/tw with breakfast RM35/105/130; ❀@❀) The lush foliage sprouting around and tumbling off the tiered balconies of this high-quality guest-house is eye-catching and apt for its name. Inside, bright red walls and timber-lined rooms (some without windows) are visu-ally distinctive along with the collection of Chinese pottery figurines. Friendly staff also make it a very appealing option.

Lodge Paradise Hotel   HOTEL **$$**
(Map p42; ☑2142 0122; www.lodgeparadize.com; 2 Jln Tengah; d from RM120; ❀@) Although its

kidney-shaped swimming pool is just for show, this nicely revamped hotel in a four-storey 1940s building couldn't be better placed. The budget rooms at the back are a great deal and are more sheltered from traffic noise than the superior rooms in the main building. Long-stay deals are also available.

YY38 Hotel   HOTEL **$$**
(Map p42; ☑2148 8838; www.yy38hotel.com.my; 38 Tingkat Tong Shin; s/d from RM100/120; ❀❀) Pastel pink, lemon, lime and blue adorn the exterior and interior of this appeal-ing new budget hotel with no-frills rooms. Breakfast isn't available, but there's a con-venience store downstairs plus plenty of other nearby options for Malaysian eats. Add RM20 to rates for stays on Friday and Saturday nights.

Classic Inn   HOSTEL **$**
(Map p42; ☑2148 8648; www.classicinn.com.my; 52 Lg 1/77A, Changkat Thambi Dollah; dm/s/d

RM35/88/118; ✳@) Occupying a smartly renovated, yellow-painted shophouse on the southern edge of the Golden Triangle, this is a retro-charming choice with dorms and private rooms, a small grassy garden and welcoming staff.

Hotel Istana HOTEL $$$
(Map p42; 2141 9988; www.hotelistana.com. my; 73 Jln Raja Chulan; r/ste from RM850/3500; ✳@🛜🏊) The Istana's soothing rooms, where beds sport batik throws and there are fresh flowers, stand in contrast to the high glitz of its lobby with giant columns and Malay motifs. It also has a good-sized swimming pool in a garden setting.

Impiana HOTEL $$$
(Map p42; 2141 1111; www.impiana.com; 13 Jln Pinang; d with breakfast from RM450; ✳@🛜🏊) This chic property offers spacious rooms with parquet floors and lots of seductive amenities including a spa and infinity pool with a view across to the Petronas Towers (partly marred by the soon-to-open Grand Hyatt). Not to be outdone, the Impiana is adding a second tower of rooms.

Shangri-La Hotel HOTEL $$$
(Map p42; 2032 2388; www.shangri-la.com; 11 Jln Sultan Ismail; r/ste from RM660/1910; ✳@🛜🏊) A jaw-droppingly opulent hotel that features an impressive range of facilities and several top-class restaurants – the lobby lounge is particularly pleasant. The rooms are spacious and well equipped.

Westin Kuala Lumpur
HOTEL & SERVICED APARTMENTS $$$
(Map p42; 2731 8333; www.westin.com/ kualalumpur; 199 Jln Bukit Bintang; d/apt from RM800/1300; ✳@🛜🏊) The Westin's spacious rooms are modern and appealing and it's easy to see why long-term residents love its serviced apartments with their full kitchens and glassed-in balconies. It also has a good gym and stylish restaurants and bars.

Ritz Carlton HOTEL $$$
(Map p42; 2142 8000; www.ritzcarlton.com; 168 Jln Imbi; r/ste from RM1150/3600; ✳@🛜🏊) Dark wood and marble create a nostalgic old-world atmosphere, and rooms are extravagantly appointed, if conservative in taste. Ceramic tiffin pots and other pieces of Asian bric-a-brac add a hint of colonial grandeur. The on-site Spa Village (p69) is highly recommended. Promotional rates can more than halve room prices.

Piccolo Hotel HOTEL $$
(Map p42; 2303 8000; www.thepiccolohotel. com; 101 Jln Bukit Bintang; r from RM414; ✳@🛜) Although its boutique look is somewhat cheaply thrown together, we do like the striking marine life images decorating the walls at this hotel in the midst of the Bintang Walk shopping strip. Almost constant promotional rates and online bookings bring it down a budget category.

Royale Bintang Kuala Lumpur HOTEL $$$
(Map p42; 2143 9898; www.royale-bintang-hotel. com.my; 17-21 Jln Bukit Bintang; r from RM400; ✳@🛜🏊) Bright decor and tasteful details score points for this towering hotel on the Bukit Bintang strip. There's a lovely palm-shaded pool area, and rooms have all the expected mod cons, including minibars, safes and facilities to make tea and coffee.

Sky Hotel HOTEL $$
(Map p42; 2148 6777; www.skyhotel.com.my; 1A Jln Bintang; r from RM148; ✳🛜) King-size beds – or twin singles – dominate the spacious rooms at this keenly priced hotel. Just opened on our visit, it's yet to develop much of a personality. The bathrooms are nicely designed and the rooms look like they were decorated with light wood laminate furnishings from Ikea.

Radius International Hotel HOTEL $$
(Map p42; 2715 3888; www.radius-international. com; 51A Changkat Bukit Bintang; r/ste from RM170/450; ✳@🏊) This big tower hotel, at the foot of KL's most buzzing restaurant and bar strip, has all the facilities of an international chain hotel, including a decent-sized swimming pool, but at lower prices. Rates are almost always on promotion – opt for the tasteful 'premier' rooms.

Hotel Capitol HOTEL $$
(Map p42; 2143 7000; www.fhihotels.com; Jln Bulan; r/ste from RM253/518; ✳@🏊) Go online to get the best rates for this pleasing contemporary hotel. Its loft-style and premium corner rooms are worth checking out for added hip furnishings and good views. Guests have access to the nearby Federal Hotel's swimming pool.

Red Palm HOSTEL $
(Map p42; 2143 1279; www.redpalm-kl.com; 5 Tingkat Tong Shin; dm/s/d/tr incl breakfast RM30/50/70/105; @) There's no sign outside this cosy shophouse hostel, which ensures a pleasantly informal atmosphere inside. Rooms are typical for the area – small and

BAYAN INDAH

From the looks of the leafy *kampung* (village) surrounding **Bayan Indah** (☑7729 0122; www.bayanindah.com; 3343 Kg Palimbayan Indah, Sungai Penchala; d with breakfast from RM450; ✳@⊛) it's hard to credit that you're within the city limits, just 30 minutes drive from the KLCC and even closer to mammoth shopping malls such as 1 Utama. This perfect rural escape, with four lovely en-suite rooms, balconies and lush gardens, was once the home of super-friendly food writer and cook Rohani Jelani, who serves delicious breakfasts and is a mine of local information. You don't need to join one of Rohani's cooking classes (see p63) to stay here but you'd be crazy to pass up the chance to do so.

thin-walled with shared bathrooms – but the communal areas are great and the owners charming.

Green Hut Lodge
HOSTEL $
(Map p42; ☑2142 3339; www.thegreenhut.com; 48 Tingkat Tong Shin; dm/s/d incl breakfast RM25/50/65; ✳@) The ever-popular Green Hut is a wholesome travellers' choice with a varied selection of rooms and lots of communal spaces to relax in. It's bright and inviting and the air-conditioned rooms are a bargain. You can check your email and play pool. Pay more if you want a private bathroom.

Bedz KL
HOSTEL $
(Map p42; ☑2144 2339; www.bedzkl.com; 58 Changkat Bukit Bintang; dm RM30; ✳@) There are only dorms at this smart choice, shielded from busy Changkat Bukit Bintang by a grove of bamboo. Rain showers, plenty of internet terminals and souvenir T-shirts are part of the package.

Swiss-Garden Hotel
HOTEL $$
(Map p42; ☑2141 3333; www.swissgarden.com; 117 Jln Pudu; d from RM242; ✳@⊛) Good location, high-standard rooms and facilities.

KLCC & AROUND
The high price of real estate around the Petronas Towers is the reason for the dearth of budget and even midrange options in this area.

TOP CHOICE G City Club Hotel
HOTEL $$$
(Map p64; ☑2168 1919; www.thegcityclubhotel.com; 199 Jln Tun Razak; d with breakfast from RM780; ✳@⊛⊠) There's an exclusive atmosphere at this slickly designed property atop a new office complex. Only hotel guests and tenants can access the gym, two infinity pools and top-floor lounge, restaurant and bar. Arty black-and-white prints set a sophisticated tone in the bedrooms. Ask for

one of the slightly bigger corner rooms, preferably with a view to Tabung Haji.

Traders Hotel Kuala Lumpur
HOTEL $$$
(Map p42; ☑2332 9888; www.tradershotels.com; KLCC, off Jln Kia Peng; d/ste from RM610/890; ✳@⊛⊠) Lovely as it is inside, you're going to want to opt for a room with a view across to the Petronas Towers at this contemporary design addition to KL's portfolio of luxe hotels.

MiCasa All Suite Hotel
SERVICED APARTMENTS $$$
(Map p64; ☑2179 8000; www.micasahotel.com; 368B Jln Tun Razak; apt from RM400; ✳@⊛⊠) MiCasa has a choice of one-, two- or three-bedroom suites – all reasonably priced and newly renovated with wooden floors and kitchens. Relax beside the large, palm-tree-fringed pool, or enjoy their small spa and the gourmet restaurant Cilantro (see p79).

Hotel Maya
HOTEL $$$
(Map p60; ☑2711 8866; www.hotelmaya.com.my; 138 Jln Ampang; r/ste with breakfast from RM700/1000; ✳@⊛⊠) Even though it remains one of KL's most stylish hotels, the Maya is beginning to show some wear and tear in its sleek timber-floored studios and suites. Rack rates include airport transfers, as well as a host of other goodies, while promotional rates – nearly half the official ones – include only breakfast and wi-fi.

Mandarin Oriental
HOTEL $$$
(Map p60; ☑2380 8888; www.mandarinoriental.com/kualalumpur; KLCC, Jln Pinang; r/ste from RM1080/3000; ✳@⊛⊠) Backing onto the greenery of KLCC Park, the Mandarin is one for sybarites. Silks and batiks lend an Asian feel to the rooms, which have every conceivable amenity. The Oriental Club rooms are the ones to pick, allowing access to a lounge with a great view of the Petronas Towers. There's a spa and infinity

pool that seems to merge into the parkland beyond.

Pacific Regency Hotel Suites

SERVICED APARTMENTS **$$$**

(Map p42; ☎2332 7777; www.pacific-regency.com; Menara Panglobal, Jln Punchak; apt from RM650; ❄@🛜🏊) These upmarket self-catering studios and serviced apartments are good value compared with the rooms of a similar standard at KL's other five-star properties. Head to the roof to enjoy the rooftop pool and Luna (p87), one of the city's best bars.

Doubletree by Hilton, Kuala Lumpur

HOTEL **$$$**

(Map p64; ☎2172 7272, http://kl.doubletreebyhilton.com; Intermark, 182 Jln Tun Razak; r RM550; ❄@🛜🏊) This new hotel is a good addition to KL's upmarket options, with slightly lower rates than similar abodes. Rooms sport a pleasant modern design in beige tones. Executive floor rooms are the only ones to include internet access in their rates.

Royale Chulan Kuala Lumpur

HOTEL **$$$**

(Map p64; ☎2688 9688; www.theroyalechulan.com.my; 5 Jln Conlay; r/apt with breakfast from RM700/800; ❄@🛜🏊) Designed in regal Malay style, the rooms at this massive luxury property – while pleasantly decorated and spacious – don't match the glitz of the public areas. A downer is the daily RM45 charge for internet access.

LITTLE INDIA & CHOW KIT

Hotels in Little India mainly cater to visiting traders; rooms tend to be functional with little character.

TOP CHOICE Tune Hotel

HOTEL **$**

(Map p60; ☎7962 5888; www.tunehotels.com; 316 Jln TAR; r from RM50; ❄@🛜) This innovative operation uses the low-cost approach of local budget airline Air Asia: book online six months in advance and it's possible to snag a room with bathroom for under RM50 – walk-in rates are more likely to be from RM90 to RM130. This basic rate, however, just gets you the room – air-con, towel and toiletries, and wi-fi access are extra. Each floor is sponsored, which means you'll find yourself gazing at an ad for, say, Maggi or Nippon Paints, in your room and along the corridors. There's also a branch next to the LCCT (Low Cost Carrier Terminal; see p73).

Hotel Noble

HOTEL **$$**

(Map p48; ☎2691 7111; www.hotelnoble.com; 165-169 Jln TAR; d from RM120; ❄🛜) Hidden away behind a silk store, this hotel has reasonably spacious rooms with minibars, safes, coffee-and tea-making facilities and old TVs. Clean sheets and a batik throw compensate for stained carpets.

Cititel Express

HOTEL **$$**

(Map p60; ☎2691 9833; www.cititelexpress.com; 449 Jln TAR; d with breakfast from RM130; ❄🛜) Big, clean rooms and constant promotion rates. Ask for a room away from the busy main road.

Ben Soo Homestay

GUESTHOUSE **$**

(Map p60; ☎2691 8096, 012 675 6110; bensoohome@yahoo.com; 2nd fl, 61B Jln Tiong Nam; s/d RM40/45; ❄@) Down-at-heel homestay offering two plain, clean rooms with wooden floors and shared bathrooms. The family who runs it is very welcoming, with Ben offering guided tours.

BRICKFIELDS & LAKE GARDENS

TOP CHOICE Hilton Kuala Lumpur

HOTEL **$$$**

(Map p54; ☎2264 2264; www.hilton.com; 3 Jln Stesen Sentral; r/ste from RM455/850; ❄@🛜🏊) Sharing a fabulous landscaped pool and spa with the Meridien next door, the Hilton is a design diva's dream. Sliding doors open to join the bathroom to the bedroom, picture windows present soaring city views and rooms are decked out from floor to ceiling in eye-catching materials. It's almost on top of KL Sentral and there are five respected restaurants and two bars on site.

Carcosa Seri Negara

HOTEL **$$$**

(off Map p54; ☎2295 0888; www.shr.my; Taman Tasik Perdana; ste from RM1100; ❄@🛜) Secluded on the highest hill of the Lake Gardens, this elegant heritage property is split between two colonial mansions. Carcosa, once the residence of British government representative Sir Frank Swettenham, was closed for renovation at the time of research, leaving Seri Negara, formerly the official guesthouse, offering six conservatively designed, spacious suites, perfect for non-rock-star VIPs. If it's out of your price bracket, then see how the other half live by splashing out on the hotel's excellent afternoon tea (see p85).

YMCA

HOTEL **$**

(Map p54; ☎2274 1439; www.ymcakl.com; 95 Jln Padang Belia; d or tw RM80, tr without bathroom RM100; ❄🛜) This reliable property near KL Sentral offers spic-and-span rooms with TVs, telephones and proper wardrobes (not just

If all you need to do is freshen up before or after your flight, you might like to use the **Airside Transit Hotel** (✆8787 4848; www.klairporthotel.com/airside-transit-hotel; Gate 5, Satellite Bldg, KLIA; d per 6hr RM140; ✷@). The hotel includes a fitness centre, business centre, spa and sauna, and all rooms come with attached bathroom and TV.

The budget **Tune Hotel** (www.tunehotels.com; r from RM50; ✷@奈), which rewards advance online bookings with the cheapest rates, has a branch within the LCCT, while the luxurious **Pan Pacific KLIA** (✆8787 3333; www.panpacific.com; r from RM480; ✷@✸) is linked by a bridge to the main KLIA terminal.

hangers on a wall hook). There's a laundry, shop and cafe with wi-fi access, and also tennis courts for hire.

My Hotel @ Sentral   HOTEL **$$**
(Map p54; ✆2273 8000; www.myhotels.com.my; 1 Jln Tun Sambanthan 4; d from RM98; ✷) Just sneaking into the budget category if you opt for the no-breakfast rate, this simple, clean and conveniently located hotel might just be a lifesaver if you arrive at Sentral without a place to stay. If you do opt for brekkie, it's served in the Old Time chain cafe next door.

BANGSAR & MID VALLEY

TOP CHOICE **Serendah Tenggiri**   GUESTHOUSE **$$**
(off Map p59; ✆017 207 5977; www.tenggiri.com; 48 Jln Tenggiri, Taman Weng Lock, Bangsar; r from RM200; ✷奈✸) Even if it didn't provide access to landscape architect Ng Seksan's superlative private collection of contemporary Malaysian art (displayed in the rooms of the adjoing house) this would be a lovely place to stay. The rough luxe mix of concrete, wood and wire decor (with cleverly recycled materials making up lamp fixtures) is softened by abundant garden greenery and a cooling plunge pool. There's a basic kitchen, a housekeeper and several great places to eat on nearby Lg Kurau.

Terasek Brickhouse   GUESTHOUSE **$$**
(off Map p59; ✆012-2062846; www.terasekbrickhouse.com; 42a Jln Terasek, Bangsar Baru; r/house RM200/1000; ✷奈) Sporting the same minimalist chic as Serendah Tenggiri (they share the same designer) is this five-room property, part of a residential row within walking distance of Bangsar Baru's shops and restaurants. It also has a tiny plunge pool, full kitchen and roof deck with panoramic views of the area, plus they use solar power. A sister establishment, Seapark Brickhouse, is in Petaling Jaya (p106).

Gardens Hotel & Residences
HOTEL & SERVICED APARTMENTS **$$$**
(✆2268 1111; www.gardenshtlres.com; Gardens, Mid Valley City, Lingkaran Syed Putra; r/apt with breakfast from RM300/450; ✷@奈✸) Attached to the swanky Gardens Mall, this luxury hotel and serviced residences are very appealing. Wooden panelling with lattice details and striking flower prints on the walls make the room decor pop; the apartments are even better – some of the best we saw in KL.

✖ Eating

KL is a nonstop feast. You can dine in incredible elegance or mingle with locals at thousands of street stalls. A meal at a night market (p35) is one of KL's unmissable highlights.

Most often the best food is from the hawker stalls, cheap cafes (called *kopitiam*) and inexpensive restaurants (*restoran*). Hygiene standards at hawker stalls are generally good and you should have little to fear from eating at them. To be absolutely safe, stick to stalls with lots of customers. However, if eating on the street is not your thing – or you just want air-con with your meal – then food courts, usually located in shopping malls, are the solution.

To some degree, food is localised to the areas where the different ethnic minorities live. Chinatown, Bukit Bintang and Pudu are good for Chinese food, while Little India and Brickfields have excellent Indian restaurants and stalls. Kampung Baru is great for Malay and Indonesian home cooking. For international food, head to the big shopping malls, top hotels and Bangsar Baru.

At a budget ($) restaurant you'd be spending under RM20 for a meal without alcohol, from RM20 to RM50 at a midrange ($$) place, and over RM50 at top-end ($$$) place. Unless otherwise stated, the restaurants listed are open daily for lunch from noon to 2.30pm and dinner from 6pm to 10.30pm.

CHINATOWN

Chinatown has some of the best and most inexpensive street food in KL. From breakfasts of *yong tau fu* (bean curd and vegetables stuffed with fish paste) and curry noodles on Madras Lane to a supper of satay and fried fish with an ice-cold beer at the popular open-air cafes along Jln Hang Lekir, you can hardly go wrong. An air-con option is the food court on level two of Central Market (p47).

TOP CHOICE Madras Lane Hawkers

HAWKER STALLS $

(Map p48; Madras Lane; noodles RM5; ☺closed Mon) Weave your way through Chinatown's wet market to find this short alley of stalls tucked between Jln Tun HS Lee and Jln Petaling. It's best visited for breakfast or lunch, with standout operators including the one offering 10 types of *yong tau fu* in a fish broth (☺9.30am to 3.30pm) and, at the far end of the strip, the one serving *asam* and curry laksa (☺8am to 2pm).

TOP CHOICE Old China Café MALAY & NONYA $$

(Map p48; ☏2072 5915; www.oldchina. com.my; 11 Jln Balai Polis; mains RM40-50; ☺11.30am-10pm) Housed in the old guild hall of the Selangor & Federal Territory Laundry Association, this atmospheric cafe captures some of the charm of old KL. The walls are huge and covered with old bric-a-brac, and the cook prepares Nonya dishes from Melaka and Penang, including a fine beef rendang (coconut and lime-leaf curry) with coconut rice and fiery Nonya laksa soup with seafood.

Ikan Panggang HAWKER STALLS $$

(Map p48; ☏019 315 9448; spicy seafood RM12; ☺5-11pm Tue-Sun) Tuck into spicy fish and seafood dishes and luscious chicken wings from this unsigned stall outside Hong Leong Bank, tucked behind the stalls on the corner of Jln Petaling and Jln Hang Lekir. Order ahead – it generally takes 20 minutes for your foil-wrapped pouch of seafood to cook, allowing time to explore the market. Wash the meal down with a glass of *mata kucing* (meaning 'cat's eye'), a refreshing Asian fruit drink, also bought from a stall on the same corner.

Purple Cane Tea Restaurant CHINESE $$

(Map p48; ☏2272 3090; www.purplecane.com.my; 1 Jln Maharajalela; mains RM10-20; ☺11am-10pm) Tucked behind the Chinese Assembly Hall, this laid-back place uses tea as an ingredient in most of its dishes. Intriguing specials include chicken soup with tea and ginseng, and beef simmered in lychee tea. There are also branches in Mid Valley Megamall and the Shaw Centre near Pudu.

Sing Seng Nam CHINESE $

(Map p48; 2 Medan Pasar; mains RM5-10; ☺7am-5pm Mon-Sat) KL is fast filling up with new 'old-style' *kopitiam,* but this is the genuine object, busy with locals enjoying breakfast of *kaya* toast and runny boiled egg or a *kopi peng* (iced coffee with milk). Later in the day tuck into inexpensive bowls of chicken rice and 'curry fish'.

Precious MALAY & NONYA $$$

(Map p48; ☏2273 7372; www.oldchina.com.my; 1st fl, Central Market; mains RM40-60; ☺11.30am-10pm) The owners of Old China Café also run this upmarket place, which manages to recreate the mood of mining-era KL despite its mall setting. The food is good and the art and antiques on display are mostly for sale.

Peter Hoe Beyond WESTERN $$

(Map p48; 2nd fl, Lee Rubber Bldg, 145 Jln Tun HS Lee; mains RM10-20; ☺10am-7pm) You may find the affable Mr Hoe himself serving at this supremely relaxing cafe, where you can tuck into a great lunch of delicious quiche with masses of fresh salad, or just enjoy a cake and coffee in between forays around his stylishly merchandised retail space (p95).

Café Café FRENCH & ITALIAN $$$

(off Map p48; ☏2141 8141; 175 Jln Maharajalela; mains RM80-100; ☺6pm-midnight) Flickering candles and twinkling crystal decorations conjure a romantic atmosphere at this quirky restaurant a short walk south of Chinatown. Avoid the fancy foie gras dishes; stick to simpler concoctions and you'll do fine.

Khukri   NEPALESE $$
(Map p48; 2072 0663; Jln Silang; meals RM20; 9am-9pm) A gathering point for Nepalis in KL, this simple restaurant serves authentic Nepalese cuisine including great *momo* (dumplings), steamed or fried, and spicy chicken and mutton dishes.

Restoran Yusoof dan Zakhir   INDIAN MUSLIM $
(Map p48; Jln Hang Kasturi; roti RM2; 24hr) This huge banana-yellow and palm tree–green canteen opposite Central Market serves huge portions of delicious *mamak* food; perfect for a roti and curry sauce snack.

Chee Cheong Fun Stall   CHINESE $
(Map p48; Cnr Jln Petaling & Jln Hang Lekir; noodles RM4; Thu-Tue 7am-4pm;) One of the best breakfasts in Chinatown can be had at this unprepossessing, decades-old stall tucked away just off the street. All it serves are melt-in-the-mouth *chee cheong fun* (rice noodles) doused with sweet and spicy sauces and a sprinkle of sesame seeds. Nearby, further down Jln Hang Lekir, is the equally good *congee* (rice porridge) stall **Hon Kee** (4.30am-3pm).

Shin Kee   CHINESE $
(Map p48; 7A Jln Tun Tan Cheng Lok; noodles RM6; 10.30am-3.30pm) Aficionados of beef ball noodles argue that this hole in the wall with just nine squished tables is *the* place to sample the dish: we found the meat sauce a little salty, but the dry noodles themselves were cooked perfectly. The noodles at **Lai Foong** (138 Jln Tun Tan Cheng Lok; noodles RM5; 10.30am-3.30pm) across the street are equally good.

Hong Ngek   CHINESE $
(Map p48; 50 Jln Tun HS Lee; noodles RM5; 10.30am-7pm Mon-Thu & Sat, to 5pm Fri, closed Sun) Office workers pack out this long-running Hokkien coffee shop, tucking into expertly made fried *beehoon* noodles, crab balls and succulent pork ribs stewed in Guinness. There's air-con upstairs, but it's more interesting to watch the world go by at a table on the naturally ventilated street level.

Restoran Sando Chapati House   INDIAN $
(Map p48; 11 Jln Tun HS Lee; chapati RM1.20; 6.30am-6.30pm Mon-Sat) Chapatis are freshly made at the entrance to this no-frills, self-serve cafe offering one of the cheapest places to snack in the area.

West Lake Restoran   CHINESE $
(Map p48; 2072 3350; 15 Jln Sultan; meals RM10-20; 7am-2am) Simple eatery known for its *yong tau fu* and *mee* (noodle) dishes.

Kafe Happy Meal   BAKERY $
(Map p48; 2072 6080; 143 Jln Tun HS Lee; pastries RM3; 7am-7pm Mon-Sat) Take-away bakery offering creamy durian puffs and other lovely pastries and packaged sandwiches – ideal for a picnic in the Lake Gardens.

Tang City   FOOD COURT $
(Map p48; Jln Hang Lekir) Set back from the open-air tables on the main drag, this food court serves a good variety of inexpensive dishes.

GOLDEN TRIANGLE
Amid this area's myriad eating possibilities, two major malls – Pavilion KL and Starhill Gallery – offer such a wide and top-quality range (from food courts to fine dining) that only the pickiest diner could find fault. Nothing seems to be dousing the white-hot popularity of the Changat Bukit Bintang dining and drinking strip, with the icing on the Golden Triangle's edible cake being ever-reliable Jln Alor and – our favourite reason for getting up early – the breakfast stalls at Imbi Market.

TOP CHOICE Imbi Market   HAWKER STALLS $
(Pasar Baru Bukit Bintang; Map p64; Jln Kampung; meal RM10; 6.30am-12.30pm Tue-Sun) The official name is Pasar Baru Bukit Bintang, but everyone knows it simply as Imbi Market. Breakfast is like a party here with all the friendly and curious locals happily recommending their favourite stalls. We like **Sisters Crispy Popiah**; **Teluk Intan Chee Cheung Fun**, where Amy Ong serves a lovely oyster-and-peanut *congee* (rice porridge) and egg puddings; **Stanley's stall** beside Amy's serving delicious fish-head noodle soup sweetened with evaporated milk; and **Bunn Choon** for the creamy mini egg tarts.

Frangipani   FRENCH $$$
(Map p42; 2144 3001; www.frangipani.com.my; 25 Changkat Bukit Bintang; 3-course menu RM140; 7.30pm-10.30pm Tue-Sun) Much feted for its innovative approach to European fusion cooking, Frangipani is leagues ahead of most of the competition. The decor is

JALAN ALOR

The great common denominator of KL's food scene – hauling in everyone from sequined society babes to penny-strapped backpackers – is the collection of roadside restaurants and stalls lining Jln Alor. From around 5pm till late every evening, the street transforms into a continuous open-air dining space with hundreds of plastic tables and chairs and rival caterers shouting out to passers-by to drum up business (avoid the pushiest ones!). Most places serve alcohol and you can sample pretty much every Malay Chinese dish imaginable, from grilled fish and satay to *kai-lan* (Chinese greens) in oyster sauce and fried noodles with frogs' legs. Thai food is also popular.

Recommended options include the small complex **One Plus One** (Map p42), one of the few places open from 8am for breakfast, where the Sisters Noodle stall does delicious 'drunken' chicken *mee* (noodles) with rice wine, and there's also a good Hong Kong–style dim sum stall; **Wong Ah Wah** (Map p42; ☺4pm-4am), unbeatable for addictive spicy chicken wings, as well as grilled seafood, tofu and satay; and the unnamed but ever-popular **frog porridge stall** (Map p42; bowl RM7) – you can choose to have 'spicy', where the frogs' legs are served separate, or 'nonspicy', where they're mixed in with the tasty rice gruel.

as slick as the menu, with a stunning dining room surrounding a reflecting pool, and there's an equally stylish bar upstairs. Their new ground-floor wine bar and shop, **Bibitus** (RM55; ☺noon-2.30pm Tue-Sun), offers a brasserie-style lunch. On the last Sunday of the month they also serve a themed brunch (RM120) in the main dining room.

Top Hat NONYA & BRITISH $$$
(Map p64; ☎2142 8611; www.top-hat-restaurants. com; 3 Jln Stonor; meals RM60-110; ☺noon-10.30pm) Set in a spacious bungalow surrounded by peaceful gardens and serving both traditional British – think oxtail stew and bread-and-butter pudding – as well as local dishes, such as Nonya laksa (RM28), which all come with signature 'top hats' (pastry shells filled with sliced veggies) and choice of local dessert.

Nerovivo ITALIAN $$
(Map p42; ☎2070 3120; www.nerovivo.com; 3A Jln Ceylon; mains RM50-100) Tasty Italian food, including crispy pizza and freshly made pastas, are served at this chic, partly open-air restaurant. Down the hill on the ground floor of the Somerset serviced residences is their cosy stable-mate, **Neroteca** (Map p42; ☎2070 0530; www.neroteca.com; Somerset, 8 Lg Ceylon; meals RM50-100; ☺10am-midnight Wed-Mon, 6pm-midnight Tue), an equally appealing place.

TOP CHOICE **Sao Nam** VIETNAMESE $$
(Map p42; ☎2144 1225; www.saonam.com. my; 25 Tingkat Tong Shin; mains RM30-70; ☺noon-2.30pm & 7.30-10.30pm Tue-Sun) This reliable

place is decorated with colourful propaganda posters and has a courtyard for dining outside. The kitchen turns out huge plates of delicious Vietnamese food, garnished with basil, mint, lettuce and sweet dips. The starter *banh xeo* (a huge Vietnamese pancake with meat, seafood or vegetables) is a meal all by itself.

Hakka CHINESE $$$
(Map p42; ☎2143 1908; meals RM80-100; 90 Jln Raja Chulan) Big, long-running restaurant specialising in Hakka-style Chinese cuisine; try the stuffed crabs and tofu dishes. The outdoor section – the most atmospheric, hung with fairy lights that complement the view of the illuminated Petronas Towers – is open only in the evening.

Sisters Kitchen MALAY & NONYA $$
(Map p42; ☎2142 6988; www.sisterscrispypopiah. com.my; 1st fl, Menara Hap Seng, Jln P Ramlee; set lunch RM15; ☺7.30am-5pm Mon-Fri, 8am-4pm Sat) Nobody in KL makes *popiah* quite like the sisters (see p77); at the franchise's main outlet you can try several different versions as well as a good range of other Malay dishes. Their set lunch – including drink, dessert and snack of the day – is good value.

TOP CHOICE **Bijan** MALAY $$$
(Map p42; ☎2031 3575; www.bijan restaurant.com; 3 Jln Ceylon; mains RM60-100; ☺noon-2.30pm & 6.30-10.30pm Mon-Sat, 4.30-10.30pm Sun) One of KL's best Malay restaurants, Bijan offers skilfully cooked traditional dishes in a sophisticated dining room that spills out into a tropical garden. Must-try

dishes include *rendang daging* (dry beef curry with lemongrass), *masak lemak ikan* (Penang-style fish curry with turmeric) and *ikan panggang* (grilled skate with tamarind).

Enak   MALAY $$$
(Map p42; ☎2141 8973; www.enakkl.com; Feast fl, Starhill Gallery, 181 Jln Bukit Bintang; meals RM70-100; ☺noon-1am) Finely presented Malay cuisine with a sophisticated twist, as befitting the trendy Starhill Gallery.

Food Republic   FOOD COURT $
(Map p42; Level 1; Pavilion KL, 168 Jln Bukit Bintang; meals RM10-20; ☺10am-10pm) Outstanding choice and slick design make this probably the best shopping mall food court in KL. It's also surrounded by scores of proper restaurants.

Dragon-i   CHINESE $$
(Map p42; ☎2143 7688; www.dragon-i.com.my; Level 1, Pavilion KL, 168 Jln Bukit Bintang; meals RM40-50; ☺10am-10pm) Very popular outlet of this chain serving Shanghaiese food including steaming dumplings and their signature dish, a multilayer sandwich of braised pork belly and sheets of tofu soaked in a delicious sauce.

Ngau Kee Beef Ball Noodles   CHINESE $
(Map p42; Tingkat Tong Shin; noodles RM5; ☺24hr) The dish at this venerable street stall comes in two parts: dry, steamed noodles topped with a thick soy-sauce mince, and the chunky beef balls in a clear soup – delicious! Refresh your palate with their salty-sweet lime drink.

Loaf   BAKERY $
(Map p42; ☎2145 3036; www.theloaf.net; Levels 3 & 4, Pavilion KL, 168 Jln Bukit Bintang; meals RM10-20; ☺10am-10pm) This bakery cafe and bistro (which has ex-PM Dr Mahathir as an investor) is a Malaysian take on a Japanese baked goods shop. Its big range of baked goods is uniformly divine and we love the mini cheesecakes for a quick snack.

Chiaroscuro   ITALIAN $$
(Map p42; ☎2144 8006; www.chiaroscurokl.com; 30 Jln Bedara; meals RM50; ☺6.30pm-midnight Mon-Sat) The Italian chef and co-owner of this relaxed trattoria really knows how to make fantastic pizza. The homemade pasta, meat and fish dishes are fine, too. Finish off with an Italian mixed cheese plate.

Magnificent Fish & Chip Bar   SEAFOOD $$$
(Map p42; ☎2142 7021; 28 Changkat Bukit Bintang; meals RM60-80; ☺8.30-1am Mon-Fri, 10.30am-1am Sat & Sun) The high quality of the fish (at least eight types, including barramundi) explains the high price you'll pay for the newspaper-wrapped fish and chips at this thoroughly English but stylish operation.

Twenty One Kitchen & Bar   FUSION $$$
(Map p42; ☎2142 0021; www.drbar.asia; 20-1 Changkat Bukit Bintang; meals RM60-80; ☺noon-3am) Lots of interesting choices on the menu here, several of which you can sample together on tasting plates. The bar upstairs, with a deck overlooking the street, gets cranking at weekends when a DJ spins chill and dance tunes. They've opened a second equally chic and happening outlet at Bangsar Shopping Centre.

LOCAL KNOWLEDGE

MEI LIM: SISTERS CRISPY POPIAH

Mei Lim is obviously doing something right: her **Sisters Crispy Popiah** (www.sisters crispypopiah.com.my) outlets can now be found in Menara Hap Seng (see p76), Mid Valley Megamall (p95), Petaling Jaya's Sunway Pyramid mall (p106) and Putrajaya's Alamanda mall (p111), as well as at its humble original location in the Imbi Market (p75).

How long have you been rolling popiah?

I've been in this business over 20 years.

What are the ingredients in the roll?

I use egg frost (flakes of deep-fried egg), crushed peanuts, fried shallots, slivers of cucumber and carrot, and turnip boiled in soy sauce and garlic. I prepare this in the afternoon so it has time to rest overnight – that way it tastes better.

What's the secret to your rolls?

There is a secret, but I'm not telling you.

TOP CHOICE **Mythai Jim Thompson** THAI $$$

(Map p42; ☑2148 6151; www.jimthompson. com; Feast fl, Starhill Gallery, 181 Jln Bukit Bintang; mains RM20-60) Silk cushions and drapes abound at this Thai place that aims to create the colonial mood of Jim Thompson's villa in Bangkok. Refreshingly, style does not triumph over substance – the Thai food is excellent, with numerous regional dishes from around Thailand.

Vansh INDIAN $$$

(Map p42; ☑2142 6162; www.vansh.com.sg; Feast fl, Starhill Gallery, 181 Jln Bukit Bintang; mains from RM30) High-quality Indian cuisine, from a respected Singaporean operation, at prices that match the posh surroundings. Look out for imaginative fusion dishes such as tandoori-marinated lobster, or try their signature *kulzza* – leavened breads topped with tomato, coriander and onion seeds.

Gonbei JAPANESE $$$

(Map p42; ☑2782 3801; Relish fl, Starhill Gallery, 181 Jln Bukit Bintang; mains RM30-100) This brilliantly conceived Japanese restaurant is entered through a Zen walkway of leaning beams. There's a broad sushi and sashimi menu, including seasonal *fugu* (blowfish) for the brave. Diners sit around a series of open kitchens.

Blue Boy Vegetarian Food Centre CHINESE & MALAY $

(Map p42; ☑2144 9011; Jln Tong Shin; mains RM3-10; ☺7.30am-9.30pm; ☑) It's hard to believe that everything prepared at this spotless hawker-style cafe at the base of a backstreet apartment block is vegetarian, but it's true. The *char kway teow* (broad noodles fried in chilli and black-bean sauce) is highly recommended.

Restoran Oversea CHINESE $$

(Map p42; ☑2144 7567; www.oversea.com.my; 84-88 Jln Imbi; mains RM15-50) The main branch of this unpretentious banquet restaurant has been pleasing locals for over 30 years. Specialities include pork belly, fish (cooked in various styles) and streaky bacon cooked in a pot with dried chillies.

Le Bouchon FRENCH $$$

(Map p42; ☑2142 7633; www.lebouchonrestaurant.com; 14-16 Changkat Bukit Bintang; mains RM60-100; ☺noon-2pm Tue-Fri, 7.30-10.30pm Tue-Sun) The dining room at this tasteful French-owned place could have been plucked straight from a Burgundy chateau. The wine list is extensive and the house

bouillabaisse (seafood soup with saffron) is highly recommended.

Prego ITALIAN $$$

(Map p42; ☑2773 8013; Westin Kuala Lumpur, 199 Jln Bukit Bintang; mains RM60-100) Delectable Italian pizzas and pasta in chic but family-friendly surroundings. Come on Sunday for the free-flowing champagne brunch (RM128/188 for three/five courses) with a balloon-twisting clown to entertain the kids.

Restoran Sahara Tent ARABIC $$

(Map p42; ☑2144 8310; www.saharatent.com; Jln Sultan Ismail; mains RM10-30; ☺11am-2am) A new location for this long-established favourite has not diminished the quality and value for money of its Mid East cuisine. Come here for Turkish coffee, meaty kebabs and couscous, then sit back with a bubbling *shisha* (RM15).

Daikanyama JAPANESE $$$

(Map p42; ☑2141 032; 42 Changkat Bukit Bintang; mains RM25-35; ☺5.30pm-12.30am Mon-Thu, 5pm-2am Fri & Sat) This high-class canteen and sake bar is a lovely, relaxed place to sample a quality range of Japanese nibbles – the salmon, soft-shell crab and avocado sushi roll is very good, and you shouldn't miss the flavourful salmon belly soup.

Betty's Café MALAY & NONYA $

(Map p42; ☑2031 7880; www.bettysgroup.com; Wisma Conway, Jln Raja Chulan; meals RM8-15; ☺10am-6pm) Cute canteen offering simple local dishes such as curry laksa, prawn *mee* and Ipoh *kway teow* soup. There's also a branch in CapSquare (p57).

Restoran Nagansari Curry House MALAY & INDIAN $

(Map p42; Jln Nagansari; meals RM5-10; ☺7am-midnight) This simple hawker-style restaurant serves a good selection of Malay dishes – soup *mee, tom yam* and so on – with a few Indian favourites thrown in for good measure. Fans blow moist air around the dining hall to keep diners cool.

Seri Melayu MALAY & NONYA $$

(Map p42; ☑2145 1833; www.serimelayu.com; 1 Jln Conlay; set lunch/dinner RM35/60) Housed in a vast wooden pavilion, Seri Melayu firmly targets the coach-tour crowd, but the dinner show (starting at 8.30pm) of traditional music and dance is nevertheless professional, the food tasty and the buffet all-you-can-eat.

TOP BRUNCHES & BREKKIES

The following are worth attending for either daily breakfasts or blow-out Sunday brunches:

» **Dish** (p80) Free-flowing Veuve Clicquot at their Sunday brunch (RM250; RM150 without champagne).

» **Prego** (p78) Another Sunday food fest with unlimited bubbly (RM230; RM170 without champagne).

» **Sky Bar** (p87) Unlimited cocktails plus a 15-minute head or shoulder rub and swim at Sunday brunch (RM150).

» **Frangipani** (p75) Brunch only on the last Sunday of the month but it's a good one (RM120).

» **Imbi Market** (p75) Best local-style breakfast in town – and a bargain at around RM10. Closed Monday.

» **Chee Cheong Fun Stall** (p75) Best rice noodles (RM4).

» **Sing Seng Nam** (p75) Classic Malaysian toast, *kaya* and strong coffee breakfast (RM3).

» **Yogitree** (p83) Breakfast available all day long (around RM20).

Ibunda
MALAY $$$

(Map p64; ☑2142-8488; www.ibunda-finedine.com.my; 251 Jln Bukit Bintang; ☑11.30am-2.30pm & 6.30-10.30pm Mon-Sat) In a restored colonial mansion Ibunda makes a valiant attempt at Malay-fusion fine dining, serving up eye-popping creations with subtle flavours and textures. It also hosts a cultural show from 8pm on Friday and Saturday.

Elcerdo
SPANISH $$$

(Map p42; ☑2145 0511; www.elcerdokl.com; 43-45 Changkat Bukit Bintang; meals RM80-100) It's pork lovers' heaven at this classy 'nose-to-tail eating' joint. If you're not hungry as a hog, next door is their tapas bar El Cerdito.

Lot 10 Hutong
FOOD COURT $$

(Map p42; Basement, Lot 10, 50 Jln Sultan Ismail; mains RM3-20; ☑10am-10pm) The concept is a collection of greatest hits from around Malaysia's culinary map made by experienced vendors. In the warren-like set-up you can dine on classic renditions of dishes such as pork stew *bak kut the,* chicken rice and Hokkien *mee.*

Din Tai Fung
CHINESE $$

(Map p42; www.dintaifung.com.tw; Level 6, Pavilion KL, 168 Jln Bukit Bintang; mains RM10-20; ☑10am-10pm) Fantastic Taiwan-style soup dumplings and noodles. There's also a branch in Mid Valley Megamall.

Restaurant Muar
MALAY & NONYA $$

(Map p42; ☑2144 2072; 6G Tingkat Tong Shin; mains RM10-20; ☑11am-3pm & 6-10pm Tue-Sun) Ever-reliable home cooking.

Xenri D' Garden Terrace
JAPANESE $$$

(Map p42; ☑2078 6688; 2nd fl, Menara Hap Seng, Jln P Ramlee; mains RM30 50; ☑noon 3pm & 6-10pm) Looks out on a calming bamboo-and-stone garden. Call to see if the week-end eat-all-you-can buffet's on.

KLCC & AROUND

There are over 30 different dining options in Suria KLCC, plus two food courts: **Signatures**, on Level 2, specialises in international food; and **Rasa Food Arena**, on Level 4, offers local dishes.

Cilantro
FRENCH $$$

(Map p64; ☑2179 8082; www.cilantrokl.com; Mi-Casa All Suite Hotel, 68B Jln Tun Razak; set lunch/dinner RM150/270; ☑noon-2pm Fri, 6pm-1am Mon-Sat) Takashi Kimura is often lauded as one of KL's most accomplished chefs. When we visited his elegantly revamped restaurant for lunch, two out of the four courses were memorable standouts: breadcrumbed foie gras on a perfectly poached egg, and a succulent, lightly seared rack of lamb.

Little Penang Kafé
MALAY & NONYA $$

(Map p60; ☑2163 0215; Level 4, Suria KLCC; mains from RM15; ☑11.30am-9.30pm) At peak meal times expect a long line outside this mall joint serving authentic food from Penang, including specialities such as curry *mee* (spicy soup noodles with prawns) and spicy Siamese *lemak laksa* (curry laksa) available only from Friday to Sunday. There's also a branch at Mid Valley Megamall.

DISH
STEAK $$$

(Map p64; ☎2164 1286; www.delicious.com.my; Dua Annexe, Jln Tun Razak; mains RM50-100; ⊙11.30am-10pm) This sophisticated gourmet haven, known for its steaks (priced by the 100g), has a relaxed vibe. The premium imported ingredients used in their cooking are sold in the attached deli – one of KL's best. Graze across the menu at their Sunday brunch buffet (with/without free-flow champagne RM249/149). Upstairs there's a wider, more wallet-friendly selection of dishes at **Delicious** (☎2166 2066; mains RM30-56).

il Lido
ITALIAN $$$

(Map p60; ☎2161 2291; www.il-lido.com.my; mains RM45-70; Mayang, Jln Mayang; ⊙noon-2.30pm & 6.30-10.30pm Mon-Fri, dinner only Sat) If it's fine dining Italian style you're after, then il Lido delivers handsomely with lovely homemade pasta, fish and meat dishes. There's an exclusive club feel to the sophisticated dining room and a bar upstairs for lingering over of nightcap of grappa. A three-course set lunch is RM50.

Seri Angkasa
MALAY $$$

(Map p42; ☎2020 5055; www.serimelayu.com; Menara KL, Jln Puncak; buffet lunch/dinner RM69/155; ⊙noon-2.30pm & 6.30-11pm) Watch KL pass by from this revolving restaurant atop Menara KL (KL Tower). The lunch and dinner buffets features a wide range of Malay dishes and are consistently good. Book for evening meals, especially sunset dining. There's a dress code but the staff will provide men wearing shorts with a sarong (to cover the legs).

Bisou
BAKERY $

(Map p60; www.bisou.com.my; Level 3, Suria KLCC; ⊙10am-10pm) Offers 13 irresistible flavours of cupcake, plus a monthly special, and other light snacks. There's another outlet on the first floor of Bangsar Village I.

Nasi Kandar Pelita
INDIAN MUSLIM $

(www.pelita.com.my; ⊙24hr) Bangsar Baru (Map p59; Jln Telawi 5); KLCC (Map p60; 149 Jln Ampang) Serves exquisite Indian Muslim food, including magnificent *roti canai* and *hariyali tikka* (spiced chicken with mint, cooked in the tandoor). The swish, fan-cooled pavilion near the KLCC is probably the flashiest of all the *mamak* canteens in KL.

LITTLE INDIA, CHOW KIT & KAMPUNG BARU

You won't regret going on grazing safaris at the Saturday *pasar malam* of both Little India and Kampung Baru (see p35). The best hawker food in Chow Kit is found inside the Bazaar Baru Chow Kit market (p57); the atmosphere is lively, the food tasty and cheap and you can pick up an astonishing variety of tropical fruit for dessert at the surrounding market stalls.

TOP CHOICE Yut Kee
CHINESE & WESTERN $$

(Map p60; ☎2698 8108; 35 Jln Dang Wangi; meals RM10-15; ⊙7.30am-4.45pm) It doesn't matter how busy it gets at this beloved Hainanese *kopitiam,* the staff remain calm and polite. Skip the Western dishes and go for the house specialities such as toast with homemade *kaya, roti babi* (deep-fried bread filled with shredded pork and onions) or the fried Hokkien *mee* noodles. Their roast rolled pork with apple sauce, available from Friday to Sunday, usually sells out by 2.30pm.

Saravanaa Bhavan
INDIAN VEGETARIAN $$

(www.saravanabhavan.com; ☎) Bangsar Baru (Map p59; ☎2287 1228; 52 Jln Maarof, Bangsar; ⊙8am-11pm) Masjid India (Map p48; ☎2698 3293; 1007 Selangor Mansion, Jln Masjid India; ⊙8am-10.30pm) This global chain of restaurants offers some of the best quality Indian food you'll find in KL. Their banana-leaf and mini-tiffin feasts are supremely tasty and you can also sample southern Indian classics such as *masala dosa.*

Ikan Bakar Berempah
HAWKER STALLS $

(Map p60; Gerak Pak Lang, Jln Raja Muda Musa; meals RM5-10; ⊙24hr) If you can't make it to Kampung Baru for its Saturday *pasar malam* (see p35), head to this excellent barbecued-fish stall, within a hawker-stall market covered by a zinc roof. Once you've picked your fish off the grill there's a long buffet of great Malay *kampung*-style side dishes you can add to it.

Coliseum Café
WESTERN $$

(Map p60; ☎2692 6270; 100 Jln TAR; meals RM15-60; ⊙10am-10pm) Resisting the passage of time, the cafe at the Coliseum still enjoys a good reputation for its sizzling steaks. Even if you don't come for dinner, it's worth stopping by for a cocktail at the atmospheric wood-panelled bar next door.

Capital Café
MALAY $

(Map p60; 213 Jln TAR; dishes RM3.50-5; ⊙10am-8pm Mon-Sat) This nostalgic cafe has been in business since 1956 and hardly looks like it's changed since. Try their excellent beef or chicken satay with peanut sauce, *mee goreng* or *rojak* – all very cheap and good.

Bilal Restoran
INDIAN MUSLIM **$**

(Map p48; ☑2078 0804; 33 Jln Ampang; mains RM4-10; ☺8am-9pm) No points for ambience, but the South Indian Muslim food here is fine. Reliable dishes include their *roti canai* (unleavened, flaky flat bread), which come in egg and *bawang* (onion) versions, and *ikan* (fish) and *kambing* (mutton) curries.

Sagar
INDIAN **$**

(Map p60; ☑2691 3088; Semua House, Jln Masjid India; meals RM10; ☺8am-8pm) Enjoy the good-value *thali* meals (rice or bread served with assorted vegetables and curries for under RM10) at this footpath cafe, and soak up the street life of Little India. There's also an air-con section inside.

Restoran Buharry
INDIAN MUSLIM **$**

(Map p60; 22-24 Jln Doriaswamy; meals RM10-15; ☺6am-late Mon-Sat, 8.30am-1am Sun) Popular hang-out for office workers during the day and late-night clubbers on Asian Heritage Row. All the usual *mamak* favourites are on offer, plus excellent *tom yam* soup and delicious mango smoothies.

Thai-la
THAI **$$**

(Map p60; ☑2698 4933; ground fl, CapSquare; dishes RM8-13; ☺noon-10pm Mon-Sat) One of the best dining options at the CapSquare complex. The food's tasty and made by Thai chefs, the decor has a chic charm, and Zaki, the entertainingly camp owner, can talk the hind legs off a donkey.

Chop 'n' Steak
WESTERN & ITALIAN **$$**

(Map p60; 16 Jln Daud; steaks RM30-40; ☺5pm-2am) This quirky place occupies an actual fishing boat that's run aground in the midst of Kampung Baru. Their sizzling steak platters offer juicy meat slavered with tasty sauce.

Masjid India Hawker Court
HAWKER STALLS **$**

(Map p48; Jln Masjid India; meals RM2-10; ☺8am-9pm) A bustling covered hawker court serving all the usual Malay, Indian and Chinese favourites. Good to visit if you can't make it to the Saturday *pasar malam*.

PUDU

TOP CHOICE **Sek Yuen**
CHINESE **$$**

(☑9222 9457; 313-315 Pudu; mains RM20-40; ☺noon-3pm & 6-10pm Tue-Sun) Occupying the same beautiful, time-worn, Art Deco building for the past 60 years, Sek Yuen serves up meals that offer an experience of KL food history. There's no written menu but you can trust the aged chefs toiling in the wood-fired kitchen to make something delicious. Their *kau yoke* (belly pork), *char siew* (barbecued pork) and fried rice are all classics, as is their sweet-and-sour fish.

TOP CHOICE **Jalan Sayur Stalls**
HAWKER STALLS **$**

(Jln Sayur; noodles RM5; ☺11am-midnight) Off the tourist radar, these high-quality hawker stalls are found on a street opposite Sek Yuen. Visit during the day to try the famous **Hakka mee stall**, right on the corner with Jln Pudu: order these egg noodles with chopped pork dry, with a side of 'white sauce' (aka melted lard) rather than 'black sauce' (all soy, no lard). Evening grazing could include a luscious *chee cheong fun* with curry sauce or the rich and peppery *sup kambing* (mutton broth).

BRICKFIELDS, THE LAKE GARDENS & AROUND

TOP CHOICE **Robson Heights**
CHINESE **$$**

(☑2274 1633; www.robsonheights.com; 10B Jln Permai, off Jln Syed Putra; mains RM30-60; ☺10.30am-2.30pm & 5.30-11.30pm) Folks drive from far and wide to feast on the top-class food served at this rickety hillside joint. While their specialities such as stir-fried pig intestines with dried prawn and chilli, braised terrapin, or Marmite crab may not appeal to all, we can vouch for their delicious baked spare ribs in honey sauce and stir-fried udon noodles in black pepper sauce (RM8).

Sui Sui
CHINESE **$$**

(☑016 370 8555; 15-11 Lg Syed Putra Kiri; mains RM40-60; ☺11am-11pm Tue-Sun) On the way to the Tian How Temple, this no-frills, partly alfresco place is very similar to Robson Heights and nearly as good. Order the milk curry prawns with buns to soak up the tasty gravy, or any type of fish.

Hornbill Restaurant
MALAY & WESTERN **$$**

(Map p54; ☑2693 8086; www.klbirdpark.com; KL Bird Park, 920 Jln Cenderawasih, Lake Gardens; mains RM40-60; ☺9am-8pm; ☎) Providing a ringside view of the feathered inhabitants of KL Bird Park, this slick restaurant and cafe offers very good food without gouging the tourists too much. Go local with their *nasi lemak* and fried noodles or please the kids with fish and chips or their homemade chicken or beef burgers.

Ikan Bakar Jalan Bellamy HAWKER STALLS $$
(Jln Bellamy; meals RM10; ⊙11am-11pm Mon-Sat)
It's said the king occasionally sends his min-
ions to get an order of grilled stingray from
one of the justifiably popular barbecued-fish
hawker stalls on the hill behind the royal
palace – there's little to choose between the
three of them. Wander around and see what
takes your fancy.

Kompleks Makan Tanglin HAWKER STALLS $$
(Map p54; Jln Cendarasari, Lake Gardens; meals
RM10; ⊙7am-4pm Mon-Sat) Yet another good
reason for hanging out in the Lake Gardens
is the chance to grab a meal at this hawker-
stall complex – **Ikan Bakar Pak Din's stall**
is a popular one.

Annalakshmi INDIAN $
(Map p54; ☑2272 3799; Temple of Fine Arts, 116 Jln
Berhala, Brickfields; ⊙11.30am-3pm & 6.30-10pm
Tue-Sun; ☑) 'Eat as you wish, give as you feel'
is the mantra at this vegetarian Indian restaurant. There's a dress code, probably to
deter freeloaders.

Vishal INDIAN $
(Map p54; ☑2274 0502; 15 Jln Scott, Brickfields;
meals RM5; ⊙7am-10.30pm; ☑) Punters sit at
two long rows of tables for the great banana-
leaf meals served up at this long-running
Brickfields favourite. Good for tiffin snacks
and a refreshing lassi, too.

Gem Restaurant INDIAN $$
(Map p54; ☑2260 1373; 124 Jln Tun Sambanthan,
Brickfields; mains RM5-20; ⊙11.30am-11.30pm;
❄) A Brickfields stalwart, this calm, air-
conditioned restaurant serves good south
Indian food, including specialities from
Chettinad, Andhra Pradesh and the Malabar
coast. The *thali* is great value.

Chynna CHINESE $$$
(Map p54; ☑2264 2266; Hilton Kuala Lumpur, KL
Sentral, Brickfields; mains RM60-150; ⊙noon-
2.30pm & 6.30-10.30pm) The best of the Hilton's set of restaurants, ranged around
Frank Woo's giant sculpture, *Dancing Shadow*. Dress up for the fancy Shanghai-chic
decor and lots of upmarket Cantonese and
east-coast Chinese cooking.

BANGSAR & MID VALLEY
Bangsar's brilliant range of dining options
include a whole bunch of new ones at the
revamped Bangsar Shopping Centre. Sunday night's *pasar malam* (see p35), held in
the parking lot opposite the mosque on Jln
Telawi 1, is an institution, while those in the

know frequent Lucky Gardens and the collection of eateries hidden away on Lg Kurau.
Still hungry? Then the many places to eat
in Mid Valley's pair of malls will surely sort
that problem out.

TOP CHOICE **Sri Nirwana Maju** INDIAN $
(Map p59; ☑2287 8445; 43 Jln Telawi
2; meals RM10-20; ⊙7am-2am) There are far
flashier Indian restaurants in Bangsar, but
who cares about the decor when you can
tuck into food this good and cheap? Serves
it all from roti for breakfast to banana-leaf
curries throughout the day.

TOP CHOICE **House+Co** MALAY & WESTERN $$
(☑2094 3139; www.houseandco.com.my;
3rd fl, Bangsar Shopping Centre, 285 Jln Maarof;
mains RM20; ⊙11am-10pm; ☎) The most pleas-
ant thing about this cool cafe that's part of
a stylish homewares shop is that they really
can make great local dishes – try their deli-
cious *kway teow* soup or the spicy *mee hoon
kerabu* salad, and come hungry as the por-
tions are huge.

Alexis Bistro MALAY & WESTERN $$
(Map p59; ☑2284 2880; www.alexis.com.my; 29 Jln
Telawi 3, Bangsar Baru; mains from RM30; ⊙noon-
midnight Sun-Thu, to 1am Fri & Sat) Consistently
good food is delivered at this Bangsar stal-
wart where Asian favourites such as Sarawak laksa (the owner is originally from
this Malaysian state) mix it up with European fare. After your meal, move on to its
ultrasmooth Bar Upstairs (see p88). There's
another good branch in the Bangsar Shopping Centre.

Delicious WESTERN $$
(Map p59; ☑2287 1554; www.delicious.com.my;
ground fl, Bangsar Village II, Jln Telawi 1, Bangsar
Baru; mains from RM40; ⊙11am-midnight Sun-
Thu, to 1am Fri & Sat) One of the most success-
fully conceived dining brands in KL, serving
healthy salads, pasta, sandwiches and pies
among many other things in a cool con-
temporary setting. Apart from this buzzing
branch you'll find others near KLCC and in
Mid Valley Megamall.

Chawan MALAY $
(Map p59; ☑2287 5507; 69-G Jln Telawi 3; meals
RM5-10; ⊙8am-midnight) A chic contemporary
take on a *kopitiam*, offering mega-strength
coffees from all of the country's states to
wash down dishes such as beef *rendang* and
a brown-paper-wrapped *nasi lemak*.

Pressroom
FRENCH $$$

(☎2095 8098; www.pressroom.com.my; Lot G110, ground fl, Bangsar Shopping Centre, 285 Jln Maarof; mains RM45-75; ☺8am-midnight; ☎) The La Bodega group are behind this classy modern bistro out the front of this gourmet destination mall. The copper-plated open-air dining space is sophisticated but relaxed and the menu of reliable items, such as steak frittes and lamb chops, are supplemented by blackboard specials.

Sage
FRENCH/FUSION $$$

(☎2268 1328; www.sagekl.com; Level 6, Gardens Residences, Mid Valley, Jln Syed Putra; set lunch/dinner RM100/150; ☺noon-2pm & 6-10.30pm Mon-Fri, dinner only Sat) Sister restaurant to Cilantro (see p79) this spacious, fine-dining restaurant and wine bar offers inventive cuisine using high-quality ingredients, and boasts a panoramic view across to Bangsar.

Woods Macrobiotics
VEGETARIAN $$

(www.macrobiotics-malaysia.com; ☎) Bangsar Baru (Map p59; ☎2287 0959;25 Jln Telawi 2; dishes RM8-12; ☺11am-9.30pm Tue-Sun) Golden Triangle (Woods Bio Marche; Map p42; ☎6201 0726; Bukit Kiara; ☺7am-2pm Tue-Sun) An air of calm hangs over this worthy operation that ticks all the organic, vegan and wholefood boxes. Even their brownies are organic. They also offer cooking classes.

Devi's Corner
FOOD COURT $

(Map p59; 14 Jln Telawi 2; meals RM10; ☺24hr) A pavement-cafe mood prevails at this food court facing the Bangsar Village II mall. The tray curries are excellent, with plenty of fish, prawns and other seafood. You can get *dosa*, biryani and great satay here.

Reunion
CHINESE $$$

(Map p59; ☎2287 3770; www.delicious.com.my; 2nd fl, Bangsar Village II, Jln Telawi 1; meals RM80-100; ☺noon-3pm & 6-10.30pm) The Delicious group bring their restaurant know-how to bear at this elegantly designed contemporary Chinese restaurant that's ideal for a business dinner or intimate date. It's very affordable for a lunch treat with most dishes under RM20.

Restaurant BAHT
THAI $$

(off Map p59; ☎2282 0991; 15 Lg Kurau; mains RM7-10; ☺11am-9pm Mon-Sat) Local foodies drool over this casual Thai cafe, serving all the expected dishes like green chicken curry, fish cakes and *tom yum* soup. Set lunches (RM11) are great value.

La Bodega
SPANISH $$

(Map p59; ☎2287 8318; www.bodega.com.my; 14 & 16 Jln Telawi 2, Bangsar Baru; mains RM10-40; ☺8am-1am) This long-running place is four venues in one: an all-day deli-cafe serving good sandwiches; a chilled-out tapas bar; a formal dining room; and a lively lounge bar. Good wine and authentic tapas and paella complete the Spanish mood. They also have big outlets at Bangsar Shopping Centre and Pavilion KL, which is known for its hearty cooked English breakfast.

Smokehouse Restaurant
BRITISH $$$

(Map p59; ☎2288 1510; 67-G Jln Telawi 3; mains RM30-50; ☺noon-11pm, bar closes at 1am) Half-timbered, Surrey-meets-KL decor signals that this is traditional English cooking territory, with such dishes as fish and chips with mushy peas and beef Wellington on the menu. They also offer a traditional afternoon tea – just the kind of pick-me-up you'll need after trawling the Bangsar Village malls across the street.

Yogitree
MALAY & WESTERN $$

(☎2282 6763; www.yogitree.com; 1st fl, Gardens Mid Valley, Jln Syed Putra; meals RM20-70; ☺10am-10pm) We love anywhere that serves breakfast until 6pm. This 'real food' cafe and yoga clothing boutique uses plenty of organic produce in its mix-and-match local and Western food menu.

ELSEWHERE

TOP CHOICE Nathalie's Gourmet Studio
FRENCH $$

(☎6207 9572; www.nathaliegourmetstudio.com; Unit 4-1-5 Publika, 1 Jln Dutamas, Mont Kiara; mains RM25-35; ☺9am-6pm Mon-Sat) Swoon over self-taught chef Nathalie's colourful collection of melting macaroons and then discover how the girl can *really* cook with a lunch of tomato crumble with goat's cheese cream, crispy scallop tart with melted onion and pepper sauce, and an ingeniously revised nicoise salad. These are dishes that deserve to be savoured over dinner rather than lunch, which Nathalie offers twice a month (call or check the website for dates). There's also a cooking school here (p83).

Wau Penyu
MALAY $$

(☎6207 9177; www.waupenyu.com; Unit A3-G1-03, Publika, 1 Jln Dutamas, Mont Kiara; ☺8am-midnight) Another dining option at Publika is this laid-back place, which specialises in the Malay dishes of Kelantan and Terrenganu;

LUCKY GARDENS

South of Jln Ara, **Lucky Gardens** (Map p59) may not be as ritzy as the grid of Telawis, but locals love to hit the morning fruit and veg market here and it is blessed with some delicious and inexpensive dining options. Time your visit to the **Nam Chuan Coffee Shop** (Lg Ara Kiri 2; ☉7am-10pm), a busy, no-frills food court, so that you can enjoy a bowl of Christina Jong's fantastic **Sarawak laksa** (RM5), Jimmy Saw's **Myanmar laksa** (RM5) or Ah Mun's **kuih** (rice cakes; RM1) – his *onde onde* (glutinous rice balls filled with palm sugar) are flavoured with real pandan and are considered the best in KL.

There's also a fantastic strip of outdoor hawker stalls along Lg Ara Kiri: sample vegan Indian delights at **Chelo's Appam Stall** (RM5; ☉7am-10pm Mon-Sat; 🖉); more vegetarian food at **Poomy's** (RM5; ☉3pm-11pm Mon-Sat; 🖉), including the sweet *appam* (coconut milk pancakes); and the tastebud explosion of **Bangsar Fish Head Corner** (meals from RM30; ☉7am-4pm Mon-Sat).

try *nasi kerabu* (rice salad with fish) or the meat version, *nasi dagang*.

Mei Keng Fatt Seafood Restaurant
CHINESE SEAFOOD **$$$**
(🖉4256 6491; www.meikengfatt.com; 1 Lg Awan 6, Kuala Ampang; meals RM80-100; ☉11am-2.30pm & 4pm-midnight) Less than 10 minutes in a taxi from KLCC is this fab seafood restaurant favoured by locals and clued-up expats. Great for group dining, its many specialities include crab cooked in a number of ways – check the prices, though, before ordering.

Steak Hut at Suzi's Corner
STEAK **$$**
(Ampang Point, Jln Ampang; steak from RM32; ☉6pm-11pm Wed-Mon) With the price of meat in one of KL's upmarket steakhouses being what it is, it's easy to understand the allure of this long-running hawker stall operation that gets most expats' stamp of approval. Their tenderloin, which comes sizzling on a platter with a choice of sauces, hits the spot. You can BYO alcohol, too.

D'Istana Jalamas Café
MALAY **$**
(Map p63; 🖉4025 3161; Jln Tun Razak, Titiwangsa; mains from RM5; ☉7am-8pm) The cafe at Istana Budaya serves a serve-yourself buffet of Malay and *mamak* favourites such as fish-head curry, salads, snacks and fresh fruit in classier than average surroundings. Balcony seats overlook nearby Titiwangsa Park.

Yu Ri Tei
JAPANESE **$$**
(🖉4044 0422; Sentul Park Koi Centre, Jln Strachan; mains RM15; ☉11am-9pm) If you come up to KLPac (p90) to see a show, drop into this charming Japanese teahouse surrounded by ponds at the Sentul Park Koi breeding centre. The menu runs to ramen, tempura and various types of dumplings and fried rice. Jln Strachan is off Jln Ipoh.

Restoran Nelayan Titiwangsa
MALAY **$$**
(Map p63; 🖉4022 8400; www.nelayan.com.my; Jln Temerloh, Taman Tasik Titiwangsa; buffet lunch/dinner RM19/28.50; ☉noon-2.30pm & 6.30-10.30pm, dinner only Fri) Housed in a wooden pavilion at Titiwangsa Lake Gardens, Restoran Nelayan offers a decent Malaysian buffet that also includes steamboat (fondue-style) items. There's an à la carte menu, too, and traditional instrumental music is played live at dinner.

🍷 Drinking

Bubble tea, iced *kopi-o*, a frosty beer, or a flaming Lamborghini – KL's cafes, teahouses and bars offer a range of ways to whet your whistle. Muslim mores mean a night on the town in KL tends to be restrained, unless you visit one of the clubs or dance bars dotted around the city (see p89).

Attitudes to drinking are founded in religion – places catering to Chinese and Indian Malaysians and foreigners normally serve alcohol; places that target Malays stick to tea, coffee and juices. The Golden Triangle caters to both crowds with Jln Bukit Bintang and Changkat Bukit Bintang being the busiest streets. Bangsar also continues to hold its own for classy expat bars and cafes. Unless otherwise noted, standard opening hours for bars are 5pm to 2am.

Apart from ubiquitous Starbucks and Coffee Bean & Tea Leaf branches (normally with free wi-fi), there are Malaysian chains such as Old Town and several independent cafes that will give you a more local experience with your beverage.

CHINATOWN & AROUND

Chinatown has few formal bars, and sipping beers at the open-air restaurants around Jln Petaling night market is what many visitors quite rightly prefer to do. For inexpensive drinks, the Original Backpackers Travellers Inn (p67) has a grungy traveller bar on its roof.

Reggae Bar   BAR
(www.reggaebarkl.com; ☺noon-late) Chinatown (Map p48; 158 Jln Tun HS Lee) Golden Triangle (Map p42; 31 Changat Bukit Bintang) Travellers gather in droves at this pumping bar in the thick of Chinatown, which has outdoor seats if you'd like to catch the passing parade. No prizes for guessing what dominates the sound system most nights. There are beer promos, pool tables and pub grub served till late. The Golden Triangle branch is a bit fancier.

Malay Teahouse   TEAHOUSE
(Map p48; www.malayteahouse.com.my; Central Market, Jln Hang Kasturi; ☺10am-9pm) Sip traditional Malay herbal teas s each one helpful for particular bodily complaints and functions – at this innovative operation also serving simple Malay meals and snacks. The teas are nicely packaged for gifts. If you have time, take a trip out to their idyllic main outlet at FRIM (p103).

Purple Cane Tea House   TEAHOUSE
(Map p48; 3rd fl, 6 Jln Panggong; ☺11am-8pm) Serves a broad range of Chinese green and jasmine teas; their tea shop is around the corner on Jln Sultan.

Moontree House   CAFE
(Map p48; www.moontree-house.blogspot.com; 1st fl, 6 Jln Panggong; ☺10am-8pm Wed-Mon; ☎) Quiet space for a coffee, also selling cute handicrafts and feminist literature.

GOLDEN TRIANGLE

Bar-hopping along Changat Bukit Bintang is a must. Apart from the following, No Black Tie (p90) is a sophisticated place for a drink, usually with live music. If you just want to chill with a beer or iced coffee and watch the passing parade, then settled into a sidewalk seat on Jln Alor.

TOP CHOICE Palate Palette   CAFE-BAR
(Map p42; www.palatepalette.com; 21 Jln Mesui; ☺noon-midnight Tue-Thu, to 2am Fri & Sat; ☎) Colourful, creative, quirky and super cool this cafe-bar is our favourite place to eat, drink, play board games, and mingle with KL's boho crowd. The menu (mains RM10 to RM30) features dishes as diverse as shepherd's pie and teriyaki salmon. Check the website for details of event such as free indie movie nights.

DON'T MISS

AFTERNOON TEA OR TIFFIN

One of Malaysia's best colonial hangovers is the ritual of afternoon tea. Here are some of our favourite places to indulge in the minifeast of English sweetmeats or the more Asian-inspired nibbles of tiffin.

» **Carcosa Seri Negara** (p72) This VIP hotel's afternoon tea (weekday/weekend RM69/75; 3pm to 6pm daily) is one not to miss. As well as the traditional English style of finger sandwiches and scones, there's a Malay-inspired version with curry puffs and the like. Book ahead as it's a long hike up the hill and sometimes the lounge is closed for weddings and other events.

» **Delicious** (p82) All branches of this chic restaurant–cafe serve a delectable afternoon tea including such treats as duck confit in filo pastry, chocolate-dipped strawberries and rosemary-and-cheese cookies (RM59.90 for two).

» **Luk Yu Tea House** (p86) Tea in the refined Chinese style, along with dim sum (RM30 to RM50, depending on how many dim sum you have).

» **Saravanaa Bhavan** (p80) Go for their minitiffin platters (RM9) of delicious vegetarian Indian snacks including *masala dosa*.

» **Seri Angkasa** (p80) Go for a spin at the top of KL Tower as you dig into the afternoon tea buffet (weekday/weekend RM40.25/55.20).

» **Smokehouse Restaurant** (p83) RM18 gets you a blow-out feast including scones, apple pie, sandwiches and brownies.

TOP CHOICE **Village Bar** BAR

(Map p42; Feast fl, Starhill Gallery, 181 Jln Bukit Bintang; ☺noon-1am) Columns of glasses and bottles and cascades of dangling lanterns lend an *Alice in Wonderland* quality to this basement bar. Prices are high, but the decor is rather spectacular.

Neo Tamarind BAR

(Map p42; www.samadhiretreats.com; 19 Jln Sultan Ismail; ☺11.30am-2.30pm & 6.30-10.30pm) Next to its sister operation, Tamarind Hill, this sophisticated restaurant–bar feels like a slice of Bali smuggled into the heart of KL. There's sometimes live-music performances to enjoy while you sip cocktails by flickering tealights under leafy trees. At the time of research the operation company was about to launch Villa Samadhi, a sleek urban retreat a short drive from the city centre – it should be worth checking out for overnight stays.

Celsius CAFE-BAR

(Map p42; www.celsiuskl.com; LG2-01, Fahrenheit88, 179 Jln Bukit Bintang; ☺11am-1am Sun-Thu, until 2am Fri & Sat) Picking up on Fahrenheit88's temperature theme, this slick street-level restaurant–bar is a chic space dominated by a circular bar with illuminated panels. It's round the back of the revamped mall, facing Jln Walter Greiner. Their spicy mango caipirinha is a killer cocktail.

Teeq Brasserie CAFE-BAR

(Map p42; ☎2782 3555; www.teeq.com.my; Level 8, Lot 10, 50 Jln Sultan Ismail; ☺6.30pm-10.30pm, bar open to 1am Tue-Sun) Beside the rooftop garden of Lot 10 is this contemporary-styled brasserie with a relaxed alfresco bar from which you can observe the commercial frenzy of Bintang Walk at a calm distance.

Levain CAFE

(Map p64; www.levain.com.my; 7 Jln Delima; ☺8am-8pm) Appealing bakery, cake shop and cafe in a quiet part of the city centre. The outdoor patio is a pleasant spot for a Western-style breakfast, light lunch or tea-time treat, and the pastries are very good.

Typica CAFE

(Map p42; GL-08, Shaw Parade, Changkat Thambi Dollah; www.typicacafe.blogspot.com; ☺11am-9pm Sun-Thu, to 10pm Fri & Sat) Sit at old wooden desks and savour excellent drip and siphon-brewed coffees, many made from a selection of gourmet beans, and lovely homemade cakes – try the yam-coconut one if they have it. They also do some other interesting drinks such as pandan latte.

Luk Yu Tea House TEAHOUSE

(Map p42; Feast fl, Starhill Gallery, 181 Jln Bukit Bintang; ☺10am-1am) Enjoy a premium brew inside a charming traditional Chinese teahouse along with dim sum and other dainty snacks.

Sixty Nine Bistro CAFE

(Map p42; 14 Jln Kampung Dollah; ☺noon-1.30am, from 2pm Fri & Sat) A very funky youth venue that has a junk-shop chic vibe to its decor, a fun menu of bubble teas and the like, and resident fortune tellers.

Wings CAFE-BAR

(Map p42; www.wingsmusicafe.com; 16 Jln Kampung Dollah; ☺6.30am-1am, to 2am Fri & Sat) A few doors down from Sixty Nine Bistro, this cheerful student hang-out has regular live music, though most drinkers prefer to chill out on the front terrace.

Green Man PUB

(Map p42; www.greenman.com.my; 40 Changkat Bukit Bintang; ☺noon-1am, to 2am Fri-Sun) There are several Irish-style pubs along Changkat Bukit Bintang these days, but this is the original one and has a very loyal crowd. It's calmer indoors than on the busy terrace. Join in the regular Thursday night quiz for RM15.

Ceylon Bar BAR

(Map p42; 20-2 Changkat Bukit Bintang; ☺4pm-1am, from 11am Sun) Big, comfy lounges, inexpensive drinks and a genuinely convivial mood make this one of the friendliest drinking holes in KL, one that's noticeably more relaxed than others along this frantic strip. Come early to bag one of the terrace tables or the sofas inside.

J Co Donuts & Coffee CAFE

(Map p42; www.jcodonuts.com; Basement, Pavilion KL, 168 Jln Bukit Bintang; ☺10am-10pm) Their wacky donut creations may have cheesy names (Tira Miss U or Mona Pisa anyone?) but they look so damn tasty that it's difficult to pass by this fried dough and coffee operation.

Snowflake CAFE

(Map p42; Level 4, Pavilion KL, 168 Jln Bukit Bintang; ☺10am-10pm) We're prepared to believe the cute marketing blurb saying that Jimmy learned how to make these refreshing jelly-based drinks and desserts from his Taiwanese gran – they make you realise how much more there is to soft drinks in Asia than canned pop.

There's a fairly active and visible gay scene in KL; the lesbian scene is less obvious but exists for those wanting to seek it out. Check out www.utopia-asia.com and www.fridae.com for the latest happenings. Prince World KL (www.princeworldkl.com) organises big gay dance parties several times a year – they're usually held at Maison (see p90) and other big club venues.

Frangipani Bar   DJ BAR
(Map p42; ☎2144 3001; 25 Jln Changkat Bukit Bintang; cover Fri RM30; ☻5pm-1am Tue-Thu & Sun, 5pm-3am Fri & Sat) Friday is the official gay night at this chic DJ bar, above the restaurant of the same name (p75) but on other nights of the week you'll find a gay-friendly crowd here, too.

Marketplace   RESTAURANT/LOUNGE
(Map p60; ☎2166 0750; www.marketplacekl.com; 4A Lg Yap Kwan Seng; cover Sat RM35; ☻Sat 10pm-3am) As Saturday night turns into Sunday morning at this restaurant, with a superb rooftop view of the Petronas Towers, really packs them in. There's a super relaxed vibe, which is just as well since it's body to body on the dance floor.

Garçon   CLUB
(Map p60; ☎2381 2088; 8 Jln Yap Ah Shak; cover RM30; ☻9pm-3am Sun) For Sunday night clubbers this boy-friendly dance event at the glam Maison (p90) is the place to be seen.

Blue Boy   CLUB
(Map p42; ☎2142 1067; 54 Jln Sultan Ismail; ☻8.30pm-2am) The skanky workhorse of the KL gay scene just keeps on going. Come before 11pm if you wish to sing karaoke with the winking lady boys. Later it gets packed with rent boys and their admirers.

Thermos   SAUNA
(Map p42; ☎3214 4968; www.daythermos.com; 40-6 Jln Sultan Ismail; cover RM28; ☻2-11pm) If you're just looking to hook up, there's this relatively stylish and clean sauna with mini-gym and internet lounge. It's near Blue Boy on an alley running parallel to Jln Sultan Ismail.

Bakita   BAR
(Map p42; www.bakita.com.my; 33 Jln Berangan) This multilevel, partly alfresco bar, taking up a good-sized chunk of the corner of Jln Berangan and Jln Nagansari, has proved an instant hit with its maximum people-watching potential, big-screen TV action and chilled DJ mixes.

Whisky Bar Kuala Lumpur   BAR
(Map p42; www.thewhiskybarkl.com; Changat Bukit Bintang) Part of the Werner's empire of restaurants and watering holes that have colonised this end of CBB – if you don't fancy a dram of the amber nectar then there's his wine bar next door.

KLCC & AROUND
Apart from the following there's a very stylish alfresco roof bar attached to il Lido (p80) with faux grass, Philippe Starck–designed chairs and sophisticated lounge music.

TOP CHOICE Luna   BAR
(☎2332 7777; Menara PanGlobal, Jln Punchak; ☻3pm-1am, to 3am Fri & Sat) Staff can't mix a dirty martini but you certainly get the twinkling view of KL's skyline right at this super-sophisticated rooftop bar surrounding a swimming pool. Also up here, inside and facing towards KL Tower, is the smoke-free **Cristallo**, a playboy-esque bar lined with silver velour sofas and draped with strings of glittering crystals.

TOP CHOICE Sky Bar   BAR
(Map p42; ☎2332 9888; Level 33, Traders Hotel, KLCC; ☻7pm-1am, to 3am Fri &Sat) Head to the rooftop pool area of this hotel for a grand circle view across to the Petronas Towers – it's the perfect spot for sundowner cocktails or late-night flutes of bubbly. For serious inebriation, spend a hazy afternoon enjoying their Sunday free-flow cocktail brunch.

Apartment Downtown   CAFE-BAR
(Map p60; 1st fl, Suria KLCC, Jln Ampang; ☻11am-10pm) Imagine you actually live at KLCC with outdoor seating overlooking the park – a lovely spot to revive after a hard day's shopping at the mall.

7AteNine BAR
(Map p60; ☎2167 7789; www.sevenatenine.com; Ground fl, Ascot, 9 Jln Pinang; ⏲4.30pm-2am Mon-Fri, from 6pm Sat) White sheets hang over the tables and sofas at this sleek nightspot near KLCC. There's a sophisticated dinner menu. Ladies night is every Wednesday, and there's a free cocktail for anyone who turns up dressed all in white on Saturday.

Jln P Ramlee has numerous lively theme bars with live music or DJs and happy-hour specials. These places tend to attract lots of sex workers and sexpats, the following two long-term and perpetually pumping survivors of the strip included:

Beach Club Café BAR
(Map p42; 97 Jln P Ramlee; ⏲6pm-3am Tue-Sun)

Rum Jungle BAR
(Map p60; 1 Jln P Ramlee; ⏲5pm-3am)

LITTLE INDIA & AROUND

The mothballed colonial-era bar at the Coliseum Hotel (see p58) is one of the few reputable places in Little India for alcohol. There are also several bars and cafes at **Cap-Square** (p57) and **Asian Heritage Row** (www.asianheritagerow.com) but neither location has managed to consistently attract the party crowd.

Wine Room WINE BAR
(Map p60; ☎2691 8672; www.w-wineroom.com; Asian Heritage Row, 56-60 Jln Doraisamy; ⏲6pm-2am Wed-Sat) An eclectic mix of decorative elements – velvet drapes, marble and stainless steel surfaces, antique and retro furniture – conjure up a luxe atmosphere at this relaxed wine bar, one of the best places on Asian Heritage Row for a quiet drink.

BRICKFIELDS

Zeta Bar BAR
(Map p54; ☎2264 2264; www.kl-studio.com; Hilton Kuala Lumpur, 3 Jln Stesen Sentral, Brickfields; ⏲6pm-1.30am, to 3am Fri & Sat) If you're down in Brickfields, this classy hotel bar pulls in a well-to-do 30-something crowd. Big-name DJs and artists sometimes appear in the hotel ballroom.

BANGSAR BARU & AROUND

Apart from the following there are several more good bars and cafes clustered in the shopping malls Bangsar Shopping Centre and Bangsar Village I and II – see p95.

WIP BAR
(☎2094 1789; www.wip.com.my; G111 ground fl, Bangsar Shopping Centre, 285 Jln Maarof; ⏲noon-2am) Standing for 'whipped into place', this partly alfresco restaurant–bar is riding the wave of being Bangsar's trendiest watering hole. It's perpetually busy, attracting a stylish crowd who prefer to hang in the suburbs rather than shuffle into town.

Bar Upstairs BAR
(Map p59; ☎2284 2880; www.alexis.com.my; 29 Jln Telawi 3, Bangsar Baru; ⏲6pm-1am, to 2am Fri & Sat) Above the popular bistro Alexis and probably the most chilled-out drinking spot in Bangsar Baru. Sink into comfortable chairs and relax to the soothing sounds on the decks.

Poco Homemade CAFE
(off Map p59; www.pocohomemade.blogspot.com; 1 Lg Kurau; ⏲noon-9.30pm Tue-Sun) Super-cute cafe and craft atelier with a modern Japanese cafe concept of comfort foods such as *katsu* (breaded chicken fillets) curry rice. Their tofu cheesecake is a creamy delight and there are some pretty handbags, accessories and simple artworks to buy.

Social CAFE-BAR
(www.thesocial.com.my; ⏲10-2am) Bangsar Baru (Map p59; 57-59 Jln Telawi 3) Golden Triangle (Map p42; Changkat Bukit Bintang) The Social is a classy sports bar offering pool tables and good food as well as the booze, including a

TRADITIONAL DANCE & MUSIC SHOWS

If you'd like to see and hear traditional Malaysian dances and music, there are good shows at the **Malaysian Tourism Centre** (p98; adult/child RM5/free) at 3pm Tuesday to Thursday and 8.30pm Saturday. There's also an evening dance show at 8.30pm daily in the attached restaurant **Saloma** (Map p60; ☎2161 0122; show only RM40, buffet & show RM75).

Several other **tourist restaurants** offer live performances of traditional music and dance including Seri Melayu (p78), Ibunda (p79) and Restoran Nelayan Titiwangsa (p84). Also drop by the information desk at Central Market (p47) as there are sometimes free cultural events staged here, too.

BEST CONTEMPORARY ART GALLERIES

Whether or not you're in the market for a piece of art, the following commercial galleries are all rewarding places to swing by to take the pulse of Malaysia's vibrant art scene and to view other interesting works from across Asia.

» **Annexe Gallery** (Map p48; ☑2070 1137; www.annexegallery.com; 1st & 2nd floors, Annexe, Central Market, Jln Hang Kasturi; ☺11am-8pm) Nonprofit centre for contemporary arts that also hosts occasional film screenings, theatre and dance workshops, talks and launches.

» **Art Seni** (Map p42; ☑2144 0782; www.artseni.com; 4th fl, Starhill Gallery, 181 Jln Bukit Bintang; ☺10am-10pm) Also on the Muse floor of this mall is the **Gallery at Starhill**, dedicated to Malaysian artists.

» **Galeri Tangsi** (Map p48; ☑2691 0805; PAM Centre, 6 Jln Tangsi; ☺10am-6.30pm Mon-Fri, 10am-1pm Sat) Explore the jumble of canvases at this space in a heritage building west of Merdeka Sq.

» **MAP** (☑6207 9732; www.facebook.com/mapkl Publika,1 Jln Dutamas, Dutamas) This ambitious new space, part of the innovative Publika retail destination (p97), consists of the White Box exhibition gallery and the Black Box, a 250-seat experimental theatre.

» **Valentine Willie Fine Art** (Map p59; ☑2284 2348; www.vwfa.net/kl/index.php; 1st fl, 17 Jln Telawi 3, Bangsar Baru; ☺noon-8pm Mon-Fri, to 6pm Sat) One of KL's best galleries, with frequent shows representing some of the country's top artists.

» **Wei-Ling Gallery** (Map p54; www.weiling-gallery.com; 8 Jln Scott, Brickfields; ☺noon-7pm Mon-Fri, 10am-5pm Sat) The top two floors of this old shophouse have been imaginatively turned into a contemporary gallery to showcase local artists.

good wine list. The Golden Triangle branch is super popular.

☆ Entertainment

KL's entertainment options range from numerous cinemas and venues for live music, including a spectacular classical music concert hall, to sporting events and theatre. Big international rock and pop artists often add KL to their Asia tours, but sometimes have to adapt their stage shows to accommodate what's considered respectable (for example Linkin Park had to agree not to scream, jump around, wear shorts or use foul language on stage!).

The city's **club** scene is fairly fluid with places constantly flitting in and out of fashion – for the latest information check the local media listings (see p96). Most clubs impose a cover charge of RM20 to RM50 from Thursday to Saturday, which includes one drink.

Many big shopping centres have plush **multiplexes** showing international blockbusters, plus Malay, Chinese, Cantonese and Hindi films. Tickets range from RM6 to RM12, depending on the time of day. Also

see p90 for information about arthouse film screenings by some of KL's cultural centres.

As with live music, what gets performed in **theatres** is subject to the whims of KL's conservative censors. That said, some surprisingly issue-charged and boundary-pushing works sneak through alongside innocuous crowd-pleasing musicals and traditional dance and music shows. Kakiseni (www.kak iseni.com) has listings of events and performances around the capital, with a promised ticket booking facility in the future.

For some events you may find yourself straying out of the city limits to venues in Petaling Jaya (see p108) and around.

TOP CHOICE **Dewan Filharmonik Petronas**

CONCERT HALL

(Map p60; ☑2051 7007; www.malaysianphilhar monic.com; Box Office, Tower 2, Petronas Towers, KLCC; tickets RM10-210; ☺box office 10am-6pm Mon-Sat) Don't miss the chance to attend a concert at this gorgeous concert hall at the base of the Petronas Towers. The polished Malaysian Philharmonic Orchestra plays here (usually Friday and Saturday evenings and Sunday matinees, but also other times) as well as other local and international ensembles. There is a dress code.

TOP CHOICE No Black Tie
LIVE MUSIC

(Map p42; ☎2142 3737; www.noblacktie.com.my; 17 Jln Mesui; cover RM20-50; ⊗5pm-2am Tue-Sun) Blink and you'd miss this small chic live-music venue, bar and Japanese bistro, as it's hidden behind a grove of bamboo. NBT, as it's known to its fans, is owned by Malaysian concert pianist Evelyn Hii who has a knack for finding talented singer-songwriters, jazz bands and classical-music ensembles who play here from around 9.30pm.

TOP CHOICE Zouk
CLUB

(Map p60; www.zoukclub.com.my; 113 Jln Ampang; ⊗9pm-3am Tue-Sun) KL's top club offers spaces to suit everyone and a line-up of top local and international DJs. As well as the two-level main venue, there's the more sophisticated Velvet Underground (which is also the venue for the popular monthly **Time Out KL stand-up comedy nights**), with a dance floor that's glitter-ball heaven, Phuture for hip hop and the cutting-edge Bar Sonic.

Kuala Lumpur Performing Arts Centre
PERFORMING ARTS

(KLPac; ☎4047 9000; www.klpac.com; Sentul Park, Jln Strachan; tickets RM20-300) Part of the Sentul West regeneration project, this modernist performing-arts complex puts on a wide range of progressive theatrical events. Combine a show with a stroll in peaceful Sentul Park and dinner at Yu Ri Tei (p84), beside the Sentul Park Koi Centre.

Actors Studio @ Lot 10
THEATRE

(Map p42; ☎2142 2009; www.theactorsstudio.com.my; Lot 10, 50 Jln Sultan Ismail) Apart from staging shows at KLPac (p90), the Actors Studio theatre and comedy group has its base at this splendid, state-of-the-art venue located on the roof of Lot 10. Other theatre and dance companies also get to put on shows here. Prices depend on the performance.

Maison
CLUB

(Map p60; www.maison.com.my; 8 Jln Yap Ah Shak; ⊗9pm-3am Wed-Sun) Just off Asian Heritage Row, five shophouses have been knocked together to form this huge bar and club complex. It's a trendy spot so dress your best to make it past the bouncers. Unlike other dance clubs around here, which change names and theme each season, Maison has gone the distance and looks set to remain a fixture.

KL Live
LIVE MUSIC

(Map p42; www.kl-live.com.my; 1st fl, Life Centre, 20 Jln Sultan Ismail) One of the best things to happen to KL's live-music scene in a while has been the opening of this spacious venue, which has been packing in rock and pop fans with an impressive line-up of overseas and local big-name artists and DJs.

Rootz
CLUB

(Map p42; www.rootz.com.my; Rooftop, Lot 10, 50 Jln Sultan Ismail; ⊗10pm-3am Wed-Sat) Golden and glitzy like a Russian oligarch's dream boudoir, this gaudy-to-the-max club sits pretty and aloof atop Lot 10. The entry passage is hung with reproductions of Russian old masters, while inside you can take your pick from KL's best selection of champagnes.

MILK
CLUB

(www.mistclub.com.my; 18 Jln Liku, Bangsar; ⊗10pm-3am Wed-Sat) A spin-off from neighbouring R&B and hip-hop club Mist, MILK has been designed to cater to a more exclusive, sophisticated crowd. There's state-of-the-art lighting effects for the DJ to play with and the cocktail menu has, predictably, plenty of creamy blends.

Istana Budaya
PERFORMING ARTS

(National Theatre; Map p63; ☎4026 5555; www.istanabudaya.gov.my; Jln Tun Razak, Titiwangsa; tickets RM100-300) Big-scale drama and dance shows are staged here, as well as music performances by the National Symphony Or-

---

MOVIES AT CULTURAL CENTRES

The following international cultural centres screen foreign-language movies with subtitles – check their websites for details:

Alliance Française (☎2694 7880; www.kl.alliancefrancaise.org.my; 15 Lg Gurney)

Goethe Institut (Map p64; ☎2142 2011; www.goethe.de/ins/my/kua; 1 Jln Langgak Golf, off Jln Tun Razak; ⊗8.30am-6pm Mon-Fri)

Japan Foundation (☎2284 6228; www.jfkl.org.my; 18th fl Northpoint, Block B, Mid-Valley City, Medan Syed Putra) Free films are usually shown on the first Saturday of the month at 3pm at FINAS, Lot 1662, Bt. 8, Jln Hulu Kelang, 68000 Ampang.

Locals are big supporters of football (soccer) and basketball, and all of KL gets caught up in the Petronas Malaysian Formula 1 Grand Prix held at the Sepang International Circuit (see p111).

Footy fans can catch international matches at the **National Sports Complex, Malaysia** (Kompleks Sukan Negara, Malaysia; ☑8892 0888; www.stadium.gov.my/b.melayu; Bukit Jalil, 57700 Sri Petaling), accessible from the Bukit Jalil LRT station. For information on fixtures, contact the **Football Association of Malaysia** (☑7873 3100; www.fam.org.my). Basketball games run by the **Malaysia Amateur Basketball Association** (MABA; www.malaysia-basketball.com) take place at the **MABA Stadium** (p48; Jln Hang Jebat).

If you're into the horses, attend the sport of kings at **Selangor Turf Club** (Map p103; ☑9058 3888; www.selangorturfclub.com; Sungei Besi; admission RM6), a KL institution dating back to 1896 and originally sited where KLCC is now. The grandstand holds up to 25,000 fans and on race days there's a free shuttle bus from Serdang Komuter Train Station and Sungai Besi LRT Station.

chestra and National Choir. There's a dress code: no shorts, and men must wear long-sleeved shirts.

Sutra Dance Theatre   DANCE
(Map p63; ☑4021 1092; www.sutradancetheatre. com; 12 Persiaran Titiwangsa 3, Titiwangsa) The home of Malaysian dance legend Ramli Ibrahim has been turned into a showcase for Indian classical dance as well as a dance studio, gallery and cultural centre near Lake Titiwangsa. See the website for upcoming shows.

Hard Rock Café   LIVE MUSIC
(☑2715 5555; Hotel Concorde, 2 Jln Sultan Ismail; cover charge RM35 Fri & Sat; ☺11.30am-2.30am) Ok, so it's a tacky international chain, but if you're into live rock bands this place delivers with musicians hitting the stage from 11pm Monday to Saturday.

Golden Screen Cinemas   CINEMA
(www.gsc.com.my) Berjaya Times Square (Map p42; ☑8312 3456; 3rd fl, Berjaya Times Square, 1 Jln Imbi); Mid Valley (☑8312 3456; Mid Valley Megamall, Mid Valley City); Pavilion KL (Map p42; ☑8312 3456; Level 6, Pavilion KL, 168 Jln Bukit Bintang) Book a seat in Gold Class (RM40) for La-Z-boy–style reclining chairs and a drinks service.

Tanjung Golden Village   CINEMA
(www.tgv.com.my) CapSquare (Map p60; ☑2381 3535; Persiaran CapSquare, CapSquare); KLCC (Map p60; ☑7492 2929; Level 3, Suria KLCC)

🔒 Shopping

When it comes to giving your wallet a workout and satisfying your consumer urges, KL delivers with everything from street markets

proffering fake-label goods to glitzy, air-con shopping malls packed with the real deal. For general information on what to buy and when, see p23. Unless otherwise noted in the reviews, opening hours are 10am to 9.30pm daily.

GOLDEN TRIANGLE

TOP CHOICE ❯ **Pavilion KL**   MALL
(Map p42; www.pavilion-kl.com; 168 Jln Bukit Bintang) Pavilion has been setting the gold standard in KL's shopping scene since opening in 2007. Amid the many familiar international luxury labels and intriguing concept stores, such as Paul Frank and DC Comics, there are some good local retail options, including branches of the fashion houses **British India** (see p93); **MS Read** for larger-sized gals; **Noir** for Chinese-style casual clothing and home accessories; and **Philosophy for Men** for fun casual wear.

TOP CHOICE ❯ **Sungei Wang Plaza**   MALL
(Map p42; www.sungeiwang.com; Jln Sultan Ismail) This ragbag of retail fun promises 'all kinds of everything' and you'd better believe it. Connected with **BB Plaza**, Sungei Wan is confusing to navigate but jam-packed with youth-oriented fashions and accessories. Anchoring one corner is the **Parkson Grand** department store, and you'll find a post office, various fast-food outlets and a hawker centre on the 4th floor. Teens and youthful fashionistas should hunt out the 6th floor **Trendy Zone**, home also to the Green Box Karaoke centre.

Fahrenheit88   MALL
(Map p42; www.fahrenheit88.com; 179 Jln Bukit Bintang) The dowdy, dark KL Plaza has

been majorly brightened up by the team responsible for Pavilion KL to relaunch itself under a moniker that sums up how hot a retail concept it is. Actually, it's just more of the same, but the debut here of Malaysia's first branch of Japanese fast-fashion sensation **Uniqlo** has sent fashionistas into a frenzy, and the mall also contains plenty of local talent, including fashion diva **Bernard Chandran** (www.bernardchandran.com), KL's largest collection of shoe shops and an electronic gadgets superstore.

Lot 10 MALL
(Map p42; www.lot10.com.my; 50 Jln Bukit Bintang) Lot 10's relatively recent makeover restored some of its oomph. Apart from branches of the department stores Isetan and Debenhams, there's an interesting **National Geographic** concept store with branded travel-related goods and a tapas cafe; the Thai silk and silver jewellery shop **Sakun Silver & Silk** (4th fl; www.sakunsilk.com); Sonny San's very wearable clothes at **Eclipse** (www.eclipse.com.my); a fine basement food court and the rooftop garden with a gym, the Actors Studio performance space and hipsters' hangouts Rootz and Teeq Brasserie.

Starhill Gallery MALL
(Map p42; www.starhillgallery.com; 181 Jln Bukit Bintang) Break out the platinum charge card – this glitzy mall is the domain of exclusive fashion brands including Louis Vuitton, Salvatore Ferragamo and Alfred Dunhill. The basement level is a virtual village of upmarket restaurants, while the 'Pamper' floor has some of KL's best spas (p69) and the 'Muse' floor a collection of contemporary art galleries.

Khoon Hooi FASHION
(Map p42; www.khoonhooi.com; Explore fl, Starhill Gallery, 181 Jln Bukit Bintang) Interesting fabric textures are a signature of this up-and-coming designer's work. What sets his clothes apart is an attention to detail, such as pleated belts made from zips or shifts sewn from lace.

House of Suzie Wong ANTIQUES
(Map p42; www.houseofsuziewong.com; Muse fl, Starhill Gallery, 181 Jln Bukit Bintang) Antiques from across Asia are gathered together in informal room settings at this eccentric Starhill Gallery store. Staff can tell you the individual history of where each item was found.

Jendela BATIK
(Map p42; www.jendela-kl.com; Explore fl, Starhill Gallery, 181 Jln Bukit Bintang; ⊙10am-8pm) Unique and beautiful traditional and modern batik prints are used for the homewares and clothing here. A 3m-long batik print on Swiss cotton is RM2000, on silk RM1300.

Jim Thompson Silk FASHION & HOMEWARES
(Map p42; Explore fl, Starhill Gallery, 181 Jln Bukit Bintang; ⊙10am-7pm) Outlet of the Thai silk company founded by Jim Thompson, who disappeared in 1967 in Malaysia's Cameron Highlands. You can buy sumptuous loose silk as well as ready-made clothes, home furnishings and gifts.

Berjaya Times Square MALL
(Map p42; www.timesquarekl.com; 1 Jln Imbi) Teen fashions and toy stores abound at this mammoth mall just south of Bukit Bintang. The **Metrojaya** department store has good deals on clothes and there's a big branch of **Borders** bookstore on level 2. Regular kids' expos are held here, from comic fairs to pint-sized talent contests. The centre also has a bowling alley, karaoke, fish spa, cinema and an indoor theme park (p61).

Plaza Low Yat ELECTRONICS
(Map p42; www.plazalowyat.com; 7 Jln Bintang, off Jln Bukit Bintang) KL's best IT mall, packed with six floors of retailers big and small offering deals on laptops, digital cameras, mobile phones, computer peripherals and accessories. Digital camera memory cards, card-readers and portable hard drives are particularly good value. If you can't find what you need here (in particular electronic parts) then scout around the stalls in nearby **Imbi Plaza** (Map p42; Jln Imbi; ⊙11am-9pm).

Jadi Batek Centre BATIK & HANDICRAFTS
(Map p64; ☑2145 1133; www.jadibatek.com; 30 Jln Inai, off Jln Imbi; ⊙9am-5.30pm) On the tour bus circuit, this batik goods and Malaysian handicrafts showroom and workshop is nevertheless worth a look. You can find plenty of handmade pieces here – colourful and pretty things, but no extraordinary designs. Watch artists at work and have a go yourself.

YH Art Gallery ART GALLERY
(Map p42; www.yahongart.com; BB Park, Jln Bukit Bintang; ⊙10.30am-10.30pm) Admire the artistic batik works of the late Chuah Thean Teng (1914–2008) and his talented offspring at this gallery. Teng lived and worked in Penang where another of his galleries can be

SUEANN CHONG: FASHION BLOGGER

Not everyone can afford to rent a retail space in KL, which is where **blogshops** come in. Some, such as **Lah'Lah'Land** (lahlahlandkl.blogspot.com) and **Brollies at Pink Tattoos** (thebrollies.blogspot.com) started as blogshops and are now real shops in Subang [a commuter town in the Klang Valley]. Other really good blogshops to check out, simply because these people design their own apparel and accessories, include:

» **Things Eye Made** (http://thingseyemade.blogspot.com)

» **Chic Yamada** (www.chicyamada.com)

» **Mimpi Murni** (http://mimpimurni.blogspot.com)

» **Thirtyfour** (www.thirtyfour.net)

Tongue in Chic (www.tonguechic.com) has an online store that further highlights these young designers and we also organise the Chic Pop Street Market events around KL. Such flea and fashion markets have become very popular – there's one every Saturday at the Curve (see p107) and every Sunday at **Plaza Mont'Kiara** (www.plazamontkiara. com.my). Also look out for Bizarre Bazaar, organised by Lah'Lah'Land and the similar **Bijou Bazaar** (http://bijoubazaar.blogspot.com).

Sueann Chong is the managing editor of fashion blog Tongue in Chic (www.tonguechic.com).

visited at Batu Ferringhi. Some of his works also hang in the National Art Gallery.

Curiousity Shop INTERIOR DESIGN
(Map p42; ☑2142 6660; www.thecuriousitygallery. blogspot.com, 11 Jln Berangan; ⊙9am-7pm Mon-Sat) This very curious but interesting mix of antique and retro goods, from Asian furnishings and clothes to pop cultural ephemera, is worth a rummage. If it's closed try their second branch over on the 2nd floor of the nearby serviced apartment building Somerset House, where the same owners also run the boutique **ho.Lang**.

KLCC & AROUND

TOP CHOICE **Suria KLCC** MALL
(Map p60; www.suriaklcc.com.my; KLCC, Jln Ampang) Even if shopping bores you to tears, you're sure to find something to interest you at this fine shopping complex at the foot of the Petronas Towers, strong on both local and international brands such as **Jimmy Choo**, who as every Carrie Bradshaw knows was born in Penang. There's also an excellent branch of the bookshop **Kinokuniya** (level 4), scores of restaurants and cafes, two food courts, a cinema, gallery and a kids' museum.

Kompleks Budaya Kraf ARTS & CRAFTS
(Map ; ☑2162 7533; www.malaysiancraft.com; Jln Conlay; ⊙9am-8pm Mon-Fri, to 7pm Sat & Sun) A government enterprise, this huge complex

mainly caters to coach tours, but it's worth a visit to browse the shops and stalls selling batik, wood carvings, pewter, basketware, glassware and ceramics. You can see craftspeople and artists at work in the surrounding **Art Colony**. The complex also has a small museum and offers batik-making courses.

Pucuk Rebung ANTIQUES, ARTS & CRAFTS
(Map p60; www.pucukrebung.com; Level 3, Suria KLCC, Jln Ampang) Half museum, half shop, this upmarket arts-and-craft store offers genuine antiques and Malay ethnological items. Only some of the items are for sale – it's worth popping in for a browse around the treasures, and there are some affordable, contemporary craft and art pieces among the antiques.

MO Outlet FASHION
(www.mo-outlet.com; 62 Jln 8/91, Taman Shamelin; ⊙9.30am-7pm) End-of-line and bargain sale outlet for luxury brand retailer Melium, whose 50-plus labels include D&G, Ferla and Hugo Boss, as well as Malaysian and Asian designer ready-to-wear garments. The ten-minute taxi ride here from KLCC will save you between 40% and 70% on prices there.

British India FASHION
(www.britishindia.com.my) Ampang (Great Eastern Mall, 303 Jln Ampang); Bangsar (Bangsar Shopping Centre, 285 Jln Maarof); Golden Triangle (Map p42; Lower fl, Pavilion KL, Jln Bukit Bintang); KLCC

CENTRAL MARKET

Based in an historically significant building, **Central Market** (Pasar Seni; Map p48; www.centralmarket.com.my; Jln Hang Kasturi; ⏰10am-9pm) offers KL's best selection of souvenirs, gifts and traditional crafts such as batik and kites. The complex is divided between the old market hall and the newer Annexe – at the back of the former you'll find several Asian artefacts and antiques dealers, but you'll need to bargain hard to get good deals. Among our favourite stalls:

» **Art House Gallery Museum of Ethnic Arts** (1st fl, Annexe) Like stumbling into Indiana Jones' closet. Even if you're not interested in buying, it's fascinating to browse this impressive collection of ethnographic arts from the region and as far afield as Tibet.

» **Eco Warna & Fine Batik** (www.finebatik.com; G45 ground fl & MS04 mezzanine fl, Main Bldg) The market's best selection of modern batik cloth paintings (many of them by Indonesian artists) as well as organically dyed batik clothing and material. They also have a branch at BB Park on Jln Bukit Bintang.

» **Puteri Ledang** (G41A/42 ground fl, Main Bldg) An appealing selection of crafts, including some original-design batik items – plus essential oils and skin products.

» **Rhino** (KB17 ground fl, Main Bldg) Charming hand-painted clogs and handicrafts. The soles of the shoes are made from the wood of the durian tree.

» **Songket Sutera Asli** (M53 Mezzanine fl, Main Bldg) Fine-quality decorative weavings and embroidery in silver and gold thread.

» **Tanamera** (www.tanamera.com.my; G25 ground fl, Main Bldg) Malaysian-brand spa products made from 100% natural materials including detox infusions, essential oils and various balms.

» **Wau Tradisi** (M51 mezzanine fl, Main Bldg) Eye-catching selection of traditional paper and bamboo kites, including the giant *wau bulan* (moon kites) from Kelantan.

(Map p60; Suria KLCC, Jln Ampang) Mid Valley (Mid Valley Megamall, Mid Valley City) The flagship branch of this fashion house, selling super-sophisticated clothes with an ethnic flavour in soft cottons, linens and silks, is in Great Eastern Mall. This is where you'll also find the full range of their soft furnishings and homewares. Among the other branches, the one at Bangsar Shopping Centre is particularly well stocked.

Aseana   FASHION
(Map p60; ground level, Suria KLCC, Jln Ampang) Stylish and extensive selection of local fashion from local luminaries such as **Farah Khan** (www.farahkhan.com), who specialises in beaded and sequined glamour-wear, and the more casual **Melinda Looi** (www.melindalooi.com.my). Attached is a cafe serving pricey Malay food and drinks.

iKARRTiNi   BATIK & FASHION
(Map p60; www.ikarrtini.com; Level 2, Suria KLCC, Jln Ampang) Check out the separate men's and women's stores selling their own super-colourful and contemporary batik design print fashions on fine silk and cotton.

Tenmoku Pottery   POTTERY
(Map p60; www.tenmokupottery.com.my; Level 3, Suria KLCC, Jln Ampang) With their kilns based near Batu Caves, Tenmoku Pottery specialises in vases, bowls and other ceramics inspired by natural forms. It's possible to arrange pottery workshops there (see the website for details) but if you just want to buy the product there's this outlet as well as branches in Central Market and Mid Valley Megamall.

Cocoa Boutique   CHOCOLATES
(Map p60; www.cocoaboutique.com.my; 139 Jln Ampang) Brave the tour groups being pushed through this chocolate emporium and small-scale production line to sample unusual local variations such as durian-filled chocolates, or have a favourite photo embossed on chocolate for a unique souvenir.

CHINATOWN

Petaling Street Market   NIGHT MARKET
(Map p48; Jln Petaling; ⏰noon-11pm) Malaysia's relaxed attitude towards counterfeit goods is well illustrated at this heavily hyped night market. In fact, traders start to fill Jln Petal-

ing from midmorning until the whole street is jam-packed with market stalls selling everything from fake Gucci handbags and pirate DVDs to *nasi lemak* (coconut rice) and bunches of lychees. The best time to visit is after dark when the hordes of tourists scouring the stalls for convincing fakes of brand-name clothes, perfumes, watches and luggage is a mesmerising sight.

Peter Hoe Evolution
HOME DECOR
(Map p48; 2 Jln Hang Lekir; ⏱10am-7pm) Both here and at the much bigger **Peter Hoe Beyond** (Map p48; 2nd fl, Lee Rubber Bldg, 145 Jln Tun HS Lee; ⏱10am-7pm) around the corner you can satisfy practically all your gift-and-souvenir-buying needs, with selections from the KL-based designer's creative and affordable range of original batik designs on sarongs, shirts and dresses and home furnishings. The shops also stock an impressive range of Asian home-decor items and silver jewellery. The Beyond branch has a **cafe** (p74) that's worth visiting in its own right.

Justin Yap
FASHION
(Map p48; www.justinyap.com; 2nd fl, Lee Rubber Bldg, 145 Jln Tun HS Lee; ⏱10am-7pm) The atelier of one of Malaysian fashion's rising young stars is tucked away inside his uncle Peter Hoe's shop. Come here for elegant custom-made gowns and pretty shoes, as well as some off-the-peg items.

Koh Chuan Huat Tea Merchants
TEA
(Map p48; Jln Tun HS Lee; ⏱7.30am-5pm Mon-Sat) In business since 1931, when the founder bicycled around the peninsula hawking tea from a tin crate on the back. Sampling and chatting with the owners is free as long as you buy some tea, which costs as little as RM5. Their signature *lo poh* and *puer eh* teas are fermented in Malaysia from leaves imported from China, and they are also known for their 555 Blue Ribbon brand of Ceylon black tea.

Purple Cane Tea Arts
TEA
(Map p48; www.purplecane.com.my; 11 Jln Sultan) One of several specialist tea shops in Chinatown where you can sample and buy exotic teas, plus all the tea-making paraphernalia to go with them. You can also buy their teas and utensils at their restaurants (see p74).

Basket Shop
BASKETS & BOXES
(Map p48; www.thebasketshop.com.my; 10 Jln Panggong; ⏱9.30am-5.30pm Mon-Sat, to 2pm Sun) All kinds of bamboo and woven straw baskets and decorative boxes – lots of rib-
bons too – are to be found here, perfect for perfectionist present wrappers!

PUDU

Eu Yan Sang
CHINESE MEDICINE
(www.euyansang.com.my; Lot GL-01 Shaw Parade, Changkat Thambi Dollah) Eu Kong opened his first Yang Sang (meaning 'caring for mankind') Chinese medicine shop in 1879 in Malaysia. There are now scores of outlets carrying the company's herbal remedies across the globe, including this impressive one, which also has a herbal restaurant using some of the ingredients.

Kenanga Wholesale City
FASHION
(www.kenangacity.com.my; 28 Jln Gelugor, off Jln Kenanga; ⏱24hr) This wholesale fashion complex spread across 22 floors and 800 lots, which aims to rival similar centres in Bangkok and Seoul, was still under construction at the time of research, but promises to be a unique retail experience. It's also interesting to poke around the surrounding garment district.

LAKE GARDENS & BRICKFIELDS

The shop at the Islamic Arts Museum (p51) has one of KL's best selections of gift items including pieces imported from around Asia.

Lavanya
INDIAN CRAFTS
(Map p54; www.lavanya.org.my; 114-116 Jln Berhala, Brickfields; ⏱10am-9.30pm Tue-Sat, to 3pm Sun) Sells colourful craft goods made by single women working at the charitable Shiva Shukthi Trust in Coimbatore, India, including adorable kids and adults clothes, home decorations and furniture.

BANGSAR & MID VALLEY

TOP CHOICE Mid Valley Megamall
MALL
(www.midvalley.com.my; Mid Valley City, Lingkaran Syed Putra) Mega is the only way to describe this enormous mall, where you could easily lose yourself for days in the 300 stores, two department stores (**Metrojaya** and **Jusco**), an 18-screen cinema, a bowling alley, a huge food court and even a colourful Hindu temple. One unusual emporium is the **World of Feng Shui** (3rd fl; www.wofs.com) specialising in goods to balance the positive energy in your life. The KL Komuter Mid Valley station makes getting here a cinch. There are also Rapid KL buses to Chinatown and a free shuttle bus to Bangsar LRT station.

Bangsar Village I & II
MALL

(Map p59; www.bangsarvillage.com; cnr Jln Telawi 1 & Jln Telawi 2, Bangsar Baru) These twin malls – linked by a covered bridge – offer upmarket fashions, including international brands such as Ted Baker and Zara, and local Malaysian designers such Richard Tsen at **Dude & the Duchess** (Upper ground fl, Bangsar Village II), which marries tailored fits and design to interesting fabric choices, or the chic shoes and bags of **Vinci+** (Ground fl, Bangsar Village II). Asian interior-design shop **Lasting Impressions** (www.lasting-impressions.com.my; 2nd fl, Bangsar Village II) has great decorative pieces. Also here are some shops and play centres for kids, a decent Western-style supermarket, a gym, several good restaurants and cafes and the Moroccan-style spa **Hamman** (p69).

Gardens Mall
MALL

(www.thegardens.com.my; Mid Valley City, Lingkaran Syed Putra) If the Megamall is proving too plebeian for your shopping tastes – or perhaps isn't quite mega enough – then there's the luxe Gardens mall just across the way. They even have concierge-attended toilets (RM5 entry)! Anchored by Isetan and Robinsons department stores, here you'll also find many lovely fashion emporiums, including the funky unisex designs of local lad **Key Ng** (www.keyng.com.my), a food court branded after Penang's famous Gurney Rd, a multiplex and the Cocoon spa and beauty floor. For details of how to get here see Mid Valley Megamall.

Bangsar Shopping Centre
MALL

(off Map p59; www.bsc.com.my; 285 Jln Maarof) The refurbished BSC has carved a niche with KL's gourmets thanks to its fabulous food hall and collection of chic, happening restaurants, cafes and bars. Other retail reasons for heading here are to get a new outfit at **British India** (p93), homewares at **House & Co** (www.houseandco.com.my), fancy footwear in **Shoes Shoes Shoes**, and traditional fashions at **Terengganu Sonket** and **Balinese Lace**. There are also some very pukka tailors should you need a dress shirt or suit run up.

Maizen
FASHION

(off Map p59; www.maizenkl.com; 112 Jln Maarof; ⊙11am-7pm) One of KL's larger and best-stocked boutiques.

Nurita Harlth
FASHION

(Map p59; www.nuritaharith.com; 10-2 Jln Telawi 3; ⊙10am-7.30pm Tue-Sun) Darling frocks and accessories from one of KL's top young designers.

Silverfish Books
BOOKS

(Map p59; ✏2284 4837; www.silverfishbooks.com; 67-1 Jln Telawi 3, Bangsar Baru; ⊙10am-8pm Mon-Fri, to 6pm Sat) Good local bookshop and publisher of contemporary Malaysian literature and writings.

ELSEWHERE

Royal Selangor Pewter Factory
ARTS & CRAFTS

(✏4145 6122; www.visitorcentre.royalselangor.com; 4 Jln Usahawan Enam, Setapak Jaya; ⊙9am-5pm) Located 8km northeast of the city centre, the world's largest pewter manufacturer offers some very appealing souvenirs made from this malleable alloy of lead and silver. You can try your own hand at creating a pewter dish at the School of Hard Knocks (p64). The factory has an interesting visitor centre (to get here, take the LRT to Wangsa Maju station and then a taxi) or you can visit the retail outlets in KL's malls including Suria KLCC.

ℹ️ Information

Dangers & Annoyances

KL is generally very safe, but watch for pickpockets on crowded public transport. One ongoing irritation is the state of the pavements. The covers thrown over drains can give way suddenly, dumping you in the drink or worse, so walk around them. Flooding can also be a problem – carry an umbrella and be prepared to roll up your trousers to wade through giant puddles.

Emergency

Ambulance & Fire (✏994)

Police (✏999)

Tourist police (✏2166 8322)

Immigration Offices

Immigration office (✏2095 5077; Block I, Pusat Bandar Damansara; ⊙8.30am-5pm Mon-Fri, closed 12.15-2.45pm Fri) Handles visa extensions and is 2km west of Lake Gardens.

Internet Access

Internet cafes are everywhere; the going rate per hour is RM3. If you're travelling with a wi-fi–enabled device, you can get online at hundreds of cafes, restaurants, bars and many hotels for free; sign up for an account with **Wireless@KL** (www.wirelesskl.com).

Media

Juice (www.juiceonline.com) Free clubbing-oriented monthly magazine available in top-end hotels, restaurants and bars.

WORTH A TRIP

PUBLIKA FOR THE PEOPLE

Set to fully open during 2011, **Publika** (1 Jln Dutamas, Dutamas) is shaping up to be one of the most innovative and interesting of KL's retail experiences. The property developer Sunrise realised there was a bit of a problem with its latest project Dutamas – a giant but visually boring mixed-use tower complex – so called in the architectural design team responsible for giving Suria KLCC and other hit malls the star treatment.

The ambitious revamp mixes up art, culture, shopping and dining in a way not done before in Malaysia. Within the rebranded complex will be a triple-decked covered shopping arcade and a large public stage for outdoor events surrounded by modern sculptures. Low rents have been set to encourage new talents to open up shop and spaces are already being let to NGOs, charities and creative business in the offices above.

The White and Black Box gallery and performance spaces of **MAP** (p89) are up and running and attracting a steady influx of visitors with their busy schedule of events. Among the shops open at the time of research that rate a look are **Pink Jambu** (www. pinkjambu.com; unit A4-UG1-05) selling vividly coloured, hand-painted batiks made into beautiful clothing, and homewares; and **Switchblade** (unit A2-G1-07; ☺noon-midnight) where rock'n'roll fashions for babies through to adults are married with a funky US diner–style cafe. There's also delicious dining and adorable macaroons at **Nathalie's Gourmet Studio** (p83).

KL Lifestyle (www.kl-lifestyle.com.my; free in select hotels, RM6.80 in bookshops) Covers activities and attractions in the city, including nightlife options; comes with a useful list and map of airline offices.

KLue (www.klue.com.my; RM5) The KLue team provide their savvy insight into the city's social life and up-to-the-moment listings.

Time Out (www.timeoutkl.com; RM5) Monthly magazine in a globally familiar format; sign up online for their weekly 'what's going on' digest.

Medical Services

Pharmacies are all over town; the most common is Guardian, in most malls. Medical centres and dentists are also found in all the big malls – a private consultation will cost around RM35.

DENTISTS **Dental Pro** (☎2287 3333; www.dentalpro.org; 8 Lengkok Abdullah, Bangsar Utama; ☺10am-6pm Mon-Sat)

Pristine Dental Centre (☎2287 3782; 2nd fl, Mid Valley Megamall, Mid Valley City, Lingkaran Syed Putra; ☺10am-6pm)

HEALTH CENTRES **Klinik Medicare** (☎2287 7180; 2nd fl, Mid Valley Megamall, Mid Valley City, Lingkaran Syed Putra; ☺10am-10pm)

Twin Towers Medical Centre KLCC (Map p60; ☎2382 3500; www.ttmcklcc.com.my; Level 4, Suria KLCC, Jln Ampang; ☺8.30am-6pm Mon-Sat)

HOSPITALS **Hospital Kuala Lumpur** (Map p63; ☎2615 5555; www.hkl.gov.my; Jln Pahang)

Tung Shin Hospital (Map p42; ☎2072 1655; http://tungshin.com.my; 102 Jln Pudu)

PHARMACIES **Kien Fatt Medical Store** (☎2072 1648; 59 Jln Petaling; ☺8.30am-5.30pm Mon-Sat) In business since 1943, this traditional pharmacy sells both Chinese and Western medicines. A qualified English-speaking doctor is available for consultations (RM113).

Money

Most banks and shopping malls provide international ATMs (typically on the ground floor or basement level). Moneychangers offer better rates than banks for changing cash and (at times) travellers cheques; they're usually open later and at weekends and are found in shopping malls.

Post

For international postal services, go to the main **Pos Malaysia** (Map p48; Jln Raja Laut; ☺8.30am-6pm Mon-Sat, closed 1st Sat of month) office, across the river from Central Market. Branch post offices are found all over KL, including:

Bangsar Baru (Map p59; 48 Jln Telawi)

Little India (Jln TAR near the crossing with Jln Sultan Ismail)

Sungei Wang Plaza (Map p42; 3rd fl, Jln Sultan Ismail)

Suria KLCC (Map p60; Basement level, Suria KLCC, Jln Ampang)

DHL (www.dhl.com.my) Bangsar Baru (60 Jln Telawi; ☺9am-9pm Mon-Fri, 10am-6pm Sat, 11am-5pm Sun) Central Market (Ground fl, Central Market, Jln Hang Kasturi; ☺10am-9.30pm).

Telephone & Fax

Payphones abound in the capital and most take coins, credit cards and phonecards (available from convenience stores). Alternatively, streetside phone counters sell prepaid SIM cards for mobile phones (see p231). Most internet cafes offer Skype and other net-phone services.

Telekom Malaysia (Map p48; Jln Raja Chulan; ☺8.30am-4.30pm Mon-Fri, 8.30am-12.30pm Sat) Quiet booths for international calls and a desk where you can send and receive faxes.

Tourist Information

KL Tourist Association (Map p54; ☑2287 1831; www.klta.org.my; National Museum, Jln Damansara; ☺9am-5pm Mon-Fri, till 1pm Sat) Good for brochures and general information on the city.

Malaysian Tourism Centre (MaTiC; Map p60; ☑9235 4900; www.mtc.gov.my; 109 Jln Ampang; ☺8am-10pm) Housed in a mansion built in 1935 for rubber and tin tycoon Eu Tong Seng, this is KL's most useful tourist office. Also hosts good cultural performances (see p88).

Tourism Malaysia (www.tourismmalaysia. gov.my) KL Sentral (Map p54; ☑2274 5823; ☺9am-6pm); Kuala Lumpur International Airport (KLIA; ☑8776 5651; International Arrival Hall, Sepang); Putra World Trade Centre (☑2615 8188; Level 17, 45 Jln Tun Ismail; ☺9am-6pm Mon-Sat)

Travel Agencies

The agencies listed here are reliable for discount fares. See p65 for companies offering tours inside Malaysia.

MSL Travel (☑4042 4722; www.msltravel.com; 66 Jln Putra; ☺9am-5pm Mon-Fri, to 1pm Sat)

Sutra (☑2382 7575; www.sutra.my; Level 3, Suria KLCC, Jln Ampang; ☺9am-9.30pm Mon-Fri, 10am-9.30pm Sat & Sun)

STA Travel (☑2148 9800; www.statravel.com. my; Level 10, AMODA, 22 Jln Imbi; ☺9am-5pm Mon-Fri, 9am-12.30pm Sat)

🛈 Getting There & Away

Air

KL's main airport is **Kuala Lumpur International Airport** (KLIA; Map p103; ☑8777 8888; www.klia.com.my), 75km south of the city centre at Sepang.

All of AirAsia's flights are handled by the nearby **Low Cost Carrier Terminal** (LCCT; Map p103; ☑8777 8888; http://lcct.klia.com.my). There's a shuttle bus between here and KLIA.

Berjaya Air and Firefly flights arrive at **Sultan Abdul Aziz Shah Airport** (Map p103; ☑7845 8382) at Subang, around 20km west of the city centre. See p233 for listings of airline offices in KL.

Boat

Ferries sail to Tanjung Balai on Sumatra (one way RM145, 3½ hours, 11am Monday to Saturday) in Indonesia from Pelabuhan Klang (Port Klang), accessible by KTM Komuter train from KL Sentral or by public bus (RM3.50) from Klang bus stand by Pasar Seni LRT station.

Australian, American, British and some European citizens can get a visa on arrival in Indonesia; otherwise you must have an Indonesian visa before boarding. To check on ferry details call **Aero Speed Enterprises** (☑3165 2545), at the ferry terminal.

Bus

KL's main bus station is Puduraya just east of Chinatown. The only long-distance destinations that Puduraya doesn't handle are Kuala Lipis and Jerantut (for access to Taman Negara) – buses to these places leave from Pekeliling bus station; and Kota Bharu and Kuala Terengganu, buses for which leave from Putra bus station.

More luxurious long-distance bus services offering meals, massage chairs, in-seat entertainment, and sometimes wifi are operated by the following:

Aeroline (☑6258 8800; www.aeroline.com. my) Daily services to Singapore (from RM60) and Penang (RM55) leave from outside the Corus Hotel, Jln Ampang, just east of KLCC.

Compass Coaches (☑1300 888 131; www. compasscoaches.com.my) Berjaya Times Square in KL to Marina Bay Sands in Singapore (RM88, twice daily).

Nice (☑2272 1586; www.nice-coaches.com. my) Services run from outside the old KL Train Station on Jln Sultan Hishamuddin to Singapore (RM88, 10 daily), Penang (RM75, 7 daily), Butterworth (RM68, twice daily) and Melaka (RM27, twice daily) as well as other destinations.

Transtar Travel (☑2141 1771; www.transtar. com.sg) To Singapore (RM28 to RM90, depending on size of bus) and Penang (RM45) from the Pasarakyat Bus Terminal, Jln Melati, off Jln Imbi.

BUS STATIONS Hang Tuah Next to Hang Tuah LRT and monorail stations, buses leave here every 15 minutes for Seremban (RM6; one hour) and Tanjung Malim (RM7; one hour).

Klang (Map p48) Near the Pasar Seni LRT station, frequent buses leave here to Klang (RM3), Pelabuhan Klang (Port Klang; RM3.80), Petaling Jaya (RM2) and Shah Alam (RM2).

Pekeliling (Map p63) Next to the Titiwangsa LRT and monorail stations, just off Jln Tun Razak, buses leave here for Kuala Lipis (RM14.60, three hours, four daily) and Raub (RM10.80, two hours, four daily). Several companies including **Plusliner** (www.plusliner.com) run services to Kuantan (RM22, four hours; eight daily); many

DESTINATION	FARE (RM)	DURATION (HR)
Alor Setar	39.10	5
Butterworth	31.30	5
Cameron Highlands	30	4
Ipoh	17.40	2½
Johor Bahru	31.20	5
Kuantan	22	4
Melaka	12.40	2
Penang	35	5
Singapore	46.20	5½

go via Temerloh (RM11.30, 2½ hours). Buses to Jerantut (RM15, three hours) also go via Temerloh. Buses to Genting Highlands (RM6, one hour) leave half-hourly from 6.30am to 9pm.

Puduraya Recently given a major facelift, this frantic and crowded bus station remains the kind of place you want to get in and out of quickly. The crowds provide plenty of cover for pickpockets and bag-snatchers, and agents for the bus companies will pounce on you as soon as you walk in the door, determined to convince you that their company is the best choice for your destination. Inside the main entrance on Jln Pudu, you'll find a small information counter and to the rear a **left-luggage counter** (⊙6am-midnight; per day per bag RM3). There's also a food court on the roof and a hotel here.

Buses depart from the basement level, but tickets are purchased from the ticket desks at the back of the main concourse. To find a bus, wander up and down the aisles checking the lists of departure times – staff will shout out their destinations as you walk past but make sure the departure time suits you, as agents sometimes sell tickets for buses that won't be leaving for several hours. **Transnasional Express** (☑1300 888 582; www.transnasional.com.my) is the largest operator, with buses to most major destinations. To find your bus, look for the name of the bus company on the signboards by the steps that lead down to the basement.

Services are so numerous that you can often turn up and get a seat on the next bus but, to be safe, book the day before, or a few days before during peak holiday periods. When taking night buses, check what time the bus arrives in the morning; if you arrive too early you'll have to wait until the hotels open their doors before you can check in.

Putra (☑4042 9530) Several services to the east coast leave from this quieter and less intimidating station opposite the Putra World Trade Centre. To get here, take the LRT to PWTC station, or a KTM Komuter train to Putra station. Buses from here go to Kota Bahru (RM40.20, eight hours, 9.30am and 9.30pm) and Kuala Terengganu (RM39, seven hours, 10.30am and 10pm).

Car

KL is the best place to hire a car for touring the peninsula; for sample rates see p236. Driving out of KL, however, is complicated by a confusing one-way system and contradictory road signs that can throw off your sense of direction completely All the major rental companies have offices at KLIA. City offices – generally open from 9am to 5.30pm weekdays and 9am to 1pm Saturday – include the following:

Avis (☑2144 4487; www.avis.com.my; main lobby, Crowne Plaza Mutiara Kuala Lumpur, Jln Sultan Ismail)

Hertz (☑2148 6433; www5.hertz.com; ground fl, Kompleks Antarabangsa, Jln Sultan Ismail)

Mayflower (☑6253 1888; www.mayflowercar rental.com.my; 18 Jln Segambut Pusat)

Orix (☑2142 3009; www.orixauto.com.my; ground fl, Federal Hotel, 35 Jln Bukit Bintang)

Long-Distance Taxi

With plenty of cheap flights and comfortable trains and buses, there is little reason to use long-distance taxis – they take just as long as buses but they cost more and they leave only when they have a full complement of passengers, or when one passenger agrees to pay the whole fare. However, they are cheaper than ordinary taxis for long journeys.

If you feel inclined to take a shared taxi, whole-taxi fares from the depot on the 2nd floor of the Puduraya Bus Station include Melaka (RM300), Penang (RM600), Johor Bahru (RM500), Ipoh (RM300) and the Cameron Highlands (RM350). Toll charges are normally included, though some unscrupulous drivers make passengers pay extra.

ℹ TRAVEL PASSES

Bus and LRT operator Rapid KL offers the **Rapidpass** (1/3/7/15/30 days RM10/25/50/90/150) valid on their company's services only.

If you're going to be in KL or Malaysia for an extended period and plan to use public transport or the highways a lot, it may be worth getting a **Touch 'n' Go card** (www.touchngo.com.my). These electronic credit storage cards can be used on all public transport in the Klang Valley, at highway toll booths across the country and at selected parking sites. The cards, which can be purchased at KL Sentral and the central LRT stations KLCC, Masjid Jamek and Dang Wangi, cost RM10 and can be reloaded with values from RM20 to RM500.

Train

KL Sentral station is the national hub of the **KTM** (Keretapi Tanah Melayu Berhad; Map p54; ☏1300 88 5862; www.ktmb.com.my; ☺info office 9am-9pm, ticket office 7am-10pm) railway system. There are daily departures for Butterworth, Wakaf Baharu (for Kota Bharu and Jerantut), Johor Baharu, Thailand and Singapore; fares are cheap, especially if you opt for a seat rather than a berth (for which there are extra charges), but journey times are slow – see p238 for more information. KTM Komuter trains also link KL with the Klang Valley and Seremban (see p101).

ℹ Getting Around

KL Sentral (Map p54) is the hub of a rail-based urban network consisting of the KTM Komuter, KLIA Ekspres, KLIA Transit, LRT and Monorail systems. Unfortunately the systems – all built separately – remain largely unintegrated. Different tickets generally apply for each service, and at stations where there's an interchange between the services they're rarely conveniently connected. This said, you can happily get around much of central KL on a combination of rail and monorail services.

See the transit network map, p38 and the Public Transport at a Glance table, p101, for useful stops on the different lines.

To/From the Airports

KLIA The fastest way to the city from KLIA is on the comfortable **KLIA Ekspres** (www.klia ekspres.com; adult/child one way RM35/15, return RM70/30; 28 mins) with departures every 15 to 20 minutes from 5am to 1am. From KL

Sentral you can transfer to your final destination by monorail, LRT, KTM Komuter train or by taxi.

The **KL Transit train** (adult/child one way RM35/15; 35 mins) also connects KLIA with KL Sentral, stopping at three other stations en route (Salak Tinggi, Putrajaya and Cyberjaya, and Bandar Tasik Selatan). If flying from KL on Malaysia Airlines, Cathay Pacific, Royal Brunei or Emirates you can check your baggage in at KL Sentral before making your way to KLIA.

The cheaper option is the **Airport Coach** (www.airportcoach.com.my; one way/return RM10/18), taking an hour to KL Sentral; for RM18, however, they will also take you to any central KL hotel from KLIA and pick up for the return journey for RM25. The bus stand is clearly signposted inside the terminal.

Taxis from KLIA operate on a fixed-fare coupon system. Standard taxis cost RM67.10 (up to three people), premier taxis for four people RM93.40 and family-sized minivans seating up to eight RM180.40. The journey will take around one hour. Buy your taxi coupon before you exit the arrivals hall, to avoid the aggressive pirate taxis that hassle you to pay a few hundred ringgit for the same ride. Going to the airport by taxi, make sure that the agreed fare includes tolls; expect to pay RM65 from Chinatown or Jln Bukit Bintang.

If you're changing to a flight on AirAsia, there's a **shuttle bus** (RM1.50; every 20 mins; ☺6am to midnight) between KLIA and the LCCT. Penny-pinchers can use this bus to get to Nilai (RM3.50) to connect with the KTM Komuter train to KL Sentral (RM4.70). A taxi between the two airports costs RM33.

LCCT Skybus (www.skybus.com.my; one way RM9) and **Aerobus** (one way RM8) services depart at least every 15 minutes from 4.30am to 12.45am and take an hour. Travelling from LCCT, prepaid taxis charge RM62 to Chinatown or Jln Bukit Bintang (50% more from midnight to 6am). Buy your coupon at the desk near the arrivals hall exit. A taxi from the city to LCCT will cost around RM65.

There's also a shuttle bus to and from the LCCT to Salak Tinggi station where you can pick up the KL Transit Train into the city.

SULTAN ABDUL AZIZ SHAH AIRPORT Best reached by taxi (around RM40).

Bus

Most buses are provided by either **Rapid KL** (☏7885 2585; www.rapidkl.com.my) or **Metrobus** (☏5635 3070). There's an **information booth** (☺7am to 9pm) at the Jln Sultan Mohammed bus stop in Chinatown.

Rapid KL buses are divided into four classes, and tickets are valid all day on the same class of bus. Bas Bandar (routes starting with B, RM2) services run around the city centre. Bas Utama

STATION	TRANSPORT TYPE	USEFUL FOR
Bangsar	LRT	Bangsar Baru
Bukit Bintang	KL Monorail	Golden Triangle, Lot 10, Sungai Wang Plaza, Pavilion KL, Jln Alor
Bukit Nanas	KL Monorail	Malaysian Tourist Centre (Ma-TiC), KL Tower
Chow Kit	KL Monorail	Chow Kit Market
Dang Wangi	LRT	Cap Square, Little India
Imbi	KL Monorail	Golden Triangle, Berjaya Times Square, Low Yat Plaza
Kampung Baru	LRT	Kampung Baru
KLCC	LRT	Petronas Towers, KLCC
KL Sentral	All lines	Brickfields, buses & trains to the airports
Kuala Lumpur	KTM Kommuter	Lake Gardens, Islamic Arts Museum, National Mosque
Maharajalela	LRT	Chinatown, Stadium Merdeka
Masjid Jamek	LRT	Masjid Jamek, Dataran Merde-ka, Little India
Medan Tuanku	KL Monorail	Asian Heritage Row
Midvalley	KTM Kommuter	Mid Valley Megamall
Pasar Seni	LRT	Chinatown, Dataran Merdeka
Plaza Rakyat	LRT	Puduraya bus station, China-town
Pudu	LRT	Pudu Market
Putra	KTM Kommuter	Putra Bus Station
PWTC	LRT	Putra Bus Station
Raja Chulan	KL Monorail	Golden Triangle, Changkat Bukit Bintang
Titiwangsa	LRT & KL Monorail	Pekeliling Bus Station, Lake Titiwangsa Park, National Art Gallery, Istana Budaya
Tun Sambanthan	KL Monorail	Brickfields, Thean Hou Temple

(routes starting with U, RM2) services run from the centre to the suburbs. Bas Tempatan (routes starting with T, RM1) services run around the suburbs. Bas Ekspres (routes starting with E, RM4) are express buses to distant suburbs. You can also buy an all-day ticket covering all non-express buses (RM4) and a ticket covering all Rapid KL buses and trains (RM7).

Local buses leave from half a dozen small bus stands around the city – useful stops in Chinatown include Jln Sultan Mohamed (by Pasar Seni), Klang Bus Station (south of Pasar Seni), Bangkok Bank (on Lebuh Pudu), Medan Pasar (on Lebuh Ampang), Central Market (on Jln Hang Kasturi)

and the Kota Raya department store (on Jln Cheng Lock); see map p48.

KL Monorail

The air-conditioned **monorail** (www.klmonorail.com.my; RM1.20-2.50; ☺6am-midnight) zips from KL Sentral to Titiwangsa, linking up many of the city's sightseeing areas.

KTM Komuter Trains

The **KTM Komuter** (☎1300 88 5862; http://ktmkomuter.com.my; every 15-20 min; ☺6am-11.45pm) service provides a suburban rail link using long-distance railway lines, with its main hub at KL Sentral. There are two lines: Ipoh–Seremban and Batu Caves–Pelabuhan Klang.

Light Rail Transit

As well as the buses, Rapid KL runs the **Light Rail Transit** (LRT; RM1-2.80; every six to 10 min; ☺6am-11.45pm) system. There are three lines: Ampang–Sentul Timur, Sri Petaling–Sentul Timur and Kelana Jaya–Terminal Putra. The network is poorly integrated because the lines were constructed by different companies. As a result, you need a new ticket to change from one line to another, and you may also have to follow a series of walkways, stairs and elevators, or walk several blocks down the street.

Buy tickets from the cashier or electronic ticket machines. An electronic control system checks tickets as you enter and exit via turnstiles. You can buy an all-day pass for RM7, which also covers you for Rapid KL buses.

Taxi

KL has plenty of air-conditioned taxis, which queue up at designated taxi stops across the city. You can also flag down moving taxis, but drivers will stop only if there is a convenient place to pull over. Fares start at RM3 for the first two minutes, with an additional 20 sen for each 45 seconds. From midnight to 6am there's a surcharge of 50% on the metered fare, and extra passengers (more than two) are charged 20 sen each. Luggage placed in the boot is an extra RM1 and there's a RM12 surcharge for taxis to KLIA.

Unfortunately, some drivers have limited geographical knowledge of the city. Some also refuse to use the meter, even though this is a legal requirement. Taxi drivers lingering outside luxury hotels or tourist hot spots such as KL Bird Park are especially guilty of this behaviour. Note that KL Sentral and some large malls such as BB Plaza and Pavilion have a coupon system for taxis where you pay in advance at a slightly higher fee than the meter.

If a driver demands a fixed fare, bargain hard, or walk away and find another taxi. As a guide, you can get right across the centre of town for RM10 on the meter even in moderate traffic. Always ask for a receipt and check to see that they haven't included spurious extra charges, such as for baggage you don't have.

AROUND KUALA LUMPUR

Selangor, Malaysia's most urbanised, industrialised and prosperous state, surrounds KL and within its boundaries are many great attractions that can easily be visited as day trips from the capital. Most can be reached by public transport and, if not, hiring a taxi or renting a car for the day is affordable and simple to arrange.

North of Kuala Lumpur

FREE **Batu Caves**   CAVE TEMPLES
(admission free, car park RM2; ☺8am-9pm) The Hindu temples in downtown KL are just appetisers for Batu Caves, 13km north of the capital. Discovered around 120 years ago by American naturalist William Hornaday, the caves were soon after adopted by the Hindu community as their principle place of worship. A small Hindu shrine was built in the vast open space, later known as **Temple Cave**, and at the foot of the outcrop is another temple guarded by the monkey god Hanuman.

An enormous golden statue of Lord Murugan (also known as Lord Subramaniam), to whom the caves are dedicated, fronts a flight of 272 steps leading up to Temple Cave. Beyond the towering main cavern, the space opens to an atrium-like cave at the rear. Cheeky macaque monkeys use the caves as their own adventure playground, leaping from stalactite to stalagmite and soliciting snacks from pilgrims and tourists. The monkeys bite, so keep your distance.

The caves are busy most days, but each year in late January or early February a million pilgrims converge here during the three days of **Thaipusam** (see p104), which features surreal acts of self-mortification. Lord Murugan's silver chariot takes pride of place as the procession makes its way from the Sri Mahamariamman Temple in KL's Chinatown (p46) to the caves. Get here by dawn, if you want to see anything amid the crowds, and bring food and water with you.

Dark Cave
(www.darkcave.com.my; adult/child RM35/25) At step 204, a path branches off to the Dark Cave. On the 30-minute guided tour you can explore some 2km of surveyed passageways with seven different chambers. There are some dramatic limestone formations but the caves are damp and muddy – a head torch and Wellington boots are provided. See the website about organising a more challenging two- to three-hour tour that involves crawling through the cave's narrow tunnels.

Cave Villa
(☑012 910 8389; www.cavevilla.com.my; adult/child RM15/7; ☺9am-6pm) The commercialisation of the caves continues at the base where

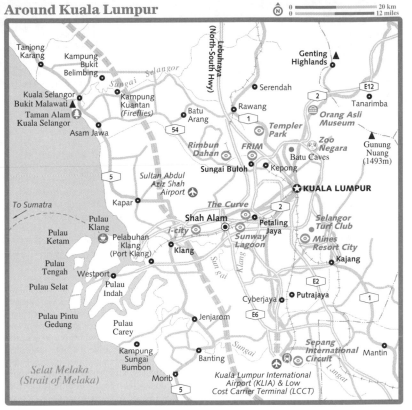

you have to pay to enter the Cave Villa, fronted by a pond packed with koi carp. The cave here features psychedelically painted sculptures of various Hindu gods arranged to tell parables from the *Bhagavad Gita* and other Hindu scriptures, while outside there's a small bird sanctuary, an area containing over 100 different species of reptiles (including a 7.6m-long python) and classical Indian dance shows on the half hour.

KTM Komuter trains terminate at the new Batu Caves station (RM1.30 from KL Sentral, 25 mins). Alternatively bus 11 (RM2, 45 minutes) leaves from where Jln Tun HS Lee meets Jln Petaling, just south of Medan Pasar in KL. The bus also stops along Jln Raja Laut in the Chow Kit area. A taxi from KL cost around RM20.

Forest Research Institute of Malaysia (FRIM)
RAINFOREST RESEARCH CENTRE

(FRIM; ☎6279 7575; www.frim.gov.my; Selangor Darul Ehsan; admission RM5; information centre ⊗8am-5pm Mon-Fri, 9am-4pm Sat & Sun) Birdsong and wall-to-wall greenery replaces the drone of traffic and air-conditioning at FRIM, at **Kepong** around 16km northwest of KL. Covering 600 hectares, FRIM was established in 1929 to conduct research into the sustainable management of Malaysia's rainforests. Its work has become increasingly important with the growing threats from logging and urban expansion.

Popular with locals who come to stroll in the shade of soaring trees, the forest's highlight is its **Canopy Walkway** (adult/child RM10/1; ⊗9.30am-1.30pm Tue-Thu, Sat & Sun), hanging a vertigo-inducing 30m above the forest floor. It is reached by a steep trail from the information centre, where you should go first to register and to pick up maps of the other trails in the park. The 200m walkway will take you right into the canopy, offering great views of the rainforest, with the towers of KL rising in the distance behind. If you've

THAIPUSAM

Malaysia's most spectacular Hindu festival is Thaipusam, a wild orgy of seemingly hideous body piercings. The festival happens every year in the Hindu month of Thai (January/February) and is celebrated with the most gusto at Batu Caves.

The greatest spectacle is the *kavadi* carriers, the devotees who subject themselves to seemingly masochistic acts as fulfilment for answered prayers. Many of the devotees carry offerings of milk in *paal kudam* (milk pots) often connected to the skin by hooks. Even more striking are the *vel kavadi* – great cages of spikes that pierce the skin of the carrier and are decorated with peacock feathers, pictures of deities, and flowers. Some penitents go as far as piercing their tongues and cheeks with hooks, skewers and tridents.

The festival is the culmination of around a month of prayer, a vegetarian diet and other ritual preparations, such as abstinence from sex, and sleeping on a hard floor. While it looks excruciating, a trance-like state stops participants from feeling pain; later the wounds are treated with lemon juice and holy ash to prevent scarring. Like firewalking, only the truly faithful should attempt the ritual. It is said that insufficiently prepared devotees keep doctors especially busy over the Thaipusam festival period with skin lacerations, or by collapsing after the strenuous activities.

Originating in Tamil Nadu (but now banned in India), Thaipusam is also celebrated in Penang at the Nattukotai Chettiar Temple.

---

ever imagined what life is like for monkeys, this is your chance to find out.

Heading down from the walkway the trail picks its way through the jungle (follow the water pipe) to a shady picnic area where you can cool off in a series of shallow waterfalls. The return hike incorporating the walkway takes around two hours. Bring water with you.

Elsewhere in the park there's a couple of handsome traditional wooden houses, relocated from Melaka and Terengganu, and a **museum** (☺9am-4pm Tue-Sun) which has some interesting displays explaining the rainforest habitat and about the forest-related research carried out by FRIM. Several arboreta highlight different types of trees and there's also a wetland area.

If you haven't brought a picnic, FRIM has a decent canteen near the information centre and, deeper into the forest, the charming **Malay Teahouse** (www.malayteahouse.com.my; ☺9am-7pm) serving traditional herbal infusions and tasty Malay food. The setting amid the trees in a colonial bungalow is lovely and you can also buy good souvenirs here, including locally made soaps, batik sarongs and flower-pattered tops.

Numerous tours run to FRIM from KL, but you can easily make your way by public transport. Take the KTM Komuter train to Kepong (RM1.30) and then a taxi (RM5). Ask the driver to come back and pick you up a few hours later.

Zoo Negara ZOO
(National Zoo; ☎03-4108 3422; www.zoonegara malaysia.my; adult/child RM15/6; ☺9am-5pm) Laid out over 62 hectares around a central lake 13km northeast of KL, this zoo is home to wide variety of native wildlife, including tigers and orang-utans, as well as other animals from Asia and Africa. Although some of the enclosures could definitely be bigger, it is one of Asia's better zoos: successful breeding programmes include ones that have produced false gharials, African dwarf crocodiles and 200 of the highly endangered milky stork.

You can buy bags of carrot chips and bunches of green bamboo to feed the elephants, camels, deer and giraffes yourself – these foodstuffs are selected to complement the animals' natural diet. New additions to the zoo include an excellent aquarium focusing on river life and an **insect zoo and butterfly park** (adult/child RM5/3) packed with fascinating creepy crawlies. It's possible to spend a day as a volunteer here – the website has details of how to arrange this.

Taxis charge around RM30 from central KL or you can take Metrobus 16 (RM2) from in front of the Central Market in Chinatown.

FREE **Orang Asli Museum** MUSEUM
(☎6189 2113; www.jheoa.gov.my/web/ guest/25; Gombak; ☺9am-5pm Sat-Thu) In the sleepy village of Gombak, 25km north of KL, this museum is devoted to the history,

rituals and customs of Malaysia's aboriginal people. It is run as a social project by Jabatan Hal Ehwal Orang Asli (JHEOA), the department of aboriginal affairs.

Inside you can see some thought-provoking displays on the various tribes of the region, and there's a small shop selling the eye-catching wood carvings by the Hma' Meri people who live on Pulau Carey and *tongkat ali* – a form of wild ginseng alleged to have Viagra-like properties!

Rapid KL Bus U12 from Central Market (RM2; 1½ hours) runs here. The museum entrance is hidden so ask the driver to let you know when you've arrived.

Templer Park   NATURE PARK
(☺24hr) About 22km north of KL beside Hwy 1, Templer was once part of a rubber estate, but the Forestry Department took over in the 1980s, preserving 1200 hectares of primary jungle from the developers. Today it's a popular weekend retreat for nature-oriented locals, with walking and jogging trails (also good for mountain bikes), picnic tables and a series of ponds, streams and waterfalls where you can swim (modestly dressed of course). There are no signs saying 'Templer Park' – look instead for the sign saying 'Hutan Lipur Kanching', which marks the path to the waterfalls area.

Metrobus 43 runs here every 15 minutes from the Bangkok Bank bus stand on Lebuh Pudu in Chinatown (RM2).

GENTING HIGHLANDS
The tacky casino, theme-park, hotel resort and shopping centre, 50km north of KL, Genting Highlands (www.rwgenting.com) is in stark contrast to the Old English style of other Malaysian hill stations. In its slender favour is the resort's cool weather; at 2000m above sea level there's no need for air-conditioning.

◉ Sights
Genting's *raison d'être* is its glitzy casino – the only one in the country. It can get busy – very busy – here; the resort's five hotels have beds for 10,000 people and three times as many punters usually turn up each day.

Bird lovers should also note that the highlands are great for **bird spotting**. The 3.4km-long Genting Skyway (one-way RM5; ☺7.30am-11pm Mon-Thu, 7.30am-midnight Fri-Sun) is a gentle, 11-minute cable-car glide above the dense rainforest.

Kids will also enjoy the indoor and outdoor theme parks (outdoor park adult/child from RM26/18; indoor park RM18/12, both parks RM46/32); they include water slides, thrill rides, a climbing wall, Snow World, and a fierce wind tunnel for a simulated skydive!

🛏 Sleeping & Eating
Genting is an easy day trip from KL, but if you decide to stay, the resort has five hotels, none of which is particularly outstanding. Rates vary enormously, the most expensive nights generally being Saturday and public holidays; check the website or KL booking offices.

First World Hotel   HOTEL **$$**
(r from RM155; @) With 6500 beds, this is Malaysia's largest hotel, with plain but quite acceptable rooms.

Genting Hotel   HOTEL **$$**
(r from RM265; @⊠) Genting's most luxurious hotel.

WORTH A TRIP

RIMBUN DAHAN

For most of the year only the Hijjas family, their friends and a handful of talented writers and artists have access to Rimbun Dahan (☎6038-3690; www.rimbundahan.org/home.html) about 20 minutes' drive west of Kepong and 45 minutes from KL. The artists' residency programme, set up by architect Hijjas Kasturi (who designed the striking Tabung Haji and Menara Maybank buildings in KL) and his Australian wife Angela in 1994, culminates in a public show in the subterranean gallery in their private estate.

The **Art for Nature** exhibition of visual arts, which helps raise funds for WWF Malaysia, is also held here, usually in late July or early August. These events are well worth attending, not only to see works by some of the brightest stars of Malaysia's art scene but also for the glimpse it allows into this serene compound that also has an indigenous herb and spice garden and two beautifully restored heritage buildings – a traditional Malay wooden house dating from 1901 that shows elements of Chinese design, and a handsome colonial bungalow transported from Penang.

Olive FUSION $$$
(☏610 1118; Genting Hotel; meals RM50-100; ⊘lunch & dinner) The pick of the fine-dining options, serving fusion cuisine in (for Genting) surprisingly classy surroundings.

Coffee Terrace MALAY/INTERNATIONAL $$$
(Genting Hotel; lunch/dinner RM55/65; ⊘lunch & dinner) A reasonably good buffet-style restaurant offering a wide range of food.

❶ Getting There & Away

Buses leave at hourly intervals from 8.30am to 8.30pm from KL's Pasarakyat bus station (adult/child RM9.60/8.50, 1½ hours) and on the hour from 8am to 7pm from KL Sentral (RM9.30/8.20); the price includes the Skyway cable car. A taxi from KL will cost around RM70.

The best deal is the **Go Genting Golden Package** (RM41), including return transport from KL, an outdoor theme park pass or buffet lunch at the Coffee Terrace. Buy the pass from Genting's ticket office at KL Sentral or from its main **sales office** (☏03-2718 1118; www.rwgenting. com; Wisma Genting, 28 Jln Sultan Ismail, KL; ⊘8.30am-6pm Mon-Fri, 8.30am-1pm Sat), where you can also book resort accommodation.

Klang Valley

Heading southwest of KL along the Klang Hwy, the **Kota Darul Ehsan** ceremonial arch marks the transition between the city and Selangor. Just over the boundary, Petaling Jaya blends into Shah Alam, the state capital, which blends into Klang, the old royal capital – pretty much all in one seamless stretch of housing estates and industrial parks.

PETALING JAYA

Many of the people you'll meet in KL actually live in the neighbouring city of Petaling Jaya (commonly shortened to PJ). This sprawling community is defined by its giant indoor shopping malls, such as Sunway Pyramid and the Curve, and the commercial areas of various Sections (or SS) of the city such as SS2 stacked with good neighbourhood restaurants and cafes plus a glutton's paradise of hawker stalls.

◉ Sights

Sunway Lagoon & Sunway Pyramid
THEME PARK
There are few more fun ways to cool down on a sticky day than splashing around at **Sunway Lagoon** (☏5639 0000; www.sunway lagoon.com; 3 Jln PJS, 11/11 Bandar Sunway; adult/child from RM45/30; inc water park RM60/45; ⊘11am-6pm Mon & Wed-Fri, 10am-6pm Sat & Sun). Built on the site of a former tin mine and quarry, the highlight of this multizone theme park are the water slides, and what's claimed to be the world's largest artificial surf beach. There's also a Wild West–themed section with all the regular thrill rides, an interactive wildlife zoo (ie, you're allowed to stroke the giant tortoises and cuddle the hamsters) and an extreme park with all-

---

WORTH A TRIP

SEAFOOD & DESSERTS IN PJ

When Martha Stewart visited KL in 2010 and fancied eating crab, the folks at Fried Chillies knew exactly where to take her: **Fresh Unique Seafood 23** (☏7960 2088; www.unique-seafood.com.my; Lot 9B, Jln Kemajuan, SS13, Petaling Jaya; ⊘noon-2.30pm & 6-10.30pm), a five-minute taxi ride from Asia Jaya LRT station. On entering you'll see a wall of tiered tanks holding a global bounty of flapping, squirming fish and crustaceans forming the backdrop to a busy dining hall packed with families digging in.

Scotland clams, Boston lobsters, mantis prawns, Australian snow or Ireland roe crabs, even California geoduck – if it's got fins, scales or a shell there's a good chance that Unique will have it. All the prices are clearly labelled – your choice is weighed first and the total given – if the price is too high it's OK to have them throw the fish back and choose something else. Once you've done the deal on the raw materials, the waiters will suggest how best it should be cooked, for which there will be an extra charge. Bring a group and choose judiciously and you could average RM50 to RM80 per head – a bargain for such fresh, expertly cooked food. It's easy, though, for the bill to head way north, especially if you opt for lobster or the like.

For dessert, motor over to nearby area SS2 where delicious shaved ice *sago loh* and *tong sui* sweet bean, nut and fruit soups are enthusiastically slurped by an appreciative crowd at **KTZ Food** (☏7877 2499; 66 & 68 Jln SS2/67; ⊘4pm-1am).

TANARIMBA

Marketed as a location for Malaysians to build their dream house, **Tanarimba**, 40km northeast of KL, is a 2954-hectare private development spread across cool-temperature rainforested hills shortly after the turn-off to Genting Highlands. Less than a quarter of the land has been allocated for low-density development, with each home sitting on a plot of 0.6 hectares. The rest of the estate is permanent forest reserve, home to, among others, wild boars and goats, dusky and silver leaf monkeys, macaques, tapirs and even tigers.

At Tanarimba's entrance is a cathedral-like visitors centre with a cafe, while further into the estate you can stay at **Enderong House** (☎09-233 0655; www.tanarimba.com.my; d Mon-Thu RM350; Fri-Sun RM500; 🔊🖥), another memorable piece of architecture constructed from local pine and stone. Rates include breakfast, with other meals available in the nearby Malay village of **Janda Baik** or Chinese village of **Bukit Tingi**.

You don't need to spend the night here to enjoy Tanarimba: locally based guides **Rainforest Experience** (☎012 219 1377; www.junglescape.com.my) lead treks along a 3km trail providing a fascinating insight into the forest environment and what it takes to survive in the jungle. These enjoyable treks (RM150 per person, minimum 4 people, maximum 10) are led by two knowledgeable guides and last around six hours, including lunch.

terrain vehicles, a rock-climbing wall and paintball fights.

The park is behind the vast **Sunway Pyramid** (☎7494 3100; www.sunwaypyramid.com) mall distinguished by its giant lion gateway, faux Egyptian walls and crowning pyramid! Inside is a **skating rink** (admission incl skate hire Mon-Fri RM13, Sat & Sun RM16; ☺9am-8pm) as well as a bowling alley, a multiplex cinema and the usual plethora of shops and dining outlets. There's also the mega dance club **EUPHORIA by Ministry of Sound** (www.euphoria.com.my), a branch of the famous London club and big enough for 1500 people.

The easiest way here is take the Putra LRT to Kelana Jaya (RM2.10), then feeder bus T623 (RM1) or a taxi (RM11) to the Sunway Pyramid. Shuttle buses U63, U67 and U756 run here from Subang Jaya station on the KTM Komuter line. A taxi from central KL will cost around RM21.

Curve SHOPPING CENTRE
(☎7710 6868; www.thecurve.com.my; Mutiara Damansara; ☺10am-10pm) It's got Ikea, it's got Tesco, and it's got oodles more shops and restaurants. However, there are other reasons for heading to the Curve about 15km west of the centre in Petaling Jaya. One of the best is to attend concerts by up-and-coming local bands and singers at **Laundry Bar** (☎7728 1715; www.laundrybar.net; G75 & 76 Western Courtyard; ☺11-1am). Also there's a flea and craft market held here at weekends that

can turn up some interesting handmade souvenirs.

A free shuttle bus runs three times a day between the mall and the Melia Kuala Lumpur Hotel on Jln Imbi and the Royale Bintang Hotel on Jln Bukit Bintang (see the website for details). Otherwise hop on Rapid KL bus U88 from KL's Central Market (RM2; 40 minutes).

🛏 Sleeping

Sunway Lagoon has several appealing accommodation options gathered together in the **Sunway Resort Hotel & Spa** (☎7492 8000; http://kualalumpur.sunwayhotels.com; rm/villa from RM280/1150; ❄@🖥🔊): the **Sunway Pyramid Hotel** is a modern and quirkily designed business hotel; the **Duplex** offers townhouses each with three chicly designed bedrooms and fully equipped kitchens – ideal for families; and the **Villas** are contemporary Asian-styled residences each with their own infinity-style plunge pools, sunken baths and rain showers; great for a romantic getaway.

Alternatively, **Seapark Brickhouse** (☎012-2062846; www.seaparkbrickhouse.com; 1 Jln 21/2, Seapark Petaling Jaya; r/house from RM180/720; ❄🔊) is the stylish sibling of Terasek Brickhouse in Bangsar (see p73). Explore PJ like a local on one of the bikes that come with this four-bedroom self-catering house. Paramount LRT station is within walking distance.

PUTTING THE ARTS IN PJ

With crowds packing its multiple malls it would be easy to dismiss residents of PJ as primarily interested in shopping. Out to challenge this stereotype are a couple of intimate yet ambitious arts salons.

CHAI (☑7784 979; http://blog.instantcafetheatre.com; 6 Jln 6/3, SS6) described as a 'cafe house of arts and ideas' is the latest venture of the long-running theatre group Instant Café Theatre Company. Don't let the suburban house fool you – this is an experimental space where all manner of events can and have happened including installations, poetry readings and debates. Monthly programmes are constructed around such themes as taboo, death and travel.

Ploughing a similar groove is **Small Talk with the Moon** (☑7955 0800; www.small talkwiththemoon.com; 5, Jln 12/15), an art gallery in a house that hosts the occasional performance. It specialises in nurturing local talent and also sells a variety of crafty goods.

SHAH ALAM

Thirty years ago Selangor's state capital was a rubber-and-palm plantation, but in the late 1970s a massive building programme spawned a well-developed infrastructure, huge public buildings and a rapidly growing population. A couple of sights in this staunchly Muslim city may be of interest.

◉ Sights

Masjid Sultan Salahuddin Abdul Aziz Shah   MOSQUE

(☑5159 9988; Persiaran Masjid; ☺10am-noon & 2-4pm Sat-Thu) Called the Blue Mosque for its azure dome (larger than that of London's St Paul's Cathedral), this is one of Southeast Asia's biggest mosques. Covered in a rosette of verses from the Quran, the building accommodates up to 24,000 worshippers and is a sight to behold. Its four minarets, looking like giant rockets, are the tallest in the world (over 140m). You'll need to be appropriately dressed if you want to look inside.

City of Digital Lights at i-City

TECHNOLOGY PARK

(www.i-city.my; per car RM10; ☺6pm-3am) Some bright spark had the idea to jolly up this otherwise dull technology park with a million and one LED light displays. There are forests of multicoloured trees, giant peacocks and cacti, a massive screen showing free movies, and an indoor display of Frostie's Wonderland where the air-con is cranked up to keep the fairy-lit snowmen and penguins climatically happy. Kids and collectors of supremely kitsch experiences will love it.

❶ Getting There & Away

Buses U18 goes to Shah Alam from KL's Klang bus station (RM2, one hour) and will drop you in front of the PKNS Plaza mall, from where it's

a short walk to the mosque. Frequent Komuter trains also run from KL to Shah Alam (RM2.50, 45 minutes), but from there it's another bus or taxi ride to the mosque. You'll also need a car or taxi to get to i-City.

KLANG & PELABUHAN KLANG

Around 10km towards the coast from Shah Alam, Klang, once the royal capital of Selangor, is where the British installed their first Resident in 1874. The compact town's few sights take no more than a couple of hours to see, leaving you plenty of time to enjoy the real reason for heading here: to dig into superb Indian food in Klang's vibrant Little India.

Five stops further down the line, the KTM Komuter trains terminate at ramshackle Pelabuhan Klang, once KL's main seaport until the establishment of the modern harbour on Pulau Indah, 17km to the southwest. You'll only need to come here to catch either a ferry to Sumatra or Pulau Ketam (see p110), or to grab a seafood meal at the nearby waterside village of Bagan Hailan.

◉ Sights

Klang is small enough to see on foot. Heading south from the train station, along Jln Stesyn, you'll pass several attractive rows of Chinese shophouses (to the right). Running parallel to Jln Stesyn to the right is Jln Tengku Kelana, heart of the intensely colourful Little India. Beside piles of vegetables, spices, Bollywood DVDs and a multitude of saris and silks, several fortune tellers squat on the pavement and predict the future with the aid of green parrots trained to pick out auspicious cards. The area is especially worth visiting around the Hindu festival of Deepavali.

Return to Jln Steysn to look around the grand whitewashed 1909 colonial building (designed by Arthur B Hubback) housing the **Galeri Diraja Sultan Abdul Aziz** (☑3373 6500; www.galeridiraja.com; Bangunan Sultan Suleiman; free; ☺10am-5pm Tue-Sun). The royal gallery, devoted to the history of the Selangor sultanate dating back to 1766, contains a wide array of royal regalia, gifts and artefacts, including copies of the crown jewels.

Heading uphill along Jln Istana will bring you to **Istana Alam Shah**, the sultan's palace before the capital was moved to Shah Alam; as part of a day-long **walking tour** (☑012 231 6973; per person RM150, minimum of two people) of the city (including two meals) it's possible to have a look around; bookings should be made at least a week in advance. The park opposite gives a pleasant view of the city.

East of the palace, along Jln Kota Raja, the handsome **Masjid Di Raja Sultan Suleiman** is a striking blend of Art Deco and Middle Eastern influences. Opened in 1934, this was once the state mosque and several past sultans are buried here. Step inside to admire its stained-glass dome.

🗶 Eating

Indian food is Klang's highlight, but it's not the only thing on offer: the Chinese community here claims to have invented the popular pork and herbal tea broth stew *bak kut the*. Excellent, wallet-friendly seafood is also available at a number of restaurants out at Bagan Hailan, a RM10 taxi ride from Pelabuhan Klang station.

Asoka INDIAN **$**
(105 Jln Tengku Kelana; meals RM5-10; ☺7am-11pm) Vividly orange-and-cream-painted parlour of Indian culinary goodness, including a great selection of sweets, juices and crispy *dosai* pancakes served with coconut chutney.

Jai Hind INDIAN **$**
(92 Jln Tengku Kelana; meals RM5-10; ☺6.30am-10.30pm) Also renowned for its sweets, Jai Hind has been in business for over 60 years and is the place to head when it's time for tiffin.

Sri Barathan Matha Vilas INDIAN **$**
(34-36 Jln Tengku Kelana; meals RM5-10; ☺6.30am-10.30pm) It's hard to resist a bowl of this restaurant's signature dish of spicy *mee goreng* fried noodles; the chef prepares them constantly in a giant wok beside the entrance.

Seng Huat Bak Kut Teh MALAY/CHINESE **$**
(☑012-309 8303; 9 Jln Besar; meal RM10; ☺7.30am-1pm & 5.30-8.30pm) Sample the fragrant, flavoursome pork stew at this unpretentious eatery, steps away from the train station, just beneath the Klang Bridge.

Mohana Bistro INDIAN **$$**
(☑3372 7659; 119 Jln Tengku Kelana; meals RM10-20; ☺7am-11pm) Deservedly popular spot for banana-leaf curry spreads and spice-laden biryani rice. The waiters bring round trays of tempting veg and meat dishes to choose from.

Bagan Seafood SEAFOOD **$$**
(☑3176 4546; Lot 4546, Lingkaran Sultan Hishamuddin, off Jln Pelabuhan Utara, Kg Baru Bagan Hailam; meals RM40; ☺11am-3pm & 6pm-11pm Mon-Fri, 11am-midnight Sat & Sun) Brave the long drive out to this seaside eatery to enjoy its super-fresh seafood. Order *mantou* (deep-fried bread buns) to mop up the yummy sauces.

❶ Getting There & Away

Trains run every 30 minutes to Klang from KL (RM3.60; 1hr); the KTM Komuter station is close to the sights. Regular buses from KL (RM2) arrive opposite the My Din shopping complex, on the northern side of the river.

Pelabuhan Klang is 8km past Klang. Buses from KL's Klang bus station run to Pelabuhan Klang via Klang, but they terminate about a kilometre from the port. The KTM Komuter train terminal is just a stone's throw from the ferry terminal.

South of Kuala Lumpur

PUTRAJAYA

An eye-catching array of monumental architecture is on display in the Federal Government's administrative hub of Putrajaya, 25km south of KL and 20km north of KLIA. Covering 4932 hectares of former rubber and palm-oil plantations, Malaysia's answer to Canberra and Milton Keynes was but a twinkle in the eye of its principal visionary – former PM Dr Mahathir – back in the early 1990s. In 2001 it was declared a Federal Territory.

Designed as an 'intelligent garden city', Putrajaya is an intriguing, strange place to visit. It's heart is a 600-hectare artificial lake fringed by landscaped parks and an

WORTH A TRIP

ISLAND ESCAPES

Need to flee the Klang Valley's urban sprawl? The islands of **Pulau Ketam** and **Pulau Carey** – one reached by ferry, the other by road – could be just what you're looking for.

Ketam means crab and an abundance of these creatures is what first brought Chinese settlers to the so-named island, a 30-minute ferry trip (RM6) through the mangroves from Pelabuhan Klang. On arrival you'll find a rickety yet charming fishing village built on stilts over the mudflats. Wander around the wooden buildings of the village then enjoy a Chinese seafood lunch at one of several restaurants. Air-con ferries depart roughly every hour between 8.45am and 6.30pm (until 7.10pm at weekends); the last ferry back from Pulau Ketam is at 5.45pm (6pm at weekends).

If you don't have your own wheels, hire a taxi to get you out to Pulau Carey (from Klang one-way/return RM60/130), an island largely covered with palm oil plantations. Pause either on the way there or back to enjoy a tasty seafood meal at **Kang Guan** (☑352 7737; Jln Bandar Lama, Telok Panglima Garang; meals RM30; ◷11.30am-2.45pm, 5.45-11pm) beside the mangroves.

Your final destination is tiny **Kampung Sungai Bumbon**, home to an Orang Asli tribe known as the Hma' Meri (also written as Mah Meri). Here you can see the woodcarvers who have put the Mah Meri's art on the cultural map. There's also a **community centre** (◷9am-5pm) where you can pick up pretty woven baskets and other products made from dyed pandanus palm leaves as well as the interesting booklet in English about Hma' Meri culture.

Held in August, the village's **Mystic event**, when prayers are made to ancestors and the Hma Meri display their carvings, is worth attending.

---

eclectic mix of buildings and bridges. Planned to eventually house 320,000 civil servants and their families, the city's current population is only around 30,000 (of which 90% are Malays), making it more a quiet village than pulsing capital. Several huge mosques have been built, but there are no major religious monuments for any other ethnic groups – fuelling claims of bias against Indian and Chinese Malaysians by the Malay-dominated government.

◉ Sights & Activities

Urban Putrajaya   ARCHITECTURE
As a showcase of urban planning and vaulting architectural ambition, Putrajaya is impressive. The main boulevard is Persiaran Perdana, which runs from the elevated spaceship-like **Putrajaya Convention Centre** (☑8887 6000; Presint 5), worth visiting for the views, to the circular **Dataran Putra** (Putra Square) passing the Mughal-esqe **Istana Kehakiman** (Palace of Justice) and the modernist Islamic gateway fronting the **Kompleks Perdadanan Putrajaya** (Putrajaya Corporation Complex).

Framing Dataran Putra on two sides are **Perdana Putra**, housing the offices of the prime minister, and the handsome **Putra Mosque** (◷for non-Muslims 9am-1.30pm &

3-6pm Sat-Thu, 3-6pm Fri), which has space for 15,000 worshippers and an ornate pink-and-white-patterned dome, influenced by Safavid architecture from Iran. Appropriately dressed non-Muslim visitors are welcome outside prayer times.

There are nine bridges, all in different styles. The longest, at 435m, is the **Putra Bridge**, which mimics the Khaju Bridge in Esfahan, Iran. Also worthy of a photo is the futurist sail-like **Wawasan Bridge** connecting Presint 2 and 8.

Lake Cruise   BOAT TOUR
The bridges and buildings look their best viewed from Putrajaya Lake. **Cruise Tasik Putrajaya** (☑8888 3769; www.cruisetasikputrajaya.com; ◷10am-6pm Mon-Thu, to 9pm Fri & Sat, to 7pm Sun), located just beneath the Dataran Putra end of the Putra Bridge, offers up two relaxing options: the gondola-like Perahu Dondang Sayang boats (adult/child RM40/26) departing any time for a 30-minute trip around the lake; or a 45-minute air-con cruise on the Belimbing boat (adult/child RM50/35) leaving hourly.

Taman Botani   BOTANIC GARDENS
(Botanic Gardens; ☑8888 9090; Presint 1; admission free; ◷9am-7pm daily) North of Perdana Putra, near the prime minister's official resi-

dence, the 93-hectare site features attractive tropical gardens, a visitors' centre, a beautifully tiled Moroccan pavilion and lakeside restaurant. A tourist tram (RM3) trundles between the flower beds and trestles, and you can hire bicycles for RM4 for two hours (RM4 for one hour at weekends).

Taman Wetland WETLAND PARK
(Wetland Park; ☑8889 4373; Presint 13; admission free; ⊙7am-7pm; visitors centre ⊙9am-6pm Mon-Fri, 9am-7pm Sat & Sun) Further north is this serene, contemplative space with peaceful nature trails, a colony of flamingos, fluttering butterflies and picnic tables overlooking the lake. Canoeing and boating trips can be arranged here.

🛏 Sleeping & Eating

Putrajaya Shangri-la HOTEL **$$$**
(☑8887 8888; www.shangri-la.com; Taman Putra Perdana, Presint 1; r from RM390; ✳@🛜🏊) This very classy hotel has a great hillside view across to the lake. Good value weekend packages are available, and its Azur restaurant serves up an impressive Malaysian set lunch (RM40).

Pullman Putrajaya Lakeside RESORT **$$**
(☑8890 0000; www.pullmanputrajaya.com; 2 Jln P5/5, Presint 5; r from RM260; ✳@🛜🏊) Close to the Convention Centre and beside the lake, this large new resort complex incorporates traditional Malaysian architectural elements into its design. The rooms and resort facilities are good

and include an alfresco seafood restaurant built over the lake.

Alamanda MALL **$**
(Presint 1; meals RM10; ⊙9am-9pm) Putrajaya's swish shopping mall is home to several restaurants as well as an excellent food court where you can join the local bureaucrats for a meal.

Selera Putra FOOD COURT **$**
(Presint 1; meals RM10; ⊙9am-7pm Mon-Fri, 9am-9pm Sat & Sun) Head to this food court beneath Dataran Putra and enjoy the lakeside view while enjoying a wide range of inexpensive Malaysian dishes.

ℹ Getting There & Away
KLIA transit trains from KL Sentral stop at the Putrajaya-Cyberjaya station (one way RM9.50; 20 mins).

Bus 200 runs from train station to Dataran Putra (50 sen); a taxi there is RM9 while hiring one for an hour to tour around the sights (the recommended option) is a set fee of RM30.

SEPANG INTERNATIONAL CIRCUIT
The **Sepang International Circuit** (☑8778 2222; www.sepangcircuit.com), 65km south of KL and a 10-minute drive east of KLIA, is where Formula 1 holds the Petronas Malaysian Grand Prix every March or April. Tickets go for as little as RM100. During the three days of the race, plenty of special train and bus transport to the circuit is on offer, from around RM80 return from KL city centre.

KUALA GANDAH ELEPHANT CONSERVATION CENTRE

Many tour operators in KL offer daytrip packages (for around RM180) to the **Kuala Gandah Elephant Conservation Centre** (☑09 279 0391; www.wildlife.gov.my/index.php/en/our-services/recreational-facilities/385; Kuala Gandah, Lanchang; entry by donation; ⊙10am-4.45pm), about 150km east of KL. This is the base for the Department of Wildlife and National Parks' Elephant Relocation Team, which helps capture and relocate rogue elephants from across Southeast Asia to other suitable habitats throughout the peninsula. Most of the elephants at the centre are work elephants from Myanmar or Thailand who help capture the wild elephants.

Before heading out this way solo, call to reserve a ticket (only 120 people are admitted each day) and check opening times. Visitors are first shown a video about the elephant's plight (⊙1pm, 1.30pm & 3.45pm Mon-Fri & 12.30pm Sat & Sun), then can watch and join in while the handlers wash down the big guys and feed them fruit (⊙2pm Sat-Thu, 2:45pm Fri). There's also an opportunity to ride on an elephant and to be dumped in the river off an elephant's back and take a swim with a few of the gentle beasts.

While all of this is good fun and hopes to raise awareness about the elephants' precarious situation in Southeast Asia, such groups as the Malaysian Nature Society criticise the circus-like activities at the centre, which they say are out of line with animal welfare principles.

Other car and motorcycle races are held here throughout the year – check the website for details. On nonrace days call ahead to book a tour of the facilities including a run through the **auto museum** (free; ☉9am-6pm). Also check the website for track days when the circuit is open to wannabe Michael Schumachers to rev up their own cars (RM200) or motorbikes (below 250cc RM70, over 250cc RM100).

MINES RESORT CITY

The scarred landscape left behind after the closure in 1982 of the world's largest open-cast tin mine has been crafted into this sprawling leisure **resort** (www.mineswellnesshotel.com.my/mrc.html; Seri Kembangan, Selangor Darul Ehsan) about 10km south of KL. Surrounding a 60-hectare artificial lake are a **golf course** (www.minesgolfclub.com/main.php), shopping mall (with a canal running through it!), drab children's amusement park, convention centre and a couple of luxury hotels: the glitzy Mughal-themed **Palace of the Golden Horses** (✏8946 4888; www.palaceofthegoldenhorses.com.my; d from RM270; ❋@≋); and the less tacky, health-spa–themed **Mines Wellness Hotel** (✏8943 6688; www.mineswellnesshotel.com.my; d from RM200; ❋@≋).

The best reason for heading here is to lounge on the lake-front artificial beach from which a wide variety of **water sports** (✏8944 2866; www.mineswatersports.com) can be arranged, including wakeboarding, waterskiing, inner tubing, parasailing and being dragged around the lake astride a banana boat.

The resort is about 15 minutes' walk from Serdang station on the KTM Komuter line.

Melaka

TELEPHONE CODE 06 / POPULATION 759,000 / AREA 1652 SQ KM

Best Places to Eat

» Pak Putra (p133)

» Selvam (p135)

» Low Yong Mow (p133)

» Capitol Satay (p135)

» Howard's (p133)

Best Places to Stay

» Majestic Malacca (p132)

» Heeren House (p128)

» River View Guesthouse (p128)

» Apa Kaba Home & Stay (p130)

» Hotel Puri (p129)

Why Go?

Outlined to the west by sandy coastline and filled inland with waves of jungle-carpeted hills, the sultry city-state of Melaka is the cradle of modern Malaysia. While everything from international trade to the country's political system (based on the Malaccan sultanate) began here, the city and state have avoided becoming high-rise metropolises and instead remain low-key enclaves basking in the memory of a majestic past. To many Malaysians, Melaka is where the soul of the country can be glimpsed, and even through Melaka City's rapid development there remains a coastal vibe that demands a slower pace of life. The variations on traditional cuisine, including a regional twist on Malay-Chinese Nonya food, rival what's on offer in better-known KL and Penang; many visitors find the food easier to explore in Melaka as dining is predominantly in restaurants (usually with English menus) rather than at hawker stalls.

When to Go?

Melaka has become an extremely popular tourist destination for Malaysians and Singaporeans and it gets very crowded on weekends and holidays. Weekdays are the best time to visit (when many hotels also offer lower rates) but this means you'll miss Friday and Saturday nights' Jonker's Walk Night Market.

Reserve well in advance for the big, colourful festival times such as Chinese New Year, Festa San Pedro and Christmas. As far as weather goes – it's always hot – but you're less likely to get rained on during October, April and early May.

MELAKA CITY

Back when KL was a malaria-ridden swamp and Penang had yet to become the 'Pearl of the Orient', Melaka was already one of the greatest trading ports in Southeast Asia. Today the city is a sleepy backwater compared with its high-rolling cousins, but it's developing quickly, much aided by the Chinatown area's Unesco Heritage Site status, granted in 2008. More than ever Melaka is a hot tourist destination and the pace at which shopping malls and hotels are being built is mind boggling. There's still charm to spare, however, best represented by Chinatown's resident artists, cooks and creative trishaws, which coexist happily alongside the gaudy, modern signs on storefronts and so many photo-snapping tourists.

The quiet power of the Peranakan, Portuguese and Dutch architecture that made the city famous persists through the surrounding hullabaloo. With the oldest functioning mosque, Catholic church and Buddhist temple in the country, the city today (as it has for centuries) exudes a tolerance that accepts visitors of every creed. And have we mentioned the food? If you're eating local dishes, it's unlikely you'll have a bad meal. From the distinct Peranakan dishes to Eurasian Portuguese cooking and Indian banana-leaf shops, the citywide restaurant aromas add further colour to the cultural mosaic that makes Melaka such an astonishing destination.

History

The history of the city-state of Melaka is a tale that begins with a legend then, as it progresses, becomes filled with tales of colonial battles. However it's told, the story of the state is inseparable from that of the city for which it was named. Historians have

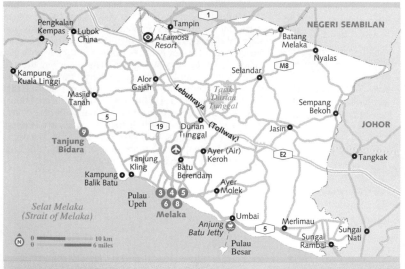

Melaka Highlights

❶ Savouring the diverse and addicting flavours of **Nonya food** (p133)

❷ Wandering aimlessly past gorgeous Malay, Chinese and Dutch **heritage architecture**

❸ Perusing and snacking at the lively **Jonker's Walk Night Market** (p134)

❹ Strolling the promenade along the eastern bank of the cleaned-up **Sungai Melaka** (Melaka River)

❺ Getting to know part of the local culture and its history at the **Baba-Nonya Heritage Museum** (p120)

❻ Shopping the eclectic boutiques, antique shops and galleries of **Chinatown** (p137)

❼ Taking a ride in a glitzy **trishaw** (p140) and rocking out to the thumping bass of your peddler's stereo

❽ Hiking to peaceful **St Paul's Church** (p116) for cool breezes and better views

❾ Driving through villages and farmland to the long white-sand beach of **Tanjung Bidara** (p141)

not been able to pinpoint the exact year when Melaka was founded but most agree it was sometime in the late 14th century. Before this time, Melaka was a simple fishing village.

Parameswara, a Hindu prince from Sumatra, was the founder of Melaka (p190). Under Parameswara, the city became a favoured port for waiting out monsoons and resupplying trading ships plying the strategic Selat Melaka (Strait of Melaka). Halfway between China and India, and with easy access to the spice islands of Indonesia, Melaka attracted merchants from all over the region.

In 1405 the Chinese Muslim Admiral Cheng Ho (p125), the 'three-jewelled eunuch prince', arrived in Melaka bearing gifts from the Ming emperor and the promise of protection from Siamese enemies. Chinese settlers followed, mixing with the local Malays to become known as the Baba and Nonya or Straits Chinese. The longest-settled Chinese people in Malaysia, they grafted many Malay customs onto their own heritage.

Despite internal squabbles and intrigues, by the time of Parameswara's death in 1414, Melaka was already a powerful trading state. Its position was consolidated by the state's adoption of Islam in the mid-15th century (see p192).

In 1509 the Portuguese came seeking the wealth of the spice and China trades, but after an initially friendly reception, the Malaccans attacked the Portuguese fleet and took a number of prisoners. This prompted an outright assault by the Portuguese, and in 1511 Alfonso de Albuquerque took the city, forcing the sultan to flee to Johor, where he re-established his kingdom. Under the Portuguese, the fortress of A'Famosa was constructed, and missionaries such as St Francis

Xavier strove to implant Catholicism. While Portuguese cannons could easily conquer Melaka, they could not force Muslim merchants from Arabia and India to continue trading there, and other ports in the area, such as Islamic Demak on Java, grew to overshadow Melaka.

The period of Portuguese strength in the East was short lived, as Melaka suffered harrying attacks from the rulers of neighbouring Johor and Negeri Sembilan, as well as from the Islamic power of Aceh in Sumatra. Melaka declined further as Dutch influence in Indonesia grew and Batavia (modern-day Jakarta) developed as the key European port of the region. Melaka passed into Dutch hands after an eight-month siege in 1641. The Dutch ruled Melaka for only about 150 years. Melaka again became the centre for peninsular trade, but the Dutch directed more time and energy into their holdings in Indonesia. In Melaka they built fine public buildings and churches, which remain the most solid suggestions of European presence, while Medan Portugis is still home to Portuguese Eurasians, many of whom are practising Catholics who speak Kristang (Cristão), a Creole dialect littered with archaic Portuguese.

When the French occupied Holland in 1795, the British – Dutch allies – temporarily assumed administration of the Dutch colonies. The British administrators, essentially traders, were opposed to the Dutch policy of trade monopoly and saw the potential for fierce rivalry in Malaysia between the Dutch and themselves. Accordingly, in 1807 they began demolishing A'Famosa fortress and forcibly removing Melaka's Dutch population to Penang to prevent Melaka rivalling British Malayan centres if Dutch control was restored. However, Sir Thomas

ORIENTING YOURSELF

The city of Melaka is a medium-sized town that's easy to navigate and compact enough to explore on foot or trishaw. While the city is the perfect size for getting around by bike, the traffic, lack of a hard shoulder and an excessive quantity of parked cars could make this option too adrenalin-charged for some people.

The colonial areas of Melaka are mainly on the eastern side of the river, focused around Town Square (which is also known as Dutch Square) and Christ Church.

Bukit St Paul (St Paul's Hill), the site of the original Portuguese fort of A'Famosa, rises above Town Sq. Located further north is Melaka's tiny Little India, while bustling, scenic Chinatown is to the west.

South of Melaka's old historical quarter are Mahkota Melaka and Taman Melaka Raya, which are two areas built on reclaimed land; bridging Mahkota Melaka to the historic quarter is the Dataran Pahlawan, a dwarfing mall and shopping and restaurant complex.

Stamford Raffles, the far-sighted founder of Singapore, stepped in before these destructive policies went too far, and in 1824 Melaka was permanently ceded to the British in exchange for the Sumatran port of Bencoolen (Bengkulu today).

Melaka, together with Penang and Singapore, formed the Straits Settlements, the three British territories that were the centres for later expansion into the peninsula. However, under British rule Melaka was eclipsed by other Straits settlements and was soon quickly superseded by the rapidly growing commercial importance of Singapore. Apart from a brief upturn in the early 20th century when rubber was an important crop, Melaka returned again to being a quiet backwater, awaiting its renaissance as a tourist drawcard.

◉ Sights

Melaka's sights veer unmistakably towards the historical. While several of the listings following (with the exception of museums) could be seen in a 30-second glance, there is a remarkable richness of stories surrounding each edifice that increases its charm

exponentially. Most central sights can be visited on the walking tour (p126).

HISTORIC TOWN CENTRE

St Paul's Church   HERITAGE BUILDING

This church is a wonderfully breezy sanctuary reached after a steep and sweaty climb up a flight of stairs. Originally built by a Portuguese captain in 1521 as the small Our Lady of the Hill chapel, St Paul's Church is a sublime testament to Catholicism in East Asia and offers bright views over Melaka from the summit of Bukit St Paul. Inside the decaying stone interior are the engraved tombstones of members of the Dutch nobility who are buried here. The church was regularly visited by St Francis Xavier, who performed several 'miracles' in the church, and following his death in China the saint's body was temporarily interred here for nine months before being transferred to Goa, where it remains today. Visitors can now look into his ancient tomb in the centre of the church, and a marble statue of the saint gazes wistfully over his beloved city.

In 1556 St Paul's was enlarged to two storeys, and a tower was added to the front in 1590. The church was renamed following

---

HANG TUAH & MELAKA'S STREET-NAME MUSKETEERS

If you look at Melaka's street names you'll notice that several begin with the word 'Hang', which was an honorary title in ancient times. The Hang of Melaka's street signs were in fact some of the region's greatest *laksmana* (admirals) of the 15th century – Hang Tuah and his friends Hang Kasturi, Hang Jebat, Hang Lekir and Hang Lekui. Their stories are some of the most beloved in Malaysia and are chronicled in both *Sejarah Melayu (Malay Annals*; a document of the establishment of the Melaka Sultanate and over 600 years of Malay history), and the *Hikayat Hang Tuah,* a romantic collection of tales involving Hang Tuah.

The undisputed leader of the band of buddies was Hang Tuah who, with his friends, mastered techniques of *silat* (a martial art) and meditation. The group was recognised early on by the sultan of the day, Tun Perak, when it managed to fight off a band of pirates who were attacking a village. Hang Tuah soon became inseparable from the sultan, to whom he pledged his absolute loyalty.

While there are many heroic tales of Hang Tuah, the most famous is the one about his battle with near-brother Hang Jebat (or, according to some versions, Hang Kasturi). A rumour had circulated that Hang Tuah was having an affair with one of the sultan's concubines. The sultan unfairly sentenced Hang Tuah to death without a trial but the executioner disobeyed the sultan's orders and secretly hid the admiral in a remote corner of Melaka. Believing that Hang Tuah had been killed for a crime he didn't commit, Hang Jebat went on a kung-fu-blockbuster-style killing spree in the palace and the sultan and his army found themselves in a losing battle. Word reached the sultan that Hang Tuah was still alive, so the sultan called his faithful servant back knowing that he was the only man alive who could defeat Hang Jebat. It took seven days, but Hang Tuah finally killed his old friend who had been fighting for his name.

The story is still highly discussed today as it represents a tension in the Malay psyche between the commitment to both loyalty and justice. It has also been adapted into several major Malay films including, most recently, *Puteri Gunung Ledang* (2004) starring M Nasir.

The red-pink paint found slathered over the Stadthuys can be attributed to the British, who brightened it up from a sombre Dutch white in 1911. The most likely reason is that the red laterite stone used to build the Stadthuys showed through the whitewashed plastering, and/or heavy tropical rain splashed red soil up the white walls – perhaps prompting the thrifty Brits to paint it all red to save on maintenance costs. The vivid colour theme extends to the other buildings around Town Sq and the old clock tower.

the Dutch takeover, but when the Dutch completed their own Christ Church at the base of the hill, it fell into disuse. Under the British it lost the tower, although a lighthouse was built, and the church eventually ended up as a storehouse for gunpowder. It has been in ruins for more than 150 years.

Porta de Santiago (A'Famosa)
HERITAGE BUILDING

A quick photo stop at this fort is a must for anyone visiting Melaka. Porta de Santiago was built by the Portuguese as a fortress in 1511. The Dutch were busy destroying the bulk of the fort when forward-thinking Sir Stamford Raffles came by in 1810 and saved what remains today. Look for the 'VOC' inscription of the Dutch East India Company on the arch; ironically, this part of the fort was saved by the Dutch after their takeover in 1670.

In 2006, work on the Menara Taming Sari revolving tower (see p125) at a riverfront site near the Tourism Melaka office, uncovered another part of the famous wall. The revolving tower was relocated further inland, the remains of the fortress walls were reconstructed and are now home to the 13-metre high **Melaka Malay Sultanate Water Wheel** replica. The original wheel would have been used to channel the river waters for the large number of traders swarming Melaka during the 15th and 16th centuries.

Stadthuys
HERITAGE BUILDING

(☑282 6526; Town Sq; admission adult/child RM5/2; ☺9am-5.30pm Sat-Thu, 9am-12.15pm & 2.45-5.30pm Fri) Melaka's most unmistakable landmark and favourite trishaw pick-up spot is the Stadthuys, the imposing salmon-pink town hall and governor's residence. It's believed to be the oldest Dutch building in the East, built shortly after Melaka was captured by the Dutch in 1641, and is a reproduction of the former Stadhuis (town hall) of the Frisian town of Hoorn in the Netherlands. With substantial, solid doors and lou-

vred windows, it is typical of Dutch colonial architecture.

Housed inside the Stadthuys is the **History & Ethnography Museum** (☺guided tours 10.30am & 2.30pm Sat & Sun), which has a recreated 17th-century Dutch dining room as well as displays of Chinese and Malay weapons and ceramics. Upstairs there's a room on Melaka's history. Also part of the complex is the mildly interesting **Literature Museum**, focusing on Malaysian writers. Admission to both museums (as well as the **Governor's House** and the **Democratic Government Museum**) is included in the admission price to Stadthuys.

Christ Church
CHURCH

Constructed from pink laterite bricks brought from Zeeland in Holland, this church still has Dutch and Armenian tombstones in the floor of its interior, while the massive 15m-long ceiling beams overhead were each cut from a single tree.

Sultanate Palace
MUSEUM

(Jln Kota; admission RM2; ☺9am-6pm) Housing a cultural museum, this wooden replica of the palace of Mansur Shah of Mansur Shah, the famous sultan who ruled Melaka from 1456 to 1477, is based on descriptions of the original palace from *Sejarah Melayu (Malay Annals;* a chronicle of the establishment of the Malay sultanate and 600 years of Malay history), and is built entirely without nails. The three-storey building is divided into eight chambers and three galleries containing a mishmash of artefacts, photographs and drawings depicting the sultan and the Malay communities of this period.

CHINATOWN

This is Melaka's most vibrant area, where you could easily entertain yourself for a few days simply by strolling through the teetertottering lanes. Surreptitiously peer into small shops where you might see a painter at work, an old man fabricating bicycle parts with a blow-torch or a stout woman

MELAKA

Melaka City

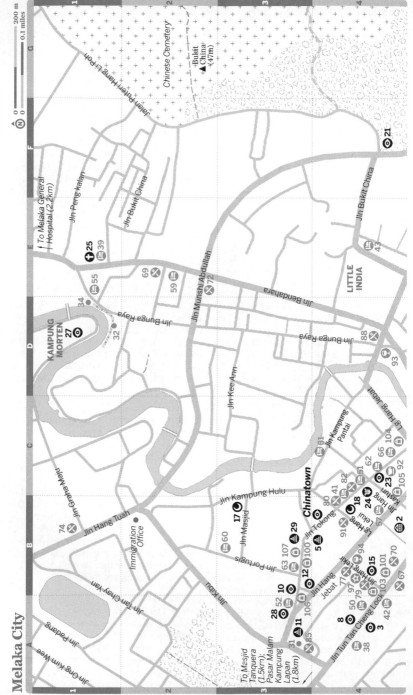

Chinese Cemetery

Bukit
China
▲ (47m)

LITTLE
INDIA

KAMPUNG
MORTEN

Chinatown

Jln Kampung Hulu

Jln Masjid

Immigration
Office

Jln Hang Tuah

Jln Gajah Meili

Jln Tan Chay Yan

Jln Padang

Jln Ong Kim Wee

Jln Kubu

Jln Portugis

Jln Hang
Jebat

Jln Tun Tan Cheng Lock

Jln Bendahara

Jln Bunga Raya

Jln Bunga Raya

Jln Munshi Abdullah

Jln Kee Ann

Jln Kampung Pantai

Jln Kampung Pantai

Jln Tokong

Jln Hang Kasturi

Jln Hang Lekiu

Jln Hang Lekir

Jln Hang Jebat

Jln Hang Jebat

Jln Hang Jebat

Jln Bukit China

Jln Bukit China

Jln Peng kalan

Jalan Puteri Hang Li Poh

To Melaka General
Hospital (2.2km)

To Masjid
Tanquera
(1.5km);
Pasar Malam
Kampung
Lapan (1.8km)

200 m
0.1 miles

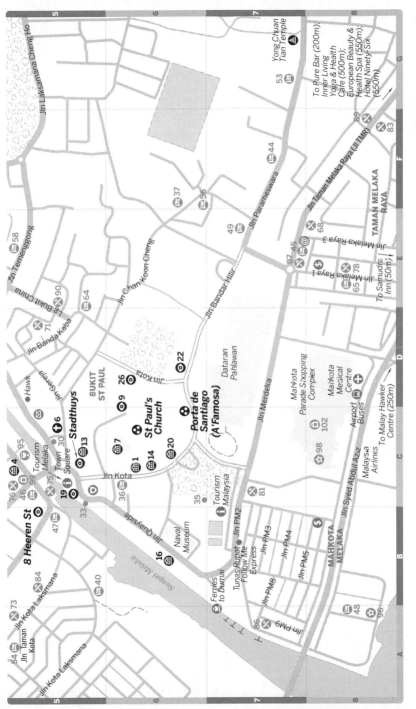

Yong Chuan
Tian Temple
53

To Pure Bar (200m);
Inner Living
Yoga & Health
Café (500m);
European Beauty &
Health Spa (550m);
Hotel Ninety-Six
(550m)

89
83

44

Jln Taman Melaka Raya (Jl TMR)

TAMAN MELAKA
RAYA

Jln Temenggong

58

Jln Bukit China

90

64

71

Jln Banda Kaba

Jln Chan Koon Cheng

37

56

49

Jln Parameswara

Jln Melaka Raya 3

68
87 45

Jln Melaka Raya 1

To Samudra
Inn (50m)

65 78

Jln Merdeka

Dataran
Pahlawan

Jln Bandar Hilir

22

Jln Kota

BUKIT
ST PAUL

26

9

St Paul's
Church

Porta de
Santiago
(A'Famosa)

Mahkota
Parade Shopping
Complex

Mahkota
Medical
Centre

Airport
Buses

To Malay Hawker
Centre (250m)

Malaysia
Airlines

98

102

81

Stadthuys

Hawk

Jln Gereja

6

13

7

14

1

20

Tourism
Melaka

Town Square

30

95

4

76
46

99

75

19

36

33

Jln Kota

35

Tourism
Malaysia

Jln PM2

Jln PM3

Jln PM4

Jln PM5

MAHKOTA
MELAKA

Jln Syed Abdul Aziz

Jln Laksamana Cheng Ho

8 Heeren St

47

Naval
Museum

16

Jln Quayside

Sungai Melaka

40

Ferries
to Dumai

Tunas Rupat ● Jln PM8
Follow Me
Express

86 Jln PM9

48

96

Jln Kota Laksamana

73

54

Jln Taman
Kota

84

Jln Kota Laksamana

plucking chickens for the restaurant next door. When your feet get sore just pop in to a reflexology or massage shop for half an hour of foot reflexology or a massage.

Baba-Nonya Heritage Museum MUSEUM
(☑283 1273; 48-50 Jln Tun Tan Cheng Lock; adult/child RM8/4; ⊙10am-12.30pm & 2-4.30pm Wed-Mon) Touring this traditional Peranakan townhouse takes you back to a time when women hid behind elaborate partitions when guests dropped by, and every social situation had its specific location within the house. The captivating museum is arranged to look like a typical 19th-century Baba-Nonya resi-dence. Furniture consists of Chinese hard-woods fashioned in a mixture of Chinese, Victorian and Dutch designs with mother-of-pearl inlay. Displays of 'Nonya ware', mul-ticoloured ceramic designs from Jiāngxī and Guǎngdōng provinces in China and made for Straits Chinese, add to the presentation. The highlight is the tour guides, who tell tales of the past with a distinctly Peranakan sense of humour. The admission price includes a tour if there are enough people.

8 Heeren Street HERITAGE BUILDING
(8 Jln Tun Tan Cheng Lock; admission free; ⊙11am-4pm Tue-Sat) Run by the Heritage Trust of

Malaysia, this 18th-century Dutch-period residential house was restored as a model conservation project. The friendly host will show you around and describe what era the differing styles of the building came from and what life would have been like inside its walls over the centuries. The project was partially chronicled by Lim Huck Chin and Fernando Jorge in their beautifully designed coffee-table book *Voices from the Street*, which is for sale at the house along with other titles on historical Melaka. You can also pick up an *Endangered Trades: A Walking Tour of Malacca's Living Heritage* (RM5) booklet and map for an excellent self-guided tour of the city centre.

Masjid Kampung Kling   MOSQUE
This hoary mosque has a multitiered meru roof (a stacked form similar to that seen in Balinese Hindu architecture) that owes its inspiration to Hindu temples, and a Moorish watchtower minaret typical of early mosques in Sumatra.

Sri Poyatha Venayagar Moorthi Temple
                                        HINDU TEMPLE
One of the first Hindu temples built in the country, this temple was constructed in 1781 on the plot given by the religiously tolerant Dutch and dedicated to the Hindu deity Venayagar.

MUSEUM ROW

Melaka has a ridiculous number of museums clustered along Jln Kota. Notables include the dusty **Islamic Museum** (admission RM1; ⊘9am-5.30pm Wed-Sun) and the small but worthwhile **Architecture Museum** (admission RM2; ⊘9.30am-5pm Tue-Sun), which focuses on local housing design. Most of the other institutions use a bland diorama format where visitors walk through a maze of wordy displays. If you're going to visit any museum here, make it the **Muzium Rakyat** (People's Museum; adult RM2; ⊘9am-5.30pm Wed-Mon) for its creepy yet compelling 'Beauty Museum' on the 3rd floor, which explores how different cultures mutilate themselves in order to look good (Western plastic surgery hasn't made it in yet).

Cheng Ho Cultural Museum   MUSEUM
(☑283 1135; 51 Lg Hang Jebat; adult/child RM20/10; ⊘9am-6pm Mon-Thu, 9am-7pm Fri-Sun) A lengthy paean to Ming Admiral Cheng Ho (Zheng He), this extensive museum charts the tremendous voyages of the intrepid Chinese Muslim seafarer. Photographs of Chinese descendants in Africa are intriguing while the puppet show is entertaining (despite its gruesome side). It's a great stop for history buffs, although there's too much information here for anyone expecting a casual visit. The ticket price includes a 15-minute film presentation on Cheng Ho.

Cheng Hoon Teng Temple   CHINESE TEMPLE
(Qing Yun Ting or Green Clouds Temple; 25 Jln Tokong; ⊘7am-7pm) Malaysia's oldest traditional Chinese temple (dating from 1646) remains a central place of worship for the Buddhist community in Melaka. Notable for its carved woodwork, the temple is dedicated to Kuan Yin, the goddess of mercy. In 2003 the structure won a Unesco award for outstanding architectural restoration. Across the street from the main temple is a traditional opera theatre.

Masjid Kampung Hulu   MOSQUE
(cnr Jln Masjid & Jln Kampung Hulu) Yet another aged superlative, this is the oldest functioning mosque in Malaysia and was, surprisingly, commissioned by the Dutch in 1728. The Portuguese had destroyed all non-Christian establishments during their occupation, including Melaka's first mosque. Later, during their colonisation, the Dutch decided to help the locals rebuild their places of worship. The resulting mosque is made up of predominantly Javanese architecture with a multitiered roof in place of the standard dome; at the time of construction, domes and minarets had not yet come into fashion.

Masjid Tanquera   MOSQUE
(Masjid Tengkera; Jln Tengkera) This mosque takes a back seat to Masjid Kampung Hulu in terms of age but is still one of the oldest in Malaysia (over 150 years old). In its graveyard is the tomb of Sultan Hussein of Johor, who signed over the island of Singapore to Stamford Raffles in 1819. The mosque is out of Chinatown about 2km towards Port Dickson along Jln Tun Tan Cheng Lock, which turns into Jln Tengkera.

AROUND THE CITY CENTRE

Kampung Chitty   NEIGHBOURHOOD
As well as the Baba-Nonya, Melaka also has a small community of Chitty – Straits-born Indians, offspring of the Indian traders who intermarried with Malay women. Having arrived in the 1400s, the Chitties are regarded as older than the Chinese-Malay Peranakan community (see the boxed text, p211). Their area of town, known as Kampung Chitty, lies west of Jln Gajah Berang, about 1km northwest of Chinatown; look for the archway with elephant sculptures beside the Mutamariman Temple. It's a pretty district in which to wander and see traditional Malay-style houses. The tiny **Chitty Museum** (☑281 1289; ⊘9.30am-5pm Tue-Sun) is a community effort with a collection of colourful artefacts such as traditional water pots, multitiered brass oil lamps, serving trays, sculptures, handicrafts and photographs.

The best time to visit is in May, during the Mariamman Festival (Pesta Datuk Charchar), a Hindu celebration during which you might also be fortunate enough to witness a traditional Indian wedding ceremony.

Little India   NEIGHBOURHOOD
Heading east from Kampung Chitty, past Chinatown and across the river, is Melaka's surprisingly plain Little India. While it's not

nearly as charming as the historic centre or Chinatown, this busy area along Jln Bendahara and Jln Temenggong is a worthwhile place for soaking up some Indian influence and grabbing an excellent banana-leaf meal. During Deepavali (see p20) a section of Jln Temenggong closes to traffic to make way for Indian cultural performances and street-food vendors.

Bukit China   GRAVEYARD
More than 12,500 graves, including about 20 Muslim tombs, cover the 25 grassy hectares of this serene hill. Since the times of British rule there have been several attempts to acquire Bukit China for road widening, land reclamation or development purposes. Fortunately, Cheng Hoon Teng Temple (p122), with strong community support, has thwarted these attempts.

In the middle of the 15th century the sultan of Melaka imported the Ming emperor's daughter from China as his bride, in a move to seal relations between the two countries. She brought with her a vast retinue, including 500 handmaidens, to Bukit China and it has been a Chinese area ever since. Along with the two adjoining hills, the area eventually became the burial ground for Chinese traders. **Poh San Teng Temple** sits at the base of the hill and was built in 1795. To the right of the temple is the **King's Well**, a 15th-century well built by Sultan Mansur Shah. It was an important source of water for Melaka and a prime target for opposition forces wanting to take the city.

St Peter's Church   CHURCH
Melaka has Malaysia's oldest traditional Chinese temple (p122) and functioning mosque (p122), so perhaps it's no surprise that **St Peter's Church** (Jln Bendahara) is the oldest functioning Catholic church in Malaysia, built in 1710 by descendants of early Portuguese settlers. The church has a striking white facade, stained-glass windows, the Latin words 'Tu es Petrus' (You are the Rock) above the altar and a bell cast in Goa (India) in 1608. On Good Friday the church comes alive when Malaccan Christians flock here, many of them making it the occasion for a trip home from far-flung parts of the country.

THE RIVERFRONT
Maritime Museum & Naval Museum
                                          MUSEUM
(admission RM3; ⊘9am-5.30pm Sun-Thu, 9am-9pm Fri & Sat) Housed in a huge recreation of the *Flor de la Mar*, a Portuguese ship that sank off the coast of Melaka (see the boxed text, p124), the Maritime Museum merits a visit. Clamber up for a detailed examination of Melaka's history, picked out by rather faded and dated props. The museum continues in the building next door with more absorbing exhibits featuring local vessels, including the striking *Kepala Burung* (a boat carved like a feathered bird) plus an assortment of nautical devices.

Kampung Morten   NEIGHBOURHOOD
Dubbed a 'living museum', this little village of 85 homes, including 52 in the traditional Malaccan style, is open to the public as a tourist destination but is still very much a real and functioning *kampung* (village). It might sound like visiting would be invasive but in fact it's not and as long as you don't get there at the same time as a tour bus, walking around is a relaxing experience and you'll meet plenty of welcoming people.

Villa Sentosa   HISTORICAL VILLA
(Peaceful Villa; ☑282 3988; entry by donation; ⊘flexible but around 9am-6pm) The highlight of a visit to the area is viewing this 1920s Malay *kampung* house on Sungai Melaka. A member of the family will show

---

TAKE A WALK ON THE CREEPY SIDE

A walk or jog around semishaded Bukit China is inner Melaka's only near-nature escape – don't let the fact that it's the largest Chinese graveyard outside China deter you. The trail begins from Poh San Teng Temple on Jln Laksmana Cheng Ho and winds up and down for about 3km, passing many ancient graves. The huge horseshoe-shaped tombs are those of the Kapitan China, the heads of the Chinese community in colonial times. Several *kermat* (sacred Muslim graves) are found on the northeast foot of the hill. The oldest tomb (located near the basketball court of SRJK Pay Fong III School) is a double burial of Mr and Mrs Huang Wei-Hung and was built in 1622. From the hill top there's a full-circle panorama of the city across paddy fields and to Pulau Besar – it's especially lovely at sunset.

SUNKEN TREASURE OF THE FLOR DE LA MAR

The Portuguese takeover of Melaka in 1511 was no peaceful affair. After 40 days of fighting the city fell to the European forces and about two months later it was sacked for its treasures for three days. The spoils were taken and stored on the *Flor de la Mar* and three other vessels bound for Portugal. Admiral Alfonso de Albuquerque claimed that the booty, including 60 tonnes of gold, the sultan's throne, 200 chests of diamonds and two bronze lion sculptures that had been a gift to the sultan from the emperor of China, were the finest treasures he had ever seen.

No sooner had the ships set sail than they encountered a storm off the coast of Sumatra, sinking the *Flor de la Mar*, which has never been recovered.

you around the house and its collection of objects including Ming dynasty ceramics, a 100-year-old copy of the Quran and a certificate of honour awarded by King George V to the late Tuan Haji Hashim Bin Dato Demang Haji Abdul Ghani (who lived here). Most of all, it's an opportunity to wander through a genuine *kampung* house and chat with your charming host.

MEDAN PORTUGIS

Roughly 3km east of the city centre on the coast is Medan Portugis (Portuguese Square). The small *kampung* centred on the square is the heart of Melaka's Eurasian community, descended from marriages between the colonial Portuguese and Malays 400 years ago. A French missionary first proposed the settlement to the British colonial government in the 1920s, but the square, styled after a typical Portuguese *mercado* (market) and lending the settlement a cultural focus, wasn't completed until the late 1980s.

The *kampung* is unexceptional, however, and the square is often empty, except on Saturday evenings when cultural events are staged. But the sea breeze is lovely while enjoying a relaxing beer or meal at the many restaurants in and around the square. Town bus 17 from the local bus station will get you here; see p139.

🏃 Activities

TOP CHOICE Eco Bike Tour   BIKE TOUR
(☑019 652 5029; www.melakaonbike. com; RM100 per person, minimum 2 people) Explore the fascinating landscape around Melaka with Alias on his three-hour bike tour through 20km of oil-palm and rubbertree plantations and delightful *kampung* communities surrounding town. Escort to and from your hotel is included. Alias

changes the tour around local events or festivals in the area. The tour can leave at either 8.30am, 3pm or 7pm for night cycling any day of the week.

TOP CHOICE Putuo Traditional Chinese Medical Therapy Centre   MASSAGE
(☑286 1052; 134 Jln Hang Jebat; 1hr reflexology RM38, 1hr chi body massage RM60; ⊙10am-10pm Mon-Thu, 10am-midnight Fri-Sun) The women here know their stuff and offer straightforward, excellent-value services. Get your feet expertly massaged while watching Chinese soap operas with the giggling staff or get a full-body chi massage in a quieter back room. If you have specific ailments, anything from migraines to water retention, the owner will create a special treatment for you. There are also ear candles, fire cupping, body scrubs and more. The centre's ambience is no-frills Chinese institutional.

Massa Sūtra   MASSAGE
(☑016 662 503; 20 Jln Kubu; www.massasutra. com; 1hr massage RM60) Described by a local expat yoga teacher as the best massage he'd ever had, so we had to find out for sure. Yup, we can say with conviction that Chris Loh is a master masseur (using Thai or Zen techniques) and he also had a massage school in the planning stages when we passed.

Inner Living Yoga & Health Cafe   YOGA
(☑017 352 4884; 3 Jln KA1; www.inner-living.com; classes RM10, mat rental RM5) Easily the prettiest and most welcoming yoga studio in Melaka; the new cafe is a place to get health-conscious meals and fresh juices over which to discuss asanas with the friendly staff. If you're in town for a while, a coupon system lowers the price of classes.

European Beauty & Health Spa   SPA & YOGA
(283 7982; 32A Jln Melaka Raya 15; classes RM15) One of the longest-running spas in Melaka caters mostly to locals but that shouldn't stop you from enjoying its long list of professional services and highly recommended yoga classes with international teachers. The setting is functional more than chic. Free shuttle services are available with just a phone call.

Biossentials Puri Spa   SPA
(282 5588; www.hotelpuri.com; Hotel Puri, 118 Jln Tun Tan Cheng Lock; spa services from RM80; ☺Thu-Mon) This international calibre spa in a sensual garden has a delicious menu of treatments including steams, body wraps, scrubs, facials and a variety of massages. There are several packages available including the sublime two-hour Vitality Purification (RM265), which includes a Thai herbal steam bath, skin tapping for circulation, detoxifying marine body mask, herbal bath and a deep-tissue massage. Bliss!

Melaka River Cruise   RIVER CRUISE
(286 5468; RM10, 40 min, minimum 8 people; ☺9-12am on demand) Riverboat cruises along Sungai Melaka (Melaka River) leave from two locations: one from the 'Spice Garden' on the corner of Jln Tun Mutahir and Jln Tun Sri Lanang in the north of town, and one at the quay behind the Maritime Museum. Cruises go 9km upriver past Kampung Morten and old *godown* (river warehouses) and there's a recorded narration explaining the riverfront's history.

Menara Taming Sari   REVOLVING VIEW TOWER
(child/adult RM10/20; ☺10am-10pm) Take a ride upwards in this 80m revolving tower that's considered an eyesore by many. Waits can be long and it's all a bit tourist-tacky but it is a good way to get your bearings and enjoy great views.

Melaka Monorail   MONORAIL RIDE
(Kampung Morten; adult/child RM10/2) The first 1.6km of Melaka's monorail system runs along

Sungai Melaka with a speed limit of 10km per hour; the monorail is more of a tourist attraction than anything else. Plans are in the works to run the line over 18km via Sentral bus station for a quick route into town but it's unclear when this will be completed.

🍜 Courses

Wok & Walk   COOKERY
(Hotel Equatorial; 2-day packages from RM340 per person) Hotel Equatorial (p131) runs the only cookery course in town. As well as two Nonya cooking workshops where you'll learn to make six signature dishes, the package includes a cookbook and apron to bring home, a two-night stay at the hotel, a walking tour and three Nonya meals at the hotel restaurant.

Eight Immortals House   TEA CEREMONY
(22 Jln Laksmana; ☺10am-7pm) If you're really into learning about tea, arrange a two-hour tea tasting and tea-ceremony course at this reputable and very authentic teashop. You can also buy loose teas and Chinese teapots.

🎊 Festivals & Events

Melaka celebrates all the major Malaysian holidays, including Chinese New Year, Thaipusam and National Day. While the festivals here might not be as big as in KL or Penang, they are more manageable and intimate.

Masimugam Festival   RELIGIOUS
A Malaccan version of Thaipusam, just as gory but without the crowds, takes place shortly after Chinese New Year in Kampong Cheng, about 15km outside Melaka city in February/March.

THE ADMIRABLE ADMIRAL CHENG HO

At the age of 13, Cheng Ho (Zheng He) was castrated and became a eunuch servant to the Chinese emperor's fourth son, Prince Zhu Di. He proved an exceptional servant, and later became an army officer and ultimately the admiral of China's 'Treasure Fleet', a convoy that solidified China's control over most of Asia during the 15th century. The admiral visited Melaka at least five times during his extraordinary voyages and set up a warehouse complex somewhere along the northern side of Sungai Melaka (Melaka River) – the exact location is unknown.

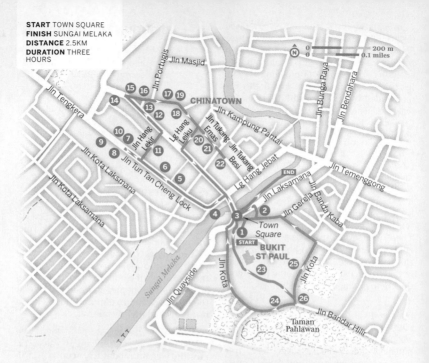

Walking Tour
Melaka's Chinatown

❯ Melaka's Chinatown is a compact area packed to the brim with interesting edifices and museums. This tour takes you to the principal sights but you'll find plenty of other ones on your own to entertain you along the way.

Start at the delightful Town Square, Melaka's historic hub. The most imposing relic of the Dutch period in Melaka is the ❶ **Stadthuys**, the salmon-pink town hall and governor's residence, and a significant example of colonial Dutch architecture dating back to 1641. Exit the Stadthuys and contemplate ❷ **Christ Church**. Dutch and Armenian tombstones still lie in the floor of the church's interior, while the massive 15m-long ceiling beams overhead were each cut from a single tree. Sit down and admire the marvellous ❸ **fountain** in Town Square, emblazoned with four bas-relief images of Queen Victoria and affixed with an inscribed plaque.

Walk northwest across the bridge over Sungai Melaka. Turn left and stroll along Jln Tun Tan Cheng Lock. Formerly called Heeren St, this narrow thoroughfare was the preferred address for wealthy Baba traders who were most active during the short-lived rubber boom of the early 20th century. These typical Peranakan houses fuse Chinese, Dutch and British influences in a style that has been described as Chinese Palladian and Chinese baroque. A finely restored example of this architectural style can be found at ❹ **8 Heeren St**.

An intriguing insight into the local vernacular can be gleaned from the ❺ **Baba-Nonya Heritage Museum**. Pop into ❻ **Malaqa House** and pick over its hoard of antiques before continuing to the elegant ❼ **Hotel Puri**; the Chinese characters emblazoned on the door literally mean 'Longevity Mountain, Fortuitous Sea'. Opposite, the impressive classical-style building set back from the street is the ❽ **Chee Mansion**, a Chinese family shrine not open to the public.

Another traditional house now serving as a hotel, ❾ **Baba House**, is just ahead. The ❿ **Eng Choon (Yong Chun) Association** is an impressively well-kept Chinese guildhall containing a small shrine to two Taoist deities. Admire the painted gods on the doors and the carved dragons adorning the stone pillars. Chinese characters written on the building mean 'peace to the country and the people' – which you see elsewhere in Chinatown.

Backtrack along Jln Tun Tan Cheng Lock and walk north up Jln Hang Lekir. Opposite **Howard's restaurant** is the dignified ⓫ **Leong San Thong** (Dragon Hill Hall), built in 1928. At the junction, turn left onto Jln Hang Jebat, formerly known as Jonker's St, once famed for its antique and craft shops and still a great street to peruse.

Continuing northwest, you'll approach the all-white ⓬ **Hang Kasturi's Tomb** on your right; there is no historical evidence that the tomb is the final resting place of the great warrior. Beyond here is the tempting ⓭ **Putuo Traditional Chinese Medicine Therapy Centre** – just the spot for a revitalising foot massage and doses of reflexology. Further along on your left is the small, modern and pink ⓮ **Guanyin Temple** (Guanyin Tang), dedicated to the Buddhist goddess of compassion. Seated in the second hall is the Taoist Jade Emperor, flanked by two attendants.

Turn right here and head up Jln Tokong (Temple St) and past a couple of small Chinese shrines, the ⓯ **Wah Teck Kiong Temple** and the ⓰ **Guangfu Temple** (Guangfu Gong). Ahead is the ⓱ **Wan Aik Shoemaker** shop on your left – the specialist manufacturer crafts doll-like shoes for bound feet, once the height of gruesome fashion for well-to-do Chinese women in Melaka.

Chinatown's most elaborate and celebrated Chinese temple, the ⓲ **Cheng Hoon Teng Temple**, is opposite the more recently constructed ⓳ **Xianglin (Fragrant Forest) Temple**, which endeavours to follow the layout of a traditional Chinese Buddhist temple. Adding splashes of colour to Jln Tokong are the Chinese shops selling red and gold lanterns, paper money and funerary preparations. The street used to be famed for its goldsmiths, but most have moved to other areas.

Continue southeast to the ⓴ **Kampung Kling Mosque** with its multitiered, stacked meru roof reminiscent of Balinese Hindu architecture, and then further along to the ㉑ **Sri Poyatha Venayagar Moorthi Temple**, one of the first Hindu temples built in the country, in 1781. Slightly further ahead is the ㉒ **Sanduo Temple** (Sanduo Miao), another Chinese shrine encapsulating effigies of Da Bo Gong, Jin Hua Niang Niang (whom women entreat for children) and Kuan Yin.

Backtrack and turn left along the exterior wall of the mosque back along Lg Hang Lekui (Fourth Cross St) to Jln Hang Jebat. Stroll back to Lg Hang Jebat (First Cross St) and the bridge, noting the decorative touches along the way – mosaics, tiling, inlaid coloured stones, carvings, Western-style balustrades, balconies, shutters and ornamentation.

Traverse the bridge, cross Town Square back to the Stadthuys and clamber up the steps leading to the top of Bukit St Paul, topped by the fabulous ruins of ㉓ **St Paul's Church**.

There are steps from St Paul's Church down the hill to ㉔ **Porta de Santiago**, once the main gate of the Portuguese fortress A'Famosa, originally constructed by Alfonso de Albuquerque in 1512.

To the northeast, at the base of Bukit St Paul, is the ㉕ **Sultanate Palace**. Across the way, in a British villa dating from 1911 is the ㉖ **Proclamation of Independence Memorial**, a museum charting the history of Malaysia's progression to independence. There's too much to read and perhaps not enough to look at (although the Japanese officer's sword from occupation days is noteworthy). Ironically, this grand building topped by Mogul-inspired domes was once the Malacca Club, a bastion of colonialism.

Follow Jln Kota around the base of Bukit St Paul and head back to Town Square. Conclude your walk by ambling along the short brick promenade on the eastern bank of Sungai Melaka (parallel with Jln Laksmana), and take in riverine views, bars, the occasional barber and walls of distinctive Dutch bricks.

Easter
RELIGIOUS

Good Friday and Easter Sunday processions are held outside at St Peter's Church in March/April.

Melaka Historical City Day
PUBLIC HOLIDAY

Public holiday on 15 April in celebration of the founding of Melaka.

Vesak Day Parade
RELIGIOUS

Celebrates the birth, enlightenment and death of Buddha on the first full moon of the fourth month of the Chinese calendar (May). In Melaka there is a big and colourful parade.

Festa San Juan
RELIGIOUS

In late June, just before the Festa San Pedro, Melaka's Eurasian community hosts this festival at the chapel on top of St John's Hill.

Festa San Pedro
RELIGIOUS

Honouring this patron saint of the Portuguese fishing community, celebrations take place at St Peter's Church in late June and normally include a float procession from the Porta de Santiago to Medan Portugis, with cooking, fishing, handicraft and carnival festivities.

Dragon Boat Festival
DRAGON BOAT

This Chinese festival, marked by a dragon-boat race in the Strait of Melaka in June/July, commemorates the death by drowning of 3rd-century BC Chinese poet and statesman Qu Yuan.

Hungry Ghosts (Phor Thor) Festival
RELIGIOUS

Smaller than the same festival in Penang, the Melaka version in August is still worthwhile. Offerings and prayers are given to dead relatives who are temporarily released to roam the earth.

Festa Santa Cruz
RELIGIOUS

This festival in mid-September finishes with a candlelight procession of Malaccan and Singaporean Catholics to Malim chapel.

Melaka Festival
ARTS

A new performance, art and film fest that draws artists from around the world livens up Melaka's historical sites for three days at the end of November. See www.melaka festival.com for details.

Christmas
RELIGIOUS

Malaccans descend on Medan Portugis to view the brightly decorated homes.

🛏 Sleeping

Note that many midrange and top-end hotels raise their tariffs on Friday and Saturday night and during holidays or peak season.

CHINATOWN

Ever since Melaka's Chinatown was named a Unesco World Heritage Site new hotels and guesthouses have been opening at an alarming rate. Staying in Chinatown puts you in the heart of the action and restaurants and activities are just a short stroll from your door. Noise can be a problem, however, especially on weekends when the Jonker's Walk Night Market buzzes on till about 11pm and cars clog the streets during the day from an early hour. Masjid Kampung Kling starts its call to prayer at 5.30am and is especially loud along Jln Tunang Emas.

TOP CHOICE Heeren House
GUESTHOUSE $$

(✆281 4241; www.melaka.net/heeren house; 1 Jln Tun Tan Cheng Lock; s RM119-139, d RM129-149, f RM259; ❀) Lodging here positions you right in the heart of Chinatown, on the waterfront and within range of top local restaurants and sights. The airy, clean and lovely rooms (six in all) in this former warehouse largely overlook the river, and have polished floorboards, traditional furniture (some with four-poster beds) and clean showers. The least expensive room (with twin beds and no river view) on the ground floor is the best choice when the weather is very hot; it stays cool in the shade of a mango tree right outside. A popular cafe is in the foyer and breakfast comes with the price of the room.

TOP CHOICE River View Guesthouse
GUESTHOUSE $

(✆012 327 7746; riverviewguesthouse@yahoo.com; 94 & 96 Jln Kampung Pantai; r RM45-60; ❀@🛜) Bordering the ambient riverfront promenade, this immaculate guesthouse is housed in a large heritage building. Plenty of detail such as some beautiful deteriorating wall coloration and the old heavy wood staircase have been left intact but rooms are modern and exceedingly comfortable. There's a big shared kitchen and common area and the hosts begin your stay with a handy map of town and directions to all their favourite sights and restaurants. Homemade cake is often on offer and you can choose to get through town via the serene riverside promenade at the back door rather than the busy streets of Chinatown at the front.

TOP CHOICE Hotel Puri
HOTEL $$

(☑282 5588; www.hotelpuri.com; 118 Jln Tun Tan Cheng Lock; r RM120-500; ✳🛜) One of Chinatown's gems, Hotel Puri is an elegant creation in a superb old renovated Peranakan mansion. Its elaborate lobby, decked out with beautiful old cane and inlaid furniture, opens to a gorgeous courtyard garden (a wi-fi area) that leads to a 'history room' where guests can peruse Melaka's past through books and photographs. Standard rooms have butter-yellow walls, crisp sheets, satellite TV, wi-fi and shuttered windows. There's an on-site spa (Biossentials Puri Spa, p125), and breakfast, taken in the courtyard or air-conditioned dining area, is included.

Courtyard@Heeren
HOTEL $$

(☑281 0088; www.courtyardatheeren.com; 91 Jln Tun Tan Cheng Lock; d RM200-250, f RM 250-300, ste RM300-400; ✳🛜) Modern rooms here are each decorated uniquely with light and bright decor paired with antique wood furniture. Some have minimalist arty stained-glass details, modern takes on Chinese latticework or drapey canopies. Not many rooms have windows but there's plenty of light pouring in from the open central courtyard. It's very professionally run with great service.

Number Twenty Guesthouse
GUESTHOUSE $$

(☑281 9761; www.twentymelaka.com; 20 Jln Hang Jebat; d incl breakfast RM95-105; 🛜✳) A 1673 Dutch mansion meets urban-Zen chic at these stylish digs, maintaining a perfect balance of old and new with its dark-wood-beam construction and high ceilings, a touch of Chinese art, low opium beds and modern lighting. The common area has elongated windows that look over Jln Hang Jebat, and you can kick back on plush, soft couches and watch DVDs on the plasma TV. Not all rooms have windows, but you can always get a little air on the rooftop garden. All rooms here have shared bathrooms. It's gay friendly.

Jonker Boutique Hotel
HOTEL $$

(☑282 5151; www.jonkerboutiquehotel.com; 52 Jln Tun Tan Cheng Lock; s/d incl breakfast RM50/80; ✳🛜) Each of the large rooms here are different but decorated in a similar style using modern black-and-cream patterned wallpaper paired with neutral-coloured walls. Most rooms have windows, and bathrooms have retro black-and-white tiles. It's well run and centrally located, but be prepared for some street noise on Friday and Saturday nights

when the night market's on. Room rates go up by about 30% on weekends and holidays.

Hangout@Jonker
HOTEL $$

(☑282 8318; www.hangouthotels.com; 19 & 21 Jln Hang Jebat; s/d/tr incl light breakfast RM100/140/180; ✳@🛜) Opened as a second site by a popular hostel in Singapore, the Jonker location shares the same high standards of cleanliness and amenities (hangout lounges, free movies, tea and coffee and internet) as its Singaporean sister but the sterile, spare modern style of concrete, tile and turquoise-and-white walls is a little out of place in Melaka. Despite the fact that the staff were still learning the ropes when we passed, this place is a good comfortable deal on weekdays – prices go up 20% on weekends and holidays.

Cafe 1511 Guesthouse
GUESTHOUSE $

(☑286 0150; www.cafe1511.com; 52 Jln Tun Tan Cheng Lock; s/d incl breakfast RM50/80; @🛜) Next door to the Baba-Nonya Heritage Museum in another beautiful Peranakan mansion, the small, simple, spotless rooms here are jazzed up by tasteful international art on the walls. The place has an old-style feeling, set to the music of a water fountain in the light-well that extends from the restaurant below. You get 20% off admission to the adjacent museum when you stay here but note that the guesthouse doesn't take guests under 30 years old – in other words, this isn't a place to party.

Casa Del Rio
HOTEL $$$

(☑292 1113; www.casadelrio-melaka.com; 88 Jln Kota Laksmana; r from RM492; ✳🛜🏊) This place was under construction and only a brick shell when we passed, but it's poised to be the biggest hotel in the Chinatown heritage area with a fabulous location right on the river. The architecture blends Portuguese with Malaysian for a much more modern look than what's available nearby and the 66 rooms are to follow cue with planned Mediterranean flair. There will also be 32 apartments available for longer-term stays.

Jalan Jalan Guesthouse
GUESTHOUSE $

(☑283 3937; www.jalanjalanguesthouse.com; 8 Jln Tukang Emas; dm RM12 s/d RM23/35; @🛜) A lovely hostel in a restored old shophouse painted periwinkle blue. Fan-cooled rooms with one shared bathroom are spread out over a tranquil inner garden-courtyard. As with some other older places, though, noise from your neighbours might keep you awake at night. The hosts get great reviews and there's bike rental available.

Sama-Sama Guest House   GUESTHOUSE $
(☎305 1980; www.sama-sama-guesthouse.com; 26 Jl Tukang Besi; dm RM12, d RM20-34) This place has a great hippie-ish vibe, with a courtyard overflowing with potted plants, mini-ponds and wind chimes. Rooms are intimately linked by creaky wood floors and the breezes that run through the wide walkways. The whole place, including the shared toilets and showers, is kept relatively clean but when anyone walks down the hall (usually barefooted) it sounds like they are stomping in combat boots. Not for light sleepers but a fun and quirky place to meet other travellers.

Tang House   GUESTHOUSE $
(☎628 3969; www.tanghouse.com.my; 80-1 Jln Tokong; s RM35, d RM55-70 incl breakfast; ❋@☎) Feel at home in tiny, shiny hardwood-floor rooms above a stylish, family-run coffee shop right in the heart of Chinatown. All rooms have air-con, are sparsely decorated with mattresses on the floor and share a bathroom. There's a deck hangout area with cooking facilities and an all-round friendly vibe.

Ringo's Foyer   GUESTHOUSE $
(☎016 354 2223; www.ringosfoyer.com.my; 46A Jln Portugis; dm RM13, s/d/tr from RM30/35/50; ❋☎) Just far enough from central Chinatown to be quiet, but close enough to be convenient, Ringo's is plain and clean, and has friendly staff and a relaxing rooftop chill-out area that plays host to impromptu barbeques. Guitars are available for guest use and played regularly by the staff, and there are also bikes for rent.

Chong Hoe Hotel   HOTEL $
(☎282 6102; 26 Jln Tukang Emas; s/d RM30/48; ❋) Chong Ho has stayed true to its no-frills functional personality and now, after all the years of staying exactly the same, it has an unpretentious charm that's lacking elsewhere. Air-con rooms with bathrooms are some of the cheapest in town and (except when Masjid Kampung Kling starts its call to prayer) it's a quiet and blissfully unexciting place to catch some Zs.

Aldy Hotel   HOTEL $$
(☎283 3232; www.aldyhotel.com.my; 27 Jln Kota; d RM118-280, r/ste from RM140/240; ❋☎) Standing out like a red, sore thumb atop a bistro opposite the foot of Bukit St Paul, this hotel

has a location to die for and is a good choice for families. Old grey carpet and decades-old decor darken the halls but things perk up a little bit in the small rooms, which are modern and equipped with satellite TV. A rooftop Jacuzzi adds to the package. There's no additional charge for children under 12 sharing a room with parents but room rates go up during holidays and peak season. Prices include a set breakfast.

Voyage Guest House   GUESTHOUSE $
(☎281 5216; Jln Tukang Besi; dm RM12) Clean, industrial-sized dorm rooms and common areas are decorated with a nouveau heritage Chinatown jazz-lounge look. It's run by Voyager Travellers Lounge (p136).

Kota Lodge   HOTEL $
(☎281 6512; Jln Taman Kota; hotelkl8@streamyx. com; r RM36-90; ❋) Heritage not your thing? Kota Lodge offers freshly painted character-less rooms all with good beds, air-con and hot showers. It's stumbling distance from central Chinatown – just follow the signs on Jln Tun Tan Cheng Lock.

Baba House   HOTEL $$
(☎281 1216; www.malacca.ws/babahouse; 125-127 Jln Tun Tan Cheng Lock; r RM86-180; ❋) In a row of restored Peranakan shophouses, this elegant Baba building is beautifully arranged with tilework, carved panels and a cool interior courtyard. Rooms, many windowless, aren't nearly as glitzy as the lobby and, even after a recent remodel, are dark and drab. Some claim the hotel is haunted but the spooks appear to be friendly in nature.

TAMAN MELAKA RAYA & AROUND

This area is close to the shopping malls and is a short walk to busy Chinatown. It's not as exciting or scenic as staying in Chinatown but many of these places offer a much quieter sleep.

TOP CHOICE **Apa Kaba Home & Stay**
  GUESTHOUSE $
(☎283 8196; apakaba28@gmail.com; 28 Kg Banda Kaba; r RM40-70 incl breakfast; ❋☎) Just when people start talking about Melaka loosing its soul, this place comes along. Nestled in a quiet and authentic Malay *kampung* that seems to magically float in a bubble in the heart of town, this homestay-style guest-house is in a simple yet beautiful old Malay house complete with creaky wood floors, louvred shutters and bright paint. You can chill out in the enormous garden (look for ripe mangos) or take a stroll out the back

gate through tiny lanes that meander straight into Chinatown. The owners take great care of their guests providing heaps of pointers around town and serving delicious breakfasts of Malay treats as well as toast for the less adventurous. It's about the quietest place in Melaka for a good night's sleep but note that the couple does have well-behaved small children who giggle or fuss from time to time.

Hotel Equatorial
HOTEL $$
(282 8333; www.equatorial.com; Jln Parameswara; r from RM250; ✳🗠🛋) Hotel Equatorial can't be beat for its location near the historic centre. While it's a bit frayed around the edges, this somehow just adds to the old charm of the hotel. Good discounts online can cut prices nearly in half, making this elegant choice excellent value. Service is well mannered and the overall presentation is crisp. There's a swimming pool, ladies-only pool, a quality fitness centre, tennis court and wi-fi access. It's worth upgrading to one of the deluxe rooms (RM500), which have either balconies or heaps of extra room space. Special packages are available through the hotel, including tours and specials such as cookery courses (p125). Check online for deals including a RM88 meal credit included in the price of the room.

Kancil Guest House
GUESTHOUSE $
(281 4044; www.machinta.com.sg/kancil; 177 Jln Parameswara; s/tw/d RM20/40/50; @) West of the small Taoist Yong Chuan Tian Temple, about a ten-minute walk from the city centre, this pleasant guesthouse offers spacious, secure lodgings on a road studded with picturesque Malaccan houses. The road itself is lethal with traffic, but the house is lovely, deep and quiet with large open hallways, grand staircases and plenty of day-lit spaces for lounging, drinking tea or reading a book from the library. There's a gorgeous garden out back, and the owners are pleasant and helpful. Bike rental is available and bus 17 from Melaka Sentral passes by here.

Emily Travellers Home
GUESTHOUSE $
(012 301 8574; 71 Jln Parameswara; dm/s RM16/24, d RM32-48; W) Enter the humble entrance off the busy road and it feels like you've stepped into another dimension filled with plants, koi ponds, a bunny hopping around (named Mr Playboy) and happy, mingling people. Every room in the heritage building and its annexes is different, from funky cottages with semi-outdoor

'jungle showers' to simple wooden rooms in the house – the dorm rooms have only two beds apiece. The whole place is decorated with recycled or found objects including a very cool coffee table that transforms into a BBQ. Rates include breakfast and all-day tea or coffee.

Malacca Straits Hotel
HOTEL $$
(286 1888; www.malaccastraitshotel.com.my; 27 Jln Chan Koon Cheng; r RM138, ste 198-268 incl breakfast; ✳🗠🛋) Smack up against Hotel Equatorial, this hotel calls itself a 'batik boutique' hotel, and it's not a bad description. While the hotel opened in 2007, it's a remodel of an older building so the hallways and lobby area still have the lingering air of a cheesy business hotel. The spacious rooms, however, have been given greater attention and are furnished with some exquisite teak furniture including four-poster beds in every room and batik fabrics everywhere. While standard rooms all have bathtubs, an upgrade to a suite adds a Jacuzzi. Don't overlook the authentic *songket* (gold-and-silver-threaded fabric) that lines the hallways and, of course, the smiling service. The à la carte breakfast is served at the on-site cafe. Prices go up about 25% on weekends and holidays.

Samudra Inn
GUESTHOUSE $
(282 7441; samudrainn@hotmail.com; 348B Jln Melaka Raya 3; dm RM15, s RM28-50, d RM30-60, tr RM60; ✳@) A short walk from the historic centre, this charming place is for lovers of peace and quiet. Caged birds chirp softly in the courtyard area but, other than that, you won't hear a peep out of anyone. TV time (satellite) is till 10pm and there are kitchen facilities if you want to cook. The ex-teacher owners take extra steps to make sure their guests are comfortable and treat you like family. You won't find a more secure or wholesome place. Pricier rooms have a shower and balcony, and laundry service is available.

Holiday Inn
HOTEL $$
(255 9000; www.melaka.holidayinn.com; Jln Sayed Abdul Aziz; r from RM221; ✳@🗠🛋) Boldly facing historic Melaka like a gleaming white, middle finger, this Holiday Inn is absurdly tall and doesn't have a single heritage quality about it. Rooms are comfy, new and carpeted yet bland. Ask for a top-storey room for fantastic views over the Straits of Melaka. The location near the pier isn't too far from Chinatown and is very near the shopping malls and even closer to Melaka's biggest

karaoke complex at the end of the pier (staff will even drive you there in a golf cart).

Hotel Ninety-Six — HOTEL $$

(☎288 1906; www.hotel906.com; 22 Jln Melaka Raya 15; d/tr/f RM98/136/176; ✸@☎) This is the best of a new cluster of fairly bland mid-range hotels located just a little too far away from the action – about 15 to 20 minutes' walk to Chinatown. The hotel itself is clean and modern with well-functioning air-con, new sheets, plenty of hot water and TVs in all the rooms. It's a bargain if you don't mind walking a lot in the hot sun. Prices go up 20% on Saturdays and 30% during holidays.

Fenix Inn — HOTEL $$

(☎281 5511; www.fenixinn.com; 156 Jln Taman Melaka Raya; d RM112-158; ✸@☎) Efficiency is the name and business is the game at this crisp hotel. Rooms are small and character-less but have clean carpets and coffee- and tea-making appliances; most have a window. Polite management, drinking water on each floor and a business centre with a good crop of terminals (RM2.5 per hour), copier and fax make this a good place for people working on the road. Prices go up about 15% on weekends and holidays.

Travellers' Lodge — HOSTEL $

(☎226 5709; 214B Jln Melaka Raya 1; d from RM30; ✸☎) Once one of the more popular backpacker places in town, the Travellers' Lodge is seeing hard times with all the new places opening up in Chinatown. Unfortunately instead of trying to woo new guests, management seems to have given up. There's still the kick-up-your-feet common area, rooftop garden and a huge assortment of good rooms so we can only hope that management will get a second wind and brighten the place up again.

LITTLE INDIA TO BUKIT CHINA

The few top-end establishments in Melaka are nearly all clustered in this area along or near busy Jln Bendahara in Little India. While this might be convenient for people coming to Melaka on business, it's a little chaotic for the casual visitor. It is, however, a short walk to all the sites.

TOP CHOICE Majestic Malacca — HOTEL $$$

(☎289 8000; www.majesticmalacca.com; 188 Jln Bunga Raya; r from US$335; ✸@☎✖) This is Melaka's most elegant choice. It's an interesting mix: the lobby is in a 1920s colonial Chinese mansion and looks quite unassuming from the exterior while the bulk of the hotel is in a tasteful modern building behind. Rooms continue with this old and new theme with hardwood floors, sheer ivory-coloured drapes and heritage-style wood furnishings (including replica claw-footed bathtubs) – yet all are very modern in their sublime level of comfort. Of course the place is stacked with amenities including a small outdoor swimming pool, a gym, a top-notch spa (all services include a 30-minute traditional Malay hair treatment), a library and stellar service. It's a lovely place but the price tag is a little exaggerated considering the size and location of the grounds.

Renaissance Melaka Hotel — HOTEL $$$

(☎284 8888; infomkz@po.jaring.my; Jln Bendahara; r/ste from RM400/435; ☎✖) The ritziest of Melaka's long-standing hotels, the Renaissance offers good service and slightly dated luxury. Large windows in the rooms take advantage of views that sweep over Melaka in all directions, while the spacious rooms, equipped with comfy Renaissance beds, are modern while incorporating classic Chinese touches. Suites aren't really worth the extra money unless you really need a windowless cave attached to your room. Build up a sweat on the squash courts or at a yoga class then sink a drink in the pub (with regular live music).

Bayview Hotel — HOTEL $$

(☎283 9888; www.bayviewhotels.com/melaka; Jln Bendahara; r from RM265; ✸☎✖) This hotel has a lively edge with a sports bar, smallish kidney-shaped pool and a dance club. Sheets and all bedding are new and crisp, and the views over the old town from some rooms are quite spectacular. This is a favourite with families (check for special family packages on the website), and kids will enjoy the rather weird computerised speaking lift. The glass lobby is refreshingly modern for such a historically oriented town.

Old Town Family Guesthouse — GUESTHOUSE $

(☎286 0796; www.melakaguesthouse.com; 119 Jln Temenggong; dm/s RM18/30, d RM30-50, tr/q from RM45/60; ✸☎) This basic French-Malay–run backpackers gets more points for its low-key ambience, cleanliness and friendly, helpful owners than for its plain but perfectly passable rooms. It's in the second storey of an apartment-type building but is quite spacious with plenty of tiled, open spaces for lounging. A toast-and-coffee breakfast is included, making this an all-round bargain. It's a good choice for families and has a kitchen for guests' use.

Eastern Heritage Guest House

GUESTHOUSE $

(☑283 3026; www.eastern-heritage.com; 8 Jln Bukit China; dm RM10, r RM26-30) It has become pretty grotty over the years but this place, housed in a crumbling 1918 mansion with Peranakan tiling, carved panelling and lots of open spaces with natural light, still holds enough charm for us to list it. Think old-school backpackers with shared dingy toilets and an adventurous Eastern feel. This is where you'd find the bad guy secretly assembling his bomb in a Bond flick. There's a dipping pool, sunroof area, a downstairs common room. The upstairs dorm is airless and bland but rooms are brightened up by murals on the walls.

Tony's Guesthouse GUESTHOUSE $

(☑688 0119; 24 Lg Banda Kaba; r from RM30; 🛜) This is a scatterbrained, hippie backpackers' place that looks like an appealingly untidy artist's living room. The host couldn't be friendlier and it's a great place to meet other budget road warriors over tea.

✖ Eating

Melaka's food reflects the city's eclectic, multicultural DNA. Nonya cuisine (prepared here with a salty Indonesian influence) is a celebrated school of cooking that stars the classic dish of Melaka, laksa. It's also the home of Portuguese Eurasian food: mostly seafood and rice, but the fiery 'devil curry' is worth an encounter. Melaka's Chinese speciality is chicken rice ball, a Hokkien-style chicken served with rice that is rolled up into savoury ping-pong-ball-sized dumplings.

Eats on the streets include *youtiao* (fried bread sticks; 40 sen), *rougan* (dried meat strips; RM26 for 250gms) and Nonya pineapple tarts. Look out for Chinese pharmacies serving tall glasses of chrysanthemum tea (RM2) on tables in front of their shops.

Most restaurants are open from 11.30am to 10pm, while more simple cafes open around 10am and close at about 5pm.

CHINATOWN

TOP CHOICE Pak Putra Restaurant INDIAN $$

(56 Jln Taman Kota Laksmana; tandoori from RM8; ☺dinner, closed every other Mon) This fabulous Pakistani place cooks up a variety of meats and seafood in clay tandoori ovens perched on the footpath. Apart from the tandoori try the *taw* prawns (cooked with onion, yoghurt and coriander, RM11) or mutton rogan josh (in onion gravy with spices and chilli oil, RM9). Side dishes of veg are around RM6 and a mango lassi costs RM4. Everything is so good that dinner conversation is often reduced to ohs and ahs of gustatory delight.

TOP CHOICE Low Yong Mow DIM SUM $

(☑282 1235; Jln Tokong; dim sum RM1-8; ☺5am-noon, closed Tue) Famous Malaysia-wide for large and delectably well-stuffed *pao* (steamed pork buns), this place is Chinatown's biggest breakfast treat. With high ceilings, plenty of fans running and a view of Masjid Kampung Kling, the atmosphere oozes all the charms of Chinatown. Take your pick from the endless variety of dumplings, sticky-rice dishes and mysterious treats that are wheeled to your table. It's great for early-bus-departure breakfasts and is usually packed with talkative, newspaper-reading locals by around 7am.

Nancy's Kitchen NONYA $$

(15 Jln Hang Lekir; meals RM10; ☺11am-5.30pm, closed Tue) In a town already known for its graciousness, this home-cooking Nonya restaurant is our favourite for friendly service. If you want an intimate meal, head elsewhere. The server is as chatty and full of suggestions as they come, and will have you making conversation with the other handful of customers in no time. It's like a happy dinner (or lunch) party with particularly good food. Try the house speciality, chicken candlenut.

Donald & Lily's NONYA $

(☑284 8907; snacks RM3; ☺9.30am-4pm, closed Tue) Just finding this place is an adventure. Take the alleyway on your left that runs behind Heeren Inn from Jln Hang Kasturi. You'll see a little stairway behind 31 Jln Tun Tan Chen Lock leading to hidden but very popular Donald & Lily's. Why bother looking? This is Melaka locals' favourite stop for the regional-style laksa and Nonya *cendol* (a popular dessert). The setting is like being in someone's living room and the service is beaming.

TOP CHOICE Howard's INTERNATIONAL $$$

(☑286 8727; 5 Jln Hang Lekir; meals RM40; ☺lunch & dinner Wed-Mon) A finely crafted ambience of creaseless linen, elegant furniture, black-and-white check tile floor, flavoursome international cuisine (lobster bisque, roast

ⓘ WHERE'S THE HAWKER FOOD?

Unlike Kuala Lumpur and Penang, Melaka isn't packed with hawker centres and food courts. Many of the areas that used to have food stalls have had buildings pop up on top of them in the city's development rush, but there are still a few good places around town to glean food from a cart:

Jonker's Walk Night Market (Jln Hang Jebat) One of the best parts of this famous night market is the food. Graze on fried dumplings on a stick and quaff sugarcane juice, fresh fruit juices, soy milk and chestnut or chrysanthemum tea.

Hang Tuah Mall (Jln Hang Tuah) This pedestrian walk swarms with open-air food stalls every evening and is the best place to go if you're looking for the hawker food experience.

Centrepoint food court (Jln Munshi Abdullah) Seek out Indian and Malay treats for lunch.

Newton Food Court (Jln Merdeka) Serving Chinese food in the main hall and Halal at the back, just west of Mahkota Parade shopping complex, this hawker centre used to be good but had just lost some of its better vendors when we passed. Others might replace them so go and check it out.

Malay hawker centre (just east of the base of Jln Melaka Raya 3 on Jln Syed Abdul Aziz) This covered area serves everything from fresh juices to fish-head curry and Nonya food.

rack of lamb) and unobtrusive service, Howard's is a thoroughly unhurried and intimate experience and a top romantic dining choice. Topped off with an impressive wine list, this is definitely Chinatown's swankiest choice.

Vegetarian Restaurant　　　　VEGETARIAN $
(43 Jln Hang Lekui; mains around RM3; ☉7.30am-2.30pm Mon-Sat; 🖉) Every Chinatown needs its basic vegetarian cafe and this is Melaka's. All the local specialties from laksa and wonton mee to 'fish balls' are here but, although they taste as good as the real thing, are completely meat-free. There's a different special every day and the staff, though they might not speak much English, will try to help you order through plenty of giggling.

Ocean Cafe　　　　　　　　NONYA $
(☎698 4917; 20 Jln Tokong; mains RM4-8; ☉10am-6pm closed Tue) In this unassuming spot you'll be treated with phenomenal local laksa along with the best, most finely spiced chicken rendang we've ever tasted. The sign on this place read 'Wo Hup Koh' when we passed but that's not its name so the signage may change; you can easily find it from the street address.

Heeren House　　　　　　　WESTERN $$
(☎281 4241; 1 Jln Tun Tan Cheng Lock; meals around RM12; ☉7.30am-6pm; 🖉) In the hotel of the same name, this is a lunch or breakfast spot for healthy Western breakfasts, a light meal of quiches and salads, and yummy brownies. You can browse the integrated shop for a wonderful selection of upscale batik and

other crafts from all around Southeast Asia, while you wait for your food to arrive.

Baboon House　　　　　　　BURGERS $$
(89 Jln Tun Tan Cheng Hok; burgers around RM14; ☉10am-5pm Mon-Thu, till 7pm Fri-Sun; @🛜) Right next to the Courtyard@Heeren Hotel, this cafe housed in a long Peranakan-style building with a light and plant-filled courtyard specialises in burgers on homemade buns. Try the spicy beef or lamb, teriyaki pork or egg, bacon and cheese burgers served with salad and fries. There's also a special burger of the day, exotic desserts, fresh juices, tea, coffee and beer.

Cafe 1511　　　　　NONYA & WESTERN $$
(☎286 0151; www.cafe1511.com; 52 Jln Tun Tan Cheng Lock; meals RM10; ☉9am-6pm, closed Wed; @) Next to the Baba-Nonya Heritage Museum is this high-ceilinged Peranakan cafe, with original tiles along the wall, lovely carved screens, a mishmash of decorative objects from Southeast Asia and a reasonably good Nonya and Western menu. There's a computer for guests and this is one of the few places in Chinatown where you'll find a Western set breakfast (RM6) at an early-ish hour.

Harper's Cafe　　　　　　　FUSION $$$
(2 & 4 Lg Hang Jebat; meals RM40; ☉4pm-1am Mon & Wed-Sat, 11am-1am Sun) Perched elegantly over Sungai Melaka, breezy Harper's serves excellent (though small) Malay-European fusion dishes in a rather stark decor. It's worth visiting for the food, though the service can be slow.

Limau-Limau Cafe
WESTERN $$
(☑698 4917; 9 Jln Hang Lekui; fruit juice from RM6, mains from RM7; @🎵🍴) Decorated with dark-coloured ceramics and an arty twist, this long-running quiet cafe moved to its current location in 2010 but still serves the same predictably good salads, sandwiches, fruit juices and milk shakes. It's also a mellow stop for internet and wi-fi.

Poh Piah Lwee
NONYA $
(Jln Kibu; ⊘9am-5pm) An authentic and lively hole in the wall with one specialist cook preparing delicious Hokkein-style *popiah* (RM2), another making near-perfect *rojak* (RM3) while the third whips up a fantastic laksa (RM3).

Hoe Kee Chicken Rice
CHICKEN RICE BALL $$$
(4 Jln Hang Jebat; meals around RM18; ⊘8.30am-3pm, closed last Wed of month) Melaka's busiest restaurant serves the local specialities, chicken rice ball and *asam* fish head (fish heads in a spicy tamarind gravy). You'll need to arrive here off-hours or expect to wait, especially on weekends. Is it worth it? The restaurant's setting, with wood floors and ceiling fans, is lovely; the food can be hit or miss (ask if the fish is fresh) and it's undeniably touristy.

TAMAN MELAKA RAYA & AROUND

Restoran Amituofoh
VEGETARIAN $
(☑292 6426; 2-20 Jln PM9, Plaza Mahkota, Bandar Hilir; meals free, contributions welcome; ⊘breakfast, lunch & dinner; 🍴) Conventional wisdom dictates that there's no such thing as a free meal. This Buddhist vegetarian restaurant – the gift of a Chinese philanthropist – generously breaks the rules by providing food on the house. You may make a contribution (and we advise you do); otherwise there are a few conditions: you must wash your own plates and cutlery, and taking food away is not permitted.

Simple Life
VEGETARIAN $$
(☑281 9211; Jln Merdeka; set lunch RM10; ⊘9am-7pm; 🍴) There's an unmistakable Zen feel to this upstairs vegetarian cafe that doubles as a health-food store. Dine on simple but delicious fare including braised tofu, Asian salads and brown rice at elegant round wooden tables.

Ind Ori
INDONESIAN $$
(☑282 4777; 236 Jln Melaka Raya 1; dishes RM1-20; ⊘8am-midnight) Mmm, Indonesian padang food, fresh and heated in a point-and-ask buffet. It's just like the real thing but with-

out the flies and dubious-sanitation issues. House specialities include delicious avocado juice with chocolate sauce and *sekotang* (sweet cream-and-peanut dumplings with green beans and hot ginger).

Restoran Banya
NONYA $$
(☑282 8297; 154 Jln Taman Melaka Raya; meals RM11; ⊘10am-10pm, closed Thu) Friendly staff will help you decode the menu at this centrally located place. The reputation here isn't as strong as at some of the other Nonya restaurants in town but we found the food delicious.

Ole Sayang
NONYA $$
(☑283 1966; 198 Jln Taman Melaka Raya, meals RM15; ⊘10am-10pm, closed Wed) Come here for ambient Nonya atmosphere, decorated with old wooden furniture and dim lighting. While this place is one of the best known in Melaka, we found that the food wasn't of a higher standard than the other Nonya places around town.

Bayonya
NONYA $$
(☑292 2192; 164 Jln Taman Melaka Raya; meals RM17; ⊘10am-10pm, closed Tue) This authentic eatery is a locals' favourite for its excellent and inexpensive home-cooked Peranakan cuisine. One of the must-tries here is the durian *cendol*.

LITTLE INDIA TO BUKIT CHINA
There's a whole string of local-style Chinese cafes around Jln Bunga Raya, full of chatting locals and which serve chicken or duck rice and a selection of noodle, rice and soup dishes at very low prices.

TOP CHOICE Capitol Satay
SATAY CELUP $
(☑283 5508; 41 Lg Bukit China; meals around RM8) Famous for its *satay celup* (a Melaka adaptation of satay steamboat), this place is usually packed and is one of the cheapest outfits in town. Stainless-steel tables have bubbling vats of soup in the middle where you dunk skewers of okra stuffed with tofu, sausages, chicken, prawns and bok choy. Side dishes include pickled eggs and ginger. Dining here is not only satisfying to the gut and palate, but also great fun and a chance for some gregarious feasting.

TOP CHOICE Selvam
INDIAN $
(☑281 9223; 3 Jln Temenggong; meals around RM8; 🍴) This is a classic banana-leaf restaurant always busy with its loyal band of local patrons ordering tasty and cheap curries, roti and tandoori chicken sets. Even

MEDAN PORTUGIS

There are really not many reasons to head out to the nondescript neighbourhood of Medan Portugis other than to eat. On Friday and Saturday evenings, head to **Restoran de Lisbon** (Medan Portugis; meals RM30), where you can sample Malay-Portuguese dishes at outdoor tables. Try the delicious local specialities of chilli crabs or the distinctly Eurasian devil curry. You can also visit any of a string of other less-famous but cuisine-savvy Portuguese seafood restaurants along a reclaimed once-seafront area next to Restoran de Lisbon. There's a pier out front where you can watch plastic bags bob around in the sea.

devout carnivores will second-guess their food preferences after trying the Friday-afternoon vegetarian special with 10 varieties of veg.

Restoran Ban Lee Siang Satay Celup
SATAY CELUP **$**

(☑284 1935; 45E Jln Om Kim Wee; meals around RM8; ☺5pm-midnight) Don't feel like waiting for a table at Capitol Satay? This place is a little out of the way but locals claim the ingredients are fresher. Go pick out your skewers from the fridge then cook them in the boiling vats of delectable satay sauce.

UE Tea House
DIM SUM **$**

(20 Lg Bukit China; meals around RM8) Another dim sum place, simpler than Chinatown's Low Yong Mow, but very tasty just the same. Sip Chinese tea and gorge yourself on the impressive array of steamed dumplings.

Bulldog Cafe
NONYA & INTERNATIONAL **$$**

(☑292 1920; 145 Jln Bendahara; meals RM10) Nonya, Chinese, Thai and Western dishes are on offer at this local-feeling joint in a lovely Peranakan-style building. For cheap snacks, sample the Nonya *popiah* – lettuce, bean sprouts, egg and chilli paste in a soft sleeve (RM2) or the *pai tee* (crispy cone-shaped morsels of rice flour, stuffed with vegetables; RM3).

☕ Drinking

Melaka is studded with watering holes, and your best bet for anything from a mellow night out to a late night of drinking is in Chinatown. The Friday and Saturday night Jonker's Walk Night Market (p137) closes down Jln Hang Lekir to traffic and the handful of bars along the lane become a mini street party with tables oozing beyond the sidewalks, live music and plenty of good-natured revelry.

Bars often open at midday and, although they technically close at 1am, will stay open longer if there's enough fun still going on.

Geographér Cafe
BAR

(☑281 6813; www.geographer.com.my; 83 Jln Hang Jebat; ☺10am-1am Wed-Sun) This ventilated, breezy bar with outside seating and late hours, in a prewar corner shophouse, is a godsend. Seat yourself with a beer amid the throng and applaud long-time resident artist and musician Mr Burns as he eases through gnarled classics from Chuck Berry to JJ Cale. A tasty choice of local and Western dishes and laid-back but professional service round it all off. The apple pie (RM8) is to die for.

Voyager Travellers Lounge
CAFE BAR

(☑281 5216; 40 Lg Hang Jebat; @☎) Ease back into a wicker chair and order a cold beer (and/or an all-day Western-style breakfast) from the glowing bar built out of recycled bottles. There are often night-time activities on, from movies to mellow live music, and Yaksa, the young owner, can help arrange activities throughout Melaka.

TOP CHOICE Cheng Ho Tea House
TEAHOUSE

(Jln Tokong; ☺10am-5pm) In an exquisite setting that resembles a Chinese temple garden courtyard, relax over a pot of fine Chinese tea (from RM15) or take a tea appreciation course with owner and tea connoisseur, Pak.

Discovery Cafe
BAR

(3 Jln Bunga Raya; @) The staff take things at a serious stroll and the food is mediocre, but the location near Sungai Melaka, the late hours and the outside seating maintain a somewhat shaky allure.

☆ Entertainment

Melaka has had some glitzy entertainment on offer in the past, from a giant Ferris wheel to a once-famous sound-and-light show, but nothing has stayed in town for long. We're guessing there will be plenty more big ideas in the future but at the time of research just a few stalwarts were up and running.

The best clubs and karaoke are found in Taman Melaka Raya near Pure Bar (see below). This area is popular with locals and expats and can make for a nontouristy-feeling night of bar-hopping.

Pure Bar CLUB
(591A Taman Melaka Raya) This has been Melaka's most fun bar and nightclub for some time. Downstairs there's a young crowd boogying to hip hop while upstairs you'll often find very good cover bands (usually from the Philippines) and plenty of happy revellers north of 30. It's gay friendly and things don't get going till after about 11pm.

TOP | Eleven CLUB
CHOICE (11 Jln Hang Lekir) This is *the* place to go if you want to get your groove on in Chinatown. Yes there's hip heritage lounge-style seating and Eurasian food, but head here after around 11pm (weekends in particular) and resident DJs spin their best and the dance floor fills. It has been dubbed Melaka's only gay bar but it's a very relaxed scene and you'll find all sorts hanging out.

Arena CLUB
(Jetty) At the foot of the Jetty in front of the Holiday Inn, this glass-walled nightspot has a big stage for live bands and a hopping bar.

Golden Screen Cinemas CINEMA
(☎281 0018; 2nd fl Mahkota Pde & 3rd fl Dataran Pahlawan; tickets RM9) These silver screens show everything from Western blockbusters to Bollywood flicks.

🛍 Shopping

'Development' for Melaka has mostly meant the building of shopping malls – huge ones – that cater primarily to throngs of weekender Singaporeans looking for better prices than they find at home. For off-mall shopping, Chinatown is one of the better haunts in Malaysia.

CHINATOWN & AROUND
Taking time to browse Chinatown's eclectic mix of shops is an activity in itself. Jln Hang Jebat (Jonker's Walk or 'Junk Street') and Jln Tun Tan Cheng Lock were once famous for their antiques but there is only a handful of 'junk' shops left nowadays, jammed with ancient relics.

Other Malaccan favourites found in this area are Nonya beaded shoes or much cheaper Nonya 'clogs' (colourful flip-flops with a wooden base and a single plastic-strip upper). Browse other shops for funky Southeast Asian and Indian clothing, shoulder bags, incense, handmade tiles, charms and crystals, cheap jewellery and more. Peek into an array of silent artists' studios where you might see a painter busy at work in a back room.

TOP | Jonker's Walk Night Market
CHOICE MARKET
(Jln Hang Jebat; ◷6-11pm Fri & Sat) Melaka's weekly shopping extravaganza keeps the shops along Jln Hang Jebat open late while trinket sellers, food hawkers and the occasional fortune teller close the street to traffic. It has become far more commercial, attracting scores of Singaporean tourists over the years, but it is an undeniably colourful way to spend an evening shopping and grazing.

Top Spinning Academy TOP SPINNING
(79 Jln Tokong; ◷10am-4pm) If you enter this shop, be prepared for a very enthusiastic traditional top-spinning lesson by *gasing uri* extraordinaire Simpson Wong. You aren't expected to purchase anything, although

DON'T MISS

COCONUT KUNG FU

While enjoying the Friday and Saturday night Jonker's Night Market don't miss the performance by Kung Fu master Dr Ho Eng Hui (southern end of Jln Hang Jebat; ◷around 6.30-9pm Fri & Sat). He eats fire and throws knives, but the real reason to stick around is to see him pummel his finger into a coconut. If you're not familiar with the strength of a coconut's husk, think back to Tom Hanks in the film *Castaway*. Remember how he spends hours hurling a coconut on the rocks trying to break the damn thing open? Now, a soft human finger just shouldn't be able to pierce through a coconut's husk – but this guy's fingers really seem to do it and have been entertaining people by doing so for over 35 years. Dr Ho Eng Hui is in fact a doctor, and the purpose of his performance is to sell a 'miracle oil' (RM10) that cures aches and pains.

PASAR MALAM KAMPUNG LAPAN

This **night market** (☉5.30-7.30pm Fri & Sat) in Kampung Lapan is where locals go to buy their fruit, vegies, meat and fish. It's invariably packed and is a fun place to peruse and snack on fried dumplings, Indian cakes and fresh juices. To get there walk northwest on Jln Heeren then turn left at Masjid Tanquera (Tanquera Mosque) – it's about half an hour's walk from central Chinatown.

.you probably will if you get the hang of the spin – a top is only RM3. Mr Wong is a charming fellow who genuinely appears to just want people to play tops with him. Go in and make his day.

Orangutan House   T-SHIRTS
(59 Lg Hang Jebat; ☉10am-6pm Thu-Tue) Having mushroomed to an impressive three outlets, this hip and brightly painted T-shirt shop adds its own brand of zest and colour to Chinatown's multifaceted personality. All shirts are the work of local artist Charles Cham and have themes ranging from Chinese astrology animals to rather edgy topics (at least for Malaysia) such as 'Use Malaysian Rubber' above a sketch of a condom. Other branches are at 96 Jln Tun Tan Cheng Lok (closed Tuesday) and 12 Jln Hang Jebat (closed Thursday).

Wah Aik Shoemaker   NONYA SHOES
(56 Jln Tokong) Raymond Yeo continues the tradition begun by his grandfather in the same little shoemaker's shop that has been in his family for generations. The beaded Nonya shoes here are considered Melaka's finest and begin at a steep but merited RM300. Tiny silk bound-feet shoes (from RM90) are also available, although nowadays they are just a curiosity rather than a necessity.

Lim Trading   NONYA SHOES
(☑292 6812; 63 Jln Tokong) Across from Wah Aik, busy Mr Lim is a second-generation craftsman (his apprenticeship began at the age of six) who also fashions gorgeous handmade Nonya beaded slippers (from RM180).

Malaqa House   ANTIQUES & DECORATION
(☑281 4770; 70 Jln Tun Tan Cheng Lock; ☉10am-6pm Mon-Fri, 10am-7pm Sat & Sun) This is a huge museumlike shop in an elegant building stuffed to the gills with antiques and replicas – it's not cheap, but it bursts with character.

TAMAN MELAKA RAYA & AROUND
As more shopping malls pop up in this area, the older ones expand. A new mall called the Explorer (www.theexplorer.com.my) should be completed in 2011 and claims to be Malaysia's 'first ecomall', meaning that it's built with 'ecofriendly' construction materials and will be solar powered. It's located across from Dataran Pahlawan and next to Mahkota Parade.

Dataran Pahlawan   MALL
(Jln Merdeka) Melaka's largest mall, with a collection of upscale designer shops and restaurants in the western half and an odd, nearly underground-feeling craft-and-souvenir market in the eastern portion.

Mahkota Parade Shopping Complex

MALL
(☑282 6151; Lot B02, Jln Merdeka) For practical needs such as cameras, pharmacy goods or electronics, head to this shopping complex, which is invariably packed with locals and often has some sort of performance or event going on.

MPH Bookstores   BOOKS
(☑283 3050; G73B, ground fl, Mahkota Parade Shopping Complex, Jln Merdeka; ☉9am-10pm) Has the city's best selection of English-language titles.

ℹ Information

Emergency
Melaka Police Hotline (☑285 1999; Jln Kota)

Immigration Office
Immigration office (☑282 4958; 2nd fl, Wisma Persekutuan, Jln Hang Tuah)

Internet Access
Several cafes in Chinatown provide internet access, and most hotels and guesthouses have free wi-fi and/or computers for guests' use.

Fenix Internet Centre (Fenix Inn, 156 Jln Taman Melaka Raya; per hr RM2.5) Also has fax and full business services.

Medical Services

Mahkota Medical Centre (📞281 3333, 284 8222; Jln Merdeka) A private hospital offering a full range of services.

Melaka General Hospital (📞282 2344; Jln Pringgit)

Money

Moneychangers are scattered about, mainly in Chinatown and near the bus stations, and there are plenty of ATMs at the shopping malls.

HSBC (Jln Hang Tuah) Has 24hr ATMs (MasterCard, Visa, Maestro, Cirrus and Plus.

Maybank (Jln Melaka Raya 2)

United Overseas Bank (Jln PM5) Has a 24hr ATM (Mastercard, Visa, Maestro, Cirrus and Plus)

Post

Post office (Jln Laksmana; ⊙8.30am-5pm Mon-Sat) Off Town Square.

Tourist information

Tourism Melaka (📞281 4803, 1800-889 483; www.melaka.gov.my; Jln Kota; ⊙9am-1pm & 2-5.30pm) Diagonally across the square from Christ Church, this place has a great location but little help is offered beyond the handing out of pamphlets.

Tourism Malaysia (📞283 6220; ⊙9am-10pm) At the Menara Taming Sari tower; has very knowledgeable, helpful staff.

Tourist police (📞281 4803; Jln Kota; ⊙8am-11pm)

ⓘ Getting There & Away

Melaka is 144km from Kuala Lumpur and 399km from Penang.

Air

Malacca International Airport's runway isn't long enough to accommodate most aircraft. **Riau Airlines** (www.riau-airlines.com) and **Wings Air** (www2.lionair.co.id) run flights to Pekanbaru in Indonesia five times per week.

Boat

High-speed **ferries** (one way/return RM119/179, 1¾ hours) make the trip from Melaka to Dumai in Sumatra daily at 10am. Tickets are available at the **Tunas Rupat Follow Me Express** (📞283 2505; 310 Taman Melaka Raya).

Bus

Melaka Sentral, the well-designed modern long-distance bus station, is inconveniently located on Jln Cempaka, off Jln Tun Razak in the north of town. Bus 17 leaves about every 15 minutes to Chinatown for RM1, or a taxi is RM20. Frequent buses head to Kuala Lumpur (RM13, two hours) and to Singapore (RM23, 4½ hours, departures approximately hourly) and Johor Bahru (RM19, 3½ hours). There are also less frequent departures for Georgetown (RM47, eight hours), Mersing (RM23, 4½ hours) and Kota Bharu (RM51, 10 hours). Luggage deposit at Melaka Sentral is RM3 per bag. There is also a reservation counter for hotels in Melaka, a money changer and restaurants.

Transnational runs **airport buses** (RM22; 5am, 8am, 12.30pm & 2.30pm; 2hr 45 min) to the KL International Airport from the Mahkota Medical Centre. Check schedules at the Tourism Malaysia office near the Menara Tamin Sari.

Car

Car-hire prices begin at around RM150 per day for an automatic; prices include insurance and tax. If you're driving, Melaka's one-way traffic system and scattered traffic require patience. Try **Hawk** (📞283 7878; 34 Jln Laksmana; www.hawkrentacar.com).

Taxi

Long-distance taxis leave from Melaka Sentral. Whole-taxi rates include KL (RM165), Kuala Lumpur International Airport (RM150) and Johor Bahru (RM240).

Train

The nearest train station is 38km north of Melaka at **Tampin** (📞441 1034) on the main north–south line from KL to Singapore. Taxis from Melaka cost around RM60, or take the Tai Lye bus (RM4.30, 1½ hours), which leaves every half hour from Melaka Sentral.

ⓘ Getting Around

Melaka is easily explored on foot, but a useful service is town bus 17, which runs every 15 minutes from Melaka Sentral to the centre of town, past the huge Mahkota Parade Shopping Complex, to Taman Melaka Raya (RM1) and on to Medan Portugis (RM1.50).

Panorama Melaka offers two types of hop-on, hop-off bus services. A double-decker bus (red line; RM5; ⊙9am-8.30pm) makes a 13-stop run while a single-decker bus (blue line; RM2; ⊙7am-9.30pm) takes in 23 stops including Melaka Sentral. Both buses run every 30 to 45 minutes – buy your ticket on the bus. Stops for both include the Hang Tua Mall, Jln Hang Jebat (Jonker's Walk), the Stadthuys, Hotel Equatorial, Renaissance Melaka Hotel and Kampung Portugis. Route

TRICKED-OUT TRISHAWS

Nowhere else in Malaysia will you find such a crazy collection of trishaws. Outrageously kitsch, the trishaws sport favourite decorations such as plastic flowers, baby-doll heads, religious paraphernalia, tinsel, Christmas lights and a sound system. While taking a ride in one of these vehicles might be the most 'I'm a tourist' things you do in Malaysia, it's good fun and supports an industry that is dying everywhere else. As a spectator, keep an eye out for Singaporean tourists hiring out trishaws en masse: the effect, with several '80s hits blaring at the same time, cameras snapping and all that glitzy decoration, turns the streets of Melaka into a circus-like parade.

maps and more information about the service are available at the Tourism Malaysia office (p139).

Bicycles can be hired at some guesthouses and hotels for around RM10 a day.

Taking to Melaka's streets by trishaw is a fun option; they should cost about RM40 per hour, but you'll have to bargain.

Taxis should cost around RM15 for a trip anywhere around town with a 50% surcharge between 1am and 6am.

AROUND MELAKA

Melaka state sits demurely in the shadow of its namesake city and consists of some peaceful off-the-beaten track *kampung* as well as two fabricated and arguably tacky resort areas popular with Malaysian and Singaporean tourists. Most of the sights outside Melaka city can be visited on a day trip from town, although staying in Alor Gajah or at Tanjung Bidara will introduce you to a sleepy-village Melaka unavailable in the capital.

Ayer Keroh

About 15km northeast of Melaka city, Ayer Keroh (also spelled Air Keroh) has several contrived tourist attractions. Kids will like the lushly landscaped **Melaka Zoo** (adult/child RM7/4, night zoo adult/child RM10/5; ◷9am-6pm daily, night zoo 8-11pm Fri & Sat) with plenty of shady, open spaces and a playground close to the entrance. It's the second-largest zoo in the country (with 200 different species) and the animals' conditions aren't bad compared with many Asian zoos.

But the main attraction in Ayer Keroh is the **Taman Mini Malaysia/Asean** (adult/child RM4/2; ◷9am-6pm), a large theme park that has examples of traditional houses from all 13 Malaysian states, as well as neighbour-

ing Asian countries. Also here is **Hutan Rekreasi Air Keroh** (Air Keroh Recreational Forest; admission free), part secondary jungle and part landscaped park with paved trails, a 250m canopy walk, picnic areas and a forestry museum.

Ayer Keroh can be reached on town bus 19 from Melaka (RM1.50, 30 minutes), or a taxi will cost around RM35.

Pulau Besar

The small island of Pulau Besar, southeast of Melaka and 5km off the coast, is a popular weekend getaway, with a few historic graves and reminders of the Japanese occupation during WWII, but the beaches tend to accumulate lots of rubbish from the polluted Strait of Melaka. Still, it's a place to get away from the city if you have time on your hands. A handful of *kedai kopi* (coffee shops) can be found near the island's only lodging option, the business-conference-oriented **Putera Island Resort** (www.pulaubesar.com; r from RM150; ❀@⌘).

Boats (RM14, 25 minutes) depart from the jetty at **Anjung Batu** (☑261 0492) at 8am, 10am, noon, 2.30pm, 5pm and 6.30pm (last boat returns at 7pm). The jetty is several kilometres past the old pier at Umbai, southeast of Melaka city.

Alor Gajah

Just off the road to KL, 24km north of Melaka, is the countryside town of Alor Gajah. In the town centre is peaceful and grassy Alor Gajah Square, which is bordered by a charming array of gaily painted and aging shophouses. Most Melaka–KL buses stop in Alor Gajah so it's possible to make a short stop here if you're willing to change buses. A taxi to A'Famosa from the bus station should cost around RM20.

☉ Sights

A'Famosa Resort   RESORT

(www.afamosa.com) Half an hour away from historic Melaka and one hour from KL, the 520-hectare A'Famosa resort is an all-encompassing resort popular with Malay and Singaporean tourists. Even though the whole place is contrived and cheesy, you'd be hard pressed not to have fun at the 8-hectare **Water World** (adult/child RM35/25 Mon-Fri, RM40/30 Sat & Sun; ☺11am-7pm Mon & Wed-Fri, 9am-8pm Sat & Sun), which has two seven-storey high-speed slides, a tube ride and even an artificial beach with a wave pool. Less adrenalin-oriented activities for families include a tots' activity pool and a giant family raft ride.

Animal Safari (admission with all rides & shows adult/child RM59/49; ☺9am-6pm) has become a focus among Malaysian animal-rights groups for the allegedly poor treatment of its animals (see www.facebook.com/pages/Stop-Animal-Abuse-at-A-Famosa/125692030790253). Critters are dressed like humans and do human activities (for example an orang-utan plays golf). The controversy came to light when a video was filmed at the park of a seemingly drugged tiger available for 'close encounters' with visitors. This prompted an investigation but no legal action was taken as of late 2010, though tiger viewings at the entrance to the park had been cancelled.

Also within the resort is a 27-hole **golf course** that is rated in the country's top 10.

🛏 Sleeping

A'Famosa Resort   RESORT

(☎522 0777; www.afamosa.com; r from RM158, villas from RM488, condotel from RM198) Stay in either the standard hotel rooms, large villas (three to five bedrooms) designed for groups and families, or 'condotels' (one to three bedrooms) with sweeping views over the resort. Prices go up on weekends, holidays and during peak season.

TOP CHOICE **Desa Paku House & Garden**
                    HOMESTAY

(☎556 2639; mush@tm.net.my; Alor Gajah; d incl 4 meals per day RM750) About 2km from the village of Alor Gajah, find an impressive collection of fruit trees, rare flowers, blooming heliconias, graceful palms and tranquil water gardens. The house is no less grand and contains some spectacular antiques and fascinating painted tiles within its distinctly Malaccan hardwood walls. Rooms are available in the main house or in a secluded bungalow bordering one of the garden's many lotus-filled ponds. A garden-and-house **tour** (per person RM50; ☺9am-noon or 3-6pm, by reservation) is available for a minimum of 10 people and includes morning or afternoon tea with a selection of Malay cakes.

Tanjung Bidara

To really get away from it all, head to lovely white-sand Tanjung Bidara, about 30km northwest of Melaka. It's well away from the main highway, requiring you to take back roads through rice paddies and farms to get to the shore. While this is a marginally popular weekend trip for Malaccan families, it's deserted midweek except for maybe one or two fishermen casting from the beach. There's a large food court at the main entrance to the beach but only one valiant stall is open outside Saturday and Sunday. The water lapping on the fine sand is brown with sediment and pollution so it's not the best place for swimming, but it is fun to sit against the jungle and watch the massive freighters head down the famous Selat Melaka (Strait of Melaka).

The main beach area is at **Tanjung Bidara Beach Resort** (☎384 2990; www.tanjungbidara.worldheritage.com.my; r RM105-235 incl breakfast; ❄🛜🏊), a quiet, relaxing but musty resort with a small swimming pool and restaurant.

Further budget accommodation is strung out over several kilometres along the beach, broken only by a large military camp. In the colourful, friendly Malay village of **Kampung Balik Batu**, about 20km south of Tanjung Bidara, are several simple beachside chalet guesthouses.

Buses 42 and 47 from Melaka go to Masjid Tanah, from where a taxi to Tanjung Bidara Beach Resort or Kampung Balik Batu costs RM10.

Penang

TELEPHONE CODE 04 / POPULATION 1.47 MILLION / AREA 1031 SQ KM

Best Places to Stay

» Clove Hall (p163)
» Straits Collection (p160)
» Cheong Fatt Tze Mansion (p160)
» Eastern & Oriental Hotel (p160)

Best Places to Eat

» Hawker Centres (p167)
» Teik Sen (p163)
» Casise (p168)
» Amelie (p164)

Why Go?

'Pearl of the Orient', Penang's nickname, conjures romantic images of trishaws pedalling past watermarked Chinese shophouses, blue joss smoke and a sting of chilli in the air; or maybe it's ornate temples, and gold-embroidered saris displayed in shop windows, next to mosques sending a call to the midday prayer; but really, whatever you're imagining, chances are that Penang *is* that reality. Add surprises like slick cafes, antiseptic shopping malls, jungles and white beaches and you'll have an even sharper image.

Historically, Penang was the waterway between Asia's two halves and the outlet to the markets of Europe and the Middle East. As such, the island straddles the juncture of Asia's great kingdoms and colonial empires. Today the culture of this region, forged over decades of colonialism, commercial activity, hosting tourists and preserving backyards, is one of Malaysia's most tolerant, cosmopolitan and exciting, especially on the palate.

When to Go?

Penang is best during its festivals and luckily you're likely to hit one at almost any time of the year. The best are Thaipusam, Chinese New Year, the Hungry Ghosts Festival and Deepavali, all which draw crowds and max out the lively volume on the streets till it makes you dizzy.

The Georgetown Festival, celebrating Penang's Unesco World Heritage status, is also poised to be an annual event lighting up the entire month of July with theatre, dance music and anything that shows off the city's multidimensional culture.

History

Little is known of Penang's early history. Chinese seafarers were aware of the island, which they called Betelnut Island, as far back as the 15th century, but it appears to have been uninhabited. It wasn't until the early 1700s that colonists arrived from Sumatra and established settlements at Batu Uban and the area now covered by southern Georgetown. The island came under the control of the sultan of Kedah, but in 1771 the sultan signed the first agreement with the British East India Company handing them trading rights in exchange for military assistance against Siam.

Fifteen years later Captain Francis Light, on behalf of the East India Company, took possession of Penang, which was formally

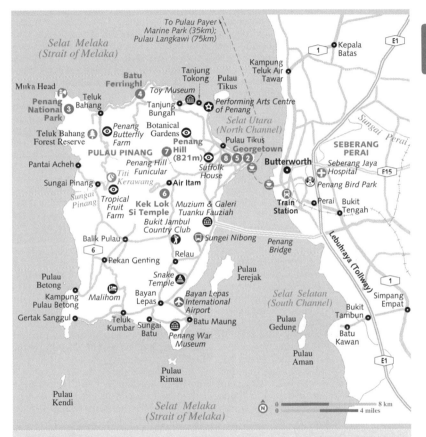

Penang Highlights

❶ Dining on the fabulous array of **hawker food** (p167)

❷ Exploring the outrageously ornate **Khoo Kongsi** (p150)

❸ Hiking through jungles to monkey beaches at **Penang National Park** (p177)

❹ Sun-tanning and cocktail drinking at a resort in **Batu Ferringhi** (p180)

❺ Understanding the meaning of Feng Shui at the **Cheong Fatt Tze Mansion** (p152)

❻ Climbing to the top of **Kek Lok Si Temple** (p175) to the 36.5m-high bronze Kuan Yin statue

❼ Enjoying the cool breezes and views from atop **Penang Hill** (p174)

❽ Eating curry and sari shopping in raucous **Little India** (p154)

signed over in 1791. Light renamed it Prince of Wales Island, as the acquisition date fell on the prince's birthday. It's said that Light fired silver dollars from his ship's cannons into the jungle to encourage his labourers to hack back the undergrowth for settlement.

Unbeknownst to the sultan of Kedah, Light had promised military protection without getting the OK from the East India Company. When Kedah was later attacked by Siam, no aid was given. The sultan tried to take back the island but was unsuccessful. His fumbled attempt resulted only in more land, a strip of the mainland now called Seberang Perai, being ceded to Light in 1800. The sultan did, however, manage to bargain for rental fees; the East India company agreed to an annual honorarium of 10,000 Spanish dollars payable to the sultan of Kedah. Through the years the amount has increased and today the state of Penang still pays the sultan of Kedah RM18,800 per year.

Light permitted new arrivals to claim as much land as they could clear and this, together with a duty-free port and an atmosphere of liberal tolerance, quickly attracted settlers from all over Asia. By the turn of the 18th century Penang was home to over 10,000 people.

In 1805 Penang became a presidency government, on a par with the cities of Madras and Bombay in India, and so gained a much more sophisticated administrative structure.

Penang briefly became the capital of the Straits Settlements (which included Melaka and Singapore) in 1826, until it was superseded by the more thriving Singapore. By the middle of the 19th century, Penang had become a major player in the Chinese opium trade, which provided more than half of the colony's revenue. It was a dangerous, rough-edged place, notorious for its brothels and gambling dens, all run by Chinese secret societies.

In 1867 the simmering violence came to a head when large-scale rioting broke out between two rival Chinese secret societies: the Cantonese-speaking Ghee Hin and the Hakka-speaking Hai San, who had each allied themselves with similar Malay groups. Today's Cannon St is so-named from the holes in the ground from cannon balls that had been fired from Khoo Kongsi (p150).

But tensions didn't prevent nostalgia from flourishing and during the early 20th century the romance of Penang attracted visits by Somerset Maugham, Joseph Conrad, Rudyard Kipling and Herman Hesse.

There was little action in Penang during WWI but WWII was a different story. When it became evident that the Japanese would attack, Penang's Europeans were immediately evacuated, leaving behind a largely defenceless population. Japan took over the island on 19 December 1941, only 12 days after the attack on Pearl Harbor in the US. The following three and a half years were the darkest of Penang's history (see p145).

Things were not the same after the war. The local impression of the invincibility of the British had been irrevocably tainted and the end of British imperialism seemed imminent. The Straits Settlements were dissolved in 1946, Penang became a state of the Federation of Malaya in 1948 and one of independent Malaysia's 13 states in 1963.

With its free-port status withdrawn in 1969, Penang went through several years of decline and high unemployment. Over the next 20 years, the island was able to build itself up as one of the largest electronics manufacturing centres of Asia and is now sometimes dubbed the 'Silicon Valley of the East'.

In 2004, 33 of the 68 deaths in Malaysia caused by the Indian Ocean tsunami occurred in Penang. While the island received minimal damage compared with its Indonesian and Thai neighbours, it's estimated that

ISLAND OR STATE?

The strip of mainland coast known as Seberang Perai (or Province Wellesley) is the mainland portion of the state that many people don't even know is Penang. The state of Penang is divided both geographically and administratively into two sections: Pulau Pinang (Penang Island), a 293 sq km island in the Strait of Melaka, and Seberang Perai, a narrow 760 sq km strip on the peninsular mainland. Georgetown, on Penang Island, is the state capital, while Butterworth is the largest town in Seberang Perai. Confusingly, the city of Geogetown is often referred to as just 'Penang', or even 'Pinang'.

The Japanese began bombing the island of Penang on 8 December 1941; after nine days of nonstop air raids the island surrendered. When the schools reopened, they taught only in Japanese, cinemas played only Japanese films and amusement parks were reborn as gambling halls. Many public buildings and private houses were taken over and rice was rationed. Soon consumer goods became hard to come by and the Japanese declared Penang's currency no longer legal. The new currency brought inflation and the development of a black market. Many Penang residents fended off starvation by growing their own fruit and vegetables and keeping chickens.

But all this was nothing compared with the terror that the new regime instilled in the people of Penang. The Japanese were accused of attempting to purge the island of its Chinese population, and the rigidity and militancy of the regime was difficult for everyone. In the early days rape was commonplace, and officers would spontaneously order beheadings as well as a slew of horrific tortures. Men were sent away to do forced labour on the Burma Railway in Thailand (aka the Death Railway) where many died of starvation, disease and overwork.

While the reign of terror was meant to scare the populace into accepting Japanese rule and culture, it had the opposite effect. An underground resistance, made up primarily of Chinese and Malay members of the communist party, quietly flourished. Meanwhile, Penang's shattered economy was no aid to the Japanese war effort. With the bombing of Hiroshima and Nagasaki in 1945, the Japanese surrendered and the British limped back to re-establish their shaken authority.

PENANG

---

the disaster cost the island's agriculture and fisheries sector tens of millions of ringgit.

More recently, the Democratic Action Party, an opposition political party popular with Malay Chinese, dominated state legislature after the 2008 elections. Penang is the only state in Malaysia that has elected a non-Malay, ethnic Chinese chief minister since independence. Changes have come in the form of shifts in foreign investment policy and a welcome ruling banning plastic bags in most retail and food outlets.

ⓘ Getting There & Away

The mainland strip of Seberang Perai is easily accessed by road and rail from other parts of the peninsula. Butterworth is the transport hub and the departure point for ferries to Penang Island, which is also linked to the mainland by bridge. Unless you're taking the train, you can easily skip over Butterworth since there's plenty of transport going direct to the island.

AIR

DOMESTIC FLIGHTS There are several daily connections between Penang and KL, Johor Bahru and Langkawi. Prices vary depending on when you book, with some fares (for all towns) hovering as low as RM38 (that's basically free with just taxes) and others as expensive as RM500 or more.

Domestic flights to/from Penang are available through the following airlines:

Air Asia (Map p148; ☑644 8701; www.airasia. com; Ground fl, Kompleks Komtar, Georgetown)

Firefly (☑03-7845 4543; www.fireflyz.com.my; Bayan Lepas International Airport)

Malaysia Airlines (Map p148; ☑262 0011; www.malaysiaairlines.com; Menara KWSP, Jl Sultan Ahmad Shah)

INTERNATIONAL FLIGHTS Penang is a major centre for cheap airline tickets, although international air fares are less competitive than they used to be. Sample fares: Singapore Airlines to Singapore RM361, Thai Airways to Bangkok RM918, and Malaysia Airlines to Sydney RM2081. Fares change from day to day so check locally for the latest prices – Air Asia has bargain flights to Bangkok online if you book well in advance.

Airline offices that have international connections to Penang Island include the following:

Air Asia (Map p148; ☑644 8701; www.airasia. com; Ground fl, Kompleks Komtar)

Cathay Pacific (Map p148; ☑226 0411; www. cathaypacific.com; Menara Boustead, 39 Jln Sultan Ahmad Shaw)

Jetstar (☑1800 81 3090; www.jetstar.com; Bayan Lepas International Airport)

Malaysia Airlines (Map p148; ☑262 0011; www.malaysiaairlines.com; Menara KWSP, Jln Sultan Ahmad Shah)

Singapore Airlines (Map p148; ☑226 6211; www.singaporeair.com; Wisma Penang Gardens, Jln Sultan Ahmad Shah)

Thai Airways International (off Map p148; THAI; ☑226 6000; www.thaiair.com; Wisma Central, 41 Jln Macalister)

DOMESTIC BUS FARES

Typical one-way fares from Sungai Nibong include the following:

DESTINATION	FARE (RM)
Cameron Highlands	23.50–28
Ipoh	10.70
Johor Bahru	49
Kuala Lumpur	27–60 (depending on bus class)
Melaka	36.20

BOAT

Both **Langkawi Ferry Service** (LFS; Map p148; ☑264 3088, 263-1398; www.langkawi
-ferry.com; PPC Bldg, Pesara King Edward) and
Ekspres Bahagia (Map p148; ☑263 1943;
PPC Bldg, Pesara King Edward) operate a shared
ferry service to Medan in Sumatra. Travel agencies will book you into whichever company has
open seats, but the boats are all the same. These
land in Belawan, and the journey to Medan is
completed by bus (included in the price), usually
taking about 4¼ hours (but sometimes as long
as five or six). The ferry leaves both Sumatra and
Georgetown at 9am every day (adult/child one
way RM110/60, return RM180/100).

The same two companies also run daily ferries
from Georgetown to Kuah on Langkawi (adult/
child one way RM60/45, return RM115/85; 1¾ to
2½ hours). Boats leave at 8.30am and 8.45am;
the second service calls in at Pulau Payar first, but
you won't be able to disembark unless you're on
a diving or snorkelling package (see p156). Boats
return from Langkawi at 2.30pm and 5.30pm.
Book a few days in advance to ensure a seat.

BUS

Long-distance bus services leave Penang from
the express bus station on Jln Sungei Nibong,
just to the south of Penang Bridge. While it may
be more convenient to buy your tickets from travel agents on Lebuh Chulia or some guesthouses
and hotels, it's a safer bet to buy your ticket in
person at the bus-company offices at the station.

Many more buses leave from next to the mainland ferry terminal in Butterworth, and a few
long-distance buses also leave from other parts

of Georgetown. **Newsia Tours & Travel** (☑261
7933; 35-36 Pengkalan Weld) is a major agent.

BUSES TO SINGAPORE From the bus station
at Komtar shopping centre: Singapore (RM53,
10 hours, two daily) and to Johor Bharu's Larkin
bus station (RM45, nine hours, one daily).

BUSES TO THAILAND From the Komtar bus
station, there are bus and minibus services
to Thailand, including Hat Yai (RM35); Phuket
(RM70); Ko Pipi (RM90); Ko Samui (RM80); and
even Bangkok (RM120). The minibuses usually
don't go directly to some destinations; you'll
probably be dumped for a change of vehicle in
Hat Yai or Surat Thani, sometimes with significant waiting times. Buy tickets from bucket
shops on Lebuh Chulia or directly at the bus
station, which can be cheaper.

TRAIN

The **train station** (☑323 7962) is next to the
ferry terminal and bus and taxi station in Butterworth. There's one daily train to KL and two
in the opposite direction to Hat Yai in Thailand;
check with www.ktmb.com.my for the latest info
on fares and schedules.

ℹ Getting Around

For information about getting around in Georgetown see p173.

BOAT

There's a **ferry service** (per adult/car
RM1.20/7.70; ☺24hr) between Georgetown and
Butterworth. Ferries take passengers and cars
every eight minutes from 6.20am to 9.30pm,
every 20 minutes until 11.15pm, and hourly
after that until 6.20am. The journey takes 15

TOO BIG FOR ITS BRIDGES

Before 14 September 1985 Penang's only link to the mainland was an overcrowded ferry.
Today an average of 70,000 people cross the 13.5km **Penang Bridge**, one of the longest
bridges in the world. Even though recent work increased the bridge's capacity by 50%,
that's not expected to meet Penang's rapid development needs. Construction is underway
on a second bridge linking Batu Maung at the southeastern tip of the island to Batu Kawan
on the mainland. It's expected to be completed by mid-2012.

In 2008 the historic centre of Georgetown was declared a Unesco World Heritage Site for having 'a unique architectural and cultural townscape without parallel anywhere in East and Southeast Asia'. Property values skyrocketed and old buildings, once abandoned, were snatched up by developers hoping to cash in on the ensuing boom. Thankfully, Penang is full of heritage activists, particularly within the Penang Heritage Trust (p173) and, in general, the city is safeguarding its age-old feel while enjoying a facelift.

minutes. Fares are charged only for the journey from Butterworth to Penang; returning to the mainland is free.

BUS

For Penang Island buses see p173. The 704 and 705 buses run from the train and ferry terminal in Butterworth to Georgetown – the 704 route ends at Komtar, while the 705 stops at Sungei Nibong, the long-distance bus terminal.

CAR

If you drive the 13.5km across Penang Bridge to the island there's a RM7.70 toll payable at the toll plaza on the mainland, but no charge to return.

GEORGETOWN

It's full of car exhaust and has a marked lack of footpaths, but Georgetown is able to woo even the most acute cityphobe with its explosive cultural mishmash that creates a scene fit for a movie set.

Dodge traffic while strolling past Chinese shophouses where people might be roasting coffee over a fire or sculpting giant incense for a ceremony. Trishaws, pedaling tourists and the occasional local, cruise around the maze of chaotic streets and narrow lanes, past British Raj–era architecture, strings of paper lanterns and retro-chic pubs, boutiques and cafes that wouldn't be out of place in a Western city. Outside the historic centre, soaring skyscrapers and massive shopping complexes gleam high above.

Just when you get the gist of Chinatown you enter Little India, which is like a street party at night with its twinkling lights, screeching Bollywood music and countless shops with a rainbow of silk saris sold on the streetsides.

Though each district is distinct, they do overlap; you'll find Chinese temples in Little India and mosques in Chinatown. Along certain streets you'll have your pick of delicious Indian curries, spicy Malay specialities or local Chinese noodle creations all lined up one after the other. Arrive on an empty stomach and graze at will. Between the city's outrageous hawker food and fine restaurants this is the food capital of Malaysia.

◉ Sights

COLONIAL DISTRICT

Penang has one of the greatest concentrations of colonial architecture in Asia. Fort Cornwallis is a good place to start a tour of the colonial district around the waterfront. Many of the buildings in the area are marked with signs explaining their history and significance. You can follow the **Heritage Trail** walking tours, which also take in temples and mosques in Chinatown – pick up a pamphlet of the routes at the tourist office or the Penang Heritage Trust. There's also a **free bus shuttle** (7am to 7pm Monday to Friday, to 2pm Saturday), which runs between the jetty and Komtar, winding its way through the colonial core of Georgetown. It's a good way to get a quick overview of the town, and you can get on and off at various numbered stops. A map of the route is in the *Penang Tourist Newspaper*.

Fort Cornwallis   HERITAGE BUILDING
(🗷261 0262; Lebuh Light; adult/child RM3/2; ⊙9am-6.30pm) For all its size, this fort isn't particularly impressive; only the outer walls stand, enclosing a pleasant park within. The star-shaped structure houses some vaguely informative exhibits, a Malaysian man stands in full British colonial uniform at the gate and a speaker system seems to play the '1812 Overture' on repeat loop; it's all wonderfully surreal.

The fort is named for Charles Cornwallis, perhaps best known for surrendering at the Battle of Yorktown to George Washington, effectively ending the American Revolution. It was at the site of the fort that Captain Light first set foot on the virtually uninhabited island in 1786 and established the free port where trade would, he hoped, be lured from Britain's Dutch rivals. Between 1808 and 1810 convict labour replaced the then-wooden

PENANG GEORGETOWN

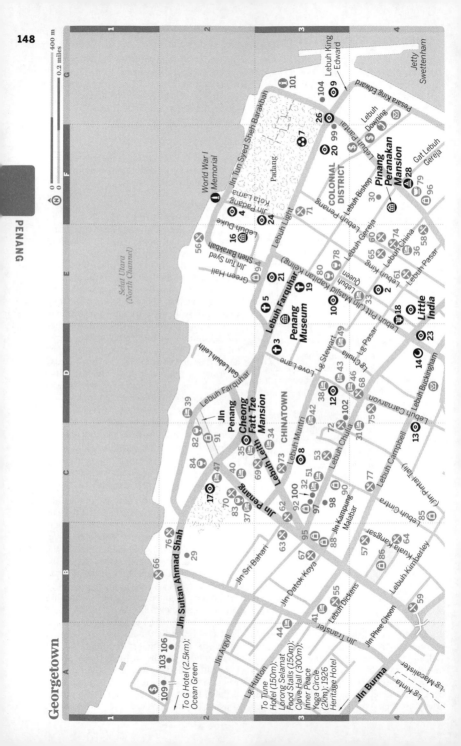

PENANG

Georgetown

Selat Utara
(North Channel)

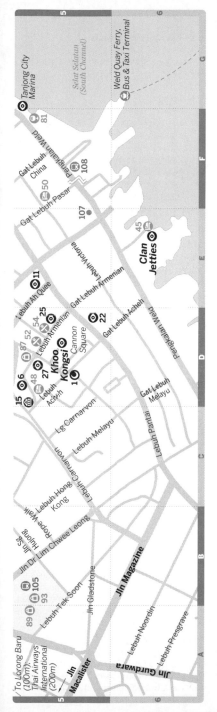

building materials with stone. The star-profile shape of the walls allowed for overlapping fields of fire against enemies.

A bronze statue of Captain Light stands near the entrance, modelled on the likeness of his son, William, because no pictures of him could be found. Said son was the founder of Adelaide in Australia. The small **chapel** in the southwest corner was the first to be built in Penang; ironically, the first recorded service was the 1799 marriage of Francis Light's widow, Martina (rumoured to have been Eurasian), to a certain John Timmers.

Seri Rambai, the most important and largest cannon, faces the north coast and was cast in 1603. It has a chequered history: the Dutch gave it to the sultan of Johor, after which it fell into the hands of the Acehnese; it was later given to the sultan of Selangor, and then stolen by pirates before ending up at the fort.

Penang Museum MUSEUM
(☎261 3144; Lebuh Farquhar; admission RM1; ⊙9am-5pm Sat-Thu) This is one of the best-presented museums in Malaysia. There are engaging exhibits on the customs and traditions of Penang's various ethnic groups, with photos, documents, costumes, furniture and other well-labelled displays. Look out for the beautifully carved opium beds, inlaid with mother-of-pearl.

Upstairs is the history gallery, with a collection of early 19th-century watercolours by Captain Robert Smith, an engineer with the East India Company, and prints showing landscapes of old Penang. You can also play videos of Penang's many cultural festivals.

Outside, one of the original Penang Hill funicular railcars is now a kiosk selling an unusual array of souvenirs including antique costume jewellery and coins; all proceeds benefit the Penang Heritage Trust.

Protestant Cemetery CEMETERY
(Jln Sultan Ahmad Shah) Here you'll find the graves of Captain Francis Light and many others, including governors, merchants, sailors and Chinese Christians who fled the Boxer Rebellion in China (a movement opposing Western imperialism and evangelism) only to die of fever in Penang, all under a canopy of magnolia trees. Also here is the tomb of Thomas Leonowens, the young officer who married Anna – the schoolmistress to the King of Siam made famous by *The King and I*.

CHINATOWN

If the imposing profile of the colonial district's buildings represent Penang at her most stately and dignified, the spaghetti of worm-narrow streets is Penang at her most quintessential. This is Chinatown, which stretches from Lebuh Pantai to Jln Penang, centres on Lebuh Chulia and encloses Little India, Chinese Assembly Halls and the backpacker ghetto. It's all here: tiny tea shops owned by stoic Chinese grandmothers, busted Indian stereo systems blaring 'Chuma chuma jai – blgrfzzzzl' and calls to prayer mingling with the loud slap of mahjong tiles.

What's there to do? Walk around, soak up, walk some more, soak, rinse, repeat. Peek into a temple, haggle at a vegetable market, slurp up some noodle soup and down a bottle of beer with the locals.

TOP CHOICE **Khoo Kongsi** CLANHOUSE
(Dragon Mountain Hall; ☎261 4609; 18 Cannon Sq; adult/child RM5/free; ⊙9am-5pm) The *kongsi*, or clanhouse, is a major node of overseas Chinese communities. It is both a

benevolent organisation for individuals with the same surname and, in its way, an economic collective. But it is also symbolises a deeper social, even spiritual contract between an extended clan, its ancestors and its social obligations. To this end, clanhouses and assembly halls are both the civic and religious backbone for many overseas Chinese, and this is the most impressive one in Penang.

The Khoo are a successful clan, and they're letting the world know. Stone carvings dance across the entrance hall and pavilions, many of which symbolise or are meant to attract good luck and wealth. Note at the entrance a turbaned Sikh guardian watchman. The interior is dominated by incredible murals depicting birthdays, weddings and, most impressively, the 36 celestial guardians (divided into two panels of 18 guardians each). The fiery overhead lighting comes courtesy of enormous paper lamps. Gorgeous ceramic sculptures of immortals, carp, dragons, and carp becoming dragons (a traditional Chinese motif symbolising success) dance across the roof ridges. As impressive as all of this is, Khoo Kongsi was

CLAN JETTIES

During the late 18th and early 19th centuries, **Weld Quay** in Georgetown was the centre of one of the world's most thriving ports and provided plentiful work for the never-ending influx of immigrants. Soon a community of Chinese grew up around the quay, with floating and stilt houses built along rickety docks; these docking and home areas became known as the clan jetties. Six of the seven jetties that developed were owned by individual clans: Lim, Chew, Tan, Lee, Yeoh and Koay; the seventh was a mixed-clan dock known as Chap Seh Keo.

Imagine: a port full of Chinese junks unloading their cargo onto the docks, where a human chain of workers carry the sacks across the gangplank out to the port clerk. *Sampan* (small boats) would row to the larger ships to unload passengers (often new immigrants) and more cargo.

Unfortunately, during the Japanese occupation in WWII (see p145) the Lim Jetty was destroyed by bombing and the Yeoh jetty had its bridge wrecked. Trading nearly came to a halt and only small smuggling operations continued from Indonesia and Thailand. Soon the jetty folk became peddlers for contraband and the jetties began to get a reputation as an area for thugs and thieves.

After the war, port activity picked up again and peaked in the late 1950s. But the era was short-lived and when the port reorganised in the '60s, many of the jetty residents left their way of life to find work.

Today the clan jetties are low-income areas with a jumble of dilapidated floating houses and planks, and are becoming popular tour bus stops. If you get here *sans* tour bus, it's a wonderful place to wander around with docked fishing boats, folks cooking in their homes and kids running around. You can also stay at the Chew Jetty – see p162.

once more ostentatious; the roof caught fire on the night it was completed in 1901, an event put down to divine jealousy. The present *kongsi* dates from 1906.

TOP CHOICE Cheong Fatt Tze Mansion
HERITAGE BUILDING

(262 0006; 14 Lebuh Leith; admission RM12; tours 11am & 3pm Mon-Sat) Built in the 1880s, the magnificent 38-room, 220-window Cheong Fatt Tze Mansion was commissioned by Cheong Fatt Tze, a Hakka merchant-trader who left China as a penniless teenager and eventually established a vast financial empire throughout east Asia, earning himself the dual sobriquets 'Rockefeller of the East' and the 'Last Mandarin'.

The mansion, rescued from ruin in the 1990s, blends Eastern and Western designs, with louvred windows, Art Nouveau stained glass and beautiful floor tiles, and is a rare surviving example of the eclectic architectural style preferred by wealthy Straits Chinese of the time. The best way to experience the house, now a boutique hotel, is to stay here (see p160); otherwise hour-long guided tours give you a glimpse of the beautiful interior. You may have seen the house shortly after its restoration in the 1992 Catherine Deneuve film *Indochine*.

Kuan Yin Teng
CHINESE TEMPLE

On Lebuh Pitt (Jln Masjid Kapitan Keling) is the temple of Kuan Yin – the goddess of mercy, good fortune, peace and fertility. Built in the early 19th century by the first Hokkien and Cantonese settlers in Penang, the temple is not impressive, but it's very central and popular with the Chinese community. It seems to be forever swathed in smoke from the outside furnaces where worshippers burn paper money, and from the incense sticks waved around inside. It's a very active place, and Chinese theatre shows take place on the goddess's birthday, celebrated on the 19th day of the second, sixth and ninth lunar months.

Tua Pek Kong
CLANHOUSE

(8 Lebuh Armenia) This recently renovated structure, resplendent in red, gold and polished black columns, has quite a few more aliases, such as Hock Teik Cheng Sin, Poh Hock Seah, Hokkien Kongsi and Tong Kheng Seah. Why so many names? Well, besides serving as a temple and assembly hall, this building has also been the registered headquarters of several secret societies. Each society occupied a different portion of the temple, which became a focal point during the 1867 riots. The fighting became so intense that a secret passage existed between

here and Khoo Kongsi for a quick escape. While you search for the corridor, be sure to admire the gilded filigree and lacquered roof beams that give this once underground HQ so much Imperial Chinese vibe.

153

FREE Dr Sun Yat Sen's Penang Base
MUSEUM

(☏262 0123; 120 Lebuh Armenia; ⊙hours vary) The leader of the 1911 Chinese revolution (which overturned the Ching dynasty and established China as the first republic in Asia), Dr Sun Yat Sen, had his headquarters in this building from 1909 to 1911. It was here the 1910 Canton uprising was planned – although unsuccessful, the uprising was a turning point for the revolution's success. The shophouse is a humble building, chosen in this obscure area of town for its low profile.

Dr Sun Yat Sen lived in Penang with his family for about six months in 1910. This house was not his residence but was the central meeting place for his political party. His office on Dato Keramat Rd was demolished.

Today the house has been restored in a low-key way. Take time to browse the interesting paraphernalia about and from the doctor's life. There are no set opening hours so you have to ring the bell and hope that someone is in (which is often the case) or call in advance.

Acheen St Mosque
MOSQUE

(Lebuh Acheh) A short walk from Khoo Kongsi, the Acheen St Mosque is unusual for its Egyptian-style minaret (most Malay mosques have Moorish minarets). Built in 1808 by a wealthy Arab trader, the mosque was the focal point for the Malay and Arab traders in this quarter – the oldest Malay *kampung* (village) in Georgetown. It's open to visitors but all the usual mosque etiquette should be exercised: wear conservative clothing, take your shoes off, avoid prayer times and be respectfully quiet.

Penang Islamic Museum
MUSEUM

(☏262 0172; 128 Lebuh Armenia; adult/child RM3/1; ⊙9.30am-6pm Wed-Mon) Penang Islamic Museum is housed in a restored villa that was once the residence of Syed Alatas, a powerful Acehnese merchant of Arab descent who led the local Acehnese community during the Penang riots of 1867. Today it holds a wordy exhibition on the history of Islam in Malaysia, along with some 19th-century furniture and a life-sized diorama of a dock scene upstairs.

Hainan Temple
CHINESE TEMPLE

(Lebuh Muntri) This small gem demands a closer look. Dedicated to Mar Chor Poh, the patron saint of seafarers, the temple was founded in 1866 but not completed until 1895. A thorough remodelling for its centenary in 1995 refreshed its distinctive swirling dragon pillars and brightened up the ornate carvings. The compound is usually buzzing with activity.

Loo Pun Hong
CHINESE TEMPLE

(70 Love Lane) The tiny Loo Pun Hong is one of the most unobtrusive of Penang's many Chinese temples. This one, built in the 1880s, is dedicated to Lo Pan, the legendary inventor of carpentry tools, and is Malaysia's oldest carpenters' guild house. Set back from the lane, it has an ornate altar inside, along with a giant drum and bell.

GEORGETOWN SIGHTS

STALWART SIKHS

You'll notice that the steps of the decadent Khoo Kongsi clan house are guarded by two life-sized granite Sikh sentinels. While this might seem strange for a Chinese edifice, the guards are a testament to an important ingredient in Penang's melting-pot background: the Sikhs from the Punjab region of India.

Brought from India in the 19th century by the British, the Sikhs were employed as guards due to their reputation as honest and reliable people. Today's Penang is home to some 2000 Sikh families but very few still work in their traditional profession of guardians; many speak Punjabi and hold high-placed jobs in several areas of Penang business.

The Sikhs' shrine was once housed inside Fort Cornwallis because most of the first Sikh arrivals were with the British military. Eventually this location proved impractical and the government allotted the Sikhs land on Jln Gurdwara (Brick Kiln Rd) for a new temple. While most of the Sikhs' religious activity revolves around the new shrine, their annual festival of Vaisakhi, the traditional harvest festival held on 14 April every year, still takes place inside the walls of ancient Fort Cornwallis. Visitors can expect plenty of Sikh folk dancing (including the lively traditional Punjabi *bhangra*), music and art.

Between the mid-1800s and the mid-1900s Penang welcomed a huge influx of Chinese immigrants, primarily from the Fujian province of China. In order to help introduce uncles, aunties, cousins, 10th cousins, old neighbourhood buddies and so on to their new home, the Chinese formed clan associations and built clanhouses to create a sense of community, provide lodging, help find employment, and more, for newcomers. In the associated temples the clan would worship patron deities.

As time went on, many clan associations became extremely prosperous and their buildings became more ornate. Clans began to compete with each other over the decadence and number of their temples. Thanks to this rivalry, today's Penang has one of the densest concentrations of clan architecture found outside China.

The houses of the five great Hokkien clans that formed the backbone of early Penang:

» **Tua Pek Kong** (p152)

» **Khoo Kongsi** (p150)

» **Yeoh Kongsi** (3 Gat Lebuh Chulia)

» **Lim Kongsi** (234 Lebuh Pantai)

» **Tan Kongsi** (Seah Tan Crt, off Lebuh Pantai).

Penang Gelugpa Buddhist Association
BUDDHIST TEMPLE
(Love Lane) This Buddhist temple next to Loo Pun Hong isn't particularly impressive compared with Penang's other religious buildings. But it is unique for being the major representative structure of the Gelugpa (Yellow Hat) school of Buddhism. The Yellow Hats are a Tibetan order, and as such there are some beautiful Tibetan wall hangings in this temple that you'd be hard pressed to find outside a museum.

LITTLE INDIA
As Little Indias go, this one fills all the criteria. It's quite small but bursts with bright lights, scratchy music, gold-edged saris and small Alps of spices that all together smash up your normal dull sensory array. Men stand on the street and yell at you to come see their shop/restaurant/stall; pausing to look will result in the inevitable hard sell. Slurp soy milk from a plastic bag or snack on *murtabak* (meat- or veg-filled pancake) from street vendors, then wander round shops full of Indian carvings and Hindu religious paraphernalia. In all, it's one of the most lively places in Georgetown, particularly at night.

Sri Mariamman Temple
HINDU TEMPLE
(Lebuh Pitt) For local Tamils, this temple fulfils the purpose of a Hokkien clanhouse; it's a reminder of the motherland and the community bonds forged within the diaspora. In this case, those bonds don't come from a benevolent society but a typically South Indian temple, dominated by its *gopuram* (entrance tower). Erupting in sculpture, the tower serves several purposes: it represents Mt Meru, the cosmic mountain that supports the heavens; and delineates the line between this world and the realm of the gods, which begins in the temple compound. Local Tamils pay homage to Tamil Nadu by worshipping Mariamman, a mother goddess popular with diaspora Indians, who represents the soil of, if not home, at least the land of their sometimes-distant origin. This temple was built in 1883 and is Georgetown's oldest Hindu house of worship.

Penang's **Thaipusam** procession begins here (see p158), and in October a wooden chariot takes the temple's deity for a spin around the neighbourhood during Vijayadasami festivities.

TOP CHOICE **Pinang Peranakan Mansion** MUSEUM
(☎264 2929; www.pinangperanakanmansion.com.my; 29 Lebuh Gereja; adult/child RM10/free; ☺9am-5pm Mon-Sat) This building rivals the Cheong Fatt Tze Mansion as the most stunning restored residence in the city. Every door, wall and archway is carved and often painted in gold leaf; the grand rooms are furnished with majestic wood furniture with intricate mother-of-pearl inlay; and knock-your-socks-off bright-coloured paintings of the family in regal Chinese dress grace the walls. The house belonged to Chung Keng Quee, a 19th-century merchant, secret society leader and commu-

nity pillar as well as being one of the most wealthy Baba-Nonyas of that era. A guided tour is included in the price.

Sire
MUSEUM

(cnr Lebuh King & Lebuh Light) This gorgeous little museum is tucked at the back of an elegant restaurant of the same name (see p168) – in fact you have to eat something at the restaurant to get in. Exquisite antique furniture and photos (from the family's mansion, which was donated to the state and is now Wawasan Open University) decorate the high-ceilinged hall along with snippets of history about family head Yeap Chor Ee, a once-prominent businessman and philanthropist, and his family.

Masjid Kapitan Keling
MOSQUE

(cnr Lebuh Buckingham & Lebuh Pitt) Penang's first Indian Muslim settlers (East India Company troops) built Masjid Kapitan Keling in 1801. The mosque's domes are yellow, in a typically Indian-influenced Islamic style, and it has a single minaret. It looks sublime at sunset. Mosque officials can grant permission to enter.

OTHER SIGHTS

Suffolk House
HERITAGE BUILDING

(Jln Ayer Itam; tour/self-guide RM15/10; ⊙10am-6pm) On the banks of the Air Itam river, 6.5km west of Georgetown's centre, is this impressive Georgian-style mansion, one of the great success stories of Penang Heritage Trust. The grand home is on the site of the original residence of Francis Light, founder of the colony and native of Suffolk, England.

It's a grand square building with sweeping verandas, a massive ballroom and a breezy colonial plantation feel.

In 1974 the house was in such poor repair that it was declared structurally unsafe and sealed off, but funds were eventually secured for its full restoration. The main building's restoration was completed in 2007, but the interior decorating is still a work in progress, each room slowly getting furnished to period style.

Many people come here for the chic semi-alfresco **restaurant** (set meals RM95-130, high tea for 2 people RM64), which serves nouveau cuisine and afternoon high tea (from 2.30pm to 6pm) and has a full bar.

Wat Chayamangkalaram
BUDDHIST TEMPLE

(Temple of the Reclining Buddha; Lorong Burma; ⊙early morning-5.30pm) The Temple of the Reclining Buddha is a typically Thai temple with it sharp-eaved roofs and ceiling accents; inside it houses a 33m-long **reclining Buddha** draped in a gold-leafed saffron robe. The icon represents the Buddha's attainment of nirvana and peaceful passage from this existence, although the claim that it's the third-longest reclining Buddha in the world is dubious.

Dhammikarama Burmese Buddhist Temple
BUDDHIST TEMPLE

(Lorong Burma) Standing opposite is a rare instance of a Burmese Buddhist temple outside Burma (now Myanmar). There's a series of panel paintings on the life of the Buddha lining the walkways, the characters dressed in typical Burmese costume, while inside

---

BUDDHISM IN PENANG

While Malaysia is officially and predominantly Muslim, the Chinese population has remained mostly Buddhist. As one of Malaysia's most Chinese states, Penang has an uncommonly diverse and burgeoning Buddhist community that embraces not only traditional Chinese Buddhism but also the Thai, Burmese, Sinhalese and Tibetan schools of Buddhist philosophy.

Kuan Yin Teng (Goddess of Mercy; p152) was built in the early 1800s, making it the oldest Chinese temple in Penang and the second oldest in the country; Cheng Hoon Teng Temple (p122) in Melaka grabs the first-place title by a hundred years or so. Later in the century the venerable Miao Lian came from China to construct the **Kek Lok Si Temple** (p175) near Penang Hill, which would become Malaysia's biggest Buddhist temple, and in 1925 the **Penang Buddhist Association** (p156) was founded.

Several Thai temples around the island attract Chinese worshippers in addition to members of the local Thai community, and Malaysia's only Burmese temple, **Dhammikarama Temple** (p155), is in central Georgetown. A Sinhalese temple, **Mahindarama Temple** (🖉282 5944; 2 Jln Kampar, Georgetown), attracts an English-educated crowd. Zen Buddhism has yet to make much of an impression, while Tibetan Buddhism is becoming increasingly popular since the Dalai Lama's much-publicised visit to Malaysia in 1981.

typically round-eyed, serene-faced Burmese Buddha statues stare out at worshippers. This was Penang's first Buddhist temple, built in 1805; it has been significantly added to over the years.

Penang Buddhist Association

BUDDHIST TEMPLE

(Jln Anson) Completed in 1931, this unusual Buddhist temple is about 1km west of town. Instead of the typical colourful design of most Chinese temples, this one shows Art Deco influences and looks like a frosted cake, all white and pastel. Interior Buddha figures are carved from Italian marble, and glass chandeliers hang above. Penang's Buddhist community gathers here on Wesak Day (April/May) to celebrate the triple holy day of the Buddha's birthday, attainment of enlightenment and death.

FREE P Ramlee House

MUSEUM

(4A Jln P Ramlee; ⊗9am-6pm Tue-Sun, closed noon-3pm Fri) This humble, and now thoroughly restored, *kampung* house was the birthplace of Malaysia's biggest megastar, P Ramlee. Ramlee was particularly known for his singing voice and acted in and directed 66 films in his lifetime. Artefacts and photos are displayed in the main room, while the other areas of the house are furnished as they would have been when Ramlee grew up and are scattered with his personal items. Heading south on Jln Perak from Jln Dato Keramat, turn right on Jln P Ramlee – the house is about 300m down this road.

Masjid Negeri

MOSQUE

(Air Itam) The glossy, modern state mosque is about 5km west of town. It's the biggest in Penang, and has a striking 50m-high minaret.

Nattukotai Chettiar Temple

HINDU TEMPLE

(Waterfall Rd) Located near the Botanical Gardens is the largest Hindu temple in Penang, dedicated to Bala Subramaniam.

Waterfall Hilltop Temple

HINDU TEMPLE

(Jln Kebun Bunga) The destination of the Thaipusam procession from Little India's Sri Mariamman Temple. About 100m before the gates to the Botanical Gardens.

🏃 Activities

Langkawi Coral

DIVING & SNORKELLING

(☑899 8822; www.langkawicoral.com; 64 Jln Tanjung Tokong; snorkelling/diving RM240/380) Take a diving or snorkelling excursions to tiny, uninhabited Pulau Payar, 32 nautical miles north of Penang. The trips include a buffet lunch and time for sunbathing and fish-feeding. The company also does day trips and overnight sojourns to the resort area of Pulau Langkawi.

Deluxcious Spa

SPA

(☑261 0288; www.deluxciousspacuisine.com; 17A Jln Sultan Ahmad Shah; ⊗9.30am-11.30pm) Penang's premier independent spa is a treat indeed. Enjoy massages (1hr around RM150), stress-melting spa packages (around RM330) and facials in a serene Balinese-style environment while sipping tea or a beer. Many packages include a meal at the spa's restaurant, which serves healthy fusion cuisine prepared by an ex–Ritz-Carlton chef. Check the website for specials.

Bukit Jambul Country Club

GOLF

(☑644 2255; 2 Jln Bukit Jambul; 18 holes from RM90) The island's premier golf course is located near Bayan Lepas International Airport; the stunning and very challenging 18

SAY WAT?

Is there a question in your life that needs answering? Head to **Wat Buppharam** (☑227 7430; 8 Perak Rd), a 1942 Buddhist temple bursting with cartoonlike sculptures of Thai, Taoist and Hindu religious figures. The ornate Thai entrance archway is the largest in the state. The wat is home to the **lifting Buddha**, a 100-year-old, gold-leaf-encrusted Buddha statue about the size of a well-fed house cat. As a seeker, kneel in front of the statue, pay respects to the figure with a clear mind and then ask, in your mind, the yes or no question you wish to have answered; ask also that you wish for the figure to become light for an affirmative answer. Try to lift the statue. To verify the answer, ask your question again, only this time ask that the statue become heavy. Lift again. (We tried this and got a very firm 'no' answer while a friend received a 'yes'. Months down the line it ended up that the statue was right in both cases.) When the statue is heavy it won't budge and when it's light it lifts off the platform like a butterfly. You can decide for yourself if there's something cosmic going on. Heading northwest on Jln Burma, turn right on Jln Perak about 500m after Hotel 1926. The wat is about 150m down this road.

ⓘ GEORGETOWN STREET NAMES

Finding your way around Georgetown can be slightly complicated since many roads have both a Malay and an English name. Fortunately, many street signs list both but it can still be confusing. In this book we use primarily the Malay name. Here are the two names of some of the main roads:

MALAY	ENGLISH
Lebuh Gereja	Church St
Jln Masjid Kapitan Keling	Pitt St
Jln Tun Syed Sheh Barakbah	The Esplanade
Lebuh Pantai	Beach St
Lebuh Pasar	Market St

To make matters worse, Jln Penang may also be referred to as Jln Pinang or as Penang Rd – but there's also a Penang St, which may also be called Lebuh Pinang! Similarly, Chulia St is Lebuh Chulia but there's also a Lorong Chulia, and this confuses even the taxi drivers.

holes were carved straight out of the rocky jungle terrain.

Penang Turf Club HORSE RACING
(☑229 3233; www.penangturfclub.com; Batu Gantong) Horse-racing events take place on two consecutive weekends every two months. Seats are cheap, but gambling on the race outcome is illegal. Horse riding is sometimes offered from Monday to Friday.

🍴 Courses

Nazlina's Spice Kitchen COOKERY SCHOOL
(www.pickles-and-spices.com/cooking-traditional -food-class.html; class RM120; ☺9am-1pm Tue-Sat) Learn to cook Penang specialities from *assam laksa* to prawn curry and take a morning market tour to get your supplies. Grind your own spices and have fun seeing how much work goes into Penang's cuisine. Classes are held at both the Tropical Spice Garden (p177) and Penang Islamic Museum (p153).

Inner Peace Yoga Circle YOGA
(☑229 2540; www.innerpeaceyogacircle.com; 293 Jln Burmah; drop-in class RM28) Offers all types of yoga plus retreats and teacher-training programmes. Ten per cent of the company's proceeds go to charity. The class schedule is available on the website.

👉 Tours

Most sights on the island are easily reached independently but expect to see only one or two in a day if you're taking local transport, perhaps three or four if you're getting lost in traffic with your own car. For people on a time budget, taking a tour can be a wise choice. Several agents around town book a range of tours at similar prices.

Ping Anchorage BUS TOURS
(☑397 7993; www.pinganchorage.com.my; 25B Jln Todok 2, Seberang Jaya) Over on the mainland this well-respected company runs several tours including the four-hour 'Hill and Temple tour', visiting Penang Hill and the Kek Lok Si Temple; round-island tours; and trips to Penang National Park. Tours cost between RM88 and RM129 (cheaper for groups of three or more), including pick-up from your hotel.

Penang Heritage Trust WALKING TOURS
(☑264 2631; www.pht.org.my; 26A Lg Stewart) A great place from which to take walking tours, including the 'Little India Experience' and the 'Heritage Trail', taking in the Cheong Fatt Tze Mansion. Both last around three hours and cost RM60, including entry fees. It also has free brochures with details of self-guided walks, such as the 'World Religions Walk' and 'Historic Georgetown Trails'.

✯ Festivals & Events

All the Malay festivals are celebrated in Penang, with the island's extraordinary enthusiasm. Current events are listed in the *Penang Tourist Newspaper*. For more on festivals and events, see p19.

WALK OF FAITH, WALK OF HERITAGE

One of the best walking tours of Penang on offer (and there are many) is presented by the **Penang Global Ethic Project** (www.globalethicpenang.net/webpages/act_02b.htm). Their **World Religion Walk** takes you past the iconography and houses of worship of Christians, Muslims, Hindus, Sikhs, Buddhists and Chinese traditional religion. We'd just add, to round out the world's belief systems: Penang's old **Jewish cemetery** (Jln Zainal Abidin), located between Jln Burma and Jln Macalister.

For a **heritage walking tour**, we recommend **Joann Khaw** (☏016 440 6823), a heritage expert who leads personalised tours of Georgetown as well as day trips to destinations as far away as Ipoh (a less-discovered heritage gem 164km south of Penang).

January–April

Thaipusam HINDU

This masochistic festival is celebrated as fervently as in Singapore and KL, but without quite the same crowds. The Sri Mariamman, Nattukotai Chettiar and Waterfall Hilltop temples are the main centres of activity. (January/February)

Chinese New Year CHINESE

Celebrated with particular gusto in Georgetown. The Khoo Kongsi is done up for the event, and dance troupes and Chinese-opera groups perform all over the city. On the night before the 15th day of the new year, a fire ceremony takes place at Tua Pek Kong temple. (January/February)

Chap Goh Meh CHINESE

The 15th day of the new year celebrations, during which local girls throw oranges into the sea. Traditionally the girls would chant 'throw a good orange, get a good husband' while local boys watched and later contacted their dream girl through matchmakers. The new year is also one of the only times to see Baba-Nonya performances of *dondang sayang* (spontaneous and traditional love ballads). (February)

May–August

Penang International Floral Festival GARDEN FESTIVAL

Held in the Botanical Gardens when many of the trees are flowering; experts show keen horticulturalists around. (May/June)

Penang International Dragon Boat Festival REGATTA

A colourful and popular regatta on the Teluk Bahang Dam, featuring traditional dragon boats. (May/June)

Georgetown Festival PERFORMING ARTS

An arts and performance festival celebrating the city's Unesco status. (July)

Penang Food & Cultural Festivals FOOD & CULTURE

Highlights the best of Penang's multi-ethnic heritage. Various locations in Georgetown. (August)

Hungry Ghosts Festival (Phor Thor) CHINESE

The gates of hell are said to be opened every year on the 15th day of the seventh month of the Chinese lunar calendar. To appease the hungry ghosts, Penangites set out food offerings and endeavour to entertain them with puppet shows and streetside Chinese-opera performances. This is a magical time to be in the city. (August)

September–December

Lantern Festival CHINESE

An island-wide festival celebrated by eating moon cakes, the Chinese sweets once used to carry secret messages for underground rebellions in ancient China. (Mid-September)

Deepavali HINDU

The Hindu Festival of Lights is celebrated with music and dancing at venues in Little India. (October)

Pesta Pulau Penang CARNIVAL

The annual Penang Island Festival (November–December) features various cultural events, parades and a funfair in Georgetown.

🛏 Sleeping

Georgetown has all the accommodation possibilities you would expect in a big, bustling tourist city, from the grungiest hostels to the swankiest hotels. Midrange options are mostly found along Jln Penang, consisting of a string of high-rises. Cacophonic Lebuh

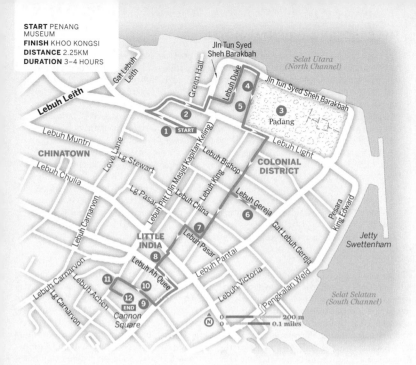

Walking Tour
Five Cultures on Two Feet

❯ This walk will give you a glimpse of Penang's cultural grab bag: English, Indian, Malay, Baba-Nonya and Chinese.

Starting at ❶ **Penang Museum**, head west and then up to the waterfront, passing the ❷ **Supreme Court**; check the statue of James Richardson Logan, advocate for nonwhites during the colonial era. Walk up Lebuh Duke to the waterfront, then right and right again down Jln Padang Kota Lama past the green ❸ **padang** (field) and grandiose architecture of the ❹ **City Hall** and ❺ **Town Hall**. Proceed left along Lebuh Light, then right on Lebuh Penang. A short detour finds the impressive ❻ **Pinang Peranakan Mansion**, the old digs of one of Georgetown's great Baba-Nonya merchant barons.

Continue down Lebuh Penang into ❼ **Little India** and take a deep breath of all that spice; if it's around lunchtime, refuel with a curry. At Lebuh Pasar, head right past shops selling milky Bengali sweets, then left at Lebuh King to the intersection of ❽ **Lebuh King and Lebuh Ah Quee**, a literal example of Penang's cultural crossroads: to your south is a Chinese assembly hall and rows of fading Chinese shopfronts; to your north is a small Indian mosque; and across the street is a large Malaysian cafeteria.

Left onto Lebuh Ah Quee, right on Jln Pantai, then right on ❾ **Lebuh Armenia** (if you want to go off-map to explore side lanes and alleyways, this is the time to do it). The street became a centre for Chinese secret societies and was one of the main fighting stages of the 1867 riots. Stroll past dusty barber shops till you reach ❿ **Tuah Pek Kong**, home to the oldest Straits Chinese clan association in Penang.

Cross the street to the corner of Lebuh Pitt and the small 1924 Hokkien clanhouse ⓫ **Yap Kongsi**, its outer altar decorated in symbols from the *Tao Teh Ching*. Left and left onto Cannon Sq brings you to the magnificently ornate ⓬ **Khoo Kongsi**, the most impressive *kongsi* in the city.

Originally built in 1884, the stylish E&O was the archetypal 19th-century colonial grand hotel, established by two of the famous Armenian Sarkies brothers, Tigram and Martin, the most famous hoteliers in the East, who later founded Raffles Hotel in Singapore.

In the 1920s the Sarkies promoted the E&O as the 'Premier Hotel East of Suez'. High-ranking colonial officials and wealthy planters and merchants filed through its grand lobby, and the E&O was established as a centre for Penang's social elite. Rudyard Kipling, Noel Coward and Somerset Maugham were just some of the famous faces who passed through its doors.

The Sarkies almost closed the E&O when the rent was raised from £200 to £350 a month. Arshak Sarkies, a third brother (and gambler by nature), persuaded the family to open Raffles Hotel instead. Arshak's generosity was legendary and some observers said that Arshak ran the E&O not to make money, but to entertain. Shortly before his death, Arshak began lavish renovations to the E&O. This expense, coupled with loans to friends that were conveniently forgotten, finally bankrupted the family business in 1931.

In the 1990s the E&O closed and fell into disrepair, but a huge renovation programme came to its rescue. In 2001 it once again opened for business, as a luxury, all-suite grand hotel with elegant, spacious rooms decorated in the best of colonial style.

Chulia and quieter Love Lane make up the heart of Penang's backpacker land, crammed with cheap hostels and hotels where it pays to check a few out before parting with your cash. There are a handful of top-end hotels, but most are strung out along Gurney Dr and Batu Ferringhi, and tend to be of the gargantuan chain-resort persuasion; the newest and most luxurious choices are heritage buildings that have been restored as boutique hotels in the city centre.

Be warned that during holidays, most notably Chinese New Year, hotels tend to fill up very quickly and prices can become ridiculously inflated; if you intend to stay at this time, book well in advance.

CHINATOWN

TOP CHOICE **Straits Collection**   APARTMENTS $$$
(www.straitscollection.com; ste from RM400; ✳@☎) Lebuh Armenia (☎262 7299; 89-95 Lebuh Armenia) Lg Stewart (☎263 7299; 47-55 Lg Stewart) If you've dreamed of living in a retro-chic restored Chinese shophouse, head here. Each residence is essentially a house (but no cooking facilities), artfully decorated with regional antiques, bright-coloured cushions and high-design rugs. Each is different but all have some sort of unforgettable detail such as light-well courtyards, wooden Japanese bathtubs or ancient sliding doors. There are five units on Lg Stewart clustering around delicious Kopi Cine (p164; owned by the same people) and four – two of which are available long-term – on Lebuh Armenia, a particularly peaceful and ambient part of the old town.

TOP CHOICE **Eastern & Oriental Hotel**   HOTEL $$$
(E&O; ☎222 2000; www.e-o-hotel.com; 10 Lebuh Farquhar; ste from RM485; ✳@☎) One of the rare hotels in the world where historic opulence has gracefully moved into the present day. Established by the Sarkies brothers in 1884, the suites seamlessly blend European comfort with Malaysian style using hardwood antiques and sumptuous linens; those with a sea view are worth the extra outlay. The sea-facing, British-manicured lawn is shaded by the biggest and oldest Java tree in Penang and conjures images of colonial suit-clad gentlemen and parasol-wielding ladies picnicking.

TOP CHOICE **Cheong Fatt Tze Mansion**   HOTEL $$
(☎262 5289; www.cheongfatttzemansion.com; 14 Lebuh Leith; r from RM250; ✳) Stay in the Blue Mansion, an 'heirloom with rooms', for the ultimate Eastern colonial experience. The house has near-perfect feng shui – even if you don't have a clue what feng shui is, once here you'll realise it's powerful stuff. The house is arranged around a plant-filled central courtyard from which the greatest *chi* energy emanates. Each room is uniquely themed and has a dreamy name like 'fragrant poem' or 'jolie', and represents a moment of Cheong Fatt Tze's life. A delicious courtyard breakfast is included in the price. Some guests say they have trouble sleeping here despite the wonderful energy, peace and quiet; old folks say it's the ghosts. The mansion is also a tourist attraction (p152) and is gay-friendly.

Muntri Mews
HOTEL $$

(☎262 3378; www.muntrimews.com; Lebuh Muntri; d around RM350; ❋@☎) The owners of Clove Hall (p163) have done it again with this superbly renovated row of shophouses in the heart of heritage Chinatown. It was still under construction when we passed but each room is essentially a suite with a sleeping area, lounge area and a retro black-and-white tiled bathroom in the centre. Wild East–feeling verandas line the rooms and overlook what is to be landscaped tropical gardens. An onsite cafe is planned for downstairs. Check the website for up-to-date rates and offers.

Penaga Hotel
HOTEL $$$

(☎261 1891; www.hotelpenaga.com; cnr Lg Hutton & Jln Transfer; r/ste from RM470/672; ❋@☎☲) The biggest of the new heritage-style hotels has three sections: one with a row of two-storey family-friendly minihomes, another with apartment-sized suites and the last with generous but more simple rooms. All are decorated with a magical mix of antiques and some surprising touches like cow-hide rugs, mid-century bright-hued couches and modern art. The stack of amenities include a pool, central gardens and a coffee shop.

Yeng Keng Hotel
HOTEL $$

(☎262 2177; www.yengkenghotel.com.my; 362 Lebuh Chulia; d/f RM300/400, ste RM400-600; ❋@☎☲) Smack in the heart of backpacker land, the Yeng Keng is a revamp of a 150-year-old hotel and is perhaps the first spark of the area's gentrification. Mustard-coloured walls and Oriental rugs in the foyer are a comfy modern take on heritage Chinese decor and the building is dotted with replica tiles that look like cartoon versions of the authentic ones at the Cheong Fatt Tze Mansion. Rooms are very small but immaculate and decorated in luxurious nouveau heritage furnishings; plenty of breezy passageways connect them all. The front patio cafe has attracted an upscale local following.

Segara Ninda
HOTEL $

(☎262 8748; www.segaraninda.com; 20 Jln Penang; r RM70-100; ❋☎) This elegant century-old villa was once the town residence of Ku Din Ku Meh, a wealthy timber merchant and colonial administrator. His home has been tastefully renovated, incorporating original features such as the carved wooden ventilation panels, staircase and tiled floors. A courtyard with fountains and plants makes this a mid-city oasis. There are 14 simply but elegantly furnished rooms of varying sizes; the cheaper ones are 'compact' and room price increases with room size.

Hutton Lodge
HOSTEL $

(☎263 6003; www.huttonlodge.com; 175 Lg Hutton; dm/s/d RM30/50/65; ❋@☎) The Hutton's exterior promises a bit more than its interior delivers. From the outside you see and expect an old-world jaunt with the allure of Asia during the Jazz Age. But the rooms, while comfy, spacious and air-conditioned, look like Ikea bed sets for children. It's a decent deal price-wise, but don't expect a heritage hotel atmosphere à la old Penang. Shared bathrooms are industrial sized and a basic continental breakfast is included in the price.

Cathay Hotel
HOTEL $

(☎262 6271; 15 Lebuh Leith; r with fan RM60, s/d with air-con RM69/75; ❋) Totally devoid of pretension, the Cathay has maintained the same lost-in-time Chinese functionality it's had for years the old guy at the front desk and woman tirelessly sweeping the floor are collecting dust they've been here so long. There's an unmistakable allure to the spacious colonial building with its light-infused courtyard, high ceilings, latticed windows and grand entrance, but the place is faded, decorated with shabby furniture and with tiles permanently stained from decades of who knows what. Rooms are huge and clean despite being worn, making this a great deal for the nostalgic. You may remember the hotel from the 1995 film *Beyond Rangoon*.

⬛ TOP CHOICE Red Inn
GUESTHOUSE $

(☎261 3931; www.redinnpenang.com; 55 Love Lane; dm/d incl breakfast from RM30/70; ❋☎) Upping the Love Lane ante, the Red Inn offers decent-sized rooms with plenty of retro flair including built-in bookcases and designer colour schemes. There's an elevated lounge area with movies on offer and the management couldn't be more helpful or professional. Dorm rooms have only three beds and, although they're a little cramped, they're clean and have good mattresses. The best room is the RM90 double with ensuite bathroom that has a rare window.

Old Penang
GUESTHOUSE $

(☎263-8805; 53 Love Lane; dm/s/d from RM20/40/55; ❋❋☎) This hotel was the first of the new relatively stylish and clean budget heritage options opening around Lebuh Chulia. Hardwood floors, white walls, high ceilings and splashes of red paint add a solid-coloured hip vibe to this hostel, otherwise set in a restored pre-WWII house that could easily serve as a set piece in a Maugham or Theroux short story. Rooms are microscopic and air-con ones with private bathrooms run to RM75.

Cititel Hotel HOTEL $$

(☎370 1188; www.cititelpenang.com; 66 Jln Penang; s/d from RM255/300; ✸@🕾) The views from the large modern rooms are particularly lovely, especially those that overlook the sea. It's brightly lit and always busy, and offers regulation business-traveller comforts, along with a few restaurants. Discounts are normally available.

Hotel Malaysia HOTEL $$

(☎263 3311; www.hotelmalaysia.com.my; 7 Jln Penang; r from RM140; ✸🕾) Crisp sheets, professional service and views over the Cheong Fatt Tze Mansion to the Penang Bridge make this place a winner in the bland category and a good deal for the price. A buffet breakfast is included.

Blue Diamond Hotel GUESTHOUSE $

(☎261 1089; 422 Lebuh Chulia; dm/s/d from RM8/20/30; ✸@) The Diamond is set in a beautiful old Chinese warehouse that contains one of the most memorable hostels in Malaysia. It's a bit grotty but beer and spirits magically coalesce into guests' hands at all hours. The worst cover band in Malaysia often plays in the courtyard; their follow-up show is to hit on every female guest within arm's reach. This may not sound appealing, yet there's an unmistakably fun vibe here, like that crazy uncle you can't help but love, and lots of return backpackers (male and female) swear by this joint. Air-con rooms with private showers cost RM45.

Banana Guest House GUESTHOUSE $

(☎262 6171; www.banananewguesthouse.com; 355 Lebuh Chulia; s/d from RM18/25; ✸@) The Banana Pancake Trail (the Southeast Asian backpacker route) lands very firmly in Banana Guest House, another one of those all-purpose hostels–bars–internet cafes–travel agencies you encounter from Bangkok to Bali. Rooms are OK, although some are sectioned off by the thinnest of walls. Come evening this is a good spot to meet other travellers, and the bar staff are the friendliest on the island. Pricier air-con digs come with or without toilet (RM50/60).

Civilians Inn GUESTHOUSE $

(☎261 6399; 52 Love Lane; s/d without bathroom from RM20/30, d with bathroom RM60; ✸) This is your standard Love Lane cheapy with plain, boxy rooms and thin mattresses, but it's the newest of the bunch so has a cleaner look than the competition. There's an airy upper level great for hanging up laundry, and a travel agency downstairs specialising in foreigner and local weddings, should you find the love of your life in Penang.

COLONIAL DISTRICT & LITTLE INDIA

China Tiger SELF-CATERING, HOMESTAY $$$

(☎264 3580; 25 & 29 Lebuh China; www.chinatiger. info; apt from RM500, homestay for 2 incl breakfast, tea & activities RM950; ✸🕾) You have a choice of experiences here: be completely independent in either of two open-concept self-catering apartments above an art gallery that are decorated in quirky antiques and the owner's modern art; otherwise, take one of the two homestay-style two-storey apartments attached to the owner's home, where you'll live in Chinese heritage elegance, get to hang out in the plant-filled courtyard and be pampered and taken around town by your hosts.

Victoria Hotel HOTEL $$

(☎262 227; 278 Lebuh Victoria; r incl breakfast from RM100; ✸🕾) This clean, modern hotel is a welcome addition for anyone wanting comfort without getting on the heritage train. There's a hint of style from the faux wood floors, designer coloured paint and arty Penang photos on the walls but other than that it's a standard hotel with good beds, TV, air-con and attached bathrooms. Filling breakfasts are either semi-full English or *nasi lemak*; wi-fi is RM8 per day.

PG Chew Jetty Homestay HOMESTAY $$

(☎🕾019 554 4909; pgcjhomestay@gmail.com; Chew Jetty; d RM128-148, f RM188; ✸) Perched at the end of the Chew Jetty, this homestay is geared towards groups but if they're empty they won't turn you away. Stay in simplicity, over the water and settle into the slow pace of jetty life. It's absurdly over-priced but offers a unique experience. Breakfast is an extra RM5.

Broadway Budget Hotel HOTEL $

(☎262 8550; www.broadwaybudgethotel.com; 35 Lebuh Pitt (Jln Masjid Kapitan Keling); s/d/tr from 35/45/55; ✸@🕾) The Broadway is a good deal if you want some comfort minus a heck of a lot of atmosphere. It's centrally located, rooms are large (if bland), there's in-room wifi for RM7 a day and the beds are comfy.

GURNEY DRIVE, JALAN BURMAH & AROUND

TOP CHOICE **Clove Hall** HOTEL $$$
(229 0818; www.clovehall.com; 11 Clove Hall Rd; ste from RM550; ※@🛜🏊) A white Edwardian Anglo-Malay mansion restored to unpretentious hardwood and tiled elegance, this is the place to go if you want to feel and be treated like a mogul of the early 1900s. In fact, this is the site of the Sarkies Brothers' first Penang home. The breezy louvred building is surrounded by gardens of birds of paradise and has a Zen-like pool with mini-waterfalls flowing into it; escape the heat in the well-ventilated foyer while taking afternoon tea and sampling the local cakes.

G Hotel HOTEL $$$
(238 0000; www.ghotel.com.my; 168 Perserian Gurney; r from RM350; ※@🛜🏊) The antithesis of the E&O is the G, which exemplifies (and aggregates) the contemporary tides of design, lifestyle and luxury amenities sweeping Malaysia's best hotels. Rooms are studies in minimalist, cubist cool, collections of geometric form set off by swatches of blocky colour. A yoga studio, spa and gym round out an exhaustive list of perks. There's a good crowd of creative and simply successful professionals blowing through the doors, giving the G a vibe that's as Manhattan as it is Malaysia.

Tune Hotel HOTEL $
(03 7962 5888; www.tunehotels.com; 100 Jln Burmah; s/d RM23/38; ※@🛜) Fly on Air Asia (who own this hotel) and you can pick up some great package deals – otherwise book early and look for specials online. It's a high-rise that's slightly out of the way for exploring the city centre but well located for good eats next to New World Park. Rooms are very clean, decent sized and decorated with an Ikea look broken by the occasional AirAsia advertisement on the wall. Room price includes no amenities – you pay extra for everything from towels to wi-fi. The price quoted above was for a weekday booked 10 days in advance, but prices vary. No matter what, it's a bargain.

1926 Heritage Hotel HOTEL $$
(228 1926; www.1926heritagehotel.com; 227 Jln Burmah; d RM105-170, f RM210-250; ※🛜🏊)

Here's another hotel that promises much more heritage allure from the outside than you'll find inside. A row of shophouses has been converted into an Olympic-length family hotel that's been gutted of every ancient artistic aspect and refilled with blandness. Rooms are comfortable, the onsite Chinese restaurant is reputable and the pool is the best in this price range.

✗ Eating

People come to Penang just to eat. Even if you thought you came here for another reason, your goals might change dramatically once you start digging into the Indian, Chinese, Malay and various hybrid treats available. Days revolve around where and what to eat, and three meals a day starts to sounds depressingly scant. It's the same for locals for whom eating out is a daily event. Any restaurant worth its salt (or chilli as the case may be) will be swarming with customers from opening to closing.

Opening hours are flexible but you can expect most places to be open from 8am to 10am for breakfast, noon to 2.30pm for lunch and 6pm to 10.30pm for dinner.

CHINATOWN

A wander down any street in Chinatown is likely to turn up hidden gems and there are basic coffee shops all over the city. A classic Penang breakfast is dim sum – search around Lebuh Cintra for the best options.

Hovering somewhere between Indian and Malay is *roti canai* (unleavened, flaky flat bread served with curry dhal), which is an all-time breakfast favourite. You'll find most stalls and restaurants serving this around Jln Penang.

For Western food, there's a concentration of smart restaurants and coffee bars on the short pedestrianised section of Jln Penang leading up towards the E&O Hotel, while Jln Chulia has dozens of backpacker cafes serving up mediocre fare.

TOP CHOICE **Teik Sen** CHINESE $
(18 Lebuh Carnavon; meals around RM10; ⊙noon-2.30pm & 5.30-8.30pm) Located just steps away from Lebuh Chulia, at first glance this open cafe looks like any other popular Chinatown establishment. On closer look you'll notice that patrons are dressed up – button shirts and high heels. Once you try the food you'll understand. This is a step up from the everyday delicacies of Chinatown. There's a menu translated into English but

DON'T MISS

PENANG MUST EATS

Don't leave town without sampling the following:

» **Char kway teow** Medium-width rice noodles stir-fried with egg, vegetables, shrimp and Chinese sausage in a dark soy sauce.

» **Curry mee** *Mee* (curly egg noodles) served in a spicy coconut-curry soup, garnished with bean sprouts, prawn, cuttlefish, cockles, beancurd and mint.

» **Hokkien mee** A busy and spicy pork-broth soup crowded with egg noodles, prawns, bean sprouts, *kangkong* (water convolvulus), egg and pork.

» **Asam laksa** Also known as Penang laksa, this is a fish-broth soup spiked with a sour tang from *asam* (tamarind paste) and a mint garnish; it comes with thick, white, rice noodles.

» **Rojak** A fruit-and-vegetable salad tossed in a sweet-tamarind-and-palm-sugar sauce and garnished with crushed peanuts, sesame seeds and chillies.

» **Won ton mee** This is a Cantonese clear-broth soup of wheat-and-egg noodles swimming with wontons (rice-paper dumplings stuffed with shrimp), vegetables and *char siew* (barbecued pork); the regional twist adds *belacan* (fermented shrimp paste).

chances are you'll be the only one among the tightly packed throngs who needs it. Try the curry prawns, crispy chicken with plum sauce or fried eggplant with bean paste. The adventurous can try other specialities like the braised sea cucumber and fish maws. Arrive by noon for lunch and 6.30pm for dinner, unless you want to wrestle a local for a table.

TOP CHOICE **Tho Yuen Restaurant**   DIM SUM **$**
(☏261 4672; 92 Lebuh Campbell; dim sum RM1-5; ☺6am-3pm, closed Tue) Our favourite place for dim sum. It's packed with newspaper-reading loners and chattering groups of locals all morning long, but you can usually squeeze in somewhere. Servers speak minimal English but do their best to explain the contents of their carts to the clueless round-eye. Try the handmade egg tarts and the *lo mai gai* (sticky rice with mushrooms) but remember not to take too much from the first cart that comes by, although you'll be tempted – there's always more to come.

Ocean Green   CHINESE SEAFOOD **$$**
(☏226 2681; 48F Jln Sultan Ahmad Shah; dishes from RM8; ☺9am-11pm) There's a menu at this waterfront seafood smorgasbord, but talk to your server about what's fresh. The dining hall is invariably packed – if it's too busy or hot ask about the air-con rooms in the adjacent Paramont Hotel. It's a good idea to reserve. We loved the crab *bee hoon* (glass noodles) and prawns with chilli dipping sauce.

TOP CHOICE **Amelie**   WESTERN **$$**
(☏469 7838; 6 Lebuh Armenian; meals around RM15; ☺10am-6pm) Our favourite stop for Western food, this three-table cafe with potted plants hanging from the ceiling, jars, baskets and hurricane lanterns perched on rickety shelves, feels like a wooden ship's kitchen while happy Hong, the chef, cooks up pasta, sandwiches and salads behind the bar. Also enjoy an excellent selection of drinks including lassis, a cooling crushed ice lime drink with longans and a full espresso bar.

Kopi Cine   WESTERN **$$**
(☏263 7299; 55 Lg Stewart; mains from RM22; ☺9am-11pm; ✍) Craving excellent Western food and a chic Italian cafe ambiance? Known for its speciality cakes, Kopi Cine does not disappoint, with its gourmet salads, sandwiches on fresh bread or copious mains like BBQ ribs or ginger bud pesto spaghetti. There's an excellent wine list, espresso drinks and plenty of refreshers like an addictive crushed mint-and-lime soda or frozen fresh fruit daiquiris.

Kheng Pin   CHICKEN RICE **$**
(80 Jln Penang; mains from RM4; ☺7am-3pm, closed Mon) Locals swear by the specialities here, most famously *lorbak* (spiced ground pork wrapped in bean curd dipped in black gravy) and Hainan chicken rice (steamed chicken with broth and rice), one of the great fast foods of East Asia. The state government used to send Kheng Pin's owner to Adelaide, Australia, every year to promote

Penang cuisine, so you know he's doing something right.

Thirty Two
FUSION $$$

(☎262 2232; 32 Jln Sultan Ahmad Shah; mains from RM50; ⊘dinner; ❋) Genteel restaurant in an elegant seaside mansion with a small garden and nice little alcoves. Dishes like six-spice marinated barbecue chicken, lobster, steaks and osso bucco lamb are on the menu but the house speciality is the crab laksa. There's a cocktail bar, and live jazz on Friday and Saturday evenings. Dress code is smart casual.

Sarkies Corner
WESTERN & ASIAN $$$

(☎222 2000; 10 Lebuh Farquahar; lunch buffet RM42, dinner buffet from RM58; ⊘lunch & dinner; ❋) Sarkies offers different themed dinner buffets every day; the focus shifts from Asian to Western to fusion to the kitchen sink, and it's uniformly good stuff (you'll want to dress up). The lunch buffet is gorgeous – it plucks menu items from across the globe, and if you can't find something you want, you're a very picky eater. Finally, for the nascent colonist deep in your soul, high tea (RM46) is served in the garden from noon to 3pm every Sunday.

1885
WESTERN $$$

(☎261 8333; 10 Lebuh Farquahar; mains from RM50; ⊘dinner; ❋) It doesn't get more elegant than a candlelit table at the E&O Hotel's main restaurant. The menu is ever-evolving, but you can always count on excellent Western cuisine such as sea bass with truffle sauce and roast duck. Service is top of the line and there's a smart-casual dress code (no T-shirts, shorts or sandals).

Ecco
MEDITERRANEAN $$

(☎262 3178; 402 Lebuh Chulia; mains around RM15; ⊘lunch & dinner, closed Sun; ❋) Those craving Mediterranean-inspired fare will find this place a godsend. It's extremely popular with locals but draws in its share of hungry Lebuh Chulia backpackers as well. The speciality is pizza, but dishes like Cajun-spiced chicken and roasted aubergine sandwiches on foccacia will keep you coming back. The chef is so concerned about quality that he purportedly grows his own basil for the pesto.

Sky Hotel
CHINESE $

(☎262 2322; 348 Lebuh Chulia; dishes around RM6; ⊘11.30am-2.30pm) It's incredible that this gem sits in the middle of the greatest concentration of travellers in Georgetown, yet is somehow almost exclusively patronised (in enthusiastic numbers) by locals. It is incumbent on you to try the *char siew* (barbequed pork), *siew bak* (pork belly), *siew cheong* (honey-sweetened pork) and roast duck. Order your pork *pun fei sau* (half fat, half lean)

LOCAL KNOWLEDGE

CK LAM: FOOD WRITER

Ask a Penangite who to talk to about where to eat and most will say CK Lam her blog **What2See: Best of Penang Food** (www.what2seeonline.com) helps even the locals discover where to eat.

Favourite Street Food

» **Duck koay chiap** (hand-rolled rice noodles in a duck soup with egg) Roadside stall near the junction of Jln Kimberly and Sungei Ujong (⊘7pm–late).

» **Mamak popiah** (Indian-style yambean, tumeric and sweet sauce spring rolls dipped in a laksa-like soup) Hawker row near Padang Brown Food Court along Jln Johor (opposite petrol station; ⊘1pm–6pm).

» **Assam laksa** Famous stall beside Air Itam Market (⊘late morning–night).

» **Chinese snacks** Coconut tarts and *khay nui ko/gai dan go* (egg cakes). Off Lebuh Cintra (⊘morning–afternoon).

Unique Eats

» **Nutmeg juice** Refreshing, slightly tangy drink often sweetened with Chinese sour plum. You can find it at Nyonya Breeze and Edelweiss Restaurants.

» **Traditional porridge** Eat rice porridge with various accompaniments while sitting (more likely balancing) on stacked stools atop benches. Stall on Jln Magazine between Jln Ria and Lebuh Lintang next to Bank Rykat (⊘11.30am-4pm Thu-Sun).

to get that proper combination of slightly wet and firm roasted goodness.

Kashmir   INDIAN $$
(Oriental Hotel, 105 Jln Penang; dishes RM5-11; ☺11am-3pm & 7-11pm; ✻) The dining area smells faintly of mothballs until the aromas of what many believe is Penang's best tandoori arrives. The restaurant is clean, with air-con and an underground feeling, but the round tables make it a fun, social experience. Revel in the bounty along with cocktails.

Kirishima   JAPANESE $$
(☏370 0108; Cititel Hotel, 66 Jln Penang; meals from RM35; ☺lunch & dinner; ✻) Japanese living in or visiting Penang head straight here; many foreigners cite it as the best sushi they've ever had. Think dark Japanese chic with saki bottles lining the walls. As well as sushi there's also excellent seafood. Reserve in advance for peak hours.

Joo Hooi   MALAYSIAN $
(Cnr Jln Penang & Lebuh Keng Kwee; laksa RM2.50; ☺12-6pm) Gorge on amazing laksa, *char kway tiaw, lorbak, cendol* (shave ice with palm sugar, coconut milk and jellies) and fresh fruit juices at this grungy-looking but clean hole-in-the-wall with minibooths and friendly service.

Hammediyah   INDIAN $
(164 Lebuh Campbell; mains from RM3; ☺lunch & dinner) There's lots of halal food available in the kitchen but, like all the locals in line, you shouldn't leave without trying the *murtabak*, a crepe-esque dish filled with beef and minced onions. Next door is the restaurant's new air-con outlet specialising in tandoori (mains RM7 to RM16).

Ee Beng Vegetarian Food   CHINESE $
(☏262 9161; 20 Lebuh Dickens; meals around RM5; ☺breakfast, lunch & dinner; ✍) Popular self-service place for cheap, mostly vegetarian food, of the tofu and green vegetables variety. It also offers fish curry for those craving something more meaty.

Passage Thru India   INDIAN $$
(☏262 0263; 132 Jln Penang; mains RM15; ☺lunch & dinner; ✻) The ambience here is nearly as enjoyable as the food: swirly Indian frescoes enliven the walls, sparkly sheer curtains drape effortlessly about and there's a collection of eclectic light fixtures. Specialities from all over India are on offer, served on a banana leaf. The tandoori and fish dishes are recommended.

Restoran Sup Hameed   MALAYSIAN $
(☏261 8007; 48 Jln Penang; mains from RM3; ☺24hr) With sprawling tables well beyond the actual restaurant like a trail of busy, dining ants down the sidewalk, this ultra-popular smorgasbord at the north end of Jln Penang has everything from spicy *sup* (soup!) and *nasi kandar* to *roti canai*. Curried squid is the house speciality.

Edelweiss   SWISS $$
(☏261 8935; 38 Lebuh Armenian; mains around RM30; ☺11am-10pm, closed Mon) Many people head here for the ambience in a gorgeously decorated, plant-filled 150-year-old Peranakan building. The food is very Swiss: think bratwurst, B52 pork sausage, rösti and smoked pork belly washed down with RM18 German beer.

Rainforest Bakery   WESTERN $
(☏261 4641; 300 Lebuh Chulia; cakes from RM2; ☺11am-7pm) This darling little take-away bakery, run by twin brothers Jesse and Jerry Tan, produces Western baked treats such as scones, cookies and bagels.

Soul Kitchen   ITALIAN $$
(102 Lebuh Muntri; mains around RM19; ☺8am-9pm) Italian specialities like lasagne, pizza and tiramisu are a few notches above the standard Lebuh Chulia bunch. Jazzy tunes are pumped out but otherwise there's not a heck of a lot of atmosphere.

COLONIAL DISTRICT & LITTLE INDIA
Finding good Indian food in Little India is a no-brainer. Wander around and you'll find endless restaurants and cafes serving up curries, roti, tandoori and biryani – restaurants usually specialise in either southern or northern Indian fare. This is also the best area to go to for vegetarian food.

Madras New Woodlands Restaurant   INDIAN $
TOP CHOICE
(☏263 9764; 60 Lebuh Penang; set lunch RM5, mains from RM1.50; ☺8.30am-10pm; ✻✍) It draws you in with its display of Indian sweets outside (try the *halwa*), but once you experience the food you might not have room for dessert. Tasty banana-leaf meals and north Indian specialities are the mainstays, as well as the thickest mango lassi in town. The daily set lunch with five servings of veg for RM5 might be Penang's greatest food bargain.

Karai Kudi   INDIAN $
(☏263 1345; 20 Lebuh Pasar; set meals from RM5; ☺11am-11pm; ✻✍) This outrageously tasty

Penang's reputation as a must-see destination hinges greatly on its food, and the best the city has to offer is served at hawker stalls and food courts. Not eating at a stall in Penang is like missing the Louvre in Paris – you simply have to do it.

Here's a list of the best in Georgetown:

Gurney Drive (Gurney Dr; ⊘dinner) Penang's most famous food area sits amidst modern high-rises bordered by the sea. It's posh for a hawker area so the food is a bit more pricey than elsewhere but you'll find absolutely everything from Malay to Western. It's particularly known for its laksa stalls (try **stall 11**). For the best *rojak* head to the Penang-famous **Aye Chye stall**.

Lorong Baru (New Lane; Lg Baru off Jln Macalister; ⊘dinner) If you ask locals where their favourite hawker stalls are, after listing a few far-flung places, they'll always mention this night-time street extravaganza, not for a particular stall but because all the food is reliably good. You'll find all the standard faves along with a few more adventurous choices like the **Chee Chong Chook stall**, which serves 'pig spare parts porridge'.

Esplanade Food Centre (Jln Tun Syed Sheh Barakbah; ⊘dinner) You can't beat the seaside setting of this food centre, which is nestled right in the heart of Penang's colonial district. One side is called 'Islam' and serves halal Malay food, and the other is called 'Cina' and serves Chinese and Malay specialities, including delicious *rojak* and fresh fruit juices. If you're sitting on the heathen side you can also enjoy some of the cheapest beer in town. When you're done with your meal, stroll along the breezy seafront esplanade with the city's budding couples.

Padang Brown Food Court (Jln Pantai off Jln Dato Keramat; ⊘lunch & dinner) Everyone in town knows that this is the spot for delectable *popiah* (spring rolls), although the *won ton mee* (egg vermicelli served with pork dumplings or sliced roast pork) and *bubur caca* (dessert porridge made with coconut milk and banana) is another good reason to try the food in this area. In the afternoons try the *yong tau foo* (clear Chinese soup with fish balls, lettuce, crab sticks, cuttlefish and more).

New World Park Food Court (Lg Swanton; ⊘lunch & dinner) Every stall serves something different at this ultramodern, covered food court with mist-blowing fans and shiny industrial decor. It's spotlessly clean and has an excellent reputation among Penangites. The *ais kacang* (shaved-ice dessert with syrup, jellies, beans and sometimes even corn on top) here gets particularly good reviews. There are also a number of great restaurants in this complex including Nonya and Indian.

Lorong Selamat (Lg Selamat off Jln Burma; ⊘dinner) This is the place to go for the city's best *char kway teow*, but you'll also find lip-smacking *won ton mee* and other Chinese Penang favourites. The setting, on a dingy lane off one of Penang's busiest streets, isn't spectacular but the locals' enthusiasm for the food here creates a lively ambience.

Kuala Kangsar Market (Jln Kuala Kangsar; ⊘6am-noon) Here you'll find vendors dexterously folding and stuffing slippery *chee cheong fun* (broad rice noodles filled with prawns or meat); watching the creation of the dish is much easier than wrestling the noodles into your mouth (good luck). Wander through the lush veggie and fish market to snack on fruit and Chinese baked goods.

Red Garden Food Paradise & Night Market (Lebuh Leith; ⊘breakfast, lunch & dinner) Not a single Penangite would list this as a best place to eat but it has an excellent location in the heart of Chinatown and offers a wide selection of food, including most local specialities, dim sum (for breakfast), pizza and even sushi. It's a good choice for families looking for something low-key and has lots of options for fussy eaters.

air-con place specialises in southern Indian Tamil Chettinad cuisine but also serves tandoori at dinner. Banana-leaf meals are huge and many sets include ice cream for dessert.

Sire WESTERN **$$**

(☎263 4359; 4 Lebuh King; mains RM20-60; ⏱11.30am-3pm & 6-10.30pm, closed Mon; ❄) The food here isn't spectacular (it's a mayonnaise-heavy Asian interpretation of fine Western cuisine) but the setting in a sky-lit air-well filled with antique Chinese tapestries and lush plants make this a special place indeed. White tablecloths and orchids on the tables seal the upscale atmosphere. Many people eat a snack here so they can visit the small yet exquisite museum at the back (see p155). If this is your angle, we suggest ordering the reasonably good walnut fudge brownie (RM16).

Sri Ananda Bahwan INDIAN **$**

(☎264 4204; 55 Lebuh Penang; mains from RM3; ⏱breakfast, lunch & dinner; ✐) Basic Indian eatery, seemingly forever full of chatting locals, which serves up tandoori chicken, *roti canai* and *murtabak* (*roti canai* filled with meat or vegetables). There's an air-con dining hall if you prefer more comfort.

Hui Sin Vegetarian Restaurant CHINESE **$**

(☎262 1443; 11 Lebuh China; meals around RM4; ⏱8am-4pm Mon-Sat; ✐) This excellent-value buffet restaurant is the place to go for a filling meat-free lunch. Take what you want from the selection of vegetables, curries and beancurds on offer, and you'll be charged accordingly. Enjoy it all with a glass of Chinese tea.

Kaliammans INDIAN **$**

(☎262 8953; 43 Lebuh Penang; mains from RM4; ⏱lunch & dinner; ✐) Smart, air-con restaurant serving north and south Indian cuisine, as well as Western food such as pizza. The best value are the tasty banana-leaf set meals, but the garlic naan with *palak paneer* (spinach and cottage cheese) is to die for.

GURNEY DRIVE, JLN BURMAH & AROUND

Penang, like Melaka and Singapore, was the home of the Straits-born Chinese, or Baba-Nonya, who combined Chinese and Malay traditions, especially in their kitchens. Penang's Nonya cuisine is a tad more fiery due to the island's proximity to Thailand. These days, Nonya cuisine is making a comeback and all the best places are found around Jln Burmah. Another good hunting ground for Nonya and international fare is on Jln Nagor, where a line of Chinese shophouses have been converted to chic restaurants and bars.

Casise FUSION **$$$**

(☎229 3858; 368-1-14 Bellisa Row, off Jln Burmah; 6-course menu RM188; ⏱noon-2:30pm & 7pm-late; ❄) New, upscale and creating a stir, Casise's chef Weng has returned to Penang from stints in San Francisco, Austria and Margaret River, Australia, to create this fusion restaurant known for its excellent wine pairing. Expect treats from duck breast with *foie gras,* cherry-pear puree and a balsamic reduction, to scallops with Yuzu vinaigrette.

Nyonya Breeze NONYA **$$**

(☎227 9646; 50 Lg Abu Siti; dishes from RM7; ⏱11.30am-2.30pm & 6.30-10pm, closed Tue; ❄) Considered by many local Peranakans to serve the best Nonya food, this humble family-run place makes you feel at home while you sample exquisite specialities like *kari kapitam* (chicken curry with coconut milk and kaffir lime) and *sambal goreng* prawns (prawns, eggplant and cashews in chilli sauce).

Bali Hai Seafood Market SEAFOOD **$$**

(☎228 8272; 90 Persiaran Gurney; meals around RM15; ⏱breakfast, lunch & dinner) A massive, always-packed seafood joint with big round tables inside and a few thatched huts outside, across from the waterfront promenade. The restaurant's motto is 'if it swims, we have it', and they do, in a mind-boggling array of tanks where you can pick out your critters. Also you can come here for dim sum in the mornings.

Mama's NONYA **$$**

(☎229 1318; 31D Lebuh Abu Siti; dishes around RM8; ⏱10am-2.30pm & 6.30-9.30pm, closed Mon; ❄) This low-key place was one of the first Nonya restaurants in Penang and it's still one of the best. Try the *otak-otak* (fish cakes), Nonya fish-head curry, *tau eu bak* (pork in soy sauce) and the unique and adventurous *daun kadok* (home-cured pickled fish innards).

Hot Wok NONYA **$**

(☎227 3368; 124 Jln Burma; mains from RM9; ⏱lunch & dinner, closed Tue; ❄) Located in a grand Nonya mansion filled with lattice-work and beautiful, distracting details, this restaurant feels upscale but is reasonably priced. Treat your tastebuds with the *or kueh* (yam cakes with chilli and onion) and *sambal sotong* (chili squid).

Miraku JAPANESE **$$**

(☎229 8702; 1st fl, G Hotel, 168A Persiaran Gurney; meals around RM35; ⏱noon-2.30pm & 6-10.30pm;

❄) Fresh fish from Japan is flown in twice a week and you can watch it get carved to perfection from the sushi counter. There's a large selection of sake and don't miss the signature dessert, tempura ice cream – ice cream encased in a fried batter ball.

Isaribi   JAPANESE $$
(☎229 8684; 60 & 62 Jln Chow Thye; set menu from RM16; ☺noon-3pm & 6-10pm) Fresh, expertly prepared sushi is served in a vine-covered hardwood setting that looks more like the heart of the jungle than the middle of the city. Beyond sushi, Japanese-style grilled fish set menus are the speciality with salmon, cod, trout and much more on offer. There's live jazz on Thursday nights.

Chock Dee   THAI $$
(☎229 1492; 231D Jln Burmah; dishes RM3-20; ☺11.30am-2.30pm & 6.30-9.30pm, closed Mon) With an elegant atmosphere and an owner who travels regularly to Thailand to stock up on ingredients, Chock Dee has garnered an impressive reputation. Menu highlights include squid in lemon sauce and Thai-style *otak-otak* (fish cakes).

🍺 Drinking

You can get a beer at most Chinese restaurants although not anywhere Malay. Food courts with Chinese vendors have the cheapest drinks prices in town; the bill goes up exponentially once you get to a restaurant or bar. Wine is available mostly by the bottle at finer restaurants and the selection quality has grown remarkably in the last few years.

One of the nicest areas for a drink is along the pedestrian section of Jln Penang, where a handful of chic bars spread out along the sidewalk and Penang's beautiful people came out in the evening to stroll and mingle.

That Little Wine Bar   BAR
(54 Jln Chow Thye; ☺5pm-midnight, closed Sun) Run by a German chef and his wife; enjoy a selection of imported wine, champagne cocktails along with tapas at this chic boutique bar and lounge. Everything from quiches to breads is made from scratch.

Slippery Senoritas   BAR
(Garage, 2 Jln Penang) Come to this see-and-be-seen club for surprisingly good live music, lots of drinking and a Tom Cruise *Cocktail*-esque show put on by the bar staff, involving lots of liquor-bottle juggling. The huge oval bar makes it possible to check out the entire diverse crowd – young and

old, expat and local – under the blaring video screens.

Jing-Si Books & Cafe   CAFE
(☎261 6561; 31 Lebuh Pantai; ☺noon-8pm) A stylish oasis of spiritual calm, this outlet for a Taiwanese Buddhist group's teachings is a wonderful place to revive in hushed surroundings over a pot of interesting teas or coffees (all only RM3).

Pitt Street Corner   BAR
(94 Lebuh Pitt) Pitt Street Corner feels like the offspring of a hipster bar crossed with a sports pub in Tamil Nadu. It's not divey but it sure isn't posh, either. Basically, it's a friendly spot for Tamil guys to get together, sink some beer, watch some football and Bollywood and play a few rounds of pool. Women are welcome, but count on being the only one.

Beach Blanket Babylon   BAR
(32 Jln Sultan Ahmad Shah) A swanky and hip bar run by the owners of Bagan and Thirty Two restaurant. Sunday night is men's night at this gay-friendly spot, with half price on standard pours and a discount on beer for males.

Soho Free House   PUB
(50 Jln Penang; ☺noon-midnight) This place starts rocking out early with cheesy '80s hits and a Chinese clientele who nosh bangers and mash and swill pints with the handful of expats. It purportedly has Malaysia's largest selection of draught beers and shows live sports on satellite TV on Saturday.

Farquhar's Bar   BAR
(10 Lebuh Farquhar) Colonial British-style bar inside the E&O Hotel, serving beer, traditional pub food and cocktails; try its signature drink, the Eastern & Oriental Sling (RM16.50) brought to you by a white-coated barman.

B@92   BAR
(92 Lebuh Gereja) Hip bar with a laidback attitude that features some live acts and hosts a pretty large – and mixed – expat and well-to-do local crowd. Has an atmosphere

---

GAY & LESBIAN PENANG

Penang is second only to KL for its gay and lesbian scene, which doesn't have to stay quite as hushed up as in many of Malaysia's more conservative cities. Popular hangouts include Bagan (p170) and Beach Blanket Babylon (p169).

somewhere between a British pub, American chain bar and small music venue.

Uptown Bistro BAR
(Cnr Jln Penang & Jln Sultan Ahmad Shah) The waitresses wear tacky sequined minis and the band is terrible but this spot is where many start the night for the buy-one-get-one-free drinks between 5pm and 8pm, the free dim sum and beer buckets for RM75.

☆ Entertainment

Penang's best dancing venues are along the stylish upper end of Jln Penang and are set up for drinking as much as, if not more than, for dancing. Karaoke can be found in several hotels along Jln Penang.

TOP CHOICE Bagan LIVE MUSIC
(☎226 4977; 18 Jln Bagan Jermal; ☺6pm-late) Think maroon-draped heritage-style lounge with a disco ball, giant mirrors and fairy lights. Sip cocktails or dine on hit-or-miss fusion fare at intimate dimly lit tables, or hang out at the bar to chat with the regular well-to-do crowd. Whatever you do, don't miss Malay trans-diva Roz, the soulful, sultry-voiced singer who performs around 10.15pm on Friday and Saturday.

Performing Arts Centre of Penang
PERFORMING ARTS
(☎891 8000; www.straitsquay.com; Straits Quay, Seri Tanjung Pinang) This centre, scheduled to open by the end of 2011, is located in the Straits Quay shopping plaza of a new housing development between Georgetown and Batu Ferringhi. It will bring the performing arts to Penang via an experimental theatre seating 150 people and a proscenium main stage seating 350, and will host art shows, films and cultural performances and even street acts by the sea. There will also be three studios for rehearsal and classes.

QEII CLUB
(☎261 2126; 8 Pengkalan Weld) Surrounded on all 360 degrees by the Straits of Malacca, QEII serves passable pizza and better ambience; this spot usually snags a good DJ who keeps funk and slow house grooving over the waterfront views.

Dome LIVE MUSIC
(Komtar, Jln Penang) This geodesic dome is one of those structures that looked dated the minute it was finished, but in any case, it still hosts some pretty good rock shows and other live acts.

LITTLE PENANG STREET MARKET

On the last Sunday of every month, the pedestrian section of Jln Penang hosts the **Little Penang Street Market** (☺10am-6pm), selling Malaysian arts and crafts such as dolls, batik, pottery, T-shirts and painted tiles, as well as items like bottled chutney.

Glo CLUB
(☎261 1066; Garage, 2 Jln Penang) If you've been longing for super-clubs/meat markets, here's a taste of what you've been missing. There's ear-splitting bass, big lights, lots of smoke, guys with slicked hair and ladies in little dresses.

Golden Screen Cinemas CINEMA
(Gurney Plaza, Gurney Dr) Penang's biggest cinema complex with 12 screens and THX sound is in the Gurney Plaza shopping complex (p172).

🛍 Shopping

Penang is a fun place to shop with plenty of outlets for local crafts and antiques, as well as cameras and electronics at competitive prices (although Kuala Lumpur has a wider range). Bargaining is usually required, except in department and upmarket stores. Jln Penang is the best shopping street in Georgetown, including several outlets selling creative and exotic women's clothing. Penang is also brimming with shops selling primarily Chinese trinkets, like calligraphy, watercolour paintings, good-luck charms and placemats.

TOP CHOICE Sam's Batik House CLOTHING
(☎261 8528; 159 Jln Penang) Nicknamed 'Ali Baba's Cave', this deep shop of silky and cottony goodness is the best place in town to buy sarongs, batik shirts and Indian fashions. Girls can go nuts over hand-embroidered dresses while the guys try on Bollywood shirts.

TOP CHOICE Fuan Wong ARTS & CRAFTS
(☎262 9079; www.fuanwong.com; 88 Lebuh Armenia; ☺11am-6pm Mon-Sat) This small gallery showcases the exquisite fused-glass creations of Penang artist Wong Keng Fuan. Colourful bowls and quirky sculptures are for sale. Be sure not to miss the photography exhibit upstairs as well.

Alpha Utara Gallery
ART GALLERY
(☎262 6840; www.alpha-utara.com; 83 Lebuh China; ☺10am-6pm Mon-Sat, noon-5pm Sun) Penang's best gallery displays the work of native son Khoo Sui Hoe and other excellent local artists like Eaton Tam and Dom Ke Pa.

Lean Giap Trading
GLASSWARE & CHINA
(☎262 0520; 443 Lebuh Chulia; ☺10.30am-6.30pm Mon-Sat) This jumbled-up little store sells a miscellany of goods including silverware, Oriental furniture, porcelain and glass.

Country Fair Boutique
CLOTHING
(☎262 1593; Level 2, Prangin Mall) Looking for a reasonably priced *kebaya* (traditional Nonya blouse)? Head here for custom and ready-made Nonya wear.

Oriental Arts & Antiques
ANTIQUES
(☎261 2748; 440 Lebuh Chulia; ☺11am-6pm Mon-Sat) Anything old seems to end up in this place, which has a selection of porcelain, furniture, jewellery, toys and general bric-a-brac.

Ten Yee Tea Trading
TEA SHOP
(33 Lebuh Pantai; ☺9.30am 6.30pm Mon-Sat) Fine teas are on sale here but the fun part is deciding which to buy. For RM10 you choose a tea (which you can share with up to five people), then a specialist shows you how to prepare it the proper Chinese way. A full explanation of all the different brews is given alongside the tea drinking.

Chowraster Bazaar
MARKET
(Jln Penang) This sweaty old market hall is where to go for a frenetic, souk-like experience. It's full of food stalls and vendors selling headscarves, batik shirts, fabrics and *kebaya*.

Gallery 29
ART GALLERY
(☎264 3580; 29 Lebuh China) Rebecca Duckett-Wilkinson's gallery shows off her modern yet traditionally inspired art in colourful splashes. There are also books, souvenirs and jewellery on offer.

Bee Chin Heong
BUDDHIST SUPPLIES
(☎261 9346; 58 Lebuh Kimberley; ☺10am-8.30pm) This interesting outlet sells a colourful, bewildering assortment of religious statues, furniture and temple supplies; if you're after a huge Chinese couch, a household shrine or have RM55,000 to spend on a 2m-tall carved-wood Buddha, this is the place to come. Even if you're not buying, it's still worth a look round.

Hong Giap Hang
PEWTER
(☎261 3288; 193-195 Jln Penang; ☺10am-8pm Mon-Sat, 11am-5pm Sun) If you're looking for pewter products, this place has one of the best ranges in town, selling all the different varieties. It also sells woodcarvings, jewellery, porcelain, crystal and batik.

Renaissance Pewter
PEWTER
(☎264 5410; Garage, 2 Jln Penang; ☺10.30am-7pm Mon-Sat) Locally made Renaissance pewter is another, much cheaper, alternative to Royal Selangor. Decorative tankards, tea caddies, vases and key rings can be had here.

Royal Selangor Pewter
PEWTER
(☎263 6742; 30 Lebuh Light) The top name in Malaysian pewter; this outlet stocks its current range, and pewter-making workshops can be arranged here, costing RM50 for about one hour. Book at least two days in advance.

ⓘ Information
Dangers & Annoyances
Although a reasonably safe place to wander around in, Georgetown, like any big city, does have its seamy side. Foreign tourists have been attacked and mugged in sidestreets at night, and it's unwise to linger in these areas alone after dark. More frequent are bag snatchers on motorbikes. Fortunately the city has cracked down on these crimes, police presence in tourist areas has increased and you're much less likely to encounter problems than a few years ago.

PENANG PEWTER

Malaysia's Royal Selangor, founded in 1885, is one of the most renowned pewter companies in the world. But with Royal Selangor's reputation comes a hefty price tag. Penang Pewter, Malaysia's second name in the metal arts, can be a real bargain compared with the picture frames, goblets, vases and the like produced by its upscale compatriots.

If you're not fussed about quality or brand names, even cheaper pewter items, many of which you can get custom engraved, are available in small shops around the Komtar shopping complex. Pewter was once made with lead, but today's varieties are made primarily of tin with a hint of copper.

MALL MANIA

There are dozens of malls in Georgetown and around the island. 1st Avenue mall, next to Prangin Mall, was under construction at the time of research and is poised to be a closer-to-town, artier version of Gurney Plaza with lots of upscale offerings.

Gurney Plaza (Gurney Dr) The most chic mall, with international chain stores like the Body Shop and Esprit. Mac users will find an Apple store here, and there's a massive music store, bookstore and several electronics outlets. There's also a mini theme park, fitness centre and a health spa.

Komtar (Jln Penang) Penang's oldest mall is housed in a 64-storey landmark tower. There are hundreds of shops in a place with the feel of an ageing bazaar. Here you'll find everything from clothes, shoes and electronics to everyday goods. There's a Tesco hypermarket, and you can take an elevator ride (RM5) from the ground floor to the 58th floor where there's a viewing area with views over the island.

Prangin Mall (Jln Penang) Adjoining Komtar, the biggest mall in downtown Georgetown houses a huge number of shops and restaurants, including smarter chain stores such as Parkson Grand, which has a wide range of clothes, cosmetics, household goods and such. There's also a cinema showing the odd Western blockbuster.

Queensbay Mall (Bayan Lepas) Penang Island's biggest and newest mall is packed with all the usual fashion suspects like Gap, Top Shop and Forever 21. It's out of the way and the other malls have the same stores but it's great if you want to get lost. It's off the Bayan Lepas Hwy near the Pulau Jerejak jetty.

Midlands Park Centre (226 8588; Jln Burma) This is like a scaled-down version of Prangin Mall, with a rooftop water park. It's on Jln Burma across from the Penang Adventist Hospital.

Robberies have occurred in some backpacker hostels, so you should never leave valuables, especially your passport, unattended. Meanwhile, drug dealing still occurs in Georgetown, despite Malaysia's very stiff antidrug laws; don't get involved.

Immigration Offices
Immigration office (261 5122; 29A Lebuh Pantai)

Internet Access
Most lodging options offer wi-fi and many also have a computer terminal for guest use. Wi-fi is also widely available at restaurants, cafes and in shopping malls. Internet cafes have lifespans slightly longer than a housefly, and loads of them can be found along Lebuh Chulia.

Libraries
Penang Library (229 3555; 2936 Jln Scotland; 9am-5pm Tue-Sat, 9am-1pm Sun)

Medical Services
The Community Directory put out by the Penang Heritage Trust (p173) has listings of traditional and modern healthcare centres.
General Hospital (229 3333; Jln Hospital)
Loh Guan Lye Specialist Centre (228 8501; 19 Jln Logan) Medical centre.

Penang Adventist Hospital (222 7200; www.pah.com.my; 465 Jln Burma)

Money
Branches of major banks are on Lebuh Pantai and Lebuh Downing near the main post office, and most have 24-hour ATMs. At the northwestern end of Lebuh Chulia there are numerous moneychangers open longer hours than banks and with more competitive rates. Moneychangers are also scattered around the banks on Lebuh Pantai and at the ferry terminal, although you'll probably get better rates on the mainland from the moneychangers at the Butterworth bus station.

Post
Post office (Lebuh Buckingham; 8.30am-6pm Mon-Sat)

Tourist Information
The extremely useful monthly **Penang Tourist Newspaper** (RM3) has comprehensive listings of shops, tourist attractions and hotel promotions, as well as detailed pull-out maps. It's usually available free from tourist offices and some hotels.

Forestry Department (262 5272; 20th fl, Komtar, Jln Penang) Provides pamphlets and information about Penang's parks and forests.

Penang Heritage Trust (☑264 2631; www.pht.org.my; 26 Lebuh Gereja; ⊗9.30am-2.30pm & 2.30-4.30pm Mon-Fri) Information on the history of Penang, conservation projects and heritage walking trails.

Penang Tourist Guide Association (☑261 4461; www.ptga.my; Komtar, 1 Jln Penang; ⊗10am-6pm Mon-Sat) Call or check the website to find a local tour guide.

Tourism Malaysia (☑262 0066; 10 Jln Tun Syed Sheh Barakbah; ⊗8am-5pm Mon-Fri) Georgetown's main tourist information office gives out maps and bus schedules.

Travel Agencies

Most, but not all, of the agencies in Georgetown are trustworthy. Reliable operators that many travellers use to purchase discounted airline tickets:

Happy Holidays (☑262 9222; 432 Lebuh Chulia)

Silver-Econ Travel (☑262 9882; 436 Lebuh Chulia)

Websites

www.globalethicpenang.net Information on the Penang Global Ethic Project, a local interfaith group that organises talks and exhibitions on religions and peace issues. See 'Walk of Faith' (p158) for information on the project's excellent World Religions walking tour.

www.igeorgetownpenang.com An excellent newsletter, aimed at Penang residents, that gives good under-the-skin information on Georgetown.

www.tourismpenang.gov.my Details of sights and restaurants in Penang.

www.ilovepenang.com Hey: we love you, Ilovepenang.com. Comprehensive information and a nicely designed website.

www.penang.ws Fairly up-to-date clearing house of hotel and restaurant listings.

www.penangfoods.com Guess what this website focuses on?

ⓘ Getting There & Away

See p173 and p173 for information on transport to and from Georgetown.

ⓘ Getting Around

Georgetown is on the northeastern corner of the island, where the channel between island and mainland is narrowest. The city centre is fairly compact and most places can easily be reached on foot or by trishaw.

To/From the Airport

Penang's **Bayan Lepas International Airport** (☑643 4411) is 18km south of Georgetown. The taxi fare to Georgetown is RM40.

Taxis take about 45 minutes from the centre of town, while the bus takes at least an hour. Bus 401 runs to and from the airport (RM3) every half hour between 6am and 11pm daily and stops at Komtar and Weld Quay.

Bus

Buses around Penang are run by the government-owned Rapid Penang. Fares range from RM1.40 to RM4. Most routes originate at Weld Quay and most also stop at Komtar and along Jln Chulia. For a full list and a map of the routes go to www.rapidpenang.com.my.

DESTINATION	ROUTE NO	PICK-UP
Batu Ferringhi	101	Pengkalan Weld, Lebuh Chulia, Komtar
Bayan Lepas International Airport	401	Pengkalan Weld, Lebuh Chulia
Gurney Dr	103	Pengkalan Weld, Air Itam, Komtar
Penang Hill Funicular	204	Pengkalan Weld, Lebuh Chulia, Komtar
Sungei Nibong bus terminal	401	Pengkalan Weld, Lebuh Chulia, Komtar
Teluk Bahang	101, 102	Pengkalan Weld, Bayan Lepas International Airport

Car

Penang's a good place to rent a car, but reserve in advance for weekends and holidays or if you need an automatic car. Rates start at around RM160 per day plus insurance but drop for longer rentals. Good deals can be found at smaller agents and online.

There are many car-hire companies in Georgetown:

Avis (☑643 9633; www.avis.com; Bayan Lepas International Airport)

Hawk (☑881 3886; www.hawkrentacar.com; Bayan Lepas International Airport)

Hertz (Map p148; ☑263 5914; www.hertz.com; 38 Lebuh Farquhar)

Motorcycle & Bicycle

You can hire bicycles and motorcycles from many places, including guesthouses and shops along Lebuh Chulia or out at Batu Ferringhi. It costs RM10 to rent a bicycle, and motorcycles start at around RM40 per day. Before heading off on a motorbike just remember that if you don't have a motorcycle licence, your travel insurance in all likelihood won't cover you.

PENANG HILL FOREST CHALLENGE

Penang's longest forest trail, the **Penang Hill Forest Challenge** runs from the upper funicular station to Teluk Bahang (p178), 6.6km away. This is a challenging trail taking the jeep track from the top to station 1 (Western Hill), a forest trail to station 10, then continuing on a forest track towards Teluk Bahang. Trees along the trail are marked with white paint and reflectors at 10m intervals. Expect a minimum of four hours to hike this trail if you are fit; the Penang Forestry Department recommends that hikers go in groups of at least four people, inform someone of where they are going, and that each person carries at least 2L of water.

Taxi

Penang's taxis all have meters, which drivers flatly refuse to use, so negotiate the fare before you set off. Typical fares around town cost around RM6 to RM15. For rates around the island see p174.

Trishaw

Bicycle rickshaws are an ideal way to negotiate Georgetown's backstreets and cost around RM30 per hour – as with taxis, it's important to agree on the fare before departure. You won't have any trouble finding one – more often than not, the drivers will hail you! From the ferry terminal, a trishaw to the hotel area around Lebuh Chulia costs from RM10 to RM15 (or you can walk there in about 15 minutes).

THE REST OF THE ISLAND

Penang isn't all Georgetown. When exploring the rest of the island, you'll find the same cultural mix but in smaller doses and with a paradisiacal backdrop. You can make the 70km circuit of the island by car, motorcycle or, if you're really fit, bicycle, but it's not possible to circle the whole island by bus. If travelling by motorcycle or car, plan to spend a minimum of five hours, including plenty of sightseeing and refreshment stops. If you're on a bicycle allow all day or maybe even stop in Teluk Bahang for the night to rest the thighs. The north-coast road runs beside the beaches.

Penang Hill

Rising 821m above Georgetown, the top of Penang Hill provides a cool retreat from the sticky heat below, being generally about 5°C cooler than at sea level. From the summit there's a spectacular view over the island and across to the mainland. There are some gardens, a simple food court, an exuberantly decorated **Hindu temple** and a **mosque** as

well as **David Brown's** (☑828 8337; near the upper station; mains from RM15; ☺9am-9pm), a colonial-style British restaurant serving everything from fish'n'chips to beef Wellington and high tea.

Penang Hill was first cleared by Captain Light, soon after British settlement, in order to grow strawberries (it was originally known as Strawberry Hill). A trail to the top was opened from the Botanical Gardens waterfall and access was by foot, packhorse or sedan chair.

In 1923 a Swiss-built **funicular** (every 10 min from 6.30am-9.30pm Sun-Fri, to 11.30pm Sat) was installed to chug up the hill; the train was upgraded throughout 2010 to accommodate more people (up to 80 at a time) and to reach the top three times faster than before without stopping at the mid-station – still, it's a bit sad to see the near-90-year-old train leave the rails. A tiny **museum** (admission free) inside the station displays some photographs and oddments from those early days. On the way, you pass the bungalows originally built for British officials and other wealthy citizens. Queues on weekends and public holidays can be horrendously long, with waits of up to 30 minutes, but on weekdays queues are minimal.

A number of roads and **walking trails** traverse the hill. From the trail near the upper funicular station you can walk the 5.5km to the Botanical Gardens (Moon Gate) in about three hours. The easier 5.1km tarred jeep track from the top also leads to the gardens, just beyond the Moon Gate. There are a couple of numbered pitstops, with views, along the trails, and you might be lucky enough to find someone stationed there to serve you a cup of tea.

ℹ Getting There & Away

From Weld Quay, Komtar or Lebuh Chulia, you can catch the frequent bus 204 (RM2). The energetic can take one of the walking trails to/from the Botanical Gardens or from Teluk Bahang.

Kek Lok Si Temple

The 'Temple of Supreme Bliss' is also the largest Buddhist **temple** (◐9am-6pm) in Malaysia and one of the most recognisable buildings in the country. Built by an immigrant Chinese Buddhist in 1890, Kek Lok Si is a cornerstone of the Malay-Chinese community, who provided the funding for its two-decade-long building (and ongoing additions).

To reach the entrance, walk through a maze of souvenir stalls, past a tightly packed turtle pond and murky fish ponds, until you reach **Ban Po Thar** (Ten Thousand Buddhas Pagoda; admission RM2) a seven-tier, 30m-high tower. The design is said to be Burmese at the top, Chinese at the bottom and Thai in between. In another three-storey shrine, there's a large **Thai Buddha image** that was donated by King Bhumibol of Thailand. There are several other temples here, as well as shops and a **vegetarian restaurant** (☑828 8142; mains from RM5; ◐10am-7pm Tue-Sun), while a **cable car** (one way/return RM4/2) whisks you to the highest level, presided over by an awesome 36.5m-high bronze **statue of Kuan Yin**, goddess of mercy. Sixteen highly decorated bronze columns support a roof over the statue, and 1000 2m-high statues of the goddess are planned to surround this area.

Also up here are a couple more temples, a fish pool, extensive gardens and statues of the twelve animals of the Chinese zodiac.

It's an impressive complex, though crowded with tourists and shoppers as much as worshippers. The temple is about a 3km walk from Penang Hill station, or you can hop on bus 204 to Air Itam (RM2). Tell the driver you want to get off near the temple.

Botanical Gardens

Don't join the throngs of Penang visitors who miss these 30-hectare **gardens** (☑227 0328; www.penangbotanicgardens.gov.my; Waterfall Rd; admission free; ◐5am-8pm). Also known as the Waterfall Gardens after the stream that cascades through from Penang Hill, they've also been dubbed the Monkey Gardens for the many long-tailed macaques that scamper around. Don't be tempted to feed them: monkeys do bite, and there's a RM500 fine if you're caught. You'll also see dusky leaf monkeys, black giant squirrels and myriad giant

bugs and velvety butterflies, which are all considerably more docile.

Once a granite quarry, the gardens were founded in 1884 by Charles Curtis, a tireless British plant lover who collected the first specimens and became the first curator. Today Penangites love their garden and you'll find groups practising t'ai chi, jogging, picnicking and even line-dancing here. The best time to visit is during the Penang International Floral Festival (see p158) around late May or early June.

Within the grounds are an orchid house, palm house, bromeliad house, cactus garden and numerous tropical trees, all labelled in English. The most famous tree in the gardens is the **cannonball tree**, which produces large pink flowers that give off stinking fruits about the size and shape of a human head.

To get here, take bus 102 (RM2) from Komtar or Weld Quay. There's also a path that leads to/from the top of Penang Hill).

Pulau Jerejak

Lying 1.5 nautical miles off Penang's southeast coast, thickly forested Pulau Jerejak has been home to a leper colony and a prison in its time, and is today occupied by the **Jerejak Resort & Spa** (☑658 7111; www.jerejakresort.com; r RM182-450; ✳❀). Packages available through the website, which usually include transport, breakfast and a massage, make staying here good value. It has some beautifully furnished chalets and a spa offering various kinds of massage, as well as a less luxurious 'adventure village' complex with simple doubles and dorms, though you will need to book the whole dorm room.

The resort has its own jetty, and day trippers are welcome. Boats leave roughly every two hours (adult/child RM25/16). There are several **activities** on the island including jungle trekking (one hour, RM20); wall climbing (RM10); mountain biking (RM15) and a suspension-bridge trail (RM15). No buses run past the jetty; a taxi from Georgetown will cost around RM50.

Snake Temple

The most misleadingly named destination in Penang is about 3km before the airport. Yes, there are snakes at the **temple** (Temple of the Azure Cloud; ◐9:30am-6pm) but, c'mon, with a name like that you expect beating drums and mad monks wielding 20-foot vipers. In reality it's just a temple with some snakes sleeping on sticks. The several resident venomous Wagler's pit vipers and green tree snakes are said to be slightly stoned by the incense smoke drifting around the temple during the day, but at night they slither down to eat the offerings and apparently throw a huge party, leaving them too messed up to do anything but lay around all the next day. There's a very depressing **snake exhibition** (adult/child RM5/3) with tanks containing various snakes in a walled-off section, and a few bored-looking snake handlers who will charge RM30 for taking your photo holding a snake.

Bus 302 runs every 30 minutes from Weld Quay and Komtar and passes the temple (RM4).

Batu Maung

About 3km after the snake temple, at the end of the Bayan Lepas Expressway, you reach the turn-off to the Chinese fishing village of Batu Maung. Once home to a biodiverse mangrove swamp, encroaching development from the Bayan Lepas Industrial Zone has resulted in extensive clearing. Development here is expected to skyrocket with the building of the new bridge linking Penang to the mainland (see the boxed text, p146). It's Penang's deep-sea fishing port so there are plenty of dilapidated, brightly painted boats along the coast.

The renovated seaside temple here, **Sam Poh Temple**, has a shrine dedicated to the legendary Admiral Cheng Ho (see p122), who was also known as Sam Poh. The temple sanctifies a huge 'footprint' on the rock that's reputed to belong to the famous navigator. Devotees pray before his statue here and drop coins into the water-filled footprint.

Perched on top of the steep Bukit Batu Maung is the **Penang War Museum** (☎626 5142; Bukit Batu Maung; adult/child RM25/12.50; ☻9am-5pm & 7-11pm). The former British fort, built in the 1930s, was used as a prison and torture camp by the Japanese during WWII. Today, the crumbling buildings have been restored as a memorial to those dark days. Barracks, ammunition stores, cookhouses, gun emplacements and other structures can be explored in this eerie, atmospheric place.

Also in town is the **Penang Aquarium** (adult/child RM5/2; ☻10am-5pm, closed Wed), which houses 25 tanks filled with colourful fish; there is a tactile tank with a young green turtle, and visitors can also feed koi.

Batu Muang is a fishing port so of course there are plenty of opportunities to sample fresh fish. The **Beginning of the World** (dishes from RM5; ☻breakfast & lunch) and **Best View Seafood** (dishes from RM5; ☻breakfast & lunch) are recommended. Bus 307 leaves for Batu Muang every half hour from Weld Quay and Komtar (RM4).

Kampung Pulau Betong

This is a fishing village utterly off the beaten track with delightful *kampung* houses, flowers and colourful docked boats. At around 5.30pm the fishing boats come in and sell their fish at the little market near the dock. Bus 403 runs from Balik Pulau as far as the market (RM1.40) but if you walk another 1.5km you'll come to **Pantai Pasir Panjang**, an empty, pristine beach with white sand the texture of raw sugar – one of the prettier spots on the island for the few who make the effort to get here. The beach is backed by a National Service Training Centre for young graduates entering the army. Be vigilant of the heavy undertow if you go into the water.

Teluk Kumbar & Gertak Sanggul

Penangites come to **Teluk Kumbar** with one thing in mind: seafood. While some housing estates have sprung up recently, the village is still a calm and beautiful stretch of sands. Stop at one of the Malay food stalls for some *mee udang* (spicy noodles with prawns) or at **Good Friend Seafood** (from RM3; ☻lunch & dinner).

Detour from Teluk Kumbar to **Gertak Sanggul**, which has gorgeous beaches, brightly painted fishing boats swaying in the sea and stalls on the shore selling fresh goodies. As enticing as it may look, don't swim here; pollution from the area's many pig farms make it a very bad idea. From the shore you can glimpse **Pulau Kendi**, the most distant island in the state of Penang.

Balik Pulau

Balik Pulau is the main town on the island circuit, with a population of 120,000. There are a number of restaurants, food stalls and a daily market here, but no accommodation.

KOPEL ECOTOURISM

A worthy ecotourism project is trying to extract tourists from the Georgetown–Northern Beaches path to Balik Pulau and the oft-ignored other sides of Pulau Pinang. **KOPEL** (☑250 5500; www.kopel.com.my), originally started as a cooperative for trishaw drivers, now puts visitors face to face with many of the traditional ways that have dominated Malay life. In Balik Pulau this includes tours of traditional handicrafts, a goat farm, paddy fields, seafood markets, palm sap harvesting and the like.

KOPEL also sponsors nine homestays in villages scattered across rarely visited corners of Penang, including the oft-ignored mainland. This is a pretty incredible opportunity for those missing a sense of 'old Asia' to connect to a way of life that is hard to grasp in rapidly modernising Malaysia. Under the auspices of a KOPEL homestay you'll be living life in tune with the rhythms of your hosts, who may be rice farmers, catfish fishermen and the like. Besides being a way of learning about a side of Malay life tourists rarely get to experience, some of the KOPEL homestay sites, like **Pulau Betong**, a small island off Pulau Penang's coast, are gorgeous, undisturbed slices of nature in their own right.

Rates vary hugely depending on season, length of stay and number of visitors – check the website and get in touch with the organisation directly for more information.

It's a good place for lunch, and the local speciality, laksa *balik pulau,* is a must – it's a tasty rice-noodle concoction with a thick fish broth, mint leaves, pineapple slivers, onions and fresh chillies, best sampled at the Balik Pulau **market**, the largest on the island.

Balik's Catholic **Holy Name of Jesus Church** was built in 1854 and its twin spires stand impressively against the jungle behind. The town's other claim to fame is its hill orchards of clove and nutmeg trees, which fruit during the month of July and between November and January. From late May to July, this is the place to come for durians.

For shopping, stop in at **Fong Ten Sent**, an ancient silversmith (and a real character) who sells his well-priced wares near the roundabout.

Balik Pulau is the terminus of bus 401 from Georgetown (RM4).

Balik Pulau to Teluk Bahang

After Balik Pulau you pass through an area of Malay *kampung* and clove, nutmeg, rubber, even durian, plantations. **Sungai Pinang**, a busy Chinese village, is built along a stagnant river. Further on is the turn-off to **Pantai Acheh**, another small, isolated fishing village.

About 2km further north along the road to Teluk Bahang is the hillside 10-hectare **Tropical Fruit Farm** (☑227 6223; ☺9am-6pm), which cultivates over 250 types of tropical and subtropical fruit trees, native and hybrid. Its two-hour tours (adult/child RM25/17) include fruit tastings and a glass of fresh juice. The hourly 501 bus runs between Balik Pulau and Teluk Bahang (RM4) four times a day, passing Sungai Pinang and the fruit farm.

After the turn-off to Pantai Acheh, the road starts to climb and twist, offering glimpses of the coast and the sea far below. During durian season stalls are set up along the road selling the spiky orbs, and you can see nets strung below the trees to protect the precious fruit when they fall. The jungle becomes denser here and soon you reach **Titi Kerawang**, until recently a waterfall flowing into a natural swimming pool just off the road – unfortunately, the nearby dam has left the stream a trickle.

Teluk Bahang & Around

If Batu Ferringhi is Penang's version of Cancun or Bali, Teluk Bahang is the quiet (sometimes deathly so) beach a few kilometres past the party. The only beach big enough for a resort has been taken over by the vacated and moulding old Mutiara, so the main thing to do is tool around Penang National Park.

◉ Sights

Penang National Park NATIONAL PARK
(Taman Negara Pulau Pinang) At just 2300 hectares, Penang National Park is the smallest in Malaysia; it's also one of the newest, attaining national park status in 2003. It has some

ESCAPING THE WORLD

Every now and then a Lonely Planet writer comes across a place so special it makes all the days of tirelessly slogging through sweaty cheap hotels worth it. **Malihom** (☎226 4466; www.malihom.com; 2 people all incl RM700; @ 🕿) is one of those places. Nine 100-year-old rice barns were imported from Thailand and brought up to this 518m peak where they have been restored to a cramped but comfortable state in a Balinese style. But you won't want to stay inside; walk around the small complex to gawk at the 360-degree view over hills of jungle, the sea and several villages. At the call to prayer you can faintly hear several mosques from around the island singing at once. The most serene infinity pool on the island is guarded by white Buddhas, the grounds are a perfect balance of shade, flowers and koi ponds, there's a conference room and yoga studio, and indoor hang-out areas perfect for sipping espresso or a glass of wine from the cellar, reading a book or watching movies. Basically you come here to completely relax because, aside from a few walks, mountain biking or fruit picking, there's blissfully little to do.

Malihom was originally built as a family retreat and always has a few artists in residence who are sponsored by the Bank of Scotland. You'll need to be shuttled up the steep hill at Malihom in their 4WD. The retreat is located off winding Route 6 between Balik Pulau and Kampung Sungai Batu.

interesting and challenging trails through the jungle, as well as some of Penang's finest and quietest beaches.

The park **office** (☎881 3500; ⊙9am-6pm) is at the park entrance with another **kiosk** (⊙7:30am-6pm) in Teluk Bahang across from the bus stop. Both have a few maps and leaflets and can help you plan your day. Just across from the main park office is the Penang Nature Tourist Guide Association office who offer **guide services** with a slew of options, such as trekking (2½ hours RM50) and many where you can hike one-way then get a ride back in a boat (four hours including boat transport for two people RM200), and also specialist tours such as bird watching, seasonal visits to a turtle hatchery, canoeing and mangrove tours. It's best to reserve longer tours in advance with agencies around Georgetown or at your hotel.

There's also a second entrance to the park at Sungai Pinang where an information counter is open from 8am to 5pm.

Trails

From the park entrance it's an easy 20-minute walk to the 250m-long **canopy walkway** (⊙10am-1pm & 2:30-4pm, closed Fri), suspended 15m up in the trees from where you can hear water flowing from the mountain and get a view over the broccoli-headed park; the walkway closes if it's raining. From here, you have the choice of heading towards Teluk Tukun and Muka Head or to Pantai Kerachut. The easiest walk is the 20-minute

stroll to **Teluk Tukun** beach where Sungai Tukun flows into the ocean. There are some little pools to swim in here. Following this trail along the coast about 25 minutes more brings you to the private **University of Malaysia Marine Research Station**, where there is a supply jetty, as well as **Tanjung Aling**, a nice beach to stop at for a rest. From here it's another 45 minutes or so down the beach to **Teluk Duyung**, also called Monkey Beach, after the numerous primates who scamper about here on the beach on **Muka Head**, the isolated rocky promontory at the extreme northwestern corner of the island. On the peak of the head, another 15 minutes along, is an off-limits 1883 **lighthouse** and an Achenese-style **graveyard**. The views of the surrounding islands from up here are worth the sweaty uphill jaunt.

A longer and more difficult trail heads left from the suspension bridge towards **Pantai Kerachut**, a beautiful white-sand beach that is a popular spot for picnics and is a green turtle nesting ground. Count on about two hours to walk to the beach on the well-used trail. On your way is the unusual **meromictic lake**, a rare natural feature composed of two separate layers of unmixed freshwater on top and seawater below, supporting a unique mini-ecosystem. From Pantai Kerachut beach you can walk about two hours onward to further-flung and isolated **Teluk Kampi**, which is the longest beach in the park; look for trenches along the coast that are remnants of the Japanese occupation in WWII.

FREE **Teluk Bahang Forest Reserve**

FOREST RESERVE

(☑Ranger's office 885 1280) The 873-hectare forest reserve contains a buzzing chunk of Penang's virgin rainforests. Guides are rarely available, so pick up a hiking leaflet at the ranger's office at the park entrance or at the Forestry Department in Georgetown (p172); the leaflets have trail maps and some information on plant identification. Also ask at either of these offices about **camping** in the reserve. There's a small **forestry museum** (☑885 2388; admission RM2; ☺9am-5pm Tue-Thu, Sat & Sun, 9am-noon & 2.45-5pm Fri) near the ranger's office.

To get to the park entrance from Batu Ferringhi, get off the bus 101 at the Teluk Bahang roundabout, turn left and walk 15 minutes. The park entrance will be on your left just past the Penang Butterfly Farm.

Trails

There are only five mapped trails in the park, the best-known being the **Penang Hill Forest Challenge**, the longest trail in Penang, which leads all the way to the top of 821m Penang Hill. This walk is obviously less strenuous in the downhill direction and is covered in the Penang Hill section (p174); from the Teluk Bahang end, expect the trek to take at least eight hours. One of the better walks is the easy 800m **Monkey-Cup Forest Trail** where you can search for carnivorous 'monkey-cups', more commonly known as pitcher plants. Intermediate trails are the 1.2km **Simpoh Gajah Trail**, which passes through virgin jungle, the 2.9km **Charcoal Kiln Trail**, which has some gnarly uphill bits through lovely forest to an old 1950s charcoal kiln; and the much more difficult 4.2km **Ridge Top Trail**, which branches off the Charcoal Kiln Trail to reach a ridge 400m above sea level. This last trail has some fantastic views over Telok Bahang, as well as pitcher plants to look out for along the way – if you don't have too much blinding sweat stinging your eyes.

Tropical Spice Garden   GARDEN

(☑881 1797; www.tropicalspicegarden.com; Jln Teluk Bahang; adult/child RM13/5, incl tour RM20/5; ☺9am-6pm) Along the road from Teluk Bahang to Batu Ferringhi is the Tropical Spice Garden, an oasis of tropical, fragrant fecundity of more than 500 species of flora, with an emphasis on spices. Ferns, bamboo,

ginger and heliconias are among the lush vegetation and you might spot a giant monitor lizard or two. The restaurant here is also excellent (see p180). To get here by bus, take any Teluk Bahang bus (RM4) and let the driver know that you want to get off here. There's a beautiful roadside white-sand **beach** just across from the gardens.

Penang Butterfly Farm   GARDEN

(☑885 1253; www.butterfly-insect.com; 830 Jln Teluk Bahang; adult/child RM20/10; ☺9am-5:30pm Mon-Fri, to 6pm Sat & Sun) Several thousand live butterflies representing over 150 species flap around here like buttery pastel clouds. There's also some fascinating beetles, lizards and spiders crawling about.

Orchid Garden   GARDEN

(☺9am-5.30pm) The colourful display of blooms is sure to delight horticulturalists.

🛏 Sleeping

Teluk Bahang is only 4km from Batu Ferringhi so if the few options here don't suit you, there are plenty more over there.

Miss Loh's Guest House   GUESTHOUSE $

(☑885 1227; 159 Jln Teluk Bahang; dm/s/d from RM8/15/30; ☀) Miss Loh's is a throwback to the good old days of long-term backpacking. Her garden-set, ramshackle guesthouse feels as much run by the guests (most of whom are sticking around for a bit) as anyone else, although we suppose the real masters of the house are the cats and dogs. Rates are negotiable for longer stays, but Miss Loh won't accept telephone reservations. There are communal shower-and-toilet blocks. To find the guesthouse, look for a store on Teluk Bahang's main street (the one street) that says 'GH Information' – this is your contact into Miss Loh's little world.

Fisherman Village Guest House

GUESTHOUSE $

(☑885 2936; 60 Jln Hassan Abbas, Kampong Nelayan; dm/d from RM7/18; ☀) Fisherman Village isn't quite as laidback as Miss Loh's, but that's being pretty relative – anywhere else in the world and this is just the sort of garden spot to fully immerse yourself in some indolent idleness. It feels more like a homestay than anything, and you'll likely be tempted to let yourself become rooted in the slow pace of life here.

Hotbay Motel   MOTEL $$

(☑016 4559062; Jln Teluk Bahang; r RM65-80; ☀) In the main shopping area east of the roundabout, Hotbay offers fair motel-style rooms, with a communal TV lounge at the front. Rooms with five and seven beds are also available (RM150/210).

✖️ Eating

With all those fishing boats in the harbour, fresh and tasty seafood is guaranteed. A group of busy hawker stalls congregate at the final bus stop after the roundabout. The main shopping area along the road heading east to Batu Ferringhi also has a few coffee shops where you'll find cheaper Chinese dishes and seafood, as well as a couple of good South Indian places which sell *murtabak* and *dosa* (savoury Indian pancakes).

TOP CHOICE **Tree Monkey** THAI $$
(☑881 3494; Tropical Spice Garden; platters from RM30; ⊘9am-11pm; 🛜) Ah, tapas platters of northeastern Thai food made with Tropical Spice Garden herbs and spices and served under a thatched roof with a view of the sea. This is alfresco at its best, surrounded by gorgeous gardens where grey misty monkeys make an appearance from time to time. Try the house speciality, the spices roll made with betelnut leaves, an array of herbs and served with a tamarind sauce. This is also an excellent place for a sunset cocktail.

Restoran Khaleel FOOD COURT $
(Jln Teluk Bahang; mains from RM4; ⊘24hr) This is a great-value little food court next to the Hotbay Motel. The usual Malay specialities such as *nasi goreng* and fish-head curry are all here.

ℹ️ Getting There & Away

Bus 101 runs from Georgetown every half-hour all the way along the north coast of the island as far as the roundabout in Teluk Bahang (RM4).

Batu Ferringhi

The road from Teluk Bahang that winds along the coast to Batu Ferringhi is a picturesque stretch of small coves and more beaches. The quaintness abruptly stops at Batu Ferringhi (Foreigner's Rock), a concrete-clad resort strip. Stretching along the main drag of Jln Batu Ferringhi, the road is lined with big hotels, Malay restaurants and tourist shops flogging neon kiddie floats and cheesy postcards. A lot of package resort types end up here, as do an increasing number of tourists from the Gulf States – you'll likely see men walking shirtless next to women in full *chador* and veil on the beach. While many resorts line the beach, the most gentle and ambient area in town is the jumble of cheap backpacker places and beachfront cafes that form a small community along the western portion of the sugary white beach.

The sand of Batu Ferringhi is fine for sunbathing, but doesn't compare to Malaysia's best; the water isn't as clear as you might expect, and often swimming means battling jellyfish. The beach itself can be dirty, especially on weekends when hordes of day trippers visit. Still, it's the best easy-access beach stop on the island.

There's a good **night market** and the **Yahong Art Gallery** (☑881 1251; 58-D Jln Batu Ferringhi) sells a vast range of Asian antiques and art, including jewellery, pewter, batik paintings, woodcarvings, and, less appealingly, ivory.

🏃 Activities

There's plenty of **watersports** rental outfits along the beach; they tend to rent wave runners (RM120 for 30 minutes), water-skiing trips (RM100 for 15 minutes) and parasailing trips (RM80 for 15 minutes).

After which you might need a relaxing **massage**. All sorts of foot masseuses will offer you their services; expect to pay around RM40 for a 30-minute deep-tissue massage.

✨ Festivals

Penang Beach Carnival CARNIVAL
This carnival in Batu Ferringhi is highlighted by traditional sporting events such as *gas uri* (top spinning) and *sepak takraw* (a ball game played over a net, much like badminton but with the players using their feet). (June)

Penang Island Jazz Festival MUSIC
Features local and international artists at changing venues in Batu Ferringhi. (November/December)

🛏️ Sleeping

Outside high season (roughly December to February), big discounts are often available. Budget places all have shared bathrooms except where indicated, and are all practically carbon copies of each other: nice-if-bland rooms in shared family-run houses with easy access to the beach. A second chain of places have recently been cropping up on the beach to the southwest of the backpacker strip – these places are shoddily built, have air-con and run by elusive managers who may or may not be around; prices hover around RM80. Midrange around these parts means a package-feel family-style resort, and top-end is like a quick trip to Bora Bora.

TOP CHOICE Lone Pine Hotel
RESORT $$$

(☏886 8686; www.lonepinehotel.com; 97 Jln Batu Ferringhi; r from RM880; ❊@☎☎) What a remodel. Reopened in late 2010, this old favourite has redefined Batu Ferringhi from a sunburned 1980s sort of place to modern, Asian-infused and chic. There's a huge selection of rooms that all have some perk, from personal plunge pools to private gardens. The ongoing theme is white and trendy with splashes of colour via bed runners and contemporary photography; rooms are well thought out, with everything exactly where you need it. The resort remains family friendly with a small pool for kids and plenty of space to run around under the hotel's namesake causarina trees next to the beach.

Shangri-La Rasa Sayang Resort
RESORT $$$

(☏881 1966; www.shangri-la.com; Jln Batu Ferringhi; r from RM780; ❊@☎☎) A vast and luxurious establishment feeling like something out of a South Sea dream. Rooms are large and decorated with fine hardwood furniture, and cloud-like white duvets float on the beds; all have balconies and many have sea views. The exclusive Rasa wing has even more decadent suites. Palms, plumeria and birds of paradise in the gardens create a lush enclave for the winding, partially shaded naturalistic swimming pool. A thin stretch of beach borders the gardens. The hotel's Chi Spa is among the most posh on Penang Island and is housed in 11 serene villas surrounded by lush plants. There's a yoga studio, tennis courts, a putting green and several restaurants.

Shangri-La Golden Sands Resort
RESORT $$$

(☏886 1191; www.shangri-la.com; r from RM490; ❊@☎) In the same Shangri-La family as the high-class Rasa Sayang, this hotel is more like the group's big-haired, cheesy-grinned little sister. You can almost imagine Julie the cruise director leading you through the orderly array of blue, rubber-woven lawn chairs, sprawling cement walkways and mushroom-like thatched huts. Rooms move into the modern age and are spacious with marble bathrooms.

Holiday Inn Resort
RESORT $$

(☏881 1601; www.holidayinnpenang.com; 72 Jln Batu Ferringhi; r from RM250; ❊@☎☎) A big, family-friendly resort with accommodation blocks on either side of the main road, which was recently subject to a cheap remodel that probably won't weather time. Still, it's all refreshingly unpretentious with a pool full of kids, a range of folks sprawled in the sun on beach chairs and themed 'kidsuites', which come with TV, video and playstation. There's also tennis courts and a gym.

Grand Plaza Park Royal
RESORT $$

(☏881 1133; www.parkroyalhotels.com; Batu Ferringhi; r from RM350; ❊@☎) The 324 rooms are pretty standard but comfortable. The grounds are more a reason to stay, with three pools, some with islands in them, lots of lawn to bask on and a great strip of beach out front.

Baba Guest House
GUESTHOUSE $

(☏881 1686; babaguesthouse2000@yahoo.com; 52 Batu Ferringhi; r RM45-80; ❊) Grandma's cooking something in the kitchen, sister is doing laundry and grandpa is snoozing in a chair. This is a wonderfully ramshackle, blue-painted house that shows off the heart and soul of its resident (and very active) Chinese family. Rooms are large and spotless, most have shared bathrooms and the dearer air-con rooms come with a fridge and shower. Grab your book, put up your feet on the colonial wood terrace and relax the day away. The beach is only about five steps away.

Ali's Guest House
GUESTHOUSE $

(☏881 1316; 53 Batu Ferringhi; tent RM10, r RM60-140, ❊) With a courtyard overflowing with tree ferns and a wooden terrace that just nails that colonial feeling, this place is the most appealing in the budget range. The simple rooms aren't as interesting as the common areas but most have air-con, attached bathrooms and TVs, and the room price includes breakfast.

ET Budget Guest House
GUESTHOUSE $

(☏881 1553; etguesthouse2006@yahoo.com; 47 Batu Ferringhi; r RM35-70; ❊) In a bright and open double-storey Chinese home with polished wood floors, this friendly, snoozy place is the best bargain on the beach. Most rooms in the charming old-time building have a common bathroom and mosquito nets. The pricier air-con rooms come with TV and shower.

Shalini's Guest House GUESTHOUSE **$**
(☎881 1859; ahlooi@pc.jaring.my; 56 Batu
Ferringhi; r RM40-70; ❀) This old, two-
storey wooden house on the beach has
an Indian family atmosphere; although
not everyone in the family is outwardly
friendly, they do warm up eventually.
Rooms are basic but neat and some have
balconies. The priciest ones have private
bathrooms.

Boomerang Guesthouse GUESTHOUSE **$**
(☎725 6619; boomeranglodge@yahoo.com;
Batu Ferringhi; r RM70-180; ❀) Probably the
quirkiest place on the new cheapy area at
the southwest of the beach, the only person we could find here when we passed
by was a 50-something German woman
smoking a hookah. Rooms are in various
stages of cleanliness and there's a terrace
bar right on the beach with plenty of
water pipes to go around.

Ismail's Beach Guest House GUESTHOUSE **$**
(☎881 2569; Batu Ferringhi; r RM70-80; ❀)
Back behind the Waverunner Beach
Chalet and right on the beach, this clean,
modern concrete complex has little in
the way of creative decor. All rooms have
air-con, attached bath and TV.

Waverunner Beach Chalet GUESTHOUSE **$**
(☎019 472 7789; 54 Batu Ferringhi; r RM80; ❀)
Right on the sand, this is a brick chalet
block that's often full. Rooms are clean,
with tiled floors, two double beds, TVs,
kettles and private showers; but there are
signs of wear and tear.

✖️ Eating & Drinking

There are some basic foodstalls on the
beachfront near the budget guesthouses,
where you can enjoy some fresh fish, while
Global Bay Food Court (cnr Jln Batu Ferringhi & Jln Sungai Emas) is a good place for
inexpensive Western and Chinese meals.
There's also a surprising number of decent
Lebanese places along the main drag.

TOP CHOICE **Ferringhi Garden** WESTERN **$$**
(☎881 1193; 34C Batu Ferringhi; mains
around RM30; ☽dinner) Everyone falls in love
with the outdoor setting here of terracotta
tiles and hardwoods surrounded by bam-
boo, tall potted plants, hanging mosses and
cut orchids in elegant vases. Inside is a cosy
lounge and bar area. The food is Western,
as interpreted by a Malaysian chef, and is
reasonably well prepared. Try the Angus

oxtail soup and sizzling Mongolian beef,
house specialities.

Sunset Bistro WESTERN **$**
(☎012 553 1313; Batu Ferringhi; mains from RM9;
☽noon-1am, to 3am Fri & Sat) Sunset does its
best to imitate a Thai beach experience with
decent, overpriced executions of pasta, burg-
ers, Chinese, seafood and Malaysian stan-
dards served by long-haired Malaysian boys.
The hiked prices are basically sand-between-
your-toes tax.

Ship SEAFOOD **$$**
(☎881 2142; 69B Jln Batu Ferringhi; mains from
RM15; ☽noon-midnight) You can't miss this
one; it's a full-size replica of a wooden sail-
ing ship, specialising in hefty steaks and
seafood. Escargot and oysters are also on
the somewhat overpriced menu. It's quite
smart inside, but rather dark.

ℹ️ Getting There & Away

Buses 101 runs from Weld Quay and from
Komtar, in Georgetown, and takes around 30
minutes to reach Batu Ferringhi (RM4).

Batu Ferringhi to Georgetown

Heading back into Georgetown from Batu
Ferringhi, you'll pass **Tanjung Bungah**
(Cape of Flowers), the first real beach
town close to the city – but it's not good
for swimming. Inexplicably, big hotels and
apartment blocks are cropping up everywhere, but Batu Ferringhi is still a better
option.

After Tanjung Bungah, you'll enter the
Pulau Tikus (Midlands) suburbs, full of
discos, wining-and-dining venues, cinemas, and megamalls like **Midlands Park
Centre** (p172) and **Island Plaza**. If your
kids have seen *Toy Story 2*, they might feel
bad for the more than 100,000 toys locked
up in the **Toy Museum** (☎460 2096; Jln
Tanjung Bungah; admission adult/child RM10/6;
☽9am-9pm) with nobody to really love
them; no one has tried to break Woody
free yet. It's a fun kitsch place to visit and
chances are that everyone will see some
old friends in the collection.

Georgetown has encroached nearly
enough for this area to be considered a
neighbourhood, rather than a separate
town. A taxi from Georgetown's Lebuh Chulia to Midlands costs RM20.

Pulau Tikus is also the beginning of scenic Gurney Dr with its great sea views and hawker food (see p167); see p172 for Gurney Plaza. Eventually it intersects with Jln Sultan Ahmad Shah, formerly Millionaire's Row, where nouveau riche Chinese in the early 20th century competed to see who could build the most impressive mansion. Many of the homes have now been demolished and abandoned, taken over by squatters, fronted by office space or even converted into fast-food outlets. Keep moving in this direction and you'll have made it back to central Georgetown.

SEBERANG PERAI

Living in the shadow of the tourist megalith of Penang Island, Seberang Perai has become the forgotten half of the state. While it doesn't hold much to entice visitors, Butterworth has one or two interesting places to visit if you're passing through. The province was previously called Wellesley Province, named for Richard Wellesley, the governor-general of Bengal from 1797 to 1805.

Butterworth

You probably won't spend much time in the industrial town of Butterworth, which lacks the historic points of interest and charm found on Penang Island. The main reason most travellers come here is to pass through and cross the channel to visit Penang. The town has a large ferry port and an air force base.

The only major point of interest is the **Penang Bird Park** (Taman Burung Pinang; ☑399 1899; Jln Todak; adult/child RM15/7.50; ☺9am-7.30pm), 7km east of the ferry terminal across the river. This landscaped park has more than 300 species of birds, mostly from Southeast Asia, including parrots, hornbills and hawks. To get there, take one of the frequent buses from Butterworth bus station to Seberang Jaya (RM1.50).

If you're a Chinese-temple freak, it's worth checking out **Rumah Berhala Tow Boo Kong** (Nine Emperor Gods Temple), which is exceedingly ornate for a modern edifice, with a dramatic roof swarming with curving pagodas and golden dragons. It's home to a Taoist group who worship the Nine Emperor Gods, the nine sons of the Queen of Heaven, who are the patron deities of, among other things, prosperity and health. During the **Nine Emperor Gods Festival** in September or October this is *the* place to be. For nine days the temple becomes a hive of followers who walk on fire and pierce their cheeks with an array of objects; on the last day a model ship is sent out to sea. Vegetarian food and snacks are prepared and sold at stalls during this time. The temple is north of the Jln Raja Uda and the Butterworth–Kulim Expressway. Look out for the temple on the right side of the road after the Butterworth Outer Ring Rd intersection.

🛏 Sleeping & Eating

'You said the train was in the afternoon!'
'I'm sorry, I can't read military time.'
'Looks like we're stuck here for the night...'

Sunway Hotel HOTEL $$
(☑370 7788; www.sh.com.my; 11 Lebuh Tenggiri Dua, Seberang Jaya; s/d RM242/288; ❄@) This modern tower close to the Penang Bird Park in the suburb of Seberang Jaya is aimed primarily at business travellers, with the usual smart international setup. Rooms sport 'oversized beds', and you can even get 'karaoke on demand' through your TV.

Hotel Berlin HOTEL $$
(☑332 1701; 4802 Jln Bagan Luar; s/d from RM100/120; ❄) A few doors down from the Ambassadress, the Berlin offers a bit more comfort, and discounts are normally available. There's a gym and sauna, and breakfast is included in the price, which is a good deal for Butterworth. We stress, for Butterworth.

Ambassadress Hotel HOTEL $
(☑332 7788; 4425 Jln Bagan Luar; r from RM40; ❄) This sleepy Chinese hotel above a cheap *kedai kopi* (coffee shop) of the same name is a fair, if rather timeworn, budget option. Air-con rooms cost RM63, and all have attached bathrooms.

Sri Ananda Bahwan Restaurant INDIAN $
(☑323 6228; 2982 Jln Bagar Luar; mains from RM3; ☺6.30am-midnight) Popular Indian place that serves vegetarian/nonvegetarian set lunches for RM3.50/5. It has a particularly good selection of colourful, handmade Indian sweets, which you can have boxed to take away.

❶ Getting There & Away

Most of the land transport (buses, trains, taxis) throughout Peninsular Malaysia and to Thailand leaves from the train station or near it, and next to the terminal for ferries going to/from Georgetown. See the Getting There & Away (p173) and Getting Around (p173) sections for information on transport services to/from Butterworth.

Pulau Aman

For anyone really wanting to get off the beaten track, head to the tiny fishing island of **Pulau Aman** (Peace Island; population 300), 4.5km off the coast of Bukit Tambun in Seberang Perai. The whole island can be covered on foot in about an hour; trees are labelled with scientific and local names, making the walk a bit educational as well. The oldest known *sukun* (breadfruit tree) in Malaysia can be found in the village, and is said to have been planted in 1891; it's marked with a basic cement sign. There is one small **beach** at the north. Several paths lead through the village and a cement path goes partway around the island.

To get to Pulau Aman take the **ferry** (one-way adult/child RM4/2), filled with fishermen and their families, that leaves the Bukit Tambun pier (departures 10am, 1pm, 4pm and 7pm; 30 minutes) for the fishing village on the northeast side of the island. The return trips to Bukit Tambun are at 8am, 12pm, 3pm and 6pm.

Understand KL, Melaka & Penang

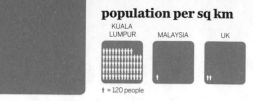

population per sq km

KUALA LUMPUR   MALAYSIA   UK

† ≈ 120 people

KL, Melaka & Penang Today

One Malaysia?

The tolerant mingling of Malay, Chinese and Indian cultures in Kuala Lumpur, Melaka and Penang are a large part of what makes these historic cities so appealing. Here, the stories of Malaysia's diverse ethnic groups and colonial empires are intertwined – south Indian cooks serve fiery curries from the doorways of Sino-Portuguese houses built as part of trade deals between European powers and the sultans of Melaka.

Interestingly, a poll by the independent Merdeka Centre published in July 2010 showed that only 39% of non-Malays believed the government's 1Malaysia policy (www.1Malaysia.com.my) was a sincere effort to unite Malaysians of all ethnicities. That such a policy was deemed necessary at all speaks volumes about the underlying tensions and suspicions that continue to simmer beneath the seeming harmony.

Gross National Income per person: US$13,770

Life expectancy: 74.4 years

Inflation: 1.9% (July 2010)

Unemployment: 3.7% (March 2010)

Improving Public Transport

If one thing does unite all Malaysians it's their frustration with public transport. You only have to look at the faces of KL citizens, squashed into a monorail or train carriage at rush hour, or stuck in a highway traffic jam, to know how they feel. 'It's not as bad as Bangkok or Jakarta,' says Steven Gan, editor of Malaysiakini (www.malaysiakini.com), referring to KL's traffic, 'but if you want people to give up using their cars you have to improve the public service.'

To address the problem the government has earmarked funds to upgrade and integrate the Mass Rapid Transit (MRT) system with the addition of three new lines, including a circular one that will span the KL–Klang Valley conurbation.

Over in Melaka the government is proud of its 1.6km-long new monorail that runs through the city centre tourist belt. Penang's second

---

Top Non-Fiction

Malaysia at Random (Editions Didier Millet) Quirky compendium of facts, figures, quotes and anecdotes.
Found in Malaysia (The Nut Graph) Compilation of 50 interviews with notable Malaysians from the news and analysis website (www.thenutgraph.com).
The Consumption of Kuala Lumpur (Zaiddin Sardar) How the once sleepy capital has evolved into a modern economic marvel.

Top Websites

www.malaysiakini.com Malaysia's best online news site.
www.malaysiandigest.com Views from across the political spectrum.
www.themalaysianinsider.com Events and personalities shaping Malaysia.

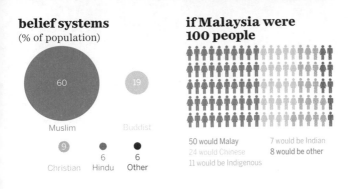

belief systems
(% of population)

60 Muslim
19 Buddist
9 Christian
6 Hindu
6 Other

if Malaysia were 100 people

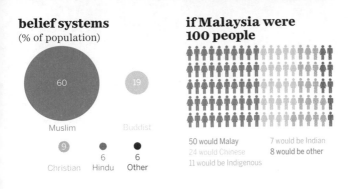

50 would Malay
24 would Chinese
11 would be Indigenous
7 would be Indian
8 would be other

bridge link to the mainland should be completed by the end of 2012 and its airport is being upgraded. However, the change of state government in 2008 (to the main opposition party) just happened to coincide with the federal government's decision to defer projects to build an outer ring road and a monorail on the island.

KL's Controversial Tower

'Really, it's just a piece of cake', concluded the call to arms on the Facebook page opposing the construction of the 100-storey Warisan Merdeka tower (www.facebook.com/NoMegaTower) in KL next to Stadium Merdeka and Stadium Negara. A month after the October 2010 announcement of what will be Malaysia's tallest building, the anti-tower pressure group had amassed over 250,000 supporters whom it was urging to gather at designated sites every Wednesday to eat birthday cake in protest. The idea is that the police wouldn't want to look foolish arresting such peaceful demonstrators.

The estimated cost of the tower, slated to be the new headquarters of PNB (Malaysia's largest fund management company and a key instrument in the government's pro-Malay affirmative action policies), is RM5 billion. 'This project is not a waste. We want a building that will become a symbol of a modern, developed country', said Prime Minister Najib, going on to remind critics that past costly construction projects, such as the Penang Bridge and the Petronas Towers, were initially greeted with antipathy.

The Development Debate

Najib is pinning hopes on economic stimulus measures such as Warisan Merdeka to win back voters who turned away from the ruling coalition in

> In October 2010 Melaka was declared a 'developed state' according to key criteria of the Organisation for Economic Cooperation and Development (OECD).

Top Fiction

My Life as a Fake (Peter Carey) Reworking of Frankenstein evokes the sultry side of KL.
The Gift of Rain (Tan Twan Eng) Set in Penang before and during WWII.
The Return (KS Manian) Indian Malaysian student returns home after studying abroad.

Top Movies

Entrapment (1999) The climax of this Sean Connery and Catherine Zeta-Jones thriller takes place at KL's Petronas Towers.
The Blue House (2009) Penang's Cheong Fatt Tze Mansion hosts this Singaporean comedy thriller

Septet (2004) Chinese boy falls for Malay girl in Yasmin Ahmad's romantic comedy.

the 2008 elections. Reforms to the pro-Malay policies that have shaped Malaysian society for the past 30 years are also on the cards (see p196) as part of the government's New Economic Model.

As the controversy over Warisan Merdeka shows, Najib may have a hard time convincing Malaysians that such developments are the best way forward. Unfinished and abandoned buildings litter central KL, and construction projects that are moving forward – such as that on the site of the former Pudu Jail (see p56) – have inflamed heritage protectionists.

Melaka and Georgetown have been somewhat protected since their inscription on the UNESCO World Heritage list in 2008. This has raised other problems, notably the impact of increased tourist numbers – Melaka hosted 8.9 million visitors in 2009, up from 1.7 million a decade ago.

A Democratic Society?

Also continuing to cause public protests is the Internal Security Act (ISA; see p197). In September 2008, Democratic Action Party (DAP) MP Teresa Kok was jailed under the ISA for a week for allegedly requesting that a local mosque turn off its loudspeakers broadcasting the call to prayer. Law minister Zaid Ibrahim resigned from the Cabinet in support of Kok and others arrested under the ISA. Thirty more arrests in Petaling Jaya and four in Penang followed in August 2010 at candlelight vigils organised to protest the ISA's 50th anniversary.

Another antidemocratic hangover from the 1960s is the lack of local government elections – KL, Georgetown and Melaka's city councillors have all been government appointees since 1964. The DAP made reintroducing these elections part of their 2008 election campaign manifesto, but since taking power in Penang they have been unable to deliver through lack of the necessary federal approval.

In 2009 *Fortune* magazine ranked the Malaysian national oil and gas company Petronas (www.petronas.com.my) as the 13th most profitable in the world. The company, which reported revenues of US$77 billion in 2009, contributes over a third of the Malaysian government's annual budget.

Playlist

Harapan (www.reshmonu.com) Dance master Reshmon's latest.

Zee Avi (www.zeeavi.com) Folksy pop from the sweet young KL-based diva.

Isaac Entry Live at No Black Tie Catchy guitar riffs from a popular KL performer.

Dos and Don'ts

» Do cover your head, arms and legs when visiting a mosque

» Do use your right hand only if eating with your fingers

» Don't embrace or kiss in public.

» Don't point with your forefinger: use the thumb of your right hand with fingers folded under.

Greetings

» A *salam* involves both parties briefly clasping each other's hand then bringing the same hand to touch their heart

» Malay women don't shake hands with men – smile and nod or bow slightly instead.

History

As a modern independent nation, Malaysia has only been around since 1963, though British colonial rule on the peninsula ended in 1957. The early history of the peninsula is hazy because of a lack of written records. The oldest remains are of the 11,000-year-old skeleton, 'Perak Man', which has genetic similarities to the Negrito who now live in the mountainous rainforests of northern Malaysia.

The Negritos were joined by Malaysia's first immigrants, the Senoi, from southern Thailand, and later by the Proto-Malay, ancestors of today's Malays, who came by sea from Indonesia between 1500 BC and 500 BC. For more on Malaysia's indigenous people see p195.

From the rise of the Melaka Sultanate in the 16th century events were well documented, both locally and by the nations that came to trade with, and later rule over, the peninsula, including the Portuguese and the Dutch.

Early Trade & Empires

By the 2nd century AD, Malaya was known as far away as Europe. Ptolemy, the Greek geographer, labelled it Aurea Chersonesus (Golden Chersonese), and Indian traders, who came in search of precious metals, tin and aromatic jungle woods, referred to the land as Savarnadvipa (Land of Gold). The first formalised religions on the peninsula – Hinduism and Buddhism – arrived with those Indian traders, giving rise to the first recorded Hindu kingdom on the peninsula, Langkasuka (from the Sanskrit for 'resplendent land').

From the 7th century to the 13th century, the area fell under the sway of the Srivijaya Empire, based in southern Sumatra. This Buddhist empire controlled the entire Malacca Straits, Java and southern Borneo and became fabulously rich from trade with India and China. Under the protection of the Srivijayans, a significant Malay trading state grew up in the Bujang Valley area in the far northwest of the Thai–Malay

TIMELINE	2nd century AD	600	1400
	Langkasuka, one of the first Hindu-Malay kingdoms, is established on the peninsula around the area now known as Kedah. It lasted in one form or another until the 15th century.	From their base in southern Sumatra, most likely around modern-day Palembang, the Buddhist Srivijaya Empire dominates Malaya, Singapore, Indonesia and Borneo for six centuries.	Hindu prince and pirate Parameswara flees his home on the island of Temasek (Singapore) following an invasion. Sailing up the peninsula, he founds what will become the great trading port of Melaka.

THE LOST KINGDOM OF LANGKASUKA

It's hardly surprising that the early Malay Peninsula kingdom of Langkasuka was lost. Even at the time, people were unable to agree on its exact location. Chinese explorers claimed it was on the east coast, while Malay histories place it on the west coast near Penang. Probably there was just one kingdom extending right across the peninsula. Between the 3rd and 6th centuries, Langkasuka's power dwindled and the Funan kingdom, centred in what is now Cambodia, assumed control of the region, before they were supplanted by the Srivijaya Empire. Langkasuka disappeared from the map, though part of its name lives in on in the islands of Langkawi.

peninsula. The growing power of the southern Thai kingdom of Ligor and the Hindu Majapahit Empire of Java finally led to the demise of the Srivijayans in the 14th century.

The Melaka Empire

The history of the Malay state begins in earnest in the late 14th century. This was when Parameswara, a renegade Hindu prince-cum-pirate from a little kingdom in southern Sumatra, washed up around 1401 in the tiny fishing village that would become Melaka. As a seafarer, Parameswara recognised a good port when he saw it and immediately lobbied the Ming emperor of China for protection from the Thais in exchange for generous trade deals. Thus the Chinese came to Malaysia.

Equidistant between India and China, Melaka became a major stop for freighters from India loaded with pepper and cloth, and junks from China loaded with porcelain and silks, which were traded for local metal and spices. Business boomed as regional ships and *perahu* (Malay-style sampans) arrived to take advantage of trading opportunities. The Melaka sultans soon ruled over the greatest empire in Malaysia's history.

It's thought that the word Malay (or Melayu) is based on the ancient Tamil word *malia*, meaning 'hill'. Other Malay words like *bahasa* (language), *raja* (ruler) and *jaya* (success) are Sanskrit terms imported to the area by Indian visitors as early as the 2nd century AD.

The Portuguese Era

By the 15th century Europe had developed an insatiable appetite for spices, which were conveyed there via a convoluted trade route through India and Arabia. The Portuguese decided to cut out the middle man and go directly to the source: Melaka. Reaching the Malay coast in 1509, the Portuguese were greeted warmly by the local sultan, but relations soon soured. The invaders laid siege to Melaka in 1511, capturing the city and driving the sultan and his forces back to Johor.

The Portuguese secured Melaka by building the robust Porta de Santiago (A'Famosa fortress) and their domination lasted 130 years, though the entire period was marked by skirmishes with local sultans. Compared

1407	1446	1509	1511
Parameswara marries the princess of Pasai, a Muslim from Sumatra, and adopts the Persian title Iskander Shah. He dies seven years later, passing control of Melaka to his son Megat Iskander Shah.	A naval force from Siam (Thailand) attacks Melaka. Warded off, they return in 1456 but are again rebuffed. Such attacks encourage Melaka's rulers to develop closer relations with China.	Portuguese traders sail into Melaka. Although at first greeted warmly, the sultan later acts on the advice of his Indian Muslim councillors and attacks the Portuguese ships, taking 19 prisoners.	Following the Portuguese conquest of Melaka, the sultan and his court flee, establishing two new sultanates on the peninsula: Perak to the north and Johor to the south.

with Indian Muslim traders, the Portuguese contributed little to Malay culture; attempts to introduce Christianity and the Portuguese language were never a big success, though a dialect of Portuguese, Kristang, is still spoken in Melaka.

The Dutch Period

Vying with the Portuguese for control of the spice trade, the Dutch formed an allegiance with the sultans of Johor to oust the Portuguese from Melaka. A joint force of Dutch and Johor soldiers and sailors besieged Melaka in 1641 and wrested the city from the Portuguese. In return for its cooperation, Johor was made exempt from most of the tariffs and trade restrictions imposed on other vassal states. Despite maintaining control of Melaka for about 150 years, the Dutch never fully realised the potential of the city. High taxes forced merchants to seek out other ports and the Dutch focused their main attention on Batavia (now Jakarta) as their regional headquarters.

East India Company

British interest in the region began with the need for a halfway base for East India Company (EIC) ships plying the India–China maritime route. The first base was established on the island of Penang in 1786.

A History of Malaya by Barbara and Leonard Andaya brilliantly explores the evolution of 'Malayness' in Malaysia's history and the challenges of building a multiracial, post-independence nation.

A HISTORY OF PIRACY

The lucrative trade routes around the Malay Peninsula have long provided rich pickings for pirates. As far back as the Srivijaya Empire, from the 7th to 13th centuries, piracy was a problem. The Srivijayans used the seafaring people the Orang Laut (also known as Sea Gypsies) to police the trade routes, but by the 11th century they had switched sides and become pirates themselves. Parameswara, founder of Melaka, was also a pirate, attacking trading ships from his temporary base of Temasek (Singapore).

A millennium later and piracy in the Strait of Melaka, one of the world's busiest waterways, remains a problem. To combat the pirates, Malaysia formed a Coast Guard that together with forces from Singapore and Indonesia have run coordinated patrols since 2004. It's had a positive impact as the International Maritime Bureau recorded that attacks in 2008 and 2009 had dipped to two compared to seven in 2007.

It's not just at sea that the authorities have to keep a look out for pirates. Malaysian markets are packed with pirated copies of DVDs, CDs, computer software and various luxury and brand-name fashion goods. The Business Software Alliance, a Malaysian antipiracy watchdog, reports that over 60% of all software used by businesses are illegal copies. The authorities, keen to preserve Malaysia's growing reputation as a hi-tech hub, are cracking down, sending inspectors into businesses and issuing fines to those found using pirated software.

1612–13	1641	1786	1795
Sejarah Melayu (Malay Annals), a literary work covering 600 years of Malay history, is believed to have been compiled by Tun Sri Lanang, the *bendahara* (chief minister) of the Johor royal court.	After a siege lasting several months, the Dutch, with the help of the Johor sultanate, wrest Melaka from the Portuguese; this marks the start of Melaka's decline as a major trading port.	Francis Light cuts a deal with the sultan of Kedah to establish a settlement on the largely uninhabited island of Penang. Under a free-trade policy the island's new economy thrives.	The British take over Melaka and Dutch Java; after the defeat of Napoleon in 1818 both are returned to the Dutch but Melaka's fortress A'Famosa is left in ruins.

THE ADOPTION OF ISLAM

Peninsular Malaysia was Buddhist and Hindu for a thousand years before the local rulers adopted Islam. The religion is believed to have spread through contact with Indian Muslim traders and gained such respect that by the mid-15th century the third ruler of Melaka, Maharaja Mohammed Shah (r 1424–44), had converted. His son Mudzaffar Shah took the title of sultan and made Islam the state religion. With its global trade links, Melaka became a hub for the dissemination of Islam and the Malay language across the region.

Meanwhile, events in Europe were conspiring to consolidate British interests on the Malay Peninsula. When Napoleon overran the Netherlands in 1795, the British, fearing French influence in the region, took over Dutch Java and Melaka. When Napoleon was defeated in 1818, the British handed the Dutch colonies back – but not before leaving the fortress of A'Famosa beyond use.

The British lieutenant-governor of Java, Stamford Raffles – yes, *that* Stamford Raffles – soon persuaded the EIC that a settlement south of the Malay Peninsula was crucial to the India–China maritime route. In 1819, he landed in Singapore and negotiated a trade deal that saw the island ceded to Britain in perpetuity, in exchange for a significant cash tribute. In 1824, Britain and the Netherlands signed the Anglo-Dutch Treaty dividing the region into two distinct spheres of influence. The Dutch controlled what is now Indonesia, and the British controlled Penang, Melaka, Dinding and Singapore, which were soon combined to create the 'Straits Settlements'.

Sabri Zain's colourful website Serajah Melayu (www.sabrizain. org/malaya) contains a wealth of historical info on the Malay Peninsula including a virtual library of nearly 500 books and academic papers.

British Malaya

In Peninsular Malaya, Britain's policy of 'trade, not territory' was challenged when trade was disrupted by civil wars within the Malay sultanates of Negeri Sembilan, Selangor, Pahang and Perak. In 1874 the British started to take political control by appointing the first colonial governor of Perak and, in 1896, Perak, Selangor, Negeri Sembilan and Pahang were united under the banner of the Federated Malay States, each governed by a British Resident.

Kelantan, Terengganu, Perlis and Kedah were then purchased from the Thais in exchange for the construction of the southern Thai railway, much to the dismay of local sultans. The 'Unfederated Malay States' eventually accepted British 'advisers', though the sultan of Terengganu held out till 1919. To this day, the states of the northeast peninsula form the heartland of the fundamentalist Malay Muslim nationalist movement. By the eve of WWII Malays were pushing for independence.

1800	1826
Penang's lieutenant governor Sir George Leith negotiates a deal to control the strip of land on the coast of Perak, opposite the island, and names it Province Wellesley after India's governor-general.	Having swapped Bencoolen on Sumatra for the Dutch-controlled Melaka, the British East India Company combines this with Penang and Singapore to create the Straits Settlements.

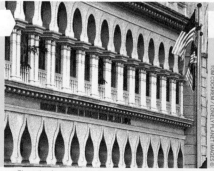

» Elegant columns grace a government building in KL

WWII

A few hours before the bombing of Pearl Harbor in December 1941, Japanese forces landed on the northeast coast of Malaya. Within a few months they had taken over the entire peninsula and Singapore.

Although Britain quickly ceded Malaya and Singapore, this was more through poor strategy than neglect. Many British soldiers were captured or killed and others stayed on and fought with the Malayan People's Anti-Japanese Army (MPAJA) in a jungle-based guerrilla war throughout the occupation.

The Japanese achieved very little in Malaya. The British had destroyed most of the tin-mining equipment before their retreat, and the rubber plantations were neglected. However, Chinese Malaysians faced brutal persecution – the atrocities of the occupation were horrific even by the standards of WWII.

The Japanese surrendered to the British in Singapore in 1945. Despite the eventual Allied victory, Britain had been humiliated by the easy loss of Malaya and Singapore to the Japanese, and it was clear that its days of controlling the region were numbered.

Colonial Sights

» A'Famosa, Melaka

» Stadthuys, Melaka

» Fort Cornwallis, Georgetown

» Merdeka Square, Kuala Lumpur

HISTORY WWII

Federation of Malaya

In 1946 the British persuaded the sultans to agree to the Malayan Union, which amalgamated all the peninsular Malayan states into a central authority and came with the offer of citizenship to all residents regardless of race. In the process, the sultans were reduced to the level of paid advisers, the system of special privileges for Malays was abandoned and ultimate sovereignty passed to the king of England.

CREATING A MULTICULTURAL NATION

British rule radically altered the ethnic composition of Malaya. Chinese and Indian immigrant workers were brought into the country as they shared a similar economic agenda and had less nationalist grievance against the colonial administration than the native Malays, who were pushed from the cities to the countryside. The Chinese were encouraged to work the mines, the Tamil Indians to tap the rubber trees and build the railways, the Ceylonese to be clerks in the civil service, and Sikhs to man the police force.

Even though 'the better-bred' Malays were encouraged to join a separate arm of the civil service, there was growing resentment among the vast majority of Malays that they were being marginalised in their own country. A 1931 census revealed that the Chinese numbered 1.7 million and the Malays 1.6 million. Malaya's economy was revolutionised, but the impact of this liberal immigration policy continues to reverberate today.

1867	1896	1914	1935
The Penang Riots see a nine-day street battle between two Chinese secret societies fighting to control commercial activities; the authorities bring reinforcements from Singapore to restore order.	Perak, Selangor, Negeri Sembilan and Pahang join as Federated Malay States, with Kuala Lumpur as the capital. The sultans lose political power to British Residents.	Penang is the scene of action in WWI when Allied warships, including the Russian Imperial Navy vessel *Zhemchug*, are sunk by the German cruiser SMS *Emden*.	The British scrap the position of Resident General of the Federated States, decentralising its powers to the individual states, in order to discourage the creation of a united, self-governing country.

The normally acquiescent Malay population were less enthusiastic about the venture than the sultans. Rowdy protest meetings were held throughout the country, and the first Malay political party, the United Malays National Organisation (UMNO; www.umno-online.com), was formed, leading to the dissolution of the Malayan Union and the creation of the Federation of Malaya in 1948, which reinstated the sovereignty of the sultans and the special privileges of the Malays.

F Spencer Chapman's memoir *The Jungle is Neutral* relates the author's experience with a British guerrilla force based in the Malaysian jungles during the Japanese occupation of Malaya and Singapore.

The Emergency

While the creation of the Federation of Malaya appeased Malays, the Chinese felt betrayed, particularly after their massive contribution to the war effort. Many joined the Malayan Communist Party (MCP), which promised an equitable and just society. In 1948 the MCP took to the jungles and embarked on a 12-year guerrilla war against the British. Even though the insurrection was on par with the Malay civil wars of the 19th century, it was classified as an 'emergency' for insurance purposes.

The effects of the Emergency were felt most strongly in the countryside, where villages and plantation owners were repeatedly targeted by rebels. In 1951 the British high commissioner was assassinated on the road to Fraser's Hill. His successor, General Sir Gerald Templer, set out to 'win the hearts and minds of the people'. Almost 500,000 rural Chinese were resettled into protected 'new villages', restrictions were lifted on guerrilla-free areas and the jungle-dwelling Orang Asli were brought into the fight to help the police track down the insurgents.

Revolusi '48 (http://revolusi48.blogspot.com, in Bahasa Malaysia), the sequel to Fahmi Reza's doco *10 Tahun Sebelum Merdeka* (10 Years Before Merdeka), chronicles the largely forgotten armed revolution for national liberation launched against British colonial rule in Malaya in 1948.

In 1960 the Emergency was declared over, although sporadic fighting continued and the formal surrender was signed only in 1989.

Merdeka & Malaysia

Malaysia's march to independence from British rule was led by UMNO, which formed a strategic alliance with the Malayan Chinese Association (MCA; www.mca.org.my) and the Malayan Indian Congress (MIC; www.mic.org.my). The new Alliance Party led by Tunku Abdul Rahman won a landslide victory in the 1955 election, and on 31 August 1957 Merdeka (Independence) was declared.

In 1961 Tunku Abdul Rahman proposed a merger of Singapore, Malaya, Sabah and Sarawak. But when modern Malaysia was born in July 1963 it immediately faced a diplomatic crisis. The Philippines broke off relations, claiming that Sabah was part of its territory (a claim upheld to this day), while Indonesia laid claim to the whole of Borneo, invading parts of Sabah and Sarawak before finally giving up its claim in 1966.

The marriage between Singapore and Malaya was also doomed from the start. Ethnic Chinese outnumbered Malays in both Malaysia and Singapore and the new ruler of the island-state, Lee Kuan Yew, refused to

1941	1946	1948	1951
Within a month of invading, the Japanese take Kuala Lumpur and occupy the peninsula. In 1942 the British capitulate Singapore, leaving the Japanese in control until 1945.	After public opposition to the proposed Malay Union, the United Malays National Organisation forms, signalling the rise of Malay nationalism and desire for political independence from Britain.	Start of the Emergency, when the Malayan Communist Party (MCP) take to the jungles and begin fighting a guerrilla war against the British that would last for 12 years.	Sir Henry Gurney, British high commissioner to Malaya, is assassinated by MCP rebels on the road to Fraser's Hill, a terrorist act that alienates many moderate Chinese from the party.

extend constitutional privileges to the Malays in Singapore. Riots broke out in Singapore in 1964 and in August 1965 Tunku Abdul Rahman was forced to boot Singapore out of the federation.

Ethnic Tensions

Impoverished Malays became increasingly resentful of the economic success of Chinese Malaysians, while the Chinese grew resentful of the political privileges granted to Malays. Things reached breaking point when the Malay-dominated government attempted to suppress all languages except Malay and introduced a national policy of education that ignored Chinese and Indian history, language and culture.

In the 1969 general elections, the Alliance Party lost its two-thirds majority in parliament and a celebration march by the opposition Democratic Action Party (DAP; http://dapmalaysia.org/newenglish) and Gerakan (the People's Movement; www.gerakan.org.my) in Kuala Lumpur led to a full-scale riot, which Malay gangs used as a pretext to loot Chinese businesses, killing hundreds of Chinese in the process.

Stunned by the savagery of the riots, the government decided that if there was ever going to be harmony between the races, the Malay com-

Orang Asli Sights

» Orang Asli Museum, Gombak

» National Museum, Kuala Lumpur

» Kampung Sungai Bumbon, Pulau Carey

HISTORY ETHNIC TENSIONS

ORANG ASLI

The indigenous people of Malaysia – known collectively as Orang Asli (Original People) – played an important role in early trade, teaching the colonialists about forest products and guiding prospectors to outcrops of tin and precious metals. They also acted as scouts and guides for anti-insurgent forces during the communist Emergency in the 1950s.

Despite this, the Orang Asli remain marginalised in Malaysia. According to the most recent data published by the Department of Orang Asli Affairs (JHEOA; www.jheoa.gov.my), in December 2004 Peninsular Malaysia had just under 150,000 Orang Asli; 80% live below the poverty line, compared with an 8.5% national average. The tribes are generally classified into three groups: the Negrito; the Senoi; and the Proto-Malays, who are subdivided into 18 tribes, the smallest being the Orang Kanak with just 87 members. There are dozens of tribal languages and most Orang Asli follow animist beliefs, despite vigorous attempts to convert them to Islam.

Although the JHEOA was originally set up to represent Orang Asli concerns to the government (ie land rights), the department has evolved into a conduit for government decisions. Asli land rights are still not recognised, and when logging, agricultural or infrastructure projects require their land, their claims are regarded as illegal.

For more information on the plight of Orang Asli people in Peninsular Malaysia, visit the websites of Temiar Web (www.temiar.com) and the Centre for Orang Asli Concerns (www.coac.org.my).

1953	1954	1957	1963
Formation of Parti Perikatan (Alliance Party) between UNMO, the Malayan Chinese Association (MCA) and Malayan Indian Congress (MIC). Two years later it wins 80% of the vote in Malaya's first national elections.	The Department of Aboriginal Affairs Malaysia is set up to protect the Orang Asli from modern encroachments and exploitation, to provide education and the means for development.	On 31 August Merdeka (Independence) is declared in Malaya; Tunku Abdul Rahman becomes the first prime minister and the nine sultans agree to take turns as the nation's paramount ruler.	Malaysia comes into being in 1963 with the addition of Singapore and the British Borneo territories of Sabah and Sarawak; Brunei pulls out at the 11th hour.

munity needed to achieve economic parity. To this end the New Economic Policy (NEP), a socio-economic affirmative action plan, was introduced (see p196).

The Alliance Party also invited opposition parties to join them and work from within. The expanded coalition was renamed the Barisan Nasional (BN; National Front), which continues to rule to this day.

Enter Mahathir

In 1981 former UMNO member Mahathir Mohamad became prime minister. Under his watch Malaysia's economy went into overdrive, growing from one based on commodities such as rubber to one firmly rooted in industry and manufacturing. Government monopolies were privatised, and heavy industries like steel manufacturing (a failure) and the Malaysian car (successful but heavily protected) were encouraged. Multinationals were successfully wooed to set up in Malaysia, and manufactured exports began to dominate the trade figures.

BUMIPUTRA PRIVILEGES

When introduced in 1971 the aim of the New Economic Policy (NEP) was that 30% of Malaysia's corporate wealth be in the hands of indigenous Malays, or *bumiputra* ('princes of the land'), within 20 years. A massive campaign of positive discrimination began which handed majority control over the army, police, civil service and government to Malays. The rules extended to education, scholarships, share deals, corporate management and even the right to import a car.

By 1990 *bumiputra* corporate wealth had risen to 19%, but was still 11% short of the original target. Poverty in general fell dramatically, a new Malay middle class emerged and nationalist violence by Malay extremists receded. However, cronyism and discrimination against Indians and Chinese increased, while Malays still account for three in four of the poorest people in the country.

Affirmative action in favour of *bumiputra* continues today but there is a growing recognition that it is hampering rather than helping Malaysia. Former law minister Zaid Ibrahim was reported in the *New York Times* as saying that Malaysia had 'sacrificed democracy for the supremacy of one race' because of the economic privileges given to *bumiputra*. In September 2010 Prime Minister Najib advocated a fundamental reform of the pro-Malay policies, but fell short of calling for the outright scrapping of the system.

In the opposite corner are those like former PM Mahathir who believes that *bumiputra* would suffer the most if the administration were to implement a 100% meritocracy-based system. A July 2010 poll by the independent Merdeka Centre shows that Malays in general are split on the matter: 45% believing the policies only benefit the rich and well-connected; 48% thinking they are good for the general public.

KARL BLACKWELL / LONELY PLANET IMAGES ©

1969

Following the general election, on 13 March a race riot erupts in KL, killing 198. In response the government devises the New Economic Policy of positive discrimination for Malays..

1976

Hussein Ohn becomes Malaysia's third prime minister following the death of Abdul Razak. His period of office is marked by efforts to foster unity and less financial inequality between Malaysia's disparate communities.

» Melaka's Proclamation of Independence Memorial

TROUBLE WITH THE ISA

Malaysia's draconian Internal Security Act (ISA) allows for arrest and detention of any person without the need for trial under circumstances in which the government deems them to be a threat to national security. Ever since the ISA's enactment in 1960 those circumstances have been wide open to interpretation, with several opposition parties and Amnesty International (www.aimalaysia.org) claiming the law has been much abused by the ruling BN coalition.

Detainees, who can be held for 60 days incommunicado, are typically incarcerated at the Kamunting Detention Centre near Taiping, a prison that's become Malaysia's Guantanamo Bay. Opposition leaders Anwar Ibrahim, Lim Kit Siang and Karpal Singh have all spent time as inmates, as has the one-time student activist, writer and film-maker Hishamuddin Raais. Raais's play *Bilik Sulit,* about the police interrogation of an ISA detainee and based on the testimonials of former detainees, has been performed around Malaysia.

During Mahathir's premiership the main media outlets became little more than government mouthpieces. The sultans lost their right to give final assent on legislation, and the once proudly independent judiciary appeared to become subservient to government wishes, the most notorious case being that of Anwar Ibrahim (see p197). Mahathir also permitted widespread use of the Internal Security Act (ISA) to silence opposition leaders and social activists, most famously in 1987's Operation Lalang when 106 people were arrested and the publishing licences of several newspapers revoked.

Economic & Political Crisis

In 1997, after a decade of near constant 10% growth, Malaysia was hit by the regional currency crisis. Characteristically, Mahathir blamed it all on unscrupulous Western speculators deliberately undermining the economies of the developing world for their personal gain. He pegged the Malaysian ringgit to the US dollar, bailed out what were seen as crony companies, forced banks to merge and made it difficult for foreign investors to remove their money from Malaysia's stock exchange. Malaysia's subsequent recovery from the economic crisis, which was more rapid than that of many other Southeast Asian nations, further bolstered Mahathir's prestige.

At odds with Mahathir over how to deal with the economic crisis had been his deputy prime minister and heir apparent, Anwar Ibrahim (www.anwaribrahim.com). Their falling out was so severe that in September 1998 Anwar was not only sacked but also charged with corruption and sodomy. Many Malaysians, feeling that Anwar had been falsely arrested,

Noel Barber's *War of the Running Dogs* is a classic account of the 12-year Malayan Emergency. The title refers to what the communist fighters called the opposition who were loyal to the British.

1981	1987	1995	1998
Dr Mahathir Mohamad becomes Malaysia's prime minister and introduces policies of 'Buy British Last' and 'Look East', in which the country strives to emulate Japan, South Korea and Taiwan.	The police launch Operation Lalang (Operation Weeding), arresting 106 activists and opposition leaders under the Internal Security Act (ISA).	Dr Mahathir announces the launch of Malaysia's new administrative capital, Putrajaya, and the creation of the Multimedia Super Corridor stretching from the centre of KL to the new international airport at Sepang.	Anwar Ibrahim's disagreements with PM Mahathir over how to deal with the Asian currency crisis, as well as his attempts to tackle government corruption, see him sacked, arrested, sent for trial and jailed.

took to the streets chanting Anwar's call for *'reformasi'*. The demonstrations were harshly quelled and in trials that were widely criticised as unfair, Anwar was sentenced to a total of 15 years' imprisonment. The international community rallied around Anwar with Amnesty International proclaiming him a prisoner of conscience.

BN felt the impact in the following year's general elections when it suffered huge losses, particularly in the rural Malay areas. The gainers were the fundamentalist Islamic party, PAS (standing for Parti Islam Se-Malaysia; www.pas.org.my), which had vociferously supported Anwar, and a new political party, Keadilan (People's Justice Party; www.keadilanrakyat.org), headed by Anwar's wife, Wan Azizah.

Amir Muhammad's 2009 documentary *Malaysian Gods* commemorates the decade since the Reformasi movement began in 1998 with the sacking of Anwar Ibrahim as deputy PM.

Abdullah vs Mahathir

Prime Minister Mahathir's successor, Abdullah Badawi, was sworn into office in 2003 and went on to lead BN to a landslide victory in the following year's election. In stark contrast to his feisty predecessor, the pious and mild-mannered Abdullah impressed voters by taking a nonconfrontational, consensus-seeking approach. He set up a royal commission to investigate corruption in the police force (its recommendations have yet to be implemented) and called time on several of the massively expensive mega projects that had been the hallmark of the Mahathir era, including a new bridge across the Strait of Johor to Singapore.

MALAYSIA'S GOVERNMENT

Malaysia is made up of 13 states and three federal territories (Kuala Lumpur, Pulau Labuan and Putrajaya). Each state has an assembly and government headed by a *menteri besar* (chief minister). Nine states have hereditary rulers (sultans), while the remaining four have appointed governors, as do the federal territories. In a pre-established order, every five years one of the sultans takes his turn in the ceremonial position of Yang di-Pertuan Agong (king). Since December 2006 the king, who is also is the head of state and leader of the Islamic faith, has been the Sultan of Terengganu.

Malaysia's current prime minister is Najib Tun Razak, who heads up the Barisan Nasional (BN), a coalition of the United Malays National Organisation (UMNO) and 13 other parties. The official opposition, Pakatan Rakyat (PR), is a coalition between Parti Keadilan Rakyat (PKR), the Democratic Action Party (DAP) and Parti Islam Se-Malaysia (PAS), the coalition leader being Anwar Ibrahim. All sit in a two-house parliament: a 70-member Senate (*Dewan Negara;* 26 members elected by the 13 state assemblies, 44 appointed by the king on the prime minister's recommendation) and a 222-member House of Representatives (*Dewan Rakyat;* elected from single-member districts). National and state elections are held every five years.

2003	2004	2007	2008
Having announced his resignation the previous year, Dr Mahathir steps down as prime minister in favour of Abdullah Badawi. He remains very outspoken on national policies.	A month after the election in which BN takes 199 of 219 seats in the lower house of parliament, Anwar Ibrahim sees his sodomy conviction overturned and is released from prison.	As the country celebrates 50 years since independence it is also shaken by two antigovernment rallies in November in which tens of thousands take to the streets of KL to protest.	In the March election BN retains power but suffers heavy defeats to the revitalised opposition coalition Pakatan Rakyat (PR); in August, Anwar Ibrahim becomes PR leader following his re-election to parliament.

This decision was the straw that broke the doctor's back, causing the former PM to publicly lambast his successor – an outburst that was largely ignored by the mainstream media. Mahathir turned to the internet (he regularly updates his blog at http://chedet.co.cc/chedetblog) to get his views across and raged against press censorship – which many found pretty rich given his own autocratic record while in power.

BN on the Ropes

Released from jail in 2004, Anwar returned to national politics in August 2008 upon winning the bi-election for the seat vacated by his wife. This was despite sodomy charges again being laid against the politician in June and his subsequent arrest in July – the case is still going through the courts but appears so full of holes that Amnesty International, Human Rights Watch Asia and Al Gore have all thrown their support behind Anwar.

The repercussions of the March 2008 election – in which UMNO and its coalition partners in BN saw their parliamentary dominance slashed to less than the customary two-thirds majority – continue to ripple through Malaysian political life. Pakatan Rakyat (PR), the opposition People's Alliance led by Anwar Ibrahim, not only bagged 82 of the parliament's 222 seats but also took control of four of Malaysia's 13 states, including the key economic bases of Selangor and Penang.

BN's fall guy was PM Abdullah Badawi, who resigned in favour of his urbane deputy Mohd Najib bin Tun Abdul Razak (typically referred to as Najib Razak) in April 2008. Son of Abdul Razak, Malaysia's second PM after independence, and nephew of Abdul's successor Hussein Onn, Najib has been groomed for this role ever since he first entered national politics at the age of 23 in 1976.

But the change of guard may be too late to resurrect the fortunes of UMNO, a party that is seen as corrupt and out of touch with the people, according to a survey by the Merdeka Centre (www.merdeka.org)

1957–2007 Chronicle of Malaysia edited by Philip Matthews is a beautifully designed book showcasing 50 years of the country's history in news stories and pictures.

2009	2010
In April, Najib Tun Razak succeeds Abdullah Badawi as prime minister; the 1 Malaysia policy is introduced to build respect and trust between the country's different races.	PM Najib introduces his New Economic Model to stimulate the country's stagnant economy by cutting bureaucracy, improving the education system and reforming affirmative action policies .

» A military march during Independence Day celebrations

Malaysian Cuisine

Robyn Eckhardt
Writer Robyn Eckhardt has lived in Asia for more than 12 years and collaborated on food-focused articles for publications such as *Travel + Leisure, Chicago Tribune, Wall Street Journal Asia* and *Time Out Kuala Lumpur.*

The author of this chapter teams with a professional photographer to publish EatingAsia (www.eatingasia. typepad.com), a blog on Southeast Asian food, ingredients and culinary culture. It also has details about their guided food and photography tours of KL and Melaka.

Malaysia is a hungry traveller's dream destination – a multiethnic nation boasting a wide-ranging cuisine shaped over the centuries by the European, Indonesian, Indian and Chinese traders, colonisers and labourers who have landed on its shores. Come mealtime you'll find yourself spoilt for choice. Fancy breakfasting on Chinese dim sum? How about an Indian *dosa* (savoury pancake) for lunch, followed by a selection of rich Malaysian curries for dinner? If the thought of choosing from the innumerable options is a bit overwhelming, seek advice from a local. Malays, opinionated but affable gourmets, love nothing more than to introduce outsiders to the joys of their cuisine. The traveller who partakes in the nation's edible delights will leave with delicious memories, as well as make a few *makan kaki* (food friends) along the way. In Malaysia it's not 'How are you?' but *'Sudah makan?'* (Have you eaten yet?).

Staples & Specialities

Curries

Though chillies are a mainstay of Malaysian cuisine, few dishes are prohibitively spicy. Curries start with *rempah* – a pounded paste of chillies and aromatics such as garlic, shallots, *serai* (lemongrass), *kunyit* (turmeric) and *lengkuas* (galangal). Dried spices – coriander seeds, fennel seeds, cumin, fenugreek – might also be included, especially if the dish is Indian-influenced.

Fresh herbs such as coriander, mint, *daun kesom* (polygonum), *kunyit, pandan* (screwpine leaves) and lime- and curry-leaves impart a fresh liveliness to curries and noodle dishes. Malays prefer their food on the

---

FOR THE LOVE OF SAMBAL

There are as many variations of *sambal* as there are Malay cooks. Mild to fiery, made with fresh or dried chillies, and incorporating ingredients from dried fish to fruit, this cross between a dip and a relish accompanies simple soup noodles, lavish feasts and every meal in between. The most common variation is *sambal belacan,* made from fresh or dried red chillies pounded with dried *belacan* (fermented prawn paste). If its pungent punch puts you off initially, try, try again – *sambal belacan* is rarely loved at first bite but often proves addictive in the long run.

Don't even think about leaving Malaysia without sampling these much-loved specialities:

» *Nasi lemak* – rice steamed in coconut milk and served with *ikan bilis* (deep-fried anchovies), fried peanuts, half a hard-boiled egg, *sambal* (chilli sauce) and a selection of curries; often eaten for breakfast.

» *Char kway teow* – wide rice noodles stir-fried with prawns, cockles, bean sprouts and egg; it vies with *nasi lemak* for the title of 'national dish'.

» *Roti canai* – flaky unleavened bread griddled with ghee until crisp and eaten with curry or dhal; it is another breakfast favourite.

» *Asam* laksa – Penang's iconic dish is a sour and chilli-hot bowlful of round rice noodles in a fish-based soup, garnished with slivered torch ginger flower, chopped pineapple and mint.

» *Cendol* – a wonderfully refreshing sweet of shaved ice mounded over toothsome mung bean noodles, all doused in fresh coconut milk and luscious palm-sugar syrup.

MALAYSIAN CUISINE STAPLES & SPECIALITIES

sweet side, but tartness is also key to the cuisine. *Asam* (sour) curries derive their piquancy from fresh tamarind, *belimbi* (a sour relative of the carambola, also known as starfruit) and *asam keping* (the dried flesh of a tart fruit related to the mangosteen; also known as *gelugor*).

Condiments & Garnishes

Belacan (fermented prawn paste) is the embodiment of the Malay love of fishy flavours. A Penang variation is the black, sticky-sweet *hae ko* that dresses *rojak* (vegetable-and-fruit salad). Other well-loved condiments from the sea include *budu* (a long-fermented anchovy sauce favoured by Malay cooks) and *cincalok* (tiny prawns treated with brine). *Ikan bilis* (dried anchovies) are deep-fried and incorporated into *sambal* or sprinkled atop noodle and rice dishes, while salted fish finds its way into stir-fries.

No Malaysian kitchen is without soy sauce and its sweetened cousin, *kecap manis*. Other seasonings and sauces integral to the cuisine are oyster sauce, hoisin sauce and *taucu* (fermented, salted bean paste).

Many Malaysian curries contain coconut milk and the fruit's flesh is grated and dry-fried to make *kerisik* (a garnish for rice dishes). Fresh *kalamansi* (a tiny, sour lime) juice dresses salads and is squeezed into *sambal belacan* just before it's served.

Rice & Noodles

Malays would be hard-pressed to choose between *nasi* (rice) and *mee* (noodles) – one or the other figures in almost every meal. *Nasi lemak*, an unofficial 'national dish' and popular breakfast food, is rice steamed in coconut milk and served with *ikan bilis,* fried peanuts, sliced cucumber, *sambal* and half a hard-boiled egg – curry is optional. Rice is also boiled with meat or seafood stock to make *bubur* (porridge), *nasi goreng* (rice fried with shallots and topped with an egg) and *lontong* (rice packed into banana leaf–lined bamboo tubes, cooked over wood, then sliced and doused with coconut milk gravy). Tinted blue with *bunga telung* (butterfly or blue-pea flower) and adorned with fresh herbs, bean sprouts and *kerisik,* rice becomes the Malay favourite *nasi kerabu*. Glutinous, or sticky, rice is a common ingredient in Malaysian sweets.

Rice flour, mixed with water and allowed to ferment slightly, becomes the batter for *idli* (Indian steamed cakes) and *apam* (pancakes). It goes into the making of noodles for dishes such as laksa: *asam* laksa is served in a fish-based sour and spicy broth, while laksa *lemak* (curry laksa)

In the beautifully photographed book *Inside the Southeast Asian Kitchen,* local experts share their knowledge of ingredients, cooking utensils and techniques, along with authentic recipes.

RECIPES

comes in a chilli coconut gravy. *Kway teow* (wide rice noodles) are stir-fried with prawns, cockles, egg and bean sprouts to make the country's other 'national dish': *char kway teow*. Other rice noodles include *beehoon* (vermicelli) and *loh see fun* (stubby 'rat tail' noodles). *Chee cheong fun* are steamed rice-flour sheets sliced into strips and topped with meat gravy or chilli and black prawn sauces.

Mee are served in soup; stir-fried with curry leaves and chilli sauce for the Indian Muslim speciality *mee mamak;* or smothered in a sweet potato-based gravy for the Malay dish *mee rebus*. A favourite Chinese noodle dish is *won ton mee* (egg vermicelli floated in broth with pork dumplings, a few leaves of Chinese mustard greens and sliced pork). It can also be served 'dry', with the broth on the side.

Seafood

Given Malaysia's multiple coastlines, it's no surprise that seafood plays a major role in the national diet. Quality is high and the options endless. Favourites for *ikan bakar* (grilled fish; also known as *ikan panggang*) include *ikan tenggiri* (Spanish mackerel) and *ikan pari* (stingray), while pomfret and *garoupa* (a white fish popular in Southeast Asia) are usually steamed Chinese-style with garlic, ginger and soy sauce. The whole head and 'shoulders' of large fish such as *ikan merah* (red snapper) and sea bass feature in the delectable Indian-Malay *kari kepala ikan* (fish-head curry). *Sotong* (squid) is battered and deep-fried, stirred into curries, and griddled on a banana leaf with *sambal*.

Malays adore shellfish: from prawns to 'top shell' (a snail-like saltwater creature with sweet, snow-white flesh), and it isn't an authentic *char kway teow* unless it includes plump blood-red cockles. Crab is steamed or stir-fried with curry, and in Penang its meat is rolled into an extravagant *popiah* (soft spring roll).

Pork

Babi (pork) is *haram* (forbidden) to Malaysia's Muslims but is the meat of choice for the Chinese, who prefer fatty cuts such as the belly and shoulder; they even dress cooked dishes with lard oil. Crispy-skinned *char yoke* (roast pork), sweet-glazed *char siew* (barbecued pork) and pork crackling are eaten on their own and incorporated into noodle dishes and snacks.

Bak kut teh (literally 'meat-bone tea'), a comforting dish of pork ribs (innards optional) stewed in a claypot with medicinal herbs, mushrooms and bean curd, and eaten with Chinese crullers, was supposedly invented in Klang, the port town west of KL. Malaysia's Hakka (a Chinese dialect group) are renowned for their succulent, long-cooked pork dishes such as sliced belly stewed with *khaw yoke* (taro).

Chicken, Duck & Beef

Ayam (chicken) is tremendously popular, with the local preference for flavourful *ayam kampong* (free-range birds). Nearly every coffee shop

Before ordering seafood at Malaysia's restaurants and hawker stalls check the *Malaysian Sustainable Seafood Guide*, available as a download from www.saveoursea food.my.

'Ketchup' is derived from the Hokkien word *ke-tsiap*, which is a fermented fish sauce brought by Chinese traders to Melaka, where it was encountered by Europeans.

NOODLES, WET OR DRY

If the thought of hanging your head over a steaming bowl in Malaysia's withering heat puts you off soupy noodle dishes, consider adding the word *konlo* to your order. You'll end up getting a bowl of warm noodles tossed in light or dark soy sauce and a bit of oil, with the hot broth served on the side. Many Malays order their noodles 'dry' to protect the pasta's al dente integrity. As any *won ton mee* (egg vermicelli floated in broth with pork dumplings) connoisseur will tell you, a noodle that doesn't offer a bit of resistance to the tooth is hopelessly overcooked.

Dine at enough *kopi tiam* (coffee shops) and you're bound to run into lamb chops and mushroom soup. Though these may seem out of place on a menu that also features *belacan* (fermented prawn paste), fried rice and fish in sour curry, these dishes are as much a part of the Malaysian culinary universe as laksa *lemak* (curry laksa). Introduced by the British but popularised in the early decades of the 20th century by Hainanese immigrants who served as their private cooks – and later became known throughout the country for their prowess in the kitchen – Western classics such as chops (pork and chicken, in addition to lamb) and fish and chips are Malaysia's intergenerational comfort foods. The best versions – found in old-time *kopi tiam* sporting original floor tiles and peeling paint – are astoundingly authentic. Seek them out when a break from local fare is in order and eat a bit of history.

houses a stall selling *nasi ayam* (Hainanese chicken-rice; poached and sliced chicken breast served with broth-infused rice, sliced cucumber and tomato, and chilli sauce). Most Malay eateries serve a variety of chicken curries, and the bird makes for Malaysia's most popular satay meat, where it's skewered, grilled and dipped in peanut-chilli sauce.

Another oft-eaten fowl is *itik* (duck), roasted or simmered in star anise–scented broth and eaten with noodles, or stewed in a spicy *mamak* (Indian Muslim) curry.

Tough Malaysian *daging* (beef) is best in slow-cooked dishes such as Indonesian-influenced rendang (an aromatic, dry-cooked, coconut-milk curry). Chinese-style beef noodles feature tender chunks of beef and springy meatballs in a rich, mildly spiced broth lightened with pickled mustard. Indian Muslims do amazing things with mutton; it's worth searching out *sup kambing* – stewed mutton riblets (and other parts, if you wish) in a thick soup flavoured with loads of aromatics and chillies, which is eaten with sliced white bread.

Vegetables

Vegetable lovers will have a field day in Malaysia. Every rice-based Malay meal includes *ulam,* a selection of fresh and blanched vegetables – wing beans, cucumbers, okra, eggplant and the fresh legume petai (or stink bean, so-named for its strong garlicky taste) – and fresh herbs to eat on their own or dip into *sambal*. Indians cook cauliflower and leafy vegetables such as cabbage, spinach and *roselle* (sturdy leaves with an appealing sourness) with coconut milk and turmeric.

Other greens – *daun ubi* (sweet potato leaves), *kangkong* (water spinach), Chinese broccoli and yellow-flowered mustard – are stir-fried with *sambal belacan* or garlic. The humble jicama is particularly versatile; it's sliced and added raw to *rojak;* grated, steamed and rolled into *popiah* (soft spring rolls); and mashed, formed into a cake and topped with deep-fried shallots and chillies for Chinese *oh kuih*. Sweetcorn is plentiful, sold by vendors grilled, or off-the-cob and steamed, at almost every night market.

Tau (soybeans) are consumed in many forms. *Taufu fa* (soy-bean milk and warm, fresh bean curd), eaten plain or doused with palm-sugar syrup, is sold from white trucks. *Yong tauhu* is a healthy Hakka dish of firm bean curd and vegetables stuffed with ground fish paste. The chewy skin that forms on the surface of vats of boiling soy milk is fried golden or eaten fresh in noodle dishes, and *tauhu pok* (flavour-absorbent, deep-fried bean curd 'puffs') are added to noodles and stews. Malays even barbecue bean curd, then stuff it with sliced cucumber and top it with sweet prawn paste and peanuts.

The word laksa derives from the Persian word for noodle, *lakhsha* (slippery). The *Oxford Companion to Food* speculates that pasta was introduced to Indonesia (from where it migrated to Malaysia) by Arab traders or Indian Muslims in the 13th century.

Vegetarians and vegans should see p208 for information on where to eat.

Sweets

A sugar high is never far away in KL, Melaka or Penang. Vendors selling *kuih muih* (sweets) lie in wait in front of stores, on street corners and at markets. Many *kuih* incorporate freshly grated coconut and *gula melaka* (a distinctive dark sugar made from the sap collected from the flower stalks of the coconut palm). Among the best are *ketayap* (*pandan* leaf–flavoured rice-flour 'pancakes' rolled around in a mix of the two; also known as *kuih dadar*) and *putu piring* (steamed rice-flour 'flapjacks' filled with palm sugar and topped with coconut).

When the heat hits, dig into *cendol* (a mound of shaved ice and chewy mung-bean noodles doused in fresh coconut milk, palm-sugar syrup and condensed milk). The more elaborate *ais kacang* or ABC (the initials stand for *air batu campur* – mixed ice) combines flavoured syrups, jellies, red beans, palm seeds and sweetcorn.

Sweet coconut-milk porridges made with *gandum* (wheat) or *bubur kacang hijau* (mung bean) are an afternoon treat, and Chinese *tong sui* (warm sweet soups) featuring ingredients such as peanuts and winter melon are said to be as healthy as they are tasty. Don't leave Malaysia without sampling the Indian subcontinental sweets stacked in colourful pyramids in Little India shop windows.

Fruits

Those who have overindulged in *kuih* might repent with a dose of healthy tropical fruits. *Nenas* (pineapple), watermelon, *jambu* (rose apple), papaya and green guava are year-round choices, with more unusual fruits available seasonally. The dull brown skin of the *ciku* (sopadilla) hides supersweet flesh that tastes a bit like a date. Strip away the yellowish peel of the *duku* (also known as *dokong* and *langsat*) to find segmented, perfumed pearlescent flesh with a lychee-like flavour.

April and May are mango months, and come December to January and June to July, follow your nose to sample notoriously odiferous love-it-or-hate-it durian. Should the king of fruits prove too repellent, consider the slightly smelly but wonderfully sweet yellow flesh of the young *nangka* (jackfruit).

Other tropical fruits you may come across at markets and street stalls:
Buah nona The custard apple; a knobbly green skin conceals hard, black seeds and sweet, gloopy flesh with a granular texture.
Buah salak Known as the snakeskin fruit because of its scaly skin; the exterior looks like a mutant strawberry and the soft flesh tastes like unripe bananas.
Cempedak The Malaysian breadfruit; a huge green fruit with skin like the Thing from the *Fantastic Four;* the seeds and flesh are often curried or fried.
Dragon fruit An alien-looking red pod with tonguelike flanges hiding fragrant, kiwi fruit–like flesh with lots of tiny edible seeds.
Guava A green, apple-like ball containing sweet pink or white flesh with seeds you can eat.
Jambu merah A Malaysian apple; elongated pink or red fruit with a smooth, shiny skin and pale, watery flesh; a good thirst quencher on a hot day.
Longan A tiny, hard ball like a mini lychee with sweet, perfumed flesh; peel it, eat the flesh and spit out the hard seeds.
Mangosteen A hard, purple shell conceals delightfully fragrant white segments, some containing a tough seed that you can spit out or swallow.
Pomelo Like a grapefruit on steroids, with a thick pithy green skin hiding sweet, tangy segments; cut into the skin, peel off the pith then break open the segments and munch on the flesh inside.

Rambutan People have different theories about what rambutans look like, not all repeatable in polite company; the hairy shell contains sweet, translucent flesh, which you scrape off the seed with your teeth.

Soursop A shapeless, sack-like fruit with tasty but tart granular flesh and hard, black seeds; it's only ripe when soft and it goes off within days so eat it quickly.

Starfruit The star-shaped cross-section is the giveaway; the yellow flesh is sweet and tangy and believed by many to lower blood pressure.

Tamarind Fresh tamarind comes in a curved, brown pod; the hard seeds are hidden inside the delicious, tart flesh.

Drinks

Half the fun of taking breakfast in one of Malaysia's Little Indias is watching the tea wallah toss-pour an order of *teh tarik* (literally 'pulled' tea) from one pitcher to another. Malays, who rank among the world's largest tea consumers, brew the leaf with *teh halia* (ginger), drink it hot or iced, *teh ais* or *teh-o-ais* (with or without milk) and tart it up with lime. For an especially rich cuppa, head for an Indian cafe and ask for *teh susu kerabau* (hot tea with boiled fresh milk). Chinese restaurants invariably serve green tea or pale-yellow chrysanthemum tea, often sweetened with sugar.

Kopi (coffee) is also popular – the dark, thick brew served in Chinese coffee shops is an excellent antidote to a case of jetlag. Caffeine-free alternatives include freshly blended fruit and vegetable juices; sticky-sweet, green, sugar-cane juice; and coconut water, drunk straight from the fruit with a straw. Other more unusual drinks include *barley peng* or *ee bee chui* (barley boiled with water, *pandan* leaf and rock sugar served over ice); *air mata kucing* (sweet dried longan beverage); and *cincau* (a herbal grass-jelly drink; to add a splash of soy milk ask for a 'Michael Jackson'). Sweetened *kalamansi* juice and Chinese salted plums may sound a strange combination but make for a thoroughly refreshing potion called *asam boi*.

Sky-high duties on alcohol can make a boozy night out awfully expensive. The cheapest beers are those brewed locally, such as Tiger and Carlsberg, and Chinese liquor shops stock less expensive, if not always palatable, hard liquors.

Regional Specialities

Penang

Mention Penang and Malays swoon. The island's reputation as gastronomic ground zero lures foodies from across the region, who come to partake in its stellar hawker fare. Must-eats include the iconic *asam laksa* (round rice noodles in a hot and sour fish-based gravy topped with slivered torch ginger flower, chopped pineapple and mint leaves) and laksa *lemak* (comes with a curry broth that's spicier and lighter on the coconut milk than versions served elsewhere).

Hokkien *mee* (yellow noodles, bean sprouts and prawn in a rich prawn and pork stock) is another signature dish of the Pearl of the Orient, as is *rojak* (fruit salad doused in Penang's unique sweet and gooey-

Tempeh (nutty-tasting 'cakes' of soybeans mixed with starter yeast and allowed to ferment) can be stewed with vegetables in mild coconut gravy or stir-fried with *kecap manis* and chillies.

Thank the knowledgable staff of Malaysian English-language food zine *Flavours* for these useful culinary guides: the *Star Street Food Guide*, covering all of Malaysia, and *Famous Street Food of Penang*.

A DISH BY ANY OTHER NAME

Be sure to keep your nomenclature straight when city-hopping. Penangites are justifiably proud of their Hokkien *mee* (a spicy dish of yellow noodles, bean sprouts and prawn in a pork-and-prawn-based broth). Order Hokkien *mee* anywhere else in Malaysia, however, and you'll end up with a plate of deliciously greasy thick noodles stir-fried with pork and egg in a dark soy-based gravy. In Penang *otak otak* is a curried coconut-milk-and-fish 'mousse' steamed in a banana leaf, but in Melaka and other parts of the southern peninsula it takes the form of a grilled coconut leaf–wrapped fish paste and chilli sausage.

black prawn paste and topped with ground nuts). One food found all over Malaysia but firmly entrenched in the island's food history is *nasi kandar* (rice eaten with a variety of curries). A speciality of Penang's *mamak* community, the dish is named for the *kandar* (shoulder pole) from which, originally, mobile vendors suspended pots of rice and curry. Drinks specific to Penang include *lau hao* (nutmeg juice) and *pat poh peng* (an iced infusion of eight Chinese medicinal herbs sweetened with rock and brown sugar).

The milk-based drink *bandung* is one of the most eye-catching you'll find sold at Malaysian street stalls. The vivid pink colour comes from rose syrup.

Melaka

Melaka boasts a number of sit-down restaurants serving local Nonya favourites such as *ikan cili garam* (fish curry) and chicken cooked with *taucu,* dark soy sauce and *ayam pong teh* (sugar). In addition to its Nonya fare, Melaka is known for its unique take on Hainanese chicken rice, which is served with a particularly zesty chilli sauce and ping pong–sized rice balls, rather than a mound of rice.

A favourite evening snack is *satay celup* (skewered vegetables, meat and seafood, which diners cook themselves in a pot at the centre of the table), which is dipped into a spicy peanut-based sauce. Pork fans shouldn't miss the Melaka version of *popiah,* which includes bits of crackling and a splash of lard oil. Though *cendol* isn't unique to Melaka, it's thought to be especially delicious there because vendors douse their ice with locally produced palm-sugar syrup.

Peranakan Restaurants

» Old China Café, Kuala Lumpur

» Top Hat, Kuala Lumpur

» Nyonya Breeze, Georgetown

» Mama's, Georgetown

» Nancy's Kitchen, Melaka

» Donald & Lily's, Melaka

Kuala Lumpur

KL doesn't really lay claim to any dishes in particular, but there are some wonderful foods more easily found there than in Penang or Melaka. *Pan meen* (literally 'board noodles') are substantial hand-cut or hand-torn wheat noodles tossed with dark soy sauce and garlic oil, garnished with chopped pork and crispy *ikan bilis,* and served with soup on the side. Some versions include a poached egg. More expensive than your average noodle dish but well worth it are *sang har meen* (literally 'fresh sea noodles'), huge freshwater prawns in gravy flavoured with Chinese rice wine and the fat from the shellfish heads, served over *yee mee* (crispy fried noodles).

Head to the city's Malay enclave of Kampung Baru to sample the specialities of Malaysia's eastern states, such as Kelantanese *nasi kerabu* and *ayam percik* (barbecued chicken smothered in chilli-coconut sauce) and, from Terengganu, *nasi dagang* (nutty, coconut milk–cooked red rice).

KL also boasts a notable range of regional Chinese cuisines. Choose from restaurants serving authentic Cantonese, Sichuanese, Dongbei (northeastern), Xinjiang, Guizhou, Teowchew, Hokkien and Hakka fare.

PERANAKAN CUISINE

Penang and Melaka are known for Nonya (also spelled Nyonya), or Peranakan, cuisine, a fusion of Chinese and Malay ingredients and cooking techniques. The Malay word *nonya* refers to prominent women in the Baba-Nonya community, descendants of early Chinese male immigrants who settled in Penang, Melaka and Singapore, and intermarried with locals (*baba* is the male counterpart). Penang Nonya food is influenced by the cuisine of nearby Thailand and tends to be spicier and more sour than that of Melaka. The preparation of Nonya dishes is laborious and time-consuming and, Malays say, best left to home kitchens. Still, there are a couple of Penang Nonya hawker specialities worth seeking out: *kerabu beehoon* (rice vermicelli tossed with fiery *sambal* and garnished with toasted coconut and herbs) and *lorbak* (a crispy treat of pork seasoned with Chinese five-spice powder, wrapped in bean curd sheets and deep-fried).

Don't be deterred from visiting Malaysia during Ramadan, the Muslim holy month of sunrise-to-sunset fasting. Indian and Chinese eateries remain open during the day to cater to the country's sizeable non-Muslim population and, come late afternoon, Ramadan bazaars pop up all over the country. These prepared-food markets offer a rare chance to sample Malay specialities from all over the country, some of which are specific to the festive season or rarely found outside private homes. One of the country's biggest Ramadan markets is held in KL's Malay enclave of Kampung Baru. Cruise the stalls and pick up provisions for an evening meal – but don't snack in public until the cry of the muezzin tells believers it's time to *buka puasa* (break the fast).

Need a break from Malaysian? KL has a cosmopolitan dining scene and you needn't look far to find – thanks to Malaysia's huge immigrant workforce – inexpensive Thai, Burmese, Nepalese, Indonesian, Bangladeshi and Pakistani fare. Restaurants serving Italian, French, fusion, Japanese and pan-Asian cuisine and ranging in style from casual to white tablecloth are among its more upmarket dining options.

Festivals & Celebrations

It's no surprise that a people as consumed with food and its pleasures as Malays mark every occasion with edible delights.

Securing a restaurant reservation in the weeks leading to Chinese New Year can be tricky, as friends, colleagues and family gather over endless banquets. Each table is sure to be graced with *yee sang* (literally 'fresh fish'; a Cantonese raw-fish dish believed to bring luck in the coming year). Other foods special to this time of the year (look for them in Chinese supermarkets) include pineapple tarts, *kuih bangkit* (snow-white, melt-in-the mouth cookies), *nga ku* (deep-fried Chinese arrowroot chips) and *ti kuih* (glutinous rice cakes wrapped in banana leaf).

For several weeks before the Indian festival Deepavali, Malaysia's Little Indias are awash in stalls selling clothing, textiles and household goods. Vendors also offer special sweets and savoury snacks, as well as foodstuffs shipped from the subcontinent, such as hand-patted pappadams and *kulfi* (frozen, milk-based dessert).

Malaysia's Ramadan bazaars are reason in themselves to visit Malaysia during the Muslim holy month. In KL vendors compete every year to secure a lucrative spot at one of the city's Ramadan markets, which swing into action late in the afternoon to serve those breaking the fast at sunset. They offer an excellent opportunity to sample home-cooked, otherwise hard-to-find Malay dishes.

Where to Eat & Drink

Hawker Stalls, Markets & Food Courts

The tastiest and best-value food is found at hawker stalls, and locals are fiercely loyal to their favourite vendors. Many hawkers have been in business for decades or operate a business inherited from their parents or even grandparents; the best enjoy reputations that exceed their geographical reach. To sample Malaysian hawker food, simply head to a stand-alone streetside kitchen-on-wheels, a coffee shop or food court. Place your order with one or multiple vendors, find a seat (shared tables are common) and pay for each dish as it's delivered to your table. You'll be approached by someone taking drink orders after you've sat down – pay for these separately as well.

Celine Marbeck's *Cuzinhia Cristang* weaves history and anecdotes with wonderful recipes to tell the story of this sadly disappearing Malakan Eurasian cuisine.

Food From the Heart: Malaysia's Culinary Heritage is a collection of mouth-watering family recipes, culinary remembrances and kitchen counsel from 86 Malays; the proceeds from the book benefit seven Malaysian charities.

Intrepid eaters shouldn't overlook *pasar* (markets). Morning markets include stalls selling coffee and other beverages, as well as vendors preparing foods such as freshly griddled roti and curry and *chee cheong fun*. *Ta pao* (takeaway) or eat 'in' – most can offer at least a stool. Night markets are also excellent places to graze.

There's really little to fear about eating outdoors at hawker stalls or food markets but if you want some air-conditioning and a little more comfort there's no shortage of indoor food courts in KL, Melaka and Penang's big shopping malls.

Coffee Shops & Restaurants

The term *kopi tiam* generally refers to old-style, single-owner coffee shops. These are simple, fan-cooled establishments that serve noodle and rice dishes, strong coffee and other drinks, and all-day breakfast fare such as half-boiled eggs and toast spread with *kaya* (coconut jam).

The word *restoran* (restaurant) applies to eateries ranging from the casual, decades-old Teowchew, Cantonese and Nonya places dotting Penang's Georgetown and small, family-run Malay restaurants in KL's Kampung Baru, to upscale establishments boasting international fare, slick decor and a full bar. Between the two extremes lie Chinese seafood restaurants (where the main course can be chosen live from a tank on the premises), as well as the numerous eateries found in many shopping malls.

Vegetarians & Vegans

Given the inclusion of prawn paste and fish in many dishes, vegetarians and vegans will find it difficult to negotiate their way around most menus. Chinese vegetarian restaurants and hawker stalls (signage will include the words *makanan sayur-sayuran*) are safe bets – they are especially busy on the 1st and 15th of the lunar month, when many Buddhists adopt a vegetarian diet for 24 hours. Indian vegetarian restaurants are another haven for snacks such as steamed *idli* served with dhal and *dosa,* as well as *thali* (full set meals consisting of rice or bread with numerous side dishes).

Justlife (www.justlifeshop.com), a chain of organic supermarkets with attached cafes, serves Western and local vegetarian fare and has stores in KL, Melaka and Penang.

When to Eat

To those of us used to 'three square meals', it might seem as if Malays are always eating. In fact, five or six meals or snacks is more the order of the day than strict adherence to the breakfast-lunch-dinner trilogy. Breakfast is often something that can be grabbed on the run: *nasi lemak* wrapped to go *(bungkus)* in a banana leaf or brown waxed paper, a quick bowl of noodles, toast and eggs, or griddled Indian bread.

Come late morning a snack might be in order, perhaps a *karipap* (deep-fried pastry filled with spiced meat or fish and potatoes). Lunch

Night Food Markets

» Kampung Baru, Kuala Lumpur

» Little India, Kuala Lumpur

» Lorong Baru (New Lane), Georgetown

» Gurney Drive, Georgetown

» Jonker's Walk, Melaka

Online Resources

» FriedChillies (www.friedchillies. com)

» Rasa Rasa (www2.rasarasa. net)

» What2See: Best of Penang Food! (www. what2seeonline. com)

BEST OF THE CHAIN GANG

While they often serve indifferent fare, a few local chain restaurants rise above the pack. Keep an eye out for the following:

Kayu Nasi Kandar (www.kayu.com.my) Penang-origin operation, named for the speciality of the house.

Saravana Bhavan (www.saravanabhavan.com) Serving delicious Keralan (South Indian) delights.

Little Penang Café Offering excellent versions of Nonya specialities in KL.

Madam Kwan's Known for *nasi lemak* and authentically sour-spicy *asam* laksa, also in KL.

» You'll rarely find a knife on the Malaysian table – fork and spoon are the cutlery of choice. Forks aren't used to carry food to the mouth, but to nudge food onto the spoon.

» Chinese food is usually eaten with chopsticks (Westerners may be offered a fork and a spoon as a courtesy).

» Malays and Indians eat rice-based meals with their right hand (the left is reserved for unclean tasks), using their thumbs to manoeuvre rice onto the balls of their fingers and then transferring the lot to their mouth. Moistening your rice with curries and side dishes helps things along and, as with any new skill, practice makes perfect.

» Before and after eating, wash your hands with water from the teapot–like container on your table (Malaysian eateries) or at a communal sink to the rear or side of the room.

» Napkins on the table (and a towel to wipe your wet hands) aren't a given, so it's always a good idea to carry a pack of tissues when heading out to graze.

» In some Chinese eateries, after you've placed your order a server will bring a basin of hot water containing saucers, chopsticks, bowls and cutlery to the table. This is meant to allay hygiene concerns – remove the items from the water and dry them off with a napkin (or shake them dry).

generally starts from 12.30pm, something to keep in mind if you plan to eat at a popular establishment.

The British left behind a strong attachment to afternoon tea, consumed here in the form of tea or coffee and a sweet or savoury snack such as *tong sui,* various Indian fritters, battered and fried slices of cassava, sweet potato, banana and – of course – *kuih.*

Mamak stalls and hawker stalls see a jump in business a few hours after dinner (which is eaten around 6.30pm or 7pm) when Malays head out in search of a treat to tide them over until morning.

MALAYSIAN CUISINE WHEN TO EAT

Culture

Visitors to Kuala Lumpur, Melaka and Penang will invariably meet friendly, welcoming Malaysians who hold a strong sense of shared experience and national identity. However, there are distinct cultural differences between the nation's three main ethnic communities – Malays, Chinese and Indians – and multicultural Malaysia is not always the perfect melting pot, with underlying religious and ethnic tensions a fact of life (see p195).

A general rivalry also exists between KL and Penang as the nation's top two urban centres: natives of each are fiercely proud of their home towns. Melaka, knowing it's a poor third in such a competition, cherishes its role as the bastion of what remains of Malaysia's Peranakan culture (see the boxed text, p211).

The Malays

All Malays, Muslim by birth, are supposed to follow Islam, but many also adhere to older spiritual beliefs and *adat* (Malay customary law, which governs a village-based social system). With its roots in the Hindu period, *adat* places great emphasis on collective responsibility and maintaining harmony within the community – almost certainly a factor in the general goodwill between the different ethnic groups in Malaysia.

The enduring appeal of the communal *kampung* spirit shouldn't be underestimated – many an urban Malay hankers after it, despite the affluent Western-style living conditions they are privy to at home. In principle, villagers are of equal status, though a headman is appointed on the basis of his wealth, greater experience or spiritual knowledge. Traditionally the founder of the village was appointed village leader *(penghulu* or *ketua kampung)* and often members of the same family would also become leaders. A *penghulu* is usually a *haji,* one who has made the pilgrimage to Mecca.

The Muslim religious leader, the imam, holds a position of great importance in the community as the keeper of Islamic knowledge and the leader of prayer, but even educated urban Malays periodically turn to *pawang* (shamans who possess a supernatural knowledge of harvests and nature) or *bomoh* (spiritual healers with knowledge of curative plants and the ability to harness the power of the spirit world) for advice before making life-changing decisions.

Status-conscious Malaysians love their honourable titles, which include, in order of importance, Tun, Tan Sri, Datuk and Dato'.

SILAT

Properly known as *bersilat,* this Malay martial art originated in Melaka in the 15th century. Originally designed as an art of war, *silat* has evolved into a highly refined and stylised activity, more akin to a choreographed dance than self-defence. You'll most likely see performances at Malay festivals, where ritualised bouts are accompanied by percussive music on drums and gongs.

Peranakan means 'half-caste' in Malay, which is exactly what they are: descendants of Chinese immigrants who, from the 16th century onwards, settled in Melaka, Penang and Singapore and married Malay women.

The culture and language of the Peranakans are a fascinating melange of Chinese and Malay traditions. The Peranakans took the name and religion of their Chinese fathers, but the customs, language and dress of their Malay mothers. They also used the terms Straits-born or Straits Chinese to distinguish themselves from later arrivals from China.

Another name you may hear for these people is Baba-Nonya, after the Peranakan words for males *(baba)* and females *(nonya)*. The Peranakans were often wealthy traders who could afford to indulge their passion for sumptuous furnishings, jewellery and brocades. Their terrace houses were gaily painted, with patterned tiles embedded in the walls for extra decoration. When it came to the interior, Peranakan tastes favoured heavily carved and inlaid furniture.

Peranakan dress was similarly ornate. Women wore fabulously embroidered *kasot manek* (beaded slippers) and *kebaya* (blouses worn over a sarong), tied with beautiful *kerasong* (brooches), usually of fine filigree gold or silver. Men, who assumed Western dress in the 19th century, reflecting their wealth and contacts with the British, saved their finery for important occasions such as the wedding ceremony, a highly stylised and intricate ritual dictated by *adat* (Malay customary law).

The Chinese

Religious customs govern much of the Chinese community's home life, from the moment of birth, which is carefully recorded for astrological consultations later in life, to funerals, which also have many rites and rituals. The Chinese, who started arriving in the region in early 15th century, came mostly from the southern Chinese province of Fujian and eventually formed half of the group known as Peranakans. They developed their own distinct hybrid culture, whereas later settlers from Guangdong and Hainan provinces stuck more closely to the culture of their homelands, including keeping their dialects.

If there's one cultural aspect that all Chinese Malaysians agree on it's the importance of education. It has been a very sensitive subject among the community since the attempt in the 1960s to phase out secondary schools where Chinese was the medium of teaching, and the introduction of government policies that favour Malays in the early 1970s (see p196). The constraining of educational opportunities within Malaysia for the ethnic Chinese has resulted in many families working doubly hard to afford the tuition fees needed to send their offspring to private schools within the country and to overseas institutions.

The Malay surname is the child's father's first name. This is why Malaysians will use your Christian name after the Mr or Miss; to use your surname would be to address your father.

The Indians

Like the Chinese settlers, Indians in Malaysia hail from many parts of the subcontinent and have different cultures depending on their religions – mainly Hinduism, Islam, Sikhism and Christianity. Most are Tamils, originally coming from the area now known as Tamil Nadu in southern India where Hindu traditions are strong. Later Muslim Indians from northern India followed along with Sikhs. These religious affiliations dictate many of the home-life customs and practices of Malaysian Indians, although one celebration that all Hindus and much of the rest of the country take part in is Deepavali (see p20).

A Variety of Religions

There is freedom of religion in Malaysia, and the variety of belief systems found in the country is a direct reflection of the diversity of races living there. As well as the religions listed below, Kuala Lumpur, Melaka and Penang all have small Christian minorities.

The one major religion you won't find represented in Malaysia is Judaism, although Penang once had a Jewish community large enough to support a synagogue (closed in 1976) and there's been a Jewish cemetery in Georgetown since 1805. Sadly, anti-Semitism, ostensibly tied to criticism of Israel, is widespread. Very few Muslims differentiate between Israelis (whose citizens cannot enter Malaysia) and Jews at large, something worth noting if you're a Jewish traveller in the region.

Islam

Islam in Malaysia: Perceptions & Facts by Dr Mohd Asri Zainul Abidin, the former Mufti of Perlis, is a collection of articles on aspects of the faith as practised in Malaysia.

Islam came to Malaysia with south Indian traders, who practised a less strict form of the faith than the orthodox Islamic traditions of Arabia. Around 60% of Malaysians identify themselves as Muslim, including all Malays, Indian Muslims and some ethnic Chinese converts.

Most Malaysian Muslims are Sunnis, but all Muslims share a common belief in the Five Pillars of Islam:

Shahadah (the declaration of faith) 'There is no god but Allah; Mohammed is his Prophet.'

Salat (prayer) Ideally five times a day, in which the *muezzin* (prayer leader) calls the faithful to prayer from the minarets of every mosque.

Zakat (alms tax) Usually taking the form of a charitable donation.

Sawm (fasting) Includes observing the fasting month of Ramadan.

Hajj (pilgrimage to Mecca) Every Muslim aspires to do the *hajj* at least once in their lifetime.

A radical Islamic movement has not taken serious root in Malaysia but religious conservatism has grown over recent years (see the boxed text, p213). For foreign visitors, the most obvious sign of this is the national obsession with propriety, which extends to newspaper polemics on female modesty and raids by the police on 'immoral' public establishments, which can include clubs and bars where Muslims may be drinking.

ISLAMIC FESTIVALS

The high point of the Islamic festival calendar is **Ramadan**, when Muslims fast from sunrise to sunset. Fifteen days before the start of Ramadan, on Nisfu Night, it is believed the souls of the dead visit their homes. During Ramadan Lailatul Qadar (Night of Grandeur), Muslims celebrate the arrival of the Quran on earth, before its revelation by the Prophet Mohammed. **Hari Raya Puasa** (also known as Hari Raya Aidilfitri) marks the end of the month-long fast, with two days of joyful celebration and feasting. Hari Raya Puasa is the major holiday of the Muslim calendar and it can be difficult to find accommodation, particularly on the coast. The start of Ramadan moves forward 11 days every year in line with the Muslim lunar calendar.

Other major Islamic festivals celebrated in Malaysia:

» **Hari Raya Haji** A two-day festival, usually in November, marking the successful completion of the hajj (pilgrimage to Mecca) and commemorating the willingness of Abraham to sacrifice his son. Many shops, offices and tourist attractions close and locals consume large amounts of cakes and sweets.

» **Mawlid al-Nabi** Usually held in March, celebrating the birth of the Prophet Mohammed.

» **Awal Muharram** The Muslim New Year falls in November or December.

Islam is the state religion of Malaysia and this influences cultural and social life at several levels. Government institutions and banks, for example, close for two hours on Friday at lunch to allow Muslims to attend Friday prayers.

Government censors, with Islamic sensitivities in mind, dictate what can be performed on public stages or screened in cinemas. This has led to pop star Beyoncé cancelling her shows when asked to adhere to strict guidelines on dress and performance style; and to the banning of movies including *Schindler's List* and *Babe,* the themes of Jews being saved from the Holocaust and a cute pig not being to Muslim tastes.

If you think those decisions sound off key, then how about the country's leading Islamic council issuing an edict against yoga in 2008, fearing the exercises could corrupt Muslims? More seriously, secular courts have been unable since 1988 to overrule decisions made by the *syariah* courts, which have jurisdiction over matters of Islamic law. This has affected cases of Muslims wishing to change their religion, and divorced parents who cannot agree on a religion by which to raise their children, prompting the question of whether Malaysia is really a secular state or an Islamic one.

Chinese Religions

The Chinese in the region usually follow a mix of Buddhism, Confucianism and Taoism. Buddhism takes care of the afterlife, Confucianism looks after the political and moral aspects of life, while Taoism contributes animistic beliefs to teach people to maintain harmony with the universe. Chinese religion upholds a belief in the innate vital energy in rocks, trees, rivers and springs. At the same time, people from the distant past, both real and mythological, are worshipped as deities. Ancestor worship is particularly important to the Chinese in Malaysia.

On a day-to-day level most Chinese are much less concerned with the high-minded philosophies and asceticism of Buddha, Confucius or Lao Zi than they are with the pursuit of worldly success, the appeasement of the dead and the spirits, and the seeking of knowledge about the future. Like Hinduism, Chinese religion is polytheistic – as well as Buddha, Lao Zi and Confucius, there are a host of house gods, auspicious deities and gods and goddesses for particular professions.

Hinduism

Hinduism in the region dates back at least 1500 years and there are Hindu influences in cultural traditions, such as *wayang kulit* (shadow puppetry) and the wedding ceremony. However, it is only in the last hundred years or so, following the influx of Indian contract labourers and settlers, that it has again become widely practised.

Hinduism has three basic practices: *puja* (worship); the cremation of the dead; and the rules and regulations of the caste system. Although still very strong in India, the caste system was never significant in Malaysia, mainly because the labourers brought here from India were mostly from the lower classes.

Hinduism has a vast pantheon of deities, although the one omnipresent god usually has three physical representations: Brahma, the creator; Vishnu, the preserver; and Shiva, the destroyer or reproducer. All three gods are usually shown with four arms, but Brahma has the added advantage of four heads to represent his all-seeing presence.

The most popular Chinese gods and local deities, or *shen,* are Kuan Yin, the goddess of mercy, Kuan Ti, the god of war and wealth, and Toh Peh Kong, a deity found only outside China, representing the spirit of the pioneers.

Women in Malaysia

Malaysian women take part in all aspects of society, from politics and big business to academia and the judicial system; in 2010 Malaysia appointed its first two female Islamic-court judges. However, women in all communities, particularly those with conservative religious values, face restrictions on their behaviour despite the general openness of Malaysian society. Arranged marriage is common among Muslim and Hindu families, and the concept of 'honour' is still a powerful force in internal family politics.

Although the wearing of the *tudong* (headscarf) is encouraged, Muslim women are permitted to work, drive and go out unchaperoned, though the religious authorities frequently crack down on *khalwat* (close proximity, ie couples who get too intimate in public), which is considered immoral. Full *purdah* (the practice of screening women from men or strangers by means of all-enveloping clothes) is rare – if you do see this it's likely to be worn by women visiting from the Persian Gulf.

Recent changes to Islamic family law have made it easier for men to marry and divorce multiple wives and claim a share of their property. Muslim parties are also campaigning to remove the crime of marital rape from the statute books and bring in new laws requiring four male witnesses before a rape case can come to trial. In response to these moves, Marina Mahathir, the daughter of the former prime minister, compared the lot of Malaysia's Muslim women to that of blacks under apartheid in South Africa.

Sisters in Islam (www.sistersinislam.org.my), run by professional Malaysian Muslim women, is campaigning to change patriarchal interpretations of Islam in Malay society.

Traditional Malay Architecture

» Rumah Penghulu, KL

» Kampung Baru, KL

» Rimbun Dahan, near KL

» Kampung Morten, Melaka

» Villa Sentosa, Melaka

» P Ramlee House, Penang

Arts

Each of Malaysia's diverse ethnic groups has its own traditional art forms, alongside which visitors can enjoy contemporary art, drama and film making.

Architecture

Malaysia has been producing noteworthy buildings since well before the colonial period. The local style of architecture reached its peak under the sultans of Melaka – the traditional Malay house is built on stilts with high peaked roofs, large windows and lattice-like grilles in

---

VOICES FROM THE STREET

'We began by listening to the voices of ordinary Malaccans. We listened to the city's streets, as we searched out hidden corners and abandoned alleyways. Listened to houses and temples, ruins and cemeteries. Even to the murmurs and whispers of empty spaces. We listened at every turn, at every step. To the living and the dead. The past and the present. In the hope that the story of an extraordinary place and its people would be told. And we heard them speak.'

Extract from Malacca: Voices from the Street
by Lim Huck Chin and Fernando Jorge (2006)

Lim Huck Chin and Fernando Jorge are two architects who worked on the restoration of a Dutch period shophouse (8 Heeren St) and have since produced *Malacca: Voices from the Street,* a gorgeous book of photos and stories about the town. You can learn about their work by visiting the website www.malaccavoices.com or by visiting the house at **8 Heeren Street** (see p120). Note that although this building is called 8 Heeren St, the street name today is Jln Tun Tan Cheng Lock.

Lim's and Jorge's words and pictures capture the magic of Melaka that many residents fear is under threat in the rush to paint heritage buildings in garish colours in the name of conservation.

The contemporary Malaysian writer who has made the biggest impression internationally is London-based Tash Aw. His debut novel, *The Harmony Silk Factory*, is set deep in the heart of Peninsular Malaysia partly during WWII and won the 2005 Whitbread First Novel award. His 2009 follow-up, *Map of the Invisible World*, which focuses on Malaysia and Indonesia in the 1960s, also garnered great reviews.

Hot on Aw's heels is Tan Twan Eng whose debut, *The Gift of Rain*, long-listed for the 2007 Man Booker Prize, is a tale of betrayal set in Penang just before and during WWII.

Not winning any accolades, but fun to read and very evocative of its KL setting, is the comedy-thriller *Devil's Place* by Brian Gomez. Kam Raslan's *Confessions of an Old Boy* is another comic tale, this time following the adventures both at home and abroad of politico Dato' Hamid.

Urban Odysseys, edited by Janet Tay and Eric Forbes, is a mixed bag of short stories set in KL that capture the city's multifaceted, multicultural flavour. It includes an entertaining story by France-based Preeta Samarasan about a man who 'power walks' through the city's many malls; Samarasan's novel *Evening is the Whole Day* has been published internationally and has the Indian immigrant experience in Malaysia as one of its themes.

A snappy read is Amir Muhammad's *Rojak: Bite-Sized Stories*, in which the multi-talented artist and writer gathers a selection of the 350-word vignettes, many of them comic, that he penned as part of the British Council–sponsored creative writing project City of Shared Stories (http://cityofsharedstorieskualalumpur.com).

the walls to maximise the cooling effect of breezes. The layout of a traditional Malay house reflects Muslim sensibilities, with separate areas for men and women, as well as areas where guests of either sex may be entertained.

The Dutch and British were jointly responsible for the distinctive colonial architecture of Melaka, but the real geniuses of architecture on the coast were the Chinese, who built distinctive stucco-fronted shophouses, ornate temples, regal mansions and stately clanhouses in Melaka, Penang and later in KL. The British colonial period also saw the architects Arthur Bennison Hubback, designer of the Jamek Mosque and Kuala Lumpur Railway Station, and Arthur Charles Norman, responsible for the collection of buildings around Dataran Merdeka, do their best work in the capital.

TY Lee is the man responsible for designing KL's Art Deco Central Market (1936) and nearby Chin Wood Stadium (1953). Among Malaysia's postcolonial architects of note is Hijjas Kasturi, who designed the Tabung Haji and Menara Maybank buildings in KL, as well as the giant shark fin–like Menara Telekom, on the border between KL and Petaling Jaya and adorned with 22 outdoor 'sky gardens', one on every third floor. It's possible at certain times of the year to visit Kasturi's home, Rimbun Dahan (see p105), also a centre for developing traditional and contemporary art forms.

Contemporary Architecture
» Petronas Towers, KL
» Istana Budaya, KL
» Tabung Haji, KL
» Kompleks Dayabumi, KL
» Wawasan Bridge, Putrajaya

Dance

A number of traditional dances are still practised on the peninsula. Similar to Thai folk dances, the masked *menora* dance (performed only by men) and female-only *mak yong* dance are used to mark Buddhist festivals. Malay dances include *rodat,* traditionally performed by fishermen to encourage a good catch, and *joget,* an upbeat dance with Portuguese origins, often performed at weddings. In Melaka it's better known as *chakunchak.*

Malaysia's premier traditional dance troupe is the Petronas Performing Art Group (PPAG), an ensemble of 30 musicians and 60 dancers. Its

Inspired by his country's 50th anniversary of independence, photojournalist Evan Hwong (www.evanhwong.com) began a project to photograph 31,857 of his fellow Malaysians (the number representing the date 31 August 1957, on which Malaya ceased to be part of the British Empire). Since starting the Citizen Malaysia project in 2008, Hwong has shot black-and-white portraits of over 2000 people, several of which were in an exhibition that was part of a festival of Malaysian contemporary arts in Singapore in August 2010.

His subjects have included local luminaries such as Marina Mahathir (daughter of the ex-PM), supermodel Amber Chia, Malaysian Idol winner Daniel Lee, the TV broadcaster William Quah, and the late film director Yasmin Ahmad. All the portraits are untitled and cropped to a square frame focusing on the subject's head and bare shoulders (Muslim women can choose to appear wearing the traditional headscarf).

For the project's next stage Hwong plans to travel around Malaysia finding subjects in each of the country's states before presenting his final portfolio as a series of giant projections across KL's city centre buildings in September 2012. The project is entirely funded out of Hwong's own pocket and, although Citizen Malaysia would be a great fit with the government's 1Malaysia policy, the photographer is adamant that he doesn't want it to become political – he purposely hasn't photographed politicians to keep it this way.

CONTEMPORARY ART

repertoire includes more than 100 ethnic dances from across the country, including Chinese and Indian dances. Various professional troupes perform in KL, and there are several tourist-oriented dance shows.

The Actors Studio on the roof of the mall Lot 10 in KL is one of the main venues where you can catch contemporary dance performances. Among the regular events here are the monthly Dancebox shows and the annual Nyoba Kan Buto Fest (www.nyobakan.blogspot.com), including performances by the local *buto* dance group Nyoba Kan, international guest artists, workshops and fringe events.

Drama

Traditional dramatic forms remain popular in Malaysia, particularly *wayang kulit,* shadow-puppet performances that tell tales from the Hindu epic the Ramayana, a distant link to Malaysia's Hindu past. The Tok Dalang (Father of the Mysteries) manipulates the buffalo-hide puppets behind a semitransparent screen, casting shadows onto the screen. Authentic shadow-plays at weddings and harvest festivals can last for many hours, though shorter performances are often laid on for visitors.

Project Wayang (http://projekwayang.blogspot.com) is a contemporary take on the *wayang* scene by a group of KL-based artists led by Fahmi Fadzil and Azmyl Yunor – the aim is to create traditional street-style performances that resonate with an urban audience. The results range from humorous sketches (all in Bahasa Malaysia but pretty understandable) to performances using light bulbs for effect.

The blog and online magazine Arteri Malaysia (www.arterimalaysia.com) is the go-to site for news and views on contemporary art in Malaysia and around the region.

Musicals about national heroes – from the sultanate-era warrior Hang Tuah to former PM Mahathir – are very popular. There is also a growing interest in English-language modern theatre, as well as in Malay, Indian and Chinese languages, though playwrights have to tread carefully when dealing with controversial topics such as race and religion.

The most interesting productions are generally staged at KL's KLPac, the Actors Studio and the Five Arts Centre. Also looking promising is the Penang Performing Arts Centre set to open in 2012.

Music

Traditional & Classical

Traditional Malay music is based largely on *gendang* (drums), but other percussion instruments include the gong and various tribal instruments made from seashells, coconut shells and bamboo. The Indonesian-style *gamelan* (a traditional orchestra of drums, gongs and wooden xylophones), also crops up on ceremonial occasions. The Malay *nobat* uses a mixture of percussion and wind instruments to create formal court music. For Western-style orchestration, attend a performance at the Dewan Filharmonik Petronas at the base of the Petronas Towers.

Chinese and Islamic influences are felt in the music of *dondang sayang* (Chinese-influenced romantic songs) and *hadrah* (Islamic chants, sometimes accompanied by dance and music). The KL-based Dama Orchestra (www.damaorchestra.com) combines modern and traditional Chinese instruments and plays songs that conjure up 1920s and '30s Malaysia.

Popular Music

The Malaysian queen of pop remains the demure Siti Nurhaliza (http://sitizone.com). Hot on her high heels is the folksy Zee Avi (www.zeeavi.com) who was snapped up by the US label Bushfire Records for her eponymous debut CD.

Winner of three AIM awards – the Malaysian equivalent of the Grammies – in 2004 for his debut album, *Monumental,* is singer-songwriter Reshmonu (www.reshmonu.com); his 2009 release *Harapan* (Hope) blends local rhythms and instruments into R'n'B and Latin grooves such as samba and bossa nova. Famous for his distinctive look of braided hair with flowing extensions, the multitalented 32-year-old has opened concerts for the likes of Alicia Keys and the Prodigy, and featured on Lonely Planet's TV programme *Six Degrees: Kuala Lumpur*.

Isaac Entry, a talented singer-songwriter in a similar vein to Zee Avi, regularly gigs around KL and released his first CD in 2010 on a label created by jazz venue No Black Tie. Khottal (www.khottal.com) are a 10-piece band from Melaka who skip all over the place between punk and melodious pop, having a lot of fun on the way.

Cinema

Although Malaysia's film industry dates back to the 1930s, its heyday was the 1950s, when P Ramlee took to the silver screen. This Malaysian icon acted in 66 films, recorded 300 songs, and even became a successful film director – his directorial debut *Penarik Becha* (The Trishaw Man; 1955) is a classic of Malay cinema.

Perhaps the best-known Malaysian director is Taiwan resident Tsai Ming Liang. His starkly beautiful but glacially slow interracial romance, *I Don't Want to Sleep Alone,* was filmed entirely on location in

---

CULTURE ARTS

Critics agreed the best thing about Glen Goei's 2009 drama *The Blue Mansion* (www.theblueman sion.com) was its setting in Georgetown's Cheong Fatt Tze Mansion. This Penang landmark also starred in the 2006 Malay love story *The Red Kabaya* and masqueraded as a location in Vietnam for the French epic *Indochine* (1992) starring Catherine Deneuve.

CHINESE OPERA

Among the Chinese communities of KL, Melaka and Georgetown, Cantonese-style *wayang* (Chinese opera) is popular. Shows feature clanging gongs, high-pitched romantic songs and outrageous dances in spectacular costumes. Performances can go for an entire evening, but plots are fairly self-explanatory and you don't have to speak Cantonese to follow the story. Street performances are held during important festivals such as Chinese New Year (January/February), the Festival of the Hungry Ghosts (August/September) and the Festival of the Nine Emperor Gods (September/October).

YASMIN AHAMAD

The multi-award winning Yasmin Ahamad was only 51 when she died after suffering a stroke in July 2009. Starting her career in advertising, Ahamad made just six movies for the cinema and one for TV but established such a reputation that she was feted both at home and abroad and is considered the most culturally important Malaysian film-maker since P Ramlee.

It was Ahamad's 2005 film *Sepet* that first shook up contemporary Malaysian cinema. About a Chinese boy and Malay girl falling in love, the movie cut across the country's race and language barriers and in turn upset many devout Malays, as did her follow up, *Gubra* (2006), which dared to take a sympathetic approach to prostitutes. Causing less of stir were *Mukshin* (2007), a romantic tale about Malay village life; and what would be her final movie, *Talentime* (2009), about the run-up to an inter-school performing arts contest.

Find out more about her work from Amir Muhammad's tribute book *Yasmin Ahamad's Films* (www.mataharibooks.com), written just a month after her funeral.

KL. It was banned and later released with massive cuts for presenting an allegedly 'negative depiction of Malaysia'.

Amir Muhammad's work also pushes the boundaries on issues that the government prefers not be discussed in the public arena. His movie *Lelaki Komunis Terakhir* (The Last Communist Man; 2006) was banned, along with his follow-up movie *Apa Khabar Orang Kampung* (Village People Radio Show; 2007) – find out more about them at www.redfilms.com.my.

Muhammad's producer and a pioneer of the Malaysian new wave of directors is James Lee, whose best-known pictures are *Room To Let* (2002) and *Beautiful Washing Machine* (2004). You can find out about and purchase some of these films and those of other local indie directors at www.dahuangpictures.com.

Visual Arts

In 2010 the federal government woke up to a fact long appreciated by art collectors around the world: Malaysia has a damned impressive contemporary art scene. The free booklet *Malaysia's Art Tourism Trail* was published (pick it up at tourist offices) and several special exhibitions organised in KL and Melaka.

Among the most interesting and internationally successful contemporary Malaysian artists are Jalaini Abu Hassan ('Jai'), Wong Hoy Cheong, landscape painter Wong Perng Fey, and Australian-trained multimedia artist Yee I-Lann. Amron Omar has focused for nearly 30 years on *silat* (a Malay martial art) as a source of inspiration for his paintings, a couple of which hang in the National Art Gallery in KL.

A young contemporary sculptor who's making a name for himself internationally is Abdul Multhalib Musa (www.multhalib.com). His work has won awards and he created several pieces in Beijing for the 2008 Olympics. One of Musa's rippling steel tube creations is in the garden at Rimbun Dahan, while another can be spotted outside Wisma Selangor Dredging, 142C Jln Ampang, in KL.

Environment & Wildlife

Kuala Lumpur, Melaka and Penang are located in Peninsular Malaysia, the long finger of land extending south from Thailand towards Indonesia. It's no accident that these three major urban centres are found on the peninsula's west coast where the land is flat and the soil fertile. The interior is made up of densely forested hills and jungle, descending steeply to the sparsely populated east coast.

The other part of the country, comprising over half of the nation's 329, 758 sq km, is Malaysian Borneo, which shares the island of Borneo with the Indonesian state of Kalimantan and the tiny Sultanate of Brunei. Malaysian Borneo is made up of Sabah and Sarawak, and is characterised by dense jungle with many large river systems. Mt Kinabalu (4101m), in Sabah, is the country's highest mountain.

Mega-Diversity Area

Malaysia is one of the world's so-called 'mega-diversity' areas. The country's jungle, believed to be 130 million years old and according to government figures covering around 70% of Malaysia, supports a staggering amount of life: around 14,500 species of flowering plant and tree, 210 species of mammal, 600 species of bird, 150 species of frog, 80 species of lizard and thousands of types of insect. Although vast areas of forests have been cleared, some magnificent stands remain mostly protected by a nationwide system of reserves and parks (p221). With patience and some luck you may well encounter the following flora and fauna in their natural habitat.

Animals

Apes & Monkeys

Malaysia's signature animal, the orang-utan, is found living wild only in the jungles of Sabah and Sarawak. Their future is threatened by habitat loss; the population, estimated to be 11,300, is thought to have dropped by 40% in the last 20 years. Drop by the zoos in KL and Melaka to see these charismatic apes.

The monkeys you're most likely to encounter living wild around KL, Melaka and Penang are macaques, the stocky, aggressive monkeys that solicit snacks from tourists at nature reserves and rural temples such as those at Batu Caves. If you are carrying food, watch out for daring raids and be wary of bites as rabies is a potential hazard.

Dogs, Cats & Civets

The animals you're most likely to see in KL, Melaka and Penang are domesticated dogs and cats. However, animal lovers should be aware that local Muslims are brought up to consider dogs unclean, hence many have

---

Conservation Organisations

» Malaysian Nature Society (www.mns.org.my)

» Orangutan Foundation (www.orangutan.org.uk)

» Sahabat Alam Malaysia (SAM; www.foe-malaysia.org)

» WWF-Malaysia (www.wwf.org.my)

The Encyclopedia of Malaysia: The Environment by Professor Sham Sani Dato, one volume of an excellent series of illustrated encyclopedias, covers everything you need to know about Malaysia's environment.

negative attitudes towards them. In 2009 villagers from Pulau Ketam in Selangor rounded up over 300 strays and dumped them on two uninhabited islands. According to reports from animal welfare agency SPCA Selangor, the starving dogs turned to cannibalism to survive.

Cats hardly fare any better with many local species of wild cats facing extinction because of hunting and the trade in body parts for traditional medicines. The Malayan tiger is now extremely rare on the peninsula, as are leopards and black panthers (actually black leopards). Smaller bay cats, leopard cats and marbled cats fare slightly better, in part because they need less territory and eat smaller prey (birds and small mammals). You may also spot various species of civet cats, a separate family of predators with vaguely catlike features but longer snouts and shaggier coats.

Elephants & Tapirs

In 2009 there was great excitement on the announcement that a population of 631 Asian elephants had been found to be living in Taman Negara National Park. Elephants help safeguard thousands of other species within a habitat: they create vital natural pathways by knocking over trees, allowing smaller species to feed, as well as dispersing plant seeds in their dung. Unfortunately, the animal is still highly endangered. Due to habitat loss, elephants are forced to hunt for food in areas surrounding natural forests such as plantations, where they raid crops on a massive scale. This leads to them either being shot by farmers or simply dying of starvation.

Deforestation is also endangering the tapir, an extraordinary animal that looks like a cross between a wild pig and a hippo. Growing up to 2m in length and weighing some 300kg, they are herbivorous and are sometimes seen at the salt licks in the further reaches of Taman Negara. For more information see www.tapirs.org.

Bats

Malaysia has more than 100 species of bat, most of which are tiny, insectivorous species that live in caves, and under eaves and bark. Fruit bats (flying foxes) are only distantly related; unlike insectivorous bats, they have well-developed eyes and do not navigate by echolocation. They are often seen taking wing from caves and trees at dusk.

Birds

Malaysia has a number of distinctive birds – 650 species live on the peninsula alone. Keep an eye out for colourful pittas, kingfishers, trogons and flycatchers, various species of bulbul, handsome long-tailed great arguses (a species of pheasant) and regal hornbills, with their huge, tou-

Wildlife Watching

» KL Bird Park, KL

» Deer Park, KL

» Zoo Negara, near KL

» Kuala Gandah Elephant Conservation Centre, Lanchang

» Melaka Zoo, Melaka

» Penang National Park, Penang

NO TIGERS ON PENANG

The Malayan tiger – as depicted on the Malaysian coat of arms and found only on the Malay Peninsula – is considered a subspecies of the Indo-Chinese tiger. The exact population is unknown but is considered by WWF to be around 500, the vast majority of which are found in the states of Pahang, Perak, Terengganu and Kelantan. Hunting and encroachments on their natural habitat by logging operations have put the species under threat.

In March 2009 a proposal to create a 40-hectare tiger park on Penang drew criticism from the Malaysian Conservation Alliance for Tigers (www.malayantiger.net) who pointed out that the island had no record of the animals ever having lived there and that the project would very likely undermine government commitments to protect jungle corridors on the mainland in order to double the wild tiger population by 2020.

canlike beak. You can spot exotic species in many urban parks, but for rarer birds you'll have to head to the jungle and the hillsides – the Malaysian Nature Society is helping to promote Genting Highlands (p105) as a prime birding location.

Reptiles & Amphibians

Some 250 species of reptile have been recorded in Malaysia, including 140 species of snake. Cobras and vipers pose a potential risk to trekkers, although the chances of encountering them are low. Large pythons are sometimes seen in national parks and you may also encounter 'flying' snakes, lizards and frogs (all these species glide using wide flaps of skin). Even in city parks, you stand a good chance of running into a monitor lizard, a primitive-looking carrion feeder notorious for consuming domestic cats.

Four species of marine turtle are native to Malaysia: hawksbills, green turtles, olive ridleys and giant leatherbacks. Although they nest on many Malaysian beaches, all four species are currently listed as endangered because of coastal development and the harvesting of turtle eggs for food. To help preserve these magnificent creatures, avoid buying any products made from turtles.

Plants

The wet, tropical climate of this region produces an amazing range of trees, plants and flowers, including such signature species as the carnivorous pitcher plant, numerous orchids and the parasitic rafflesia (or 'corpse flower'), which produces the world's largest flower – a whopping 1m across when fully open. However, vast tracts of rainforests have been cleared to make way for plantations of cash crops such as rubber and palm oil. Just look out of the window on the flight into Kuala Lumpur International Airport and you'll see endless rows of oil palms.

National Parks & Other Protected Areas

Malaysia's jungles contain some of the world's oldest undisturbed areas of rainforest. It's estimated they've existed for about 100 million years, as they were largely unaffected by the far-reaching climatic changes brought on elsewhere by the Ice Age.

Parks & Reserves

» Penang National Park, Penang

» Teluk Bahang Forest Reserve, near Penang

» Forest Research Institute of Malaysia, near KL

» Templer Park, near KL

» Hutan Rekreasi Air Keroh, near Melaka

ENVIRONMENT & WILDLIFE NATIONAL PARKS & OTHER PROTECTED AREAS

IMPROVING WILDLIFE CONSERVATION

At the end of 2010 Malaysia started to enforce its new Wildlife Conservation Act, which includes fines of up to RM100,000 and long prison sentences for poaching, smuggling of animals and other wildlife-related crimes. This first revision of such laws in over 30 years has been welcomed by local pressure groups including Traffic Southeast Asia (www.traffic.org/southeast-asia) and the Malaysian Nature Society (www.mns.my).

Smuggling of live animals and animal parts is a particular problem in the region. Pangolins, also known as scaly anteaters, are the most traded species even though they are protected under Malaysian law; their scales, believed to have medicinal properties, can fetch up to RM800 per kg. In July 2010 police looking for stolen cars also uncovered an illegal 'mini zoo' in a KL warehouse containing 20 species of protected wildlife including a pair of rare birds of paradise worth RM1 million.

A month later, the notorious animal smuggler Alvin Wong was nabbed at Kuala Lumpur International Airport after his bag burst open revealing 95 boa constrictors, two rhinoceros vipers and a mata mata turtle. In November, Wong – described as 'the Pablo Escobar of wildlife trafficking' in The Lizard King by Bryan Christy (http://thelizardking book.com), a fascinating account of international animal and reptile smuggling – was sentenced to five years in jail.

HAWKSBILL HAVEN UNDER THREAT

While Peninsular Malaysia has lost nearly all of its once-numerous leatherback turtles, hope remains for the hawksbill turtle. About 1000 hawksbills nest in Malaysia, a third of which lay on beaches around Melaka. The turtles' favoured destination is Pulau Upeh, a 2.8-hectare island 3.2km off Melaka's coast.

Since news surfaced in 2006 that the island was up for sale WWF-Malaysia has been lobbying the government to turn it into a turtle sanctuary. Environmentalists' hopes were given a blow in 2009 when Melaka's chief minister announced that Pulau Upeh would be developed for tourism. WWF-Malaysia reckons that the planned upgrade of existing facilities and building of 200 chalets on the island will seriously compromise the nesting beach.

The intrepid turtles make a perilous journey year after year through the debris, oil spills and ship traffic of the Strait of Melaka, yet their real enemy awaits on the beach. The Malaccan people have been harvesting turtle eggs throughout known memory and they believe that eating them increases male virility and can protect the health of a foetus in utero. WWF-Malaysia runs community projects sensitising local communities to the turtles' plight and offers cash to harvesters if they bring eggs to their hatchery.

Turtle tourism is not practised as yet in Melaka. If by chance you are offered a chance to watch nesting turtles, go in very small groups, be very still and quiet, keep at least 2m away from the animals, don't use flash cameras or lights, and remain behind the turtles where they can't see you. Use the same precautions during hatchings. To find out how you can help with hawksbill turtle projects, go to WWF-Malaysia's website (www.wwf.org.my).

Tropical Marine Life of Malaysia & Singapore, Tropical Birds of Malaysia & Singapore and Tropical Plants of Malaysia & Singapore are some of the titles in Periplus Editions' great series of field guides to the plants and animals of Malaysia.

Fortunately, quite large areas of some of the best and most spectacular of these rainforests have been made into national parks, in which all commercial activities are banned. The British established the first national park in Malaysia in 1938 and it is now included in Taman Negara, the crowning glory of Malaysia's network of national parks, which crosses the borders of Terengganu, Kelantan and Pahang; tour companies in KL run trips here (see p65). In addition to this and the 27 other national and state parks across the country (23 of them located in Malaysian Borneo), there are various government-protected reserves and sanctuaries for forests, birds, mammals and marine life.

Accommodation is not a problem when visiting most national parks. Various categories are available, from hostel to chalet. There are also several marine parks, including the reef conservation area at Pulau Payer, accessible on snorkelling and diving trips from Penang – see p156.

Environmental Issues

Malaysia's federal government maintains that it is doing its best to balance the benefits of economic development with environmental protection and conservation. Others, including a long list of wildlife and environment protection agencies and pressure groups, beg to differ, pointing out how big business continues to have the ear of government when decision time rolls around (witness the plight of the hawksbill turtle, p222).

A positive development was the election in 2008 of new state governments for Penang and Selangor, both of which are controlled by opposition parties to the ruling BN coalition. Penang has since announced its intention to become Malaysia's first 'green state' and Selangor has also introduced a raft of pro-environmental policies including introducing a 'no plastic bag' policy at shops at the weekends.

Deforestation

Malaysia's logging and oil palm businesses provide hundreds of thousands of jobs, yet they also wreak untold ecological damage and have caused the displacement of many tribal people and the consequent erosion of their unique cultures.

There's a disparity between government figures and those of environmental groups, but it's probable that more than 60% of Peninsular Malaysia's rainforests have been logged, with similar figures applying to Malaysian Borneo. Government initiatives such as the National Forestry Policy have led to deforestation being cut to 900 sq km a year, a third slower than previously. The aim is to reduce the timber harvest by 10% each year, but even this isn't sufficient to calm many critics who remain alarmed at the rate at which Malaysia's primary forests are disappearing.

Close to KL, the Forestry Research Institute of Malaysia (FRIM) is pioneering new ways of preserving and regenerating Malaysia's rainforests. For more information on government forestry projects visit the website of the Forestry Department (www.forestry.gov.my).

Environmental groups such as TrEES (www.trees.org.my) have also been campaigning for the protection of the rainforests and water catchment area along the eastern flank of Selangor. In 2010, 93,000 hectares of these uplands were gazetted as the Selangor State Park, making it the peninsula's third-largest protected area of forest after Taman Negara and Royal Belum State Park. Find out more about it at http://selangorstate park.blogspot.com

Overdevelopment

During the Mahathir era, Malaysia embarked on a massive campaign of construction and industrialisation. Huge swathes of countryside were sacrificed to make space for housing estates, factories and highways, displacing many indigenous communities from their ancestral lands. The administrative capital of Putrajaya, for example, gobbled up 4932 hectares of prime agricultural land.

Overdevelopment married to poor construction standards has caused several disastrous landslides, one of the most recent being in December 2008 in Bukit Antarabangsar, near KL, when four people died as 14 luxury homes tumbled down a hillside. The collapse of a 12-storey building in Selangor in December 1993 killed 49 people. The government has toughened up construction codes, but development of such precariously

The region's environment faces an ongoing threat from the so-called 'haze' – smoke from fires set by Indonesian farmers and plantation companies to clear land for agricultural purposes. The haze is at its worst usually around March and September and October, just before the rainy season.

ENVIRONMENT & WILDLIFE ENVIRONMENTAL ISSUES

THE PROBLEM OF PALM OIL

The oil palm (Elaeis guineensis), a native of West Africa and introduced into Malaysia in the 1870s, is probably now the most common tree in Peninsular Malaysia. The country's first oil palm plantation was established in 1917; today, according to the Malaysian Palm Oil Council (www.mpoc.org.my), Malaysia is the world's leading producer of palm oil, accounting for over 40% of global production. The oil is extracted from the orange-coloured fruit, which grows in bunches just below the fronds. It is used primarily for cooking, although it can also be refined into biodiesel – an alternative to fossil fuels.

For all the benefits, there have been huge environmental consequences to the creation of vast plantations that have replaced the native jungle and previously logged forests; in 2003 Friends of the Earth reported that palm-oil production was responsible for 87% of deforestation in Malaysia. The use of polluting pesticides and fertilisers in palm-oil production also undermines the crop's eco credentials.

The Palm Oil Action Group (www.palmoilaction.org.au) is an Australian pressure group raising awareness about palm oil and the need to use alternatives. Roundtable on Sustainable Palm Oil (www.rspo.org) tries to look at the issue from all sides while seeking to develop and implement global standards. ProForest (www.proforest.net) has also been working with Wild Asia (www.wildasia.org) on a programme designed to promote sustainability within the oil palm industry.

sited facilities continues apace in the cooler highland areas within easy reach of KL, such as the Cameron Highlands.

The global economic crisis has had an impact and the pace of construction shows signs of slowing. The opposition state governments of Selangor and Penang have also introduced stricter controls over development proposals, with Selangor rolling out financial incentives for developers to adhere to a Green Building Index.

Nature Escapes (www.nature -escapes-kuala -lumpur.com/ index.html) is a great online resource, run by a passionate expat dad aiming to get all ages enjoying the natural spots around KL. It also has features on environmental issues.

Cleaning Polluted Rivers

There has been some success in both Penang and Melaka when it comes to cleaning up polluted waterways. Sungai Pinang, which flows through the heart of Georgetown, was once so filthy that it had a Class V classification, meaning it was unable to sustain life and that contact with the water was dangerous. The state's clean-up programme resulted in the waterway's pollution rating dropping to Class III in 2010. By 2014 it's hoped that the river will be clean enough for people to swim in.

According to the Malaysian Nature Society, the revival of the once-sludgy Sungai Melaka flowing through Melaka is also a model of how a river can be cleaned up. Starting in 2005 the city invested about RM100 million in the project, which also included building grassy areas and walking paths along the river banks. A catamaran designed to clean up oil slicks was employed to remove rubbish, then compress it into a material that could be used to reinforce the banks. The next step was the beautification of the banks followed by domestic wastewater and cesspool treatment; reservoirs were built to trap scum, oil and refuse.

The focus has now turned to KL and the Klang Valley. The literal translation of Kuala Lumpur is 'muddy estuary' and anyone gazing on any of the milky coffee-coloured waterways that flow through the city would still find that name appropriate. Following moves in 2010 by the Selangor state government to clean up a 21km stretch of Sungai Klang around Klang, the federal government has stepped in to offer to coordinate the project. This makes sense as the 120km-long heavily polluted river flows through the capital on its way to the coast.

Ian Buchanan spent eight years creating the exquisite illustrations and text for *Fatimah's Kampung*, a parable about the how Malaysia is in the process of sacrificing nature and traditional values for economic development.

Cutting Carbon Emissions

At the 2009 climate change conference in Copenhagen, Prime Minister Najib pledged to slash Malaysia's carbon emissions by 40% by 2020. According to the International Energy Agency, the country emitted 6.68 tonnes of carbon dioxide per capita in 2007, more than twice the world's average, and the fourth-highest amount in the region after Brunei, Taipei and Singapore. Compared to these three countries, Malaysia's emission per capita percentage change between 1990 and 2007 was the highest, growing by 143%.

In order to reach its stated goal the federal government has added green technology to the portfolio of the Ministry of Energy and Water and announced the launch of a national green technology policy. The details remain sketchy, however, and the overall aim sits awkwardly with the nation's poor record on public transportation and the continuing expansion of local budget airlines such as Air Asia.

Survival Guide

Directory A–Z

Accommodation

Accommodation in Kuala Lumpur, Melaka and Penang ranges from sky-scraping five-star hotels to grungy backpacker dives that scrape the bottom of the barrel. The good news is that accommodation can be refreshingly inexpensive. Outside of public holidays (around major festivals such as Chinese New Year in January/February) most midrange and top-end hotels offer big discounts – always ask about special offers.

Budget listings in this guide (denoted with a '$') are those offering a double room with attached bathroom or dorm bed for under RM100; midrange properties ($$) have double rooms with attached baths from RM100 to RM400; top-end places ($$$) charge over RM400 including 10% service and 5% tax (expressed as ++).

Promotional rates can bring rooms at many top-end hotels into the midrange category. A 5% government tax applies to all hotel rooms (including at cheaper hotels where it is invariably included in the quoted rate), and almost all top-end hotels levy an additional 10% service charge. Credit cards are widely accepted at midrange and top-end hotels; cash payment is expected at cheaper places.

Camping

Camping is possible on Pulau Besar near Melaka and in Penang National Park, Teluk Bahang Forest Reserve and Pulau Jerejak near Penang.

Homestays

Staying with a Malaysian family is possible and a few options are listed in the accommodation sections of the KL, Melaka and Penang chapters. Contact local offices of Tourism Malaysia for more information on homestay programmes.

Hostels & Guesthouses

Kuala Lumpur, Melaka and Penang all have cheap hostels and guesthouses. Most offer dorm beds (from as little as RM10) as well as basic rooms with shared or private bathrooms and a choice of fan or air-con.

Hotels

As a rule, budget hotels offer poky box rooms, often with thin plywood partition walls and no windows; there may be a choice of private or shared bathrooms and fan or air-conditioning. In cheaper hotels, 'single' normally means one double bed, and 'double' means two double beds. To aid ventilation, the walls of cheaper rooms may not meet the ceiling, which is terrible for acoustics and privacy – bring earplugs.

At midrange hotels air-con is standard, and rooms typically have TVs, phones, proper wardrobes and private bathrooms. Some midrange hotels also offer restaurants, business centres and swimming pools.

In more upmarket hotels, 'superior' rooms are normally standard rooms, while 'deluxe' or 'club' rooms have better facilities. Top-end hotels pull out all the stops. Rooms have every conceivable amenity, from in-room internet access (typically wi-fi), to safes, minibars, slippers and robes, and even prayer mats for Muslim guests.

Business Hours

Reviews won't list operating hours unless they deviate from the following:

Banks 10am–3pm Mon–Fri, 9.30am–11.30am Sat

Restaurants noon–2.30pm & 6–10.30pm

Shops 9.30am–7pm, malls 10am–10pm

BOOK YOUR STAY ONLINE

For more accommodation reviews by Lonely Planet authors, check out hotels.lonelyplanet.com/malaysia. You'll find independent reviews, as well as recommendations on the best places to stay. Best of all, you can book online.

Climate

Lying just 2° to 7° north of the equator, Peninsular Malaysia is hot and steamy year-round, with temperatures rarely dropping below 20°C, even at night.

Although Malaysia is monsoonal, only the east coast of the peninsula has a real wet season – elsewhere there is just a little more rain than usual. Rain tends to arrive in brief torrential downpours, providing a welcome relief from the heat. During the monsoon it may rain every day, but it rarely rains all day. Humidity tends to hover around the 90% mark; escape the clammy heat by retreating to the cooler hills.

For current weather forecasts check the website of the **Malaysian Meteorological Department** (www.met.gov.my).

Customs Regulations

The following can be brought into Malaysia duty free:

» 1L of alcohol
» 225g of tobacco (200 cigarettes or 50 cigars)
» souvenirs and gifts not exceeding RM200 (RM500 when coming from Labuan or Langkawi)

Cameras, portable radios, perfume, cosmetics and watches do not incur duty. Prohibited items include weapons (including imitations), fireworks, 'obscene and prejudicial articles' (pornography, for example, and items that may be considered inflammatory or religiously offensive) and drugs. Drug smuggling carries the death penalty in Malaysia.

Visitors can carry only RM1000 in and out of Malaysia; there's no limit on foreign currency.

Electricity

240v/50hz

Kuala Lumpur

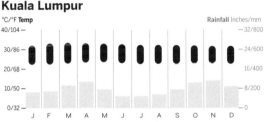

Georgetown

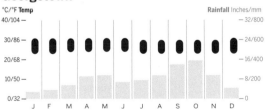

Melaka

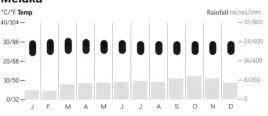

Embassies & Consulates

The following countries are among nations with diplomatic representation in Malaysia. Unless mentioned otherwise, all are in Kuala Lumpur (☏03).

Australia (☏2146 5555; www.australia.org.my; 6 Jln Yap Kwan Seng)

Brunei (; ☏2161 2800; Level 19, Menara Tan & Tan, 207 Jln Tun Razak)

Canada (☏2718 3333; www.canadainternational.gc.ca/malaysia-malaisie/; Level 18, Menara Tan & Tan, 207 Jln Tun Razak)

China (☏2163 6815; http://my.chineseembassy.org; 229 Jln Ampang)

PRACTICALITIES

» The reliable electricity supply (220V to 240V, 50 cycles) takes a UK-type three-square-pin plug.

» English-language newspapers include the *New Straits Times*, the *Star* and the *Malay Mail*. In Malaysian Borneo you'll also find the *Borneo Post*, the *Eastern Times* and the *New Sabah Times*.

» Radio stations include Traxx FM (www.traxxfm.net; 90.3 FM), HITZ FM (www.hitz.fm; 92.9 FM) and MIX FM (www.mix.fm; 94.5 FM) for pop music and Fly FM (www.flyfm.com.my; 95.8 FM) for news. Frequencies given are for KL, and may differ in other parts of Malaysia.

» Malaysia has two government TV channels, TV1 and TV2, and four commercial stations, TV3, NTV7, 8TV and TV9, as well as a host of satellite channels.

» Malaysia uses the metric system for weights and measures.

France (☏2053 5500; www.ambafrance-my.org; 196 Jln Ampang)

Germany (☏2170 9666; www.kuala-lumpur.diplo.de; Level 26, Menara Tan & Tan, 207 Jln Tun Razak)

India (☏2093 3510; www.indianhighcommission.com.my; 2 Jln Taman Duta)

Indonesia Kuala Lumpur (☏2116 4000; www.kbrikualalumpur.org; 233 Jln Tun Razak, Kuala Lumpur) Georgetown (☏04-227 5141; 467 Jln Burma, Georgetown, Penang)

Ireland (☏2161 2963; Ireland House, the Amp Walk, 218 Jln Ampang)

Italy (☏4256 5122; www.ambkualalumpur.esteri.it; 99 Jln U Thant)

Japan (☏2142 7044; www.my.emb-japan.go.jp; 11 Persiaran Stonor)

Netherlands (☏2168 6200; www.netherlands.org.my; 7th fl, South Block, the Amp Walk, 218 Jln Ampang)

New Zealand (☏2078 2533; www.nzembassy.com/malaysia; Level 21 Menara IMC, 8 Jln Sultan Ismail)

Singapore (☏2161 6277; www.mfa.gov.sg/kl; 209 Jln Tun Razak)

Spain (☏2148 4868; www.maec.es, cmb.kualalumpur@maec.es; 200 Jln Ampang)

Thailand (www.thaiembassy.org) Kuala Lumpur (☏2148 8222; 206 Jln Ampang, Kuala Lumpur) Georgetown (☏04-226 8029; 1 Jln Tunku Abdul Rahman, Georgetown, Penang)

UK (☏2170 2200; http://ukinmalaysia.fco.gov.uk/en; 185 Jln Ampang)

USA (☏2168 5000; http://malaysia.usembassy.gov; 376 Jln Tun Razak)

Gay & Lesbian Travellers

Malaysia is a predominantly Muslim country and the level of tolerance for homosexuality is vastly different from its neighbours. Sex between men is illegal at any age and *syariah* Islamic laws (which apply only to Muslims) forbid sodomy and cross-dressing. Fortunately, outright persecution of gays and lesbians is rare.

Nonetheless, gay and lesbian travellers should avoid behaviour that attracts unwanted attention. Malaysians are quite conservative about displays of public affection. Although same-sex handholding is quite common for men and women, this is rarely an indication of sexuality; an overtly gay couple doing the same would attract attention, though there is little risk of vocal or aggressive homophobia.

There's actually a fairly active gay scene in KL. The lesbian scene is more discreet, but it exists for those willing to seek it out. Start looking for information on www.utopia-asia.com or www.fridae.com, both of which provide good coverage of gay and lesbian events and activities across Asia.

The PT Foundation (www.ptfmalaysia.org) is a voluntary nonprofit organisation providing education on HIV/AIDS and sexuality, and care and support programmes for marginalised communities in Malaysia.

Insurance

We strongly recommend taking out travel insurance. Check the small print to see if the policy covers potentially dangerous sporting activities, such as diving or trekking. For medical treatment, some policies pay doctors or hospitals directly but most require you to pay on the spot and claim later (keep all receipts and documentation). Check that the policy covers ambulances or an emergency flight home.

For information on car insurance see p237.

Worldwide travel insurance is available at www.lonelyplanet.com/travel_services. You can buy, extend and claim online anytime – even if you're already on the road.

Internet Access

Internet cafes (charging around RM3 per hour) are found everywhere and many hotels offer free (or discounted) access for guests. KL is as wired a city as they come, with ubiquitous hot spots for wi-fi connections.

Among the internet providers in Malaysia are **Jaring** (www.jaring.my) and **Telekom Malaysia** (www.tm.com.my).

Legal Matters

In any dealings with the local police forces it will pay to be deferential. You're most likely to come into contact with them either through reporting a crime (some of the big cities in Malaysia have tourist police stations for this purpose) or while driving. Minor misdemeanours may be overlooked, but don't count on it.

Drug trafficking carries a mandatory death penalty. A number of foreigners have been executed in Malaysia, some for possession of amazingly small quantities of heroin. Even possession can bring down a lengthy jail sentence and a beating with the *rotan* (cane).

Maps

Periplus (https://peripluspub lishinggroup.com) has maps covering Malaysia, Peninsular Malaysia and KL. Tourism Malaysia's free *Map of Malaysia* has useful distance charts, facts about the country and inset maps of many major cities.

Money

See the inside front cover for currency exchange rates.

ATMs & Credit Cards

MasterCard and Visa are the most widely accepted brands. Banks will accept credit cards for over-the-counter cash advances, or you can make ATM withdrawals if you have your PIN. Many banks are also linked to international banking networks such as Cirrus (the most common), Maestro and

Plus, allowing withdrawals from overseas savings accounts.

Maybank (www.may bank2u.com.my), Malaysia's biggest bank with branches everywhere, accepts both Visa and MasterCard. Hongkong Bank accepts Visa, and the Standard Chartered Bank accepts MasterCard. If you have any questions about whether your cards will be accepted in Malaysia, ask your home bank about its reciprocal relationships with Malaysian banks.

Contact details for credit card companies in Malaysia:

American Express (☏2050 0000; www.americanexpress. com/malaysia)

Diners Card (☏2161 1055; www.diners.com.my)

MasterCard (☏1800 804 594; www.mastercard.com/sea)

Visa (☏1800 802 997; www. visa-asia.com)

Currency

The ringgit (RM) is made up of 100 sen. Coins in use are 1 sen, 5 sen, 10 sen, 20 sen and 50 sen; notes are RM1, RM5, RM10, RM50 and RM100.

Malaysians sometimes refer to the ringgit as 'dollars', the old name for the country's currency – if in doubt, ask if people mean US dollars of 'Malaysian dollars' (ie ringgit). Be sure to carry plenty of small bills with you when venturing outside cities – people often cannot change bills larger than RM10.

Taxes & Refunds

There is no general sales tax but there is a government tax of 5%, plus a service tax of 10% at larger hotels and restaurants.

Travellers Cheques & Cash

Banks in the region are efficient and there are plenty of moneychangers. Banks usually charge a commission for cash and cheques (around RM10 per transac-

tion, with a possible extra fee for each cheque), whereas moneychangers have no charges but their rates are more variable.

All major brands of travellers cheques are accepted. Cash in major currencies is also readily exchanged, though the US dollar has a slight edge.

Photography

Malaysians are generally relaxed about having their picture taken, though it's still polite to ask permission first. To avoid causing offence, always ask before taking pictures in mosques or temples. For advice on taking better photos, Lonely Planet's *Travel Photography: A Guide to Taking Better Pictures* is written by travel photographer Richard I'Anson.

Burning digital photos to a disk at photo development shops costs around RM10 per disk. Print film is also commonly available – a 36-exposure roll is around RM9. Slide film is a little harder to come by and more expensive – a 36-exposure roll of Fuji Velvia averages RM30. Processing prices for a 36-exposure roll of slide film range from RM15 to RM18 (mounted), and 60 sen to 70 sen per exposure for print film.

Post

Pos Malaysia Berhad (www. pos.com.my) runs a fast and efficient postal system. Post offices are open from 8am to 5pm from Monday to Saturday, but closed on the first Saturday of the month and on public holidays.

Aerograms and postcards cost 50 sen to send to any destination. Letters weighing 20g or less cost 90 sen to Asia, RM1.40 to Australia or New Zealand, RM1.50 to the UK and Europe, and RM1.80 to North America. A 1kg parcel to most destinations will cost around RM35 by sea and RM70 by air. Registered mail costs an extra RM3.90 (letters and parcels up to 2kg only).

Main post offices sell packaging materials and stationery.

Public Holidays

As well as fixed secular holidays, various religious festivals (which change dates annually) are national holidays. These include Chinese New Year (in January/February), the Hindu festival of Deepavali (in October/November), the Buddhist festival of Wesak (April/May) and the Muslim festivals of Hari Raya Haji, Hari Raya Puasa, Mawlid al-Nabi and Awal Muharram (Muslim New Year); see p14 for dates.

Fixed annual holidays include the following:

New Year's Day 1 January
Federal Territory Day 1 February (Kuala Lumpur and Putrajaya only)
Sultan of Selangor's Birthday 2nd Saturday in March (Selangor only)
Labour Day 1 May
Yang di-Pertuan Agong's (King's) Birthday 1st Saturday in June
Governor of Penang's Birthday 2nd Saturday in July (Penang only)
National Day (Hari Kebangsaan) 31 August
Christmas Day 25 December

School Holidays

Schools break for holidays five times a year. The actual dates vary from state to state but are generally in January (one week), March (two weeks), May (three weeks), August (one week) and October (four weeks).

Safe Travel

Malaysia is generally a safe country. Touting is not as big a problem as in neighbouring nations, but there are a few scams to look out for. Operators mentioned in this book have been checked by the authors and should be reliable. However, you should always check terms and conditions carefully.

Animal Hazards

Rabies occurs in Malaysia, so any bite from an animal should be treated very seriously. Be cautious around monkeys, dogs and cats. On jungle treks look out for centipedes, scorpions, spiders and snakes. Mosquitoes are likely to be the biggest menace. The risk of malaria is low and antimalarial tablets are rarely recommended but dengue fever is a growing problem, so take precautions to avoid mosquito bites by covering up exposed skin or wearing a strong repellent containing DEET.

Scams

The most common scams involve seemingly friendly locals who invite you to join rigged card games, or shops who trick travellers into buying large amounts of gold jewellery or gems at elevated prices. Anyone who accosts you in the street

> ### GOVERNMENT TRAVEL ADVICE
>
> For the latest from government travel advisories check the following websites:
> **Australia** (www.smartraveller.gov.au)
> **Canada** (www.voyage.gc.ca)
> **New Zealand** (www.safetravel.govt.nz)
> **UK** (www.fco.gov.uk/travel)
> **US** (http://travel.state.gov/travel)

asking 'where you come from' or claiming to have a 'relative studying abroad' may be setting you up for a scam – the best option is not to reply at all. At the Malaysia–Thailand border, don't believe anyone who claims that you are legally required to change sums of money into ringgit or baht before crossing the border – no such regulation exists.

Theft & Violence

Malaysia is not particularly prone to theft or violence. However, muggings and bag snatches do happen, particularly after hours and in the poorer, rundown areas of cities. Be wary of demonstrations, particularly over religious or ethnic issues, as these can turn violent.

Credit-card fraud is a growing problem. Use your cards only at established businesses and guard your credit-card numbers closely.

It's worth carrying a small, sturdy padlock for cheap hotel-room doors and hostel lockers, and to keep prying fingers out of your bags in left-luggage rooms.

Telephone

Landline services are provided by the national monopoly **Telekom Malaysia** (TM; www.tm.com.my).

Fax

Fax facilities are available at Telekom offices in the cities and at some main post offices. If you can't find one of these try a travel agency or large hotel.

International Calls

The easiest and cheapest way to make international calls is to buy a local SIM card for your mobile phone. Only certain payphones permit international calls. You can make operator-assisted international calls from local Telekom offices. To save money on landline calls,

AREA & TELEPHONE CODES

» Country code for Malaysia (☑60)

» Directory enquiries (☑103)

» International access code from Malaysia (☑00)

» International operator (☑108)

» Kuala Lumpur (☑03)

» Melaka (☑06)

» Penang (☑04)

» Singapore (☑02)

buy a prepaid international calling card (available from convenience stores).

Local Calls

Local calls cost 10 sen for three minutes. Payphones take coins or prepaid cards, which are available from Telekom offices and convenience stores. Some also take international credit cards. You'll also find a range of discount calling cards at convenience stores and mobile-phone counters.

Mobile Phones

If you have arranged global-roaming with your home provider, your GSM digital phone will automatically tune in to one of the region's digital networks. If not, buy a prepaid SIM card for one of the local networks on arrival. The rate for a local call is around 40 sen per minute. There are three mobile phone companies, all with similar call rates and prepaid packages:

Celcom (www.celcom.com.my; ☑013 or 019 numbers)

DiGi (www.digi.com.my; ☑016 numbers)

Maxis (www.maxis.com.my; ☑012 or 017 numbers).

Time

Peninsular Malaysia is eight hours ahead of GMT/UTC (London). Noon in Kuala Lumpur is

» 8pm in Los Angeles

» 11pm in New York

» 4am in London

» 2pm in Sydney and Melbourne

Toilets

Western-style sit-down loos are becoming the norm, but there are some places with Asian squat toilets. Toilet paper is not usually provided; instead, you will find a hose or a spout on the toilet seat, which you are supposed to use as a bidet, or a bucket of water and a tap. If you're not comfortable with the 'hand-and-water' technique, carry packets of tissues or toilet paper wherever you go. Public toilets in malls usually charge an entry fee, which often includes toilet paper.

Tourist Information

Tourism Malaysia (www.tourismmalaysia.gov.my) has a network of domestic offices that are good for brochures and free maps but rather weak on hard factual information. Its overseas offices are useful for predeparture planning. There are regional offices in Kuala Lumpur (p98), Melaka (p139) and Penang (p173).

Travellers with Disabilities

For the mobility impaired, KL, Melaka and Penang can be a nightmare. There are often no footpaths, kerbs can be very high, construction sites are everywhere, and crossings are few and far between. On the upside,

taxis are cheap and both Malaysia Airlines and KTM (the national rail service) offer 50% discounts on travel for travellers with disabilities.

Before setting off get in touch with your national support organisation (preferably with the travel officer, if there is one). Also try the following:

Accessible Journeys (☑800-846 4537; www.disabilitytravel.com) In the US.

Mobility International USA (☑541-343 1284; www.miusa.org) In the US.

Nican (☑02-6241 1220; www.nican.com.au) In Australia.

Tourism For All (☑0845 124 9971; www.tourismforall.org.uk) In the UK.

Visas

Visitors must have a passport valid for at least six months beyond the date of entry. You may also be asked to provide proof of a ticket for onward travel and sufficient funds to cover your stay. The following gives a brief overview of the visa requirements – full details are available on the website www.kln.gov.my.

Citizens of Israel cannot enter Malaysia. Nationals of most other countries are given a 30- or 60-day visa on arrival, depending on the expected length of stay. As a general rule, if you arrive by air you will be given 60 days automatically, though coming overland you may be given 30 days unless you specifically ask for a 60-day permit.

Visa Extensions

Depending on your nationality, it may be possible to extend your visa at an immigration office in KL, Melaka or Penang for an additional one or two months. Extensions tend to be granted only for genuine emergencies. It's normally easier to hop across the border to Thailand, Singapore or Indonesia and re-enter the country – this counts as a new visit, even if you re-enter the same day.

Volunteering

Opportunities include the following:

All Women's Action Society Malaysia (www.awam.org. my) Aims to improve the lives of women in Malaysia.

Amnesty International (www.aimalaysia.org) Help out the local branch of the human rights organisation on their various campaigns.

Eden Handicap Service Centre (www.edenhan dicap.org) Christian-run organisation caring for the handicapped of Penang – volunteers are needed to help with a variety of activities.

Malaysian AIDS Council (www.mac.org.my) Assist in their campaigning work.

Malaysian Nature Society (www.mns.org.my) Get involved in helping preserve Malaysia's natural environment.

Nur Salaam (www.chowkids. org) A charity that works with street kids living in the Chow Kit area of KL.

PAWS (www.paws.org.my) Animal rescue shelter near KL's Subang airport.

Penang Heritage Trust (www.pht.org.my) Puts out a free community directory with contact info from nonprofit organisations, including those dealing with environmental, social and cultural issues.

Selangor SPCA (www.spca. org.my) and **Penang SPCA** (www.spca-penang.net) Help

care for abandoned dogs and cats at these animal shelters in Ampang Jaya near KL and Penang.

Wild Asia (www.wildasia.net) Check this organisation's website for a variety of volunteer options generally connected with the environment and sustainable tourism in the region.

Zoo Negara (p104) Help the zoo keepers feed and care for their charges.

Women Travellers

The key to travelling with minimum hassle in Malaysia is to blend in with the locals, which means dressing modestly and being respectful, especially in areas of stronger Muslim religious sensibilities. Regardless of what local non-Muslim women wear, it's better to be safe than sorry – we've had reports of attacks on women ranging from minor verbal aggravation to physical assault. Hard as it is to say, the truth is that women are much more likely to have problems in Malay-dominated areas, where attitudes are more conservative.

In Malay-dominated areas you can halve your hassles just by tying a bandanna over your hair (a minimal concession to the headscarf worn by most Muslim women). When visiting mosques, cover your head and limbs with a headscarf and sarong (many mosques lend these at the entrance). At the beach, most Malaysian women swim

fully clothed in T-shirts and shorts, so don't even think about going topless.

Be proactive about your own safety. Treat overly friendly strangers, both male and female, with a good deal of caution. In cheap hotels check for small peepholes in the walls and doors; when you have a choice, stay in a Chinese-operated hotel. On island resorts, stick to crowded beaches, and choose a chalet close to reception and other travellers. Take taxis after dark and avoid walking alone at night in quiet or seedy parts of town.

Work

There are possibilities for those who seek them out, from professional-level jobs in finance, journalism and the oil industry to temporary jobs at some guesthouses and dive centres in popular resort areas. Those with teaching credentials can find English-teaching jobs in Malaysia, though pickings are slim compared with Japan and Korea. Teachers can check some of the many TEFL sites, including the **Edufind Jobs** (www.jobs. edufind.com).

Depending on the nature of your job, you'll need either an Expatriate Personnel Visa or Temporary Employment Visa. For details and requirements, check the website of the **Immigration Department of Malaysia** (www.imi.gov.my).

MANDARIN ORIENTAL
KUALA LUMPUR

Mandarin Oriental, Kuala Lumpur, Kuala Lumpur City Centre,
50088 Kuala Lumpur, Malaysia.
Telephone (603) 2380 8888 Facsimile (603) 2380 8833
Asas Klasik Sdn. Bhd. (Co. No. 211510)

Mission Crossing, ...
Telephone (03) 9280 0000 Facsimile (03) 9280 683
....

Transport

GETTING THERE & AWAY

Entering Malaysia

You'll need a passport that is valid for at least six months after the date of entry and proof of an onward ticket and adequate funds for your stay. In practice, you'll rarely be asked to prove this. There are no restrictions on entering Malaysia by air and leaving by land or sea, or vice versa. For details of visa and other entry requirements, see p231.

Flights, tours and rail tickets can be booked online at lonelyplanet.com/bookings.

Air

Airports & Airlines

Kuala Lumpur International Airport (see p98) shares its runways with the Low Cost Carrier Terminal (LCCT), the hub for AirAsia. Penang also handles a number of international flights – see p145.

Malaysia Airlines is the national carrier and has a good safety record, as does AirAsia, the main budget carrier.

See below for airline offices in Kuala Lumpur (the websites have listings for offices in other cities).

AirAsia (airline code AK; www.airasia.com) Tickets are best purchased online; get information and book (using online terminals) at offices in KL Sentral station (☎1300 889 933; ⊗9am-9pm) and Plaza Berjaya (12 Jln Imbi; ⊗9am-9pm).

Air China (airline code CA; ☎2166 1999; www.airchina.com.cn; Level 7, Plaza OSK, Jln Ampang)

Air India (airline code AI; ☎2142 0166; http://home.air india.in; 14th fl, Angkasa Raya Bldg, 123 Jln Ampang)

All Nippon Airways (ANA; airline code NH; ☎2032 1331; www.ana.co.jp; 11th fl, Wisma Goldhill, 67 Jln Raja Chulan)

Cathay Pacific Airways (airline code CX; ☎2035 2777; www.cathaypacific.com; ste 22.1, Level 22, Menara IMC, 8 Jln Sultan Ismail)

China Airlines (airline code CI; ☎2148 9417; www.china-airlines.com; Level 15, Amoda Bldg, 22 Jln Imbi)

Emirates (airline code EK; ☎36 207 4999; www.emir ates.com; Level 9, Pavilion Kuala Lumpur, 168 Jln Bukit Bintang)

EVA Air (airline code BR; ☎2162 2981; www.evaair.com; 12th fl, Kenanga International Bldg, Jln Sultan Ismail)

Garuda Indonesian Airlines (airline code GA; ☎2162 2811; www.garuda-indonesia.com, ground fl, Menara Park, Megan Ave II, Block D No 12 Jln Yap Kwan Seng)

Japan Airlines (airline code JL; ☎1800 813 366; www.jal.com; Level 20, Menara Citibank, 165 Jln Ampang)

CLIMATE CHANGE & TRAVEL

Every form of transport that relies on carbon-based fuel generates CO_2, the main cause of human-induced climate change. Modern travel is dependent on aeroplanes, which might use less fuel per kilometre per person than most cars but travel much greater distances. The altitude at which aircraft emit gases (including CO_2) and particles also contributes to their climate change impact. Many websites offer 'carbon calculators' that allow people to estimate the carbon emissions generated by their journey and, for those who wish to do so, to offset the impact of the greenhouse gases emitted with contributions to portfolios of climate-friendly initiatives throughout the world. Lonely Planet offsets the carbon footprint of all staff and author travel.

Jet Airways (airline code 9W; ☑2148 9020; www.jetairways. com; Level 9, Office Tower, 1 Jln Nagasari)

KLM Royal Dutch Airlines (airline code KL; ☑7712 4555; www.klm.com; 1st fl, Grand Plaza Parkroyal, Jln Sultan Ismail)

Kuwait Airways (airline code KU; ☑2031 6033; www.kuwait -airways.com; 7th fl, UBN Tower, 10 Jln Ramlee)

Lufthansa (airline code LH; ☑2052 3428; www.lufthansa. com; 18th fl, Kenanga International Bldg, Jln Sultan Ismail)

Malaysia Airlines (airline code MA; ☑1300 883 000; www.malaysiaairlines.com; Bangunan MAS, Jln Sultan Ismail)

Myanmar Airways International (MAI; ☑2072 1261; www.maiair.com; Lot 17.02, 17th fl, Wisma MPL, Jln Raja Chulan)

Nepal Airlines (airline code RA; ☑2698 7933; www.nepal airlines.com.np; ste 6.05, 6th fl, Semua House, 6 Jln Bunus)

Philippine Airlines (airline code PR; www.philippineair lines.com; Agent: Pacific World Travel, ☑2141 0767, Level 9, Office Tower, 1 Jln Nagasari)

Qatar Airways (airline code QR; ☑2118 6100; www.qatar airways.com; ground fl, Central Plaza, 34 Jln Sultan Ismail)

Royal Brunei Airlines (airline code BI; ☑2070 7166; www.bruneiair.com; 1st fl, Menara UBN, 10 Jln Ramlee)

Singapore Airlines (airline code SQ; ☑2698 7033; www. singaporeair.com; 10th fl, Menara Multi-Purpose, Capital Sq, 8 Jln Munshi Abdullah)

Sri Lankan Airlines (airline code UL; ☑2143 3353; www. srilankan.aero; 1st fl, Kompleks Antarabangsa, Jln Sultan Ismail)

Thai Airways International (airline code TG; ☑2034 6999; www.thaiair.com; 30th fl, Wisma Goldhill, 67 Jln Raja Chulan)

Vietnam Airlines (airline code VN; ☑2164 9115; www. vietnamairlines.com.vn; ste 15-12, 15th fl, Wisma UOA II, 21 Jln Pinang)

Tickets

KL is a busy international hub and there are numerous flights from Asia, Europe, Australia and further afield. Direct flights to KL are normally cheaper than those to Penang, and KL is a good place to pick up tickets to other destinations in Asia, particularly with AirAsia, which offers budget flights across the region.

Land

Peninsular Malaysia shares land borders with Thailand and Singapore (via two causeways). For useful information on train connections between Thailand, Malaysia and Singapore see www. seat61.com/Malaysia.htm.

Singapore

BUS & CAR

The Causeway linking Johor Bahru (JB) with Singapore handles most traffic between the two countries. Direct buses run from Singapore straight through to KL (from S$23, five hours), Melaka (S$25, 4½ hours) and Penang (S$40, 10 hours). However, you can save some money by taking Singapore buses over the Causeway to JB, where fares are cheaper, then catching a long-distance bus there.

Both the Causeway Express and Singapore–Johor Express air-con buses

(S$2.40) and the public SBS bus 170 (S$1.70) depart for JB every 15 minutes between 6.30am and 11pm from Singapore's Queen Street Bus Terminal. A quicker option is to go to Kranji MRT station by train and catch bus 170 (S$1.20) or Marsiling MRT and catch bus 950 ($1.20).

There is a second causeway linking Tuas, in western Singapore, with Geylang Patah in JB. This is known as the Second Link, and some bus services to Melaka and up the west coast head this way. If you have a car, tolls on the Second Link are much higher than the charge on the main Causeway. A good website with details of express buses between Singapore, Malaysia and Thailand is the **Express Bus Travel Guide** (www.myexpressbus.com).

TRAIN

KTM Intercity (☑1300 885 862; http://ktmintercity.com. my) trains connect Singapore with KL (superior/premier class R34/68, six to eight hours, three daily) and Butterworth (superior/premier class R60/127, 14 hours, daily). Fares to KL from JB start at RM33 for a seat and RM55 for a berth.

From July 2011, Singapore's historic Keppel Rd station will close and Woodlands, just across the Causeway from JB, will be the new terminus. Immigration officers at the Malay-

EASTERN & ORIENTAL EXPRESS

The Asian sector of the opulent **Eastern & Oriental Express** (www.orient-express.com) connects Singapore, KL, Butterworth (for Penang) and Bangkok. This luxuriously equipped train runs on set dates monthly (check the website for the schedule) and takes four days and three nights to complete the 1943km journey from Singapore to Bangkok. From Singapore to Bangkok, fares start at US$2320 per person in a double compartment in the Pullman coach including all meals, tea and coffee, and tours – Penang is visited for the day with lunch taken, of course, at the Eastern & Oriental.

SINGAPORE TRAIN FARES

From Singapore to KL or Butterworth you'll pay the same fare as vice versa, but in Singapore dollars. Because of the difference in exchange rates, you can therefore save money by starting your journey in JB (in which case the train ride counts as a domestic trip) and by buying the outbound and return ticket separately.

sia–Singapore border do not always stamp your passport, which can cause problems when you leave Malaysia. Keep your immigration card and train ticket to present to officials on departure.

Thailand
Note that Malaysia is an hour ahead of Thailand.

BUS & CAR
The most popular land route to Malaysia is from Hat Yai to Butterworth (crossing the border at Padang Besar or Bukit Kayu Hitam). You can also cross via the Rantau Panjang–Sungai Golok and Pengkalan Kubor–Tak Bai crossings on the east coast.

Direct buses between KL's Puduraya bus station and Hat Yai cost RM40 (seven hours). Coming from Thailand, various travel agencies and guesthouses in southern Thailand offer minibus transfers across the border to Penang.

TRAIN
KTM Intercity runs a daily service between Hat Yai and KL Sentral; seats/berths start from RM24/54. Another useful train is the daily *International Express* from Butterworth to Bangkok, which connects with trains from

KL and Singapore. Upper/lower berths cost RM95/103. You can also use this train to reach Hat Yai, which has frequent train and bus connections to other parts of Thailand.

Sea

Indonesia
From Peninsular Malaysia, all boats go to Sumatra – the most useful routes are from Medan to Penang (see p146); from Dumai to Melaka (see p139); and from Tanjung Balai and Dumai to Pelabuhan Klang, the seaport for KL (see p98).

Singapore
A number of ferry companies operate across the narrow Straits of Singapore to Malaysia. There are frequent passenger ferries from the Changi Point Ferry Terminal to the small jetties at Tanjung Belungkor and Pengerang (one way S$18, 45 minutes). Take connecting buses on the far side to reach JB from where there are buses to Melaka, Penang and KL.

Thailand
For an interesting and little-used back route into Thailand, consider taking the ferry from Penang to Pulau Langkawi (see p146) and a second ferry from Kuah jetty to Satun on the Thai coast (RM30, one hour). From the port you can take a taxi to Satun town for connections to Hat Yai or Phuket.

GETTING AROUND

Air
Domestic Air Services
The two main domestic operators are **Malaysia Airlines** (MAS; ☎1300 883 000, outside Malaysia ☎03-2161 0555; www.malaysia-airlines.com.my) and **AirAsia** (☎1300 889 933, outside Malaysia ☎603 8660 4343; www.airasia.com).

The MAS subsidiary **Firefly** (☎03-7845 4543; ww.fireflyz.com.my) has flights from KL (Subang) to Penang and from Penang to KL (Subang), JB and Langkawi.

Discounts & Special Flights
All the airlines offer discount tickets on the internet depending on how far in advance you book – in some cases you might only pay for the airport taxes. A variety of other discounts (typically between 25% and 50%) are available for flights around Malaysia on Malaysia Airlines, including for families and groups of three or more – it's worth inquiring when you book. Student discounts are available, but only for students enrolled in institutions in Malaysia.

Air Passes
Malaysia Airlines' Discover Malaysia pass costs US$199 (not including airport taxes) and travellers can take five flights anywhere in Malaysia

TRAIN SERVICES TO/FROM THAILAND

STATION	DEPARTURE	STATION	ARRIVAL
Hat Yai	3.20pm	KL Sentral	4.50am
KL Sentral	9.10pm	Hat Yai	10.35am
Butterworth	2.20pm	Bangkok	12.24pm
Bangkok	2.45pm	Butterworth	1.51pm

within a 28-day period. It also has a US$99 pass for five flights within any one province. You must have flown into Malaysia on a Malaysia Airlines flight to qualify for this pass, though.

Bicycle

While cycling around parts of Melaka and Georgetown is fine, to get anywhere in KL you must negotiate busy highways, braving the erratic city traffic. Most cyclists ride on the hard shoulder on major roads – a rear-view mirror is a valuable asset for occasions when you need to pull into the carriageway to avoid obstacles. Road signs are normally in English, or comprehensible Bahasa Malaysia, and you can get by with a racer in the cities and on major roads in the peninsula (a mountain bike is recommended for trips to backwaters, particularly national parks).

There are good jungle trails for off-roading at Templer Park (p105) and the Forest Research Institute of Malaysia (FRIM; p103). **KL Bike Hash** (www.klmbh.org) runs monthly mountain-bike forays around the capital (visitors are welcome to ride along for an RM15 donation). The website has loads of useful general information on cycling in Malaysia and dozens of links to other cycling sites.

KL is the best place to buy or find spares for bicycles – elsewhere, motorcycle mechanics can help with minor repairs. International-quality bicycles and components can be bought in bigger cities, but top-spec machines and fittings are hard to find. Bringing your own is the best bet. Bicycles can be transported on most international flights if packed correctly; check with the airline about extra charges and shipment specifications.

Boat

For details of the ferry service between Butterworth and Penang see p146.

Bus

Bus travel in Malaysia is economical, generally comfortable and seats can be reserved. It's also fast – sometimes too fast. In a bid to pack in as many trips as possible, some bus drivers speed recklessly, resulting in frequent, often fatal, accidents.

Konsortium Transnasional Berhad (www.ktb.com.my) is Malaysia's largest bus operator running services under the **Transnasional** (☎1300 888 582; www.transnasional.com.my), **Plusliner** (www.plusliner.com) and **City liner** (www.cityliner.com.my) brands. Its services tend to be slower than rivals, but their buses have also been involved in several major accidents. They have competition on the longer domestic routes from many other companies including **Aeroline** (www.aeroline.com.my) and **Supernice** (www.supernice.com.my).

On main routes most private buses have air-con and cost only a few ringgit more than regular buses. However, take note of one traveller's warning: 'Malaysian air-conditioned buses are really meat lockers on wheels with just two settings: cold and suspended animation'.

Local and regional buses often operate from one station and long-distance buses from another; in other cases, KL for example, bus stations are differentiated by the destinations they serve.

Car & Motorcycle

Driving in Malaysia is a breeze compared to most Asian countries. The government has invested heavily in the roads, which are generally of a high quality, and

motorway services are very similar to what you would find in the West. Leaded and unleaded petrol are widely available for around RM1.85 per litre and hire companies offer self-drive services at the international airports in KL and Penang. Traffic is fairly light out on the highways, and there's a 110km per hour speed limit, so you can cover long distances quickly. Small motorcycles can be hired in Georgetown for exploring Penang, but they are not really up to long-distance touring.

That's the good news. The bad news is that drivers in Malaysia have the same devil-may-care attitude as drivers elsewhere in Asia. This means inconsiderate tailgating, risky overtaking, dangerous speeding and sudden unsignalled turns. Crashes are not uncommon. Always drive defensively and be ready for unexpected manoeuvres from drivers around you. A further hassle for drivers is the confusing layout of Malaysian road junctions. Although well signposted, exits appear with little notice, giving you a narrow window of time to get into the right lane. Assuming you make the turn, exits spiral off other exits like fettuccine curled around a fork – if you're not careful, you can end up back on the highway driving back the way you came.

To help you orient yourself, the Lebuhraya (North–South Hwy) is a six-lane expressway that runs for 966km along the length of the peninsula from the Thai border in the north to JB in the south, stopping near the Causeway to Singapore. Toll charges for using the expressway vary according to the distance travelled, which keeps the traffic light. Many locals prefer the free, but more crowded, ordinary highways.

Bring Your Own Vehicle

It is technically possible to bring your vehicle into Malaysia, but there are reams of red tape and the costs are prohibitively expensive – a hire car is a much better proposition.

Driving Licence

A valid overseas licence is needed to rent a car. An International Driving Permit is usually not required but it is recommended that you bring one, just to be safe. Most rental companies also require that drivers are at least 23 years old (and less than 65), with at least one year of driving experience.

Hire

Cars can be rented in both KL and Penang. Most of the big international rental companies have airport desks and downtown offices. The big advantage of dealing with the international chains is their countrywide network of offices – you can often pick up in one city and drop off in another for a RM50 surcharge.

Unlimited-distance rates for a 1.5L Proton Wira, the cheapest and most popular car in Malaysia, start per day/week at RM180/1155 including insurance and a collision-damage waiver. Rates drop substantially for longer rentals – shop around and it is often possible to get wheels for as little as RM2500 per month, including unlimited kilometres and insurance.

Reliable car-rental companies include the following:

Avis (www.avis.com.my)

Hertz (www5.hertz.com)

Mayflower (www.mayflowercarrental.com.my)

Orix (www.orixauto.com.my) Small (100cc to 125cc) motorcycles can be hired in Penang for around RM30 per day. However, you are unlikely to be covered by insurance if you don't have a motorcycle licence.

Insurance

Rental companies will provide insurance when you hire a car, but always check what the extent of your coverage will be, particularly if you're involved in an accident. Make sure you are covered for damage to other vehicles and third-party medical treatment in the event of a crash. You might want to take out your own insurance or pay the rental company an extra premium for an insurance excess reduction.

Road Rules

Driving in Malaysia broadly follows the same rules as in Britain and Australia – cars are right-hand drive and you drive on the left side of the road. Be aware of possible road hazards, particularly stray animals, wandering pedestrians and the large number of motorcyclists. The speed limit is 110km per hour on expressways but it can slow to as little as 50km per hour on *kampung* (village) back roads, so take it easy.

Wearing safety belts is compulsory. Malaysian drivers show remarkable common sense compared to other countries in the region. However, there are still plenty of drivers who take dangerous risks. Lane-drift is a big problem and signalling, when used at all, is often unclear. Giving a quick blast of the horn when you're overtaking a slower vehicle is common practice, and helps alert otherwise sleepy drivers to your presence.

Hitching

Keep in mind that hitching is never entirely safe in any country in the world, and we don't recommend it. Travellers who decide to hitch, particularly single women, should understand that they are taking a small but potentially serious risk. Hitching is safer if you travel in pairs and let someone know where you are planning to go. Nevertheless, hitching is comparatively easy in Malaysia, though buses are so cheap that few people bother. Note that hitchers are banned from the Lebuhraya.

Local Transport

Local transport varies widely from place to place. Taxis are found in most large cities and most have meters. Fares start at RM3 for the first two minutes, with an additional 20 sen for each 45 seconds. From midnight to 6am there's a surcharge of 50% on the metered fare, and extra passengers (more than two) are charged 20 sen each.

Although drivers are legally obliged to use the meter, many prefer to make up a (usually elevated) fare on the spot. If a driver refuses to use the meter, either find another cab or bargain hard. Taxis also provide long-distance transport.

Bicycle rickshaws (trishaws) supplement the taxi service in Georgetown and Melaka, providing an atmospheric, if bumpy, means of exploring the backstreets. KL has commuter trains, a Light Rail Transit, and monorail system.

Long-Distance Taxi

Long-distance taxis cover similar routes to the buses, but few people use them to travel from KL to Melaka or Penang as buses are cheaper and much more frequent. Long-haul taxi services operate on a shared basis and taxis leave from fixed depots – look for the 'Teksi' signs. There is space for four passengers and you can either charter the whole taxi or just pay for one seat (a quarter of the whole-taxi fare) and share the cost with three other passengers. Taxis leave when there are four passengers, or when one passenger pays the whole taxi fare, which can mean a long wait. Early morning is

TRAIN SERVICES BETWEEN KL & PENANG

As well as long-haul trips to Thailand and Singapore, you can use the train to get from KL to Butterworth for Penang (seat/berth from R34/46).

STATION	DEPARTURE	STATION	ARRIVAL
KL Sentral	11.30pm	Butterworth	6.35am
KL Sentral	3.03pm	Butterworth	9.50pm
Butterworth	7.45am	KL Sentral	2.06pm
Butterworth	11.30pm	KL Sentral	6.40am

generally the best time to find people to share a taxi.

Taxi rates to specific destinations are fixed by the government and the whole-taxi fare is usually posted at the taxi stand. Air-con taxis cost a few more ringgit than those without air-con, and fares are generally about twice the comparable bus fares.

Tours

Getting around Peninsular Malaysia under your own steam is rarely difficult, but there are numerous tour companies who will make all the arrangements for you. Tour agents in KL offer day tours to Melaka and other attractions around KL, as well as Taman Negara National Park in the north of the peninsula. See Kuala Lumpur (p65) and Penang (p157) for listings of local operators and tours.

Train

Trains in Malaysia are run by the privatised national railway company **KTM** (Keretapi Tanah Melayu Berhad; ☎1300 885 862; www.ktmb.com.my), which also runs the commuter train service in KL. Although slow, the trains are modern, comfortable and inexpensive. There are basically two lines – one up the east coast, and one up the west coast, connecting with Singapore in the south and the Thai city of Hat Yai in the north.

Services & Classes

There are two main types of rail services: express and local trains. Express trains are air-conditioned and have a mixture of 'premier' (1st class), 'superior' (2nd class) and sometimes 'economy' seats (3rd class). On overnight trains you'll find 'premier night deluxe' cabins (upper/lower berth RM50/70 on top of the standard fare), 'premier night standard cabins' (upper/lower berth RM18/26 on top of the standard fare), and 'standard night' cabins (upper/lower berth RM12/17 on top of the standard fare).

Express trains stop only at main stations, while local services stop everywhere. Train schedules are reviewed biannually, so check KTM's website before you make detailed plans.

Health

Polio There have been no reported cases of polio in Malaysia in recent years. Only one booster is required as an adult for lifetime protection.

Typhoid Recommended unless your trip is less than a week and only to developed cities. The vaccine offers around 70% protection, lasts for two to three years and is given as a single shot. Tablets are also available. However the injection is usually recommended as it has fewer side effects.

Varicella If you haven't had chickenpox, discuss this vaccination with your doctor.

Internet Resources & Further Reading

Lonely Planet's *Asia & India: Healthy Travel* guide is packed with useful information. Other recommended references include *Travellers' Health* by Dr Richard Dawood and *Travelling Well* by Dr Deborah Mills. Online resources:

Centers for Disease Control and Prevention (CDC; www.cdc.gov)

MD Travel Health (www.mdtravelhealth.com)

Travelling Well (www.travellingwell.com.au)

World Health Organization (www.who.int/ith/en)

IN MALAYSIA

Availability of Health Care

There are good clinics and international-standard hospitals in Kuala Lumpur, Melaka and Penang. Over-the-counter medicines and prescription drugs are widely available from reputable pharmacies across Malaysia.

BEFORE YOU GO

» Take out health insurance.

» Pack medications in their original, clearly labelled containers.

» Carry a signed and dated letter from your physician describing your medical conditions and medications, including their generic names.

» If you have a heart condition bring a copy of your ECG (taken just prior to travelling).

» Bring a double supply of any regular medication in case of loss or theft.

HEALTH ADVISORIES

Consult your government's website on health and travel before departure:

Australia www.smartraveller.gov.au

Canada www.phac-aspc.gc.ca/tmp-pmv/index-eng.php

New Zealand www.safetravel.govt.nz

UK www.dh.gov.uk

USA wwwnc.cdc.gov/travel

Recommended Vaccinations

Proof of yellow-fever vaccination will be required if you have visited a country in the yellow-fever zone (Africa or South America) within the six days prior to entering Malaysia. The World Health Organization (WHO) recommends the following vaccinations for travellers to Malaysia:

Adult diphtheria and tetanus Single booster recommended if none in the previous 10 years.

Hepatitis A Provides almost 100% protection for up to a year. A booster after 12 months provides at least another 20 years' protection.

Hepatitis B Now considered routine for most travellers. Given as three shots over six months. A rapid schedule is also available, as is a combined vaccination with hepatitis A.

Measles, mumps and rubella (MMR) Two doses of MMR are required unless you have had the diseases. Many young adults require a booster.

Infectious Diseases

The following are the most common for travellers:

Dengue Fever Becoming increasingly common in cities. The mosquito that carries dengue bites day and night, so use insect avoidance measures at all times. Symptoms can include high fever, severe headache, body ache, a rash and diarrhoea. There is no specific treatment, just rest and paracetamol – do not take aspirin as it increases the likelihood of haemorrhaging.

Hepatitis A This food- and water-borne virus infects the liver, causing jaundice (yellow skin and eyes), nausea and lethargy. All travellers to Malaysia should be vaccinated against it.

Hepatitis B The only sexually transmitted disease (STD) that can be prevented by vaccination, hepatitis B is spread by body fluids, including sexual contact.

Hepatitis E Transmitted through contaminated food and water and has similar symptoms to hepatitis A, but is far less common. It is a severe problem in pregnant women and can result in the death of both mother and baby. There is currently no vaccine, and prevention is by following safe eating and drinking guidelines.

HIV Unprotected sex is the main method of transmission.

Influenza Can be very severe in people over the age of 65 or in those with underlying medical conditions such as heart disease or diabetes; vaccination is recommended for these individuals. There is no specific treatment, just rest and paracetamol.

Malaria Uncommon in Peninsular Malaysia and antimalarial drugs are rarely recommended for travellers. However, there may be a small risk in rural areas.

Remember that malaria can be fatal. Before you travel, seek medical advice on the right medication and dosage for you.

Rabies A potential risk, and invariably fatal if untreated, rabies is spread by the bite or lick of an infected animal – most commonly a dog or monkey. Pretravel vaccination means the postbite treatment is greatly simplified. If an animal bites you, gently wash the wound with soap and water, and apply iodine-based antiseptic. If you are not prevaccinated you will need to receive rabies immunoglobulin as soon as possible.

Typhoid This serious bacterial infection is spread via food and water. Symptoms include high and slowly progressive fever, headache, a dry cough and stomach pain. Vaccination, recommended for all travellers spending more than a week in Malaysia, is not 100% effective so you must still be careful with what you eat and drink.

Travellers Diarrhoea

By far the most common problem affecting travellers, travellers diarrhoea is commonly caused by a bacterium. Treatment consists of staying well hydrated; use a solution such as Gastrolyte. Antibiotics such as Norfloxacin, Ciprofloxacin or Azithromycin will kill the bacteria quickly.

Loperamide is a 'stopper' only (it will slow the frequency of stools/bowel movements), but it can be helpful in certain situations, eg if you have to go on a long bus ride. Seek medical attention quickly if you do not respond to an appropriate antibiotic.

Giardiasis is relatively common. Symptoms include nausea, bloating, excess gas, fatigue and diarrhoea. The treatment of choice is Tinidazole, with Metronidazole being a second option.

Environmental Hazards

Air Pollution

If troubled by the air pollution in KL, Melaka or Penang, leave the city for a few days to get some fresh air.

Heat

It can take up to two weeks to adapt to Malaysia's hot climate. Swelling of the feet and ankles is common, as are muscle cramps caused by excessive sweating. Prevent cramps by avoiding dehydration and excessive activity in the heat.

Dehydration is the main contributor to heat exhaustion. Symptoms include

---

DRINKING WATER

» Never drink tap water.

» Check bottled water seals are intact at purchase.

» Avoid ice.

» Avoid fresh juices – they may have been watered down.

» Boiling water is the most efficient method of purifying it.

» Iodine, the best chemical purifier, should not be used by pregnant women or those who suffer thyroid problems.

» Ensure your water filter has a chemical barrier such as iodine and a pore size of less than four microns.

Bedbugs live in the cracks of furniture and walls and migrate to the bed at night to feed on you. They are more likely to strike in high-turnover accommodation, especially hostels, though they can be found anywhere. An appearance of cleanliness is no guarantee there are no bedbugs. Protect yourself with the following strategies:

» Ask the hotel or hostel what it does to avoid bedbugs. It's a common problem and reputable establishments should have a pest-control procedure in place.

» Keep your luggage elevated off the floor to avoid having the critters latch on – this is one of the common ways bedbugs are spread from place to place.

» Check the room carefully for signs of bugs – you may find their translucent light-brown skins or poppy-seed-like excrement.

If you do get bitten try the following:

» Treat the itch with antihistamine.

» Thoroughly clean your luggage and launder all your clothes, sealing them afterwards in plastic bags to further protect them.

» Be sure to tell the management – if staff seem unconcerned or refuse to do anything about it complain to the local tourist office and write to us.

feeling weak, headache, irritability, nausea or vomiting, sweaty skin, a fast weak pulse and a normal or slightly elevated body temperature. Treat by getting out of the heat, applying cool wet cloths to the skin, laying flat with legs raised and rehydrating with water containing a quarter of a teaspoon of salt per litre.

Heat stroke is a serious medical emergency. Symptoms come on suddenly and include weakness, nausea, a hot dry body with a body temperature of over 41°C, dizziness, confusion, fits and eventually collapse and loss of consciousness. Seek medical help and commence cooling by getting the person out of the heat, removing their clothes and applying cool wet cloths or ice to their body, especially to the groin and armpits.

Prickly heat – an itchy rash of tiny lumps – is caused by sweat being trapped under the skin. Treat by moving out of the heat and into an air-conditioned area for a few hours and by having cool showers. Creams and ointments clog the skin so they should be avoided.

Insect Bites & Stings

Lice Most commonly inhabit your head and pubic area. Transmission is via close contact with an infected person. Treat with numerous applications of an antilice shampoo such as Permethrin.

Ticks Contracted after walking in rural areas. If you are bitten and experience symptoms such as a rash at the site of the bite or elsewhere, fever, or muscle aches, see a doctor. Doxycycline prevents tick-borne diseases.

Leeches Found in humid rainforest areas. Don't transmit disease but their bites can be itchy for weeks afterwards and can easily become infected. Apply an iodine-based antiseptic to any leech bite to prevent infection.

Bees or wasps If allergic to their stings, carry an injection of adrenaline (eg an Epipen) for emergency treatment.

Jellyfish In Malaysian waters most are not dangerous. If stung, pour vinegar onto the affected area to neutralise the poison. Take painkillers, and seek medical advice if your condition worsens.

Skin Problems

Fungal rashes can occur in moist areas that get less air such as the groin, armpits and between the toes. Treatment involves keeping the skin dry, avoiding chafing and using an antifungal cream such as Clotrimazole or Lamisil. The fungus *tinea versicolor* causes small, light-coloured patches, most commonly on the back, chest and shoulders. Consult a doctor.

Immediately wash all wounds in clean water and apply antiseptic. If you develop signs of infection (increasing pain and redness) see a doctor. Divers should be particularly careful with coral cuts as they become easily infected.

Sunburn

Always use a strong sunscreen (at least SPF 30), and always wear a wide-brimmed hat and sunglasses outdoors. If you become sunburnt, one percent hydrocortisone cream applied twice daily to the burn is helpful.

Women's Health

Sanitary products are readily available in Malaysia. Heat, humidity and antibiotics can contribute to thrush. Treat with antifungal creams and pessaries such as Clotrimazole. A practical alternative is a tablet of fluconazole (Diflucan).

Language

WANT MORE?

For in-depth language information and handy phrases, check out Lonely Planet's *Malay Phrasebook*. You'll find it at **shop.lonelyplanet.com**, or you can buy Lonely Planet's iPhone phrasebooks at the Apple App Store.

The official language of Kuala Lumpur, Melaka and Penang is Malay, or Bahasa Malaysia, as it's called by its speakers. It belongs to the Western Austronesian language family and is very similar to Indonesian.

There are several Indian and Chinese languages spoken in the region as well, such as Hokkien, Cantonese, Tamil and Malayalam. English is also widely understood.

Malay pronunciation is easy to master. Each letter always represents the same sound and most letters are pronounced the same as their English counterparts, with *c* pronounced as the 'ch' in 'chat' and *sy* as the 'sh' in 'ship'. Note also that *kh* is a guttural sound (like the 'ch' in the Scottish *loch*), and that *gh* is a throaty 'g' sound.

Syllables generally carry equal emphasis – the main exception is the unstressed *e* in words such as *besar* (big) – but the rule of thumb is to stress the second-last syllable.

BASICS

In Malaysia, *kamu* is an egalitarian second-person pronoun, equivalent to 'you' in English. The polite pronoun for the equivalent of English 'I/we' is *kami*. In polite speech, you wouldn't normally use first-person pronouns, but would refer to yourself by name or form of address, eg *Makcik nak pergi ke pasar* (Auntie wants to go to the market).

When addressing a man or a woman old enough to be your parent, use *pakcik* (uncle) or *makcik* (aunt). For someone only slightly older than yourself, use *abang* or *bang* (older brother) and *kakak* or *kak* (older sister). For people old enough to be your grandparents, *datuk* and *nenek* (grandfather and grand-mother) are used. For a man or woman you meet on the street you can also use *encik* or *cik* respectively.

Hello.	*Helo.*
Goodbye.	
(by person leaving)	*Selamat tinggal.*
(by person staying)	*Selamat jalan.*
Yes.	*Ya.*
No.	*Tidak.*
Please.	
(to ask for something)	*Tolong.*
(to offer something)	*Silakan.*
Thank you.	*Terima kasih.*
You're welcome.	*Sama-sama.*
Excuse me.	*Maaf.*
Sorry.	*Minta maaf.*
How are you?	*Apa khabar?*
Fine, thanks.	*Khabar baik.*
What's your name?	*Siapa nama kamu?*
My name is ...	*Nama saya ...*
Do you speak English?	*Bolehkah anda berbicara Bahasa Inggeris?*
I don't understand.	*Saya tidak faham.*

ACCOMMODATION

Do you have any rooms available?	*Ada bilik kosong?*
How much is it per night/person?	*Berapa harga satu malam/orang?*
Is breakfast included?	*Makan pagi termasukkah?*

air-con	pendingin udara
bathroom	bilik air
campsite	kawasan perkhemahan
double room	bilik untuk dua orang
guesthouse	rumah tetamu
hotel	hotel
mosquito coil	ubat nyamuk
single room	bilik untuk seorang
window	tingkap
youth hostel	asrama belia

DIRECTIONS

Where is ...?	Di mana ...?
What's the address?	Apakah alamatnya?
Can you write the address, please?	Tolong tuliskan alamat itu?
Can you show me (on the map)?	Tolong tunjukkan (di peta)?
Go straight ahead.	Jalan terus.
Turn left.	Belok kiri.
Turn right.	Belok kanan.

at the corner	di simpang
at the traffic lights	di tempat lampu isyarat
behind	di belakang
far	jauh
in front of	di hadapan
near	dekat
next to	di samping/di sebelah
opposite	berhadapan dengan

EATING & DRINKING

We'd like a table for (five), please.	Tolong bagi meja untuk (lima) orang.
Can I see the menu?	Minta senarai makanan?
What's in this dish?	Ini termasuk apa?
I'd like ...	Saya mahu...
I'm a vegetarian.	Saya makan sayur-sayuran sahaja.
Not too spicy, please.	Kurang pedas.
Please add extra chilli.	Tolong letak cili lebih.
Thank you, that was delicious.	Sedap sekali, terima kasih.
Please bring the bill.	Tolong bawa bil.

Key Words

bottle	botol
breakfast	makan pagi

children's menu	menu kanak-kanak
cold	sejuk
cup	cawan
dinner	makan malam
drink	minuman
food	makanan
food stall	gerai
fork	garfu
glass	gelas
grocery store	kedai makanan
highchair	kerusi tinggi
hot (warm)	panas
knife	pisau
lunch	makan tengahari
market	pasar
menu	menu
plate	pinggan
restaurant	restoran
spicy	pedas
spoon	sudu
vegetarian (food)	sayuran saja
with	dengan
without	tanpa

Meat & Fish

(dried) anchovies	ikan bilis
beef	daging lembu
brains	otak
catfish	ikan keli
chicken	ayam
cockles	kerang
crab	ketam
duck	itik
fish	ikan
freshwater fish	ikan air tawar
goat	kambing
lamb	anak biri-biri
liver	hati
lobster	udang karang
mussels	kepah
mutton	biri-biri
oysters	tiram
pig	babi
rabbit	arnab
salted dried fish	ikan kering
saltwater fish	ikan air masin
shrimp	udang
squid	sotong
tripe	perut

Signs

Masuk	Entrance
Keluar	Exit
Buka	Open
Tutup	Closed
Pertanyaan	Information
Dilarang	Prohibited
Tandas	Toilets
Lelaki	Men
Perempuan	Women

Fruit & Vegetables

apple	epal
banana	pisang
beans	kacang
cabbage	kubis
carrot	lobak
cauliflower	kubis bunga
coconut	kelapa
corn	jagung
cucumber	timun
eggplant	terung
guava	jambu
jackfruit	nangka
mango	mangga
mangosteen	manggis
mushrooms	kulat
onion	bawang
orange	oren
papaya	betik
peanuts	kacang
pineapple	nenas
potato	kentang
pumpkin	labu
soursop	durian belanda
starfruit	belimbing
watermelon	tembikai

Other

bread	roti
cake	kueh
chilli sauce	sambal
noodles	mee
oil	minyak

(black) pepper	lada hitam
rice (cooked)	nasi
rice (uncooked)	beras
salt	garam
soy sauce	kicap
sugar	gula
sweets	manisan
tofu	tahu
vinegar	cuka

Drinks

beer	bir
boiled water	air masak
citrus juice	air limau
coconut milk	air kelapa muda
coffee	kopi
cordial	pekatan
frothed tea	teh tarik
milk	susu
palm tree spirits	todi
rice wine	tuak
tea	teh
water	air
(grape) wine	wain

EMERGENCIES

Help!	Tolong!
Go away!	Pergi!
I'm lost.	Saya sesat.
There's been an accident.	Ada kemalangan.
Call a doctor!	Panggil doktor!
Call the police!	Panggil polis!
I'm ill.	Saya sakit.
It hurts here.	Sini sakit.
I'm allergic to (antibiotics).	Saya alergik kepada (antibiotik).

SHOPPING & SERVICES

I'd like to buy ...	Saya nak beli ...
I'm just looking.	Saya nak tengok saja.
May I look at it?	Boleh saya lihat barang itu?
I don't like it.	Saya tak suka ini.
How much is it?	Berapa harganya?
It's too expensive.	Mahalnya.
Can you lower the price?	Boleh kurang sedikit?
There's a mistake in the bill.	Bil ini salah.

credit card	kad kredit
mobile phone	telefon bimbit
phonecard	kad telefon
post office	pejabat pos
signature	tanda tangan
tourist office	pejabat pelancong

TIME & DATES

What time is it?	Pukul berapa?
It's (seven) o'clock.	Pukul (tujuh).
Half past (one).	Pukul (satu) setengah.

in the morning	pagi
in the afternoon	tengahari
in the evening	petang

yesterday	semalam
today	hari ini
tomorrow	esok

Monday	hari Isnin
Tuesday	hari Selasa
Wednesday	hari Rabu
Thursday	hari Khamis
Friday	hari Jumaat
Saturday	hari Sabtu
Sunday	hari Minggu

January	Januari
February	Februari
March	Mac
April	April
May	Mei
June	Jun
July	Julai
August	Ogos
September	September
October	Oktober
November	November
December	Disember

Question Words
How?	Berapa?
What?	Apa?
When?	Bila?
Where?	Di mana?
Which?	Yang mana?
Who?	Siapa?
Why?	Kenapa?

Public Transport

bicycle-rickshaw	beca
boat	bot
bus	bas
plane	kapal terbang
ship	kapal
taxi	teksi
train	keretapi

I want to go to ...	Saya nak ke ...
What time does the (bus) leave?	(Bas) bertolak pukul berapa?
What time does the (train) arrive?	(Keretapi) tiba pukul berapa?
Does the bus stop at the (restaurant)?	Bas ini berhenti di (restoran)?
Can you tell me when we get to ...?	Tolong beritahu saya bila kita sudah sampai di ...?
I want to get off at ...	Saya nak turun di ...
The (bus) has been delayed.	(Bas) itu telah terlambat.
The (train) has been cancelled.	(Keretapi) itu telah dibatalkan.

first class	kelas pertama
one-way ticket	tiket sehala
return ticket	tiket pergi-balik
second class	kelas kedual bisnis

first	pertama
last	terakhir
next	berikutnya

airport	lapangan terbang
bus stop	perhentian bas
ticket office	pejabat tiket
timetable	jadual
train station	stesen keretapi

Driving & Cycling

I'd like to hire a ...	Saya nak menyewa ...
bicycle	basikal
car	kereta
jeep	jip
motorcycle	motosikal

Numbers	
1	satu
2	dua
3	tiga
4	empat
5	lima
6	enam
7	tujuh
8	lapan
9	sembilan
10	sepuluh
20	dua puluh
30	tiga puluh
40	empat puluh
50	lima puluh
60	enam puluh
70	tujuh puluh
80	lapan puluh
90	sembilan puluh
100	seratus
1000	seribu

child seat	tempat duduk bayi
diesel	disel
helmet	topi keledar
mechanic	mekanik
petrol/gas	minyak
pump	pam
service station	stesen minyak
unleaded petrol	petrol tanpa plumbum
Is this the road to ...?	Inikah jalan ke ...?
How many kilometres?	Berapa kilometer?
Can I park here?	Boleh saya letak kereta di sini?
How long can I park here?	Beberapa lama boleh saya letak kereta di sini?
The (car) has broken down at ...	(Kereta) saya telah rosak di ...
The (motorbike) won't start.	(Motosikal) saya tidak dapat dihidupkan.
I have a flat tyre.	Tayarnya kempis.
I've run out of petrol.	Minyak sudah habis.
I've had an accident.	Saya terlibat dalam kemalangan.

GLOSSARY

adat – Malay customary law
alor – groove; furrow; main channel of a river
ampang – dam

Baba-Nonya – descendants of Chinese immigrants to Melaka and Penang who intermarried with Malays and adopted many Malay customs; also known as Peranakan, or Straits Chinese; sometimes spelt Nyonya
Bahasa Malaysia – Malay language; also known as Bahasa Melayu
bandar – seaport; town
BN – Barisan Nasional, coalition of the United Malays National Organisation (UMNO) and 13 other political parties
baru – new; common in placenames
batik – technique of imprinting cloth with dye to produce multicoloured patterns
batu – stone; rock; milepost
bendahara – chief minister

bomoh – spiritual healer
British Resident – chief British representative during the colonial era
bukit – hill
bumiputra – literally, sons of the soil; indigenous Malays
bunga raya – hibiscus flower (national flower of Malaysia)

dato' – literally, grandfather; general male nonroyal title of distinction
datuk – literally, grandfather; general male nonroyal title of distinction

Emergency – the guerrilla war between communist rebels and the Malaysian government

genting – mountain pass
gopuram – Hindu temple tower

hutan – jungle; forest

istana – palace

jalan – road

kampung – village; also spelt *kampong*
kedai kopi – coffee shop
kongsi – Chinese clan organisations, also known as ritual brotherhoods, heavenman-earth societies, triads or secret societies; meeting house for Chinese of the same clan
kopitiam – traditional coffee shop
kota – fort; city
kramat – Malay shrine
kris – traditional Malay wavy-bladed dagger
KTM – Keretapi Tanah Melayu; Malaysian Railways System
kuala – river mouth; place where a tributary joins a larger river

laksamana – admiral
laut – sea

lebuh – street
Lebuhraya – expressway or freeway; usually refers to the North-South Highway, which runs from Johor Bahru to the Thai border
lorong – narrow street; alley
LRT – Light Rail Transit (Kuala Lumpur)

mamak – Indian Muslim
masjid – mosque
MCP – Malayan Communist Party
merdeka – independence
muezzin – mosque official who calls the faithful to prayer

negara – country
negeri – state
nonya – see Baba-Nonya

Orang Asli – literally, Original People; Malaysian aborigines

padang – grassy area; field; also the city square
pantai – beach
pasar – market
pasar malam – night market

pelabuhan – port
pencak silat – see *silat*
penghulu – chief or village head
pengkalan – quay
Peranakan – refers to the Baba-Nonya or Straits Chinese
PR – Pakatan Rakyat, official opposition party
pulau – island

raja – prince; ruler
raja muda – crown prince; heir apparent
rakyat – common people
rattan – stems from climbing palms used for wickerwork and canes
roti – bread

sampan – small boat
sarong – all-purpose cloth, often sewn into a tube, and worn by women, men and children
seberang – opposite side of road; far bank of a river
silat – martial-arts dance form
Straits Chinese – see Baba-Nonya

sultan – ruler of one of Malaysia's nine states
sungai – river
syariah – Islamic system of law

tanah – land
tanjung – headland
tasik – lake
teluk – bay; sometimes spelt *telok*
temenggong – Malay administrator
tunku – prince

UMNO – United Malays National Organisation

wayang – Chinese opera
wayang kulit – shadow-puppet theatre
wet market – open food market, often selling live animals including poultry and fish
wisma – office block or shopping centre

yang di-pertuan agong – Malaysia's head of state, or 'king'

behind the scenes

SEND US YOUR FEEDBACK

We love to hear from travellers – your comments keep us on our toes and help make our books better. Our well-travelled team reads every word on what you loved or loathed about this book. Although we cannot reply individually to postal submissions, we always guarantee that your feedback goes straight to the appropriate authors, in time for the next edition. Each person who sends us information is thanked in the next edition – and the most useful submissions are rewarded with a free book.

Visit **lonelyplanet.com/contact** to submit your updates and suggestions or to ask for help. Our award-winning website also features inspirational travel stories, news and discussions.

Note: We may edit, reproduce and incorporate your comments in Lonely Planet products such as guidebooks, websites and digital products, so let us know if you don't want your comments reproduced or your name acknowledged. For a copy of our privacy policy visit lonelyplanet.com/privacy.

OUR READERS

Many thanks to the travellers who used the last edition and wrote to us with helpful hints, useful advice and interesting anecdotes:
Shermaine Abad, Samuel Bilbie, Carol Bolger, Norman Chua, Naomi Higham, Gerrit Hoekman, Claude Leglise, Rune Midtgaard, Heather Monell, Ernst Roeder-Messell, Ronald Smith, Wei Yean Choo

AUTHOR THANKS

Simon Richmond

Terima kasih to my delightful co-author Celeste whose love for all things Malaysian makes us the perfect match, and to Ilaria for enthusiastic support from Lonely Planet HQ. In KL, many thanks to Alex Yong, Eli Wong, Steven Gan, Andrew Sebastian, Elizabeth Cardosa, Ng Chee Yat, David Hogan Jr, Rohani Jelani, Peter Hoe, Pam Currie, Sueann Chong, Narelle McMurtrie, Angela and Bilqis Hijjas, Chris and Eddy and Adline binti Abdul Ghani. For great shared meals and foodie knowledge a special thanks to Robyn Eckhardt, David Hagerman, Adly Rizal and Honey Ahmad.

Celeste Brash

Most thanks to my family and to great friends Peck Choo Ho, Brandon Tan, Charles and Andrea Cham, Kiwi William, Yoga Jordan and the Melaka crew for good times. In Penang thanks to wonder-buddy Joann Khaw and brilliant Khoo Salma; to new friends Chris Ong, Narelle and Allison, Roz, Gok Ling and Leandro for Ladies' Night. *Merci beaucoup* Simon for being the most on-top-of-it coordinating author I've ever worked with and Ilaria for getting this book so fabulously together.

ACKNOWLEDGMENTS

Climate map data adapted from Peel MC, Finlayson BL & McMahon TA (2007) 'Updated World Map of the Köppen-Geiger Climate Classification', *Hydrology and Earth System Sciences*, 11, 1633–44.
Integrated Transit Network of Kuala Lumpur map (p38) provided by Tourism Malaysia.
Cover photograph: Petronas Towers in Kuala Lumpur at dusk/Anders Blomqvist/Lonely Planet Images.
Many of the images in this guide are available for licensing from Lonely Planet Images: www.lonelyplanetimages.com.

THIS BOOK

This 2nd edition of Lonely Planet's *Kuala Lumpur, Melaka & Penang* guidebook was researched and written by Simon Richmond and Celeste Brash. The previous edition was written by Joe Bindloss and Celeste Brash. The Health chapter was taken from text written by Dr Trish Batchelor. This guidebook was commissioned in Lonely Planet's Melbourne office, and produced by the following:

Commissioning Editor Ilaria Walker

Coordinating Editors Erin Richards, Louisa Syme

Coordinating Cartographer Andy Rojas

Coordinating Layout Designer Mazzy Prinsep

Managing Editors Brigitte Ellemor, Bruce Evans

Managing Cartographer Alison Lyall

Managing Layout Designers Jane Hart, Celia Wood

Assisting Editors Gabrielle Innes, Sonya Mithen

Assisting Cartographers Brendan Streager, Xavier Di Toro

Assisting Layout Designer Jessica Rose

Cover Research Naomi Parker

Internal Image Research Rebecca Skinner

Language Content Branislava Vladisavljevic

Thanks to Mark Adams, Imogen Bannister, David Connolly, Piotr Czajkowski, Melanie Dankel, Stefanie Di Trocchio, Janine Eberle, Ryan Evans, Joshua Geoghegan, Mark Germanchis, Michelle Glynn, Lauren Hunt, Laura Jane, David Kemp, Yvonne Kirk, Lisa Knights, Nic Lehman, Bella Li, Chris Love, John Mazzocchi, Annelies Mertens, Wayne Murphy, Trent Paton, Adrian Persoglia, Piers Pickard, Lachlan Ross, Michael Ruff, Julie Sheridan, Laura Stansfeld, John Taufa, Sam Trafford, Juan Winata, Emily Wolman, Nick Wood

NOTES

index

INDEX L-N

how to use this book

These symbols will help you find the listings you want:

◉ Sights	🎊 Festivals & Events	☆ Entertainment
🏃 Activities	🛏 Sleeping	🔒 Shopping
🍴 Courses	✖ Eating	ℹ Information/ Transport
☞ Tours	🍷 Drinking	

These symbols give you the vital information for each listing:

🕾 Telephone Numbers	🛜 Wi-Fi Access	🚌 Bus
⊙ Opening Hours	🏊 Swimming Pool	🚢 Ferry
P Parking	🥗 Vegetarian Selection	Ⓜ Metro
⊖ Nonsmoking	📖 English-Language Menu	Ⓢ Subway
✳ Air-Conditioning	👪 Family-Friendly	⊖ London Tube
@ Internet Access	🐾 Pet-Friendly	🚋 Tram
		🚆 Train

Reviews are organised by author preference.

Map Legend

Sights
- ◉ Beach
- ◉ Buddhist
- ◉ Castle
- ◉ Christian
- ◉ Hindu
- ◉ Islamic
- ◉ Jewish
- ◉ Monument
- ⊕ Museum/Gallery
- ◉ Ruin
- ◉ Winery/Vineyard
- ◉ Zoo
- ◉ Other Sight

Activities, Courses & Tours
- ◉ Diving/Snorkelling
- ◉ Canoeing/Kayaking
- ◉ Skiing
- ◉ Surfing
- ◉ Swimming/Pool
- ◉ Walking
- ◉ Windsurfing
- • Other Activity/ Course/Tour

Sleeping
- ◉ Sleeping
- ◉ Camping

Eating
- ✖ Eating

Drinking
- ◉ Drinking
- ◉ Cafe

Entertainment
- ◉ Entertainment

Shopping
- ◉ Shopping

Information
- ◉ Bank
- ◉ Embassy/ Consulate
- ◉ Hospital/Medical
- @ Internet
- ◉ Police
- ◉ Post Office
- ◉ Telephone
- ◉ Toilet
- ◉ Tourist Information
- • Other Information

Transport
- ◉ Airport
- ◉ Border Crossing
- ◉ Bus
- ++◉++ Cable Car/ Funicular
- -◉- Cycling
- -◉- Ferry
- Ⓜ Metro
- ═◉═ Monorail
- P Parking
- ◉ Petrol Station
- ◉ Taxi
- +◉+ Train/Railway
- ═◉═ Tram
- • Other Transport

Routes
- Tollway
- Freeway
- Primary
- Secondary
- Tertiary
- Lane
- Unsealed Road
- Plaza/Mall
- Steps
-)═ ═(Tunnel
- Pedestrian Overpass
- Walking Tour
- Walking Tour Detour
- Path

Geographic
- ◉ Hut/Shelter
- ◉ Lighthouse
- ◉ Lookout
- ▲ Mountain/Volcano
- ◉ Oasis
- ◉ Park
-)(Pass
- ◉ Picnic Area
- ◉ Waterfall

Population
- ◉ Capital (National)
- ◉ Capital (State/Province)
- ◉ City/Large Town
- ◉ Town/Village

Boundaries
- — — — International
- ----- State/Province
- — · Disputed
- — — Regional/Suburb
- Marine Park
- Cliff
- Wall

Hydrography
- River, Creek
- Intermittent River
- Swamp/Mangrove
- Reef
- Canal
- Water
- Dry/Salt/ Intermittent Lake
- Glacier

Areas
- Beach/Desert
- + + + Cemetery (Christian)
- × × × Cemetery (Other)
- Park/Forest
- Sportsground
- Sight (Building)
- Top Sight (Building)

OUR STORY

A beat-up old car, a few dollars in the pocket and a sense of adventure. In 1972 that's all Tony and Maureen Wheeler needed for the trip of a lifetime – across Europe and Asia overland to Australia. It took several months, and at the end – broke but inspired – they sat at their kitchen table writing and stapling together their first travel guide, *Across Asia on the Cheap*. Within a week they'd sold 1500 copies. Lonely Planet was born.

Today, Lonely Planet has offices in Melbourne, London and Oakland, with more than 600 staff and writers. We share Tony's belief that 'a great guidebook should do three things: inform, educate and amuse'.

OUR WRITERS

Simon Richmond

Coordinating Author, Kuala Lumpur Simon first visited KL, Melaka and Penang in 1996. A lot's changed in Malaysia since, but the country remains one of Simon's favourites for its easily accessible blend of cultures, landscapes, adventure and lip-smacking range of cuisines. His favourite experience of this research trip was learning to make the glutinous rice balls *onde onde* at the culinary retreat Bayan Indah. An award-winning travel writer and photographer, Simon has helmed Lonely Planet's Malaysia, Singapore & Brunei guide for the past three editions, as well as a shelf-load of other titles for Lonely Planet and other publishers. Find out more about his work and travels at www.simonrichmond.com.

Read more about Simon at:
lonelyplanet.com/members/simonrichmond

Celeste Brash

Melaka, Penang Celeste first visited Malaysia while studying at Chiang Mai University, Thailand in 1993 and she later moved to Singapore to teach English. The more of Malaysia she's visited over the years, the more she's fallen in love with it. She's sure Malaysian food is the world's best and the country seems to get better and better with every visit. She's contributed to over 20 Lonely Planet guidebooks including Travel with Children and her award-winning writing has appeared in publications from the LA Times to Islands Magazine. To see more of her writing go to www.celestebrash.com.

Read more about Celeste at:
lonelyplanet.com/members/celestebrash

Published by Lonely Planet Publications Pty Ltd
ABN 36 005 607 983
2nd edition – June 2011
ISBN 978 1 74179 216 4
© Lonely Planet 2011   Photographs © as indicated 2011
10 9 8 7 6 5 4 3 2 1
Printed in Singapore